VISUAL OBJECT PROCESSING: A COGNITIVE NEUROPSYCHOLOGICAL APPROACH

£15.00

Visual Object Processing: A Cognitive Neuropsychological Approach

Edited by
Glyn W. Humphreys
Department of Psychology, Birkbeck College, U.K.
and
M. Jane Riddoch
Department of Paramedical Sciences, North East London Polytechnic, U.K.

LAWRENCE ERLBAUM ASSOCIATES, PUBLISHERS
Hove and London (UK) Hillsdale (USA)

Lawrence Erlbaum Associates Ltd., Publishers
27 Palmeira Mansions
Church Road
Hove
East Sussex, BN3 2FA
U.K.

British Library Cataloguing in Publication Data

Visual object processing : a cognitive neuropsychological account.
1. Visual perception
I. Humphreys, Glyn W. II. Riddoch, M. Jane
152.1'4 BF241

ISBN 0-86377-045-2

Typeset by Spire Print Services Ltd., Salisbury, Wilts
Printed and bound by A. Wheaton & Co. Ltd., Exeter

Contents

List of Contributors ix

Preface xi

1. Introduction: Cognitive Neuropsychology and Visual Object Processing **1**
Glyn W. Humphreys and *M. Jane Riddoch*
1. Introduction 1
2. Cognitive Neuropsychology and Visual Object Processing 2
3. The Book 11

2. Visual Object Perception from a Computational Perspective **17**
Kent A. Stevens
1. Introduction 17
2. Modularity in Vision 19
3. Survey of Computational Problems 21
4. Concerning Visual Defects 35
5. Conclusion 39

3. Normal and Pathological Processes in Visual Object Constancy **43**
Glyn W. Humphreys and *Philip T. Quinlan*
1. Introduction 43
2. The Problem of Visual Object Constancy 44
3. Approaches to Object Constancy 48
4. Animal Work 82
5. Neurological Impairments of Human Vision 88
6. Some Conclusions 95

4. Picture Naming 107
M. Jane Riddoch and *Glyn W. Humphreys*
1. Introduction 107
2. Studies of Picture Naming in Normal Subjects 108
3. Data from Brain Damaged Subjects 127
4. Conclusions 139

5. Information Processing and Laterality Effects for Object and Face Perception 145
Justine Sergent
1. Introduction 145
2. Information Processing 148
3. Some Properties of the Visual System and their Implications 153
4. Hemispheric Processing Assymetry 162
5. Conclusion 167

6. The Clinical Spectrum and Localisation of Visual Agnosia 175
Andrew Kertesz
1. Introduction 175
2. Varieties of Visual Agnosia 176
3. Agnosia and Cortical Blindness 182
4. Associated Deficits 183
5. The Lesions Producing Visual Agnosia 189
6. The Functions of Visual Recognition 191

7. Apperceptive Agnosia: The Specification and Description of Constructs 197
John Campion
1. Introduction 197
2. A Neuropsychological Framework for Vision 198
3. Sensory Loss Theory and Agnosia 200
4. A Case of Apperceptive Agnosia 206
5. Two Other Patients 221
6. Conclusions 227

8. Object Concepts and Object Names: Some Deductions from Acquired Disorders of Word Processing 233
Elaine Funnell
1. Modularity and the Division of Labour 233
2. Conceptual Representations of Objects 236
3. Levels of Object Recognition 239
4. Semantic Processing and Imageable/Concrete Word Concepts 243
5. Shared Conceptual Information for Object Names and Objects 253

9. Dementia and Visual Agnosia 261
Oscar S. M. Marin
1. Dementia: Definition and Nosology 261
2. Perceptual Disorders in Dementia 264

3. Dementias as a Model for Neuropsychological Research 265
4. The Nature of Perceptual Disorders in Dementia 268
5. The Spectrum of Visual Agnosic Syndromes 275

10. The Fractionation of Visual Agnosia 281
Glyn W. Humphreys and *M. Jane Riddoch*
1. Introduction 281
2. Apperceptive Agnosia 282
3. Associative Agnosia 292
4. Classification and Lesion Sites 294
5. Re-classifying Visual Agnosia 299
6. Conclusions 304

Author Index 307

Subject Index 315

List of Contributors

John Campion *Behavioural Science Division, Admiralty Research Establishment, Queens Road, Teddington, Middlesex, U.K.*

Elaine Funnell *Cognitive Neuropsychology Research Group, Department of Psychology, University of London, Malet Street, London WC1E 7HX, U.K.*

Glyn W. Humphreys *Cognitive Neuropsychology Research Group, Department of Psychology, Birkbeck College, University of London, Malet Street, London WC1E 7HX, U.K.*

Andrew Kertesz *Clinical Neurology Department, St. Joseph's Hospital, 268 Grosvenor Street, London, Ontario N6A 4V2, Canada*

Oscar S. M. Marin *Laboratory of Cognitive Neuropsychology, Department of Neurology, Good Samaritan Hospital and Medical Center, Portland, Oregon 97210, U.S.A.*

Philip T. Quinlan *Cognitive Neuropsychology Research Group, Department of Psychology, Birkbeck College, University of London, Malet Street, London WC1E 7HX, U.K.*

M. Jane Riddoch *Department of Paramedical Sciences, North East London Polytechnic, Romford Road, Stratford, London E15 4LZ, U.K.*

Justine Sergent *Department of Neurology, McGill University, Montreal Neurological Institute, 3801 University Street, Montreal PQ, H3A 2B4, Canada*

Kent A. Stevens *Department of Computer and Information Science, University of Oregon, Eugene, Oregon 97403, U.S.A.*

Preface

This book has its origins in a meeting of the European International Neuropsychology Society (INS) at Aachen in June 1984. We had been asked to organise a symposium on visual agnosia at the conference. Our idea was to use the symposium to try to bring together workers from various disciplines in order to throw new light on the old problem of how visual object processing occurs, and on how it can be disturbed by damage to the brain. We invited a number of contributors to the book to give talks. The meeting seemed to go well, and there was interest expressed in the idea of using converging approaches to understanding object processing. Some time later, the thought occurred to us that a book covering these converging approaches might also serve some purpose, and this is the final product. In the period since the INS conference, work on all aspects of visual object processing has advanced considerably, and undoubtedly it will continue to do following the publication of this book. Our hope is to provide a state-of-the-art summary of work on the topic, and also to convey something of the excitement of working in a field subject to rapid development.

The final editing of the book has been helped by many people: all the "support staff" at Lawrence Erlbaum, the careful (though anonymous reviewers), and the Cognitive Neuropsychology Research Group at Birkbeck College, especially Philip Quinlan and Cathy Price. To all these people, our thanks. We are also grateful to Alan Cowey, Peter Dodwell, Geoff Hinton, Stephen Lupker, Stephen Palmer, and W. H. Freeman for permission to reproduce figures. All the photographs were taken by Freddie Elliot, and Daphne Ring and Sue Godfrey provided much-needed last-minute typing. Our final thanks go to Iain, Alec, and Kate, for putting up with our working in the evenings!

To Glyn and Dorothy

1 Introduction: Cognitive Neuropsychology and Visual Object Processing

Glyn W. Humphreys
*Cognitive Neuropsychology Research Group,
Department of Psychology, Birkbeck College,
University of London, Malet Street, London WC1E 7HX, U.K.*
M. Jane Riddoch
*Department of Paramedical Sciences,
North East London Polytechnic, Romford Road,
Stratford, London E15 4LZ, U.K.*

1. INTRODUCTION

The development of an efficient visual system has clearly been important for our survival. The ability to represent the position of objects with respect to our body position allows us to negotiate the world efficiently, so that we can avoid obstacles and reach appropriately for those objects we wish to grasp. The ability to recognise that an object has the same structure when seen from different viewpoints, with different lighting, etc. enables us to assign it the same response under a variety of contrasting viewing conditions. The ability to associate the viewed object with our memory facilitates such diverse activities as choosing food, taking early evasive action from predators, and selecting group members from amongst a crowd. Humans are also able to assign agreed names to objects, and so can communicate information about objects in an efficient manner. All of these different abilities reflect aspects of visual object processing.

Normally, visual object processing is so effortless and (seemingly) immediate that it is difficult to conceptualise the complexity of the processes involved. However, some inkling of this complexity can be gained when one encounters patients who, following brain damage, have selective difficulties in such apparently simple abilities as matching objects presented from different viewpoints, knowing how to use a common object or assigning a name to it. Such cases suggest that visual object processing involves a set of rather independent abilities, each of which can be selectively affected by brain damage.

In this book, we have attempted to bring together work by researchers concerned with the functional and neurological mechanisms underlying visual object processing, and the ways in which such mechanisms can be neurologically impaired. We have termed it a "Cognitive Neuropsychological" approach, because we believe it tries to relate evidence from neurological impairments of visual object processing to models of normal performance in a new and important way. Two broad aims are apparent. One is to test models of normal performance by evaluating how well the models account for the patterns of impairment and preservation of abilities that can occur following brain damage. The other is to use models of normal performance to further our understanding of acquired disorders of visual object processing. These aims distinguish the approach from neuropsychological work whose primary aim is to relate acquired deficits to the sites of damage, and from work in the field of cognitive psychology which attempts only to develop models of normal performance (see also Coltheart, 1984, 1985).

2. COGNITIVE NEUROPSYCHOLOGY AND VISUAL OBJECT PROCESSING

The characteristics of a cognitive neuropsychological approach to behaviour are only currently developing and, to some extent, they will be shaped by the nature of the particular field of study. In at least some areas, progress has been limited by the lack of well-specified information processing models (see Coltheart, 1985). It seems clear that we will remain unable to explain or to predict the various ways in which a given ability may break down if we have little idea of the component processes involved.

Recent developments in the field of visual object processing, however, provide grounds for optimism in this respect. In particular, the work on computer vision by David Marr and his associates (Marr, 1976, 1980, 1982; Marr & Nishihara, 1978) has produced a more developed information processing account of visual object processing than was hitherto available. Marr suggested that visual object processing could be considered in terms of a series of processing stages, each of which produces a more elaborated representation of a visually presented object, making different types of information explicit (see, for instance, Chapter 3 by Humphreys & Quinlan). Each of these processing stages operates as a separate module, which makes information available for subsequent stages but which is to a large extent functionally independent of those stages. Marr also outlined certain procedures which may determine how information at each stage is represented and transformed to provide the input for subsequent processing stages. Perhaps by considering the types of representation mediating visual object processing, and the procedures which create or enable access to these representations to occur, we may gain some insights into the disorders of object processing which are produced by brain damage. Also, instances of selective problems following brain damage may provide constraints on the models of normal performance.

These, then, are the general aims of a cognitive neuropsychology approach to visual object processing. However, the application of this approach to vision has not proved so straightforward. There are probably several reasons for this.

2.1. Applying Theories from Computer Vision to Humans

To begin with, there is an initial issue concerning the optimal way to "frame" the problems involved in visual object processing. As noted earlier, some of the most explicit models of the component processes involved are derived from the field of computer vision. Typically, such models are not aimed at accounting for how processing is carried out by humans. It follows that data from either normal observers or from subjects with acquired disorders of vision cannot be used to evaluate such models in their own right; the data may only be used to evaluate the models as accounts of human vision.

The question arises as to which models are then appropriate. For instance, an axiom of computational approaches to information processing is that theories may be expressed at different levels of abstraction (see Stevens, Chapter 2). At a very high level of abstraction (usually termed a computational level), theories may be concerned only with *what* the requirements of the system may be. Thus Marr (1979) states that "vision (requires) the construction of efficient symbolic descriptions from images of the world". Descriptions may be constructed which make available information which is unique to the object seen from a given viewpoint (i.e., some form of viewpoint dependent description), enabling us to manipulate the object in space. Descriptions may also be constructed which enable the object to address stored information irrespective of the viewpoint (i.e., some form of abstract object description), so that recognition can be achieved across different views (see Sutherland, 1979). According to this approach, vision requires the construction of each of the above kinds of description. Another level of theory would be concerned with *how* these descriptions are derived (the level of the algorithm), and yet another with how any processes are implemented in hardware terms (the level of the hardware; see Marr, 1982; Stevens, Chapter 2). We need to be clear about which level of theory is being addressed by any piece of behavioural evidence. Evidence that visual object processing in humans is highly constrained by viewpoint (see Humphreys & Quinlan, Chapter 3) would be pertinent to computational-level theories of the kind outlined by Marr (1982); evidence concerning the kinds of procedures used in constructing different types of visual description, however, would be pertinent to theories at the level of algorithm, not to computational level theories. The rejection of a theory as applied to human vision at the level of algorithm (e.g., in terms of the *type* of procedure used to generate a particular visual description) may not entail the rejection of the theory at a computational level (in the sense that that description may still mediate performance). Thus, the kinds of theory we accept will be dependent on the level of description to which any evidence applies.

2.2. Independence between Levels of Description

The argument that there exist separate levels of description of any complex information processing problem makes sense in computer science, where the constraints on one description of a task (e.g., in terms of a flow-chart or a description of the algorithm) may be quite independent of those at another (such as hardware). It is not clear that this is true of the brain. Details concerning the speed of neuronal transmission, the specialisation of different visual areas, the prior tuning of cells within any visual area, etc., may be crucial in determining the manner in which different processes are carried out. If this suggestion is correct, then we may not be able to apply a theory at one level of description without considering its implementation at other levels in some detail.

In cognitive neuropsychological approaches to other areas, particularly to the study of language and reading, evidence concerning the nature of the hardware has been effectively ignored (e.g. Coltheart, 1985; Mehler, Morton & Jusczyk, 1984). One reason for this selective view is that our knowledge of the brain structures mediating tasks such as reading has been insufficient to constrain theories concerned with reading mechanisms. This state of relative ignorance contrasts with that in the field of vision, where we now have quite detailed accounts of the neural systems involved, of their preferences for different types of visual input, and of their mapping (e.g. Cowey, 1985). It is possible that our developing knowledge of the neural hardware of vision will help determine theories of visual processing mechanisms. To illustrate this point, consider evidence concerning the selective preferences of cells in different visual areas of the cortex for different properties of visual stimuli. Recent work suggests that at least some cells in area V4 of the monkey cortex (see Fig. 11, Humphreys & Quinlan, Chapter 3) exhibit preferences for specific colours even when the wavelength of the illumination on a surface changes (i.e., they exhibit colour constancy; Zeki, 1980, 1983). Such cells might well be involved in colour identification (cf. Desimone, Schein, Moran, & Ungerleider, 1985;

Land, 1977). Theories concerned with how we identify, say, a letter in a particular colour may need to take account of the possibility that the neural structures subserving colour identification may differ from those finally involved in letter identification. For instance, such theories may need to posit that colour and form *identification* are functionally independent (cf. Ballard, Hinton, & Sejnowski, 1983; Treisman & Gelade, 1980). It would follow that in order to identify a particular letter in a particular colour (e.g., against a background consisting of the same letter in a different colour and different letters in the target colour), some special mechanism may be required to co-ordinate information from the different visual areas, such as linking by common retinotopic locations (cf. Quinlan & Humphreys, 1987) or by the serial application of focal attention (Treisman & Souther, 1985).

The process of interaction between the different levels of description need not be one way, however. Higher-level accounts of the mechanisms involved in visual object processing may also constrain theories at the hardware level. For instance, there is some evidence to suggest that the detection of boundaries between different visual textures can be determined by activity in sets of detectors responding to simple local, properties of stimuli, such as colour and line orientation (cf. Beck, 1967, 1982; Treisman & Gelade, 1980). These properties correspond to discriminations which may be expected from the activity of colour or orientation-tuned cells in the visual cortex (cf. Hubel & Weisel, 1968). Other behavioural evidence indicates that texture boundaries may also be distinguished on the basis of more complex visual information, such as "elongated blobs" and the number of line terminators (Julesz, 1980, 1981), or (possibly) closure (Treisman & Paterson, 1984). Given the argument that texture boundaries are signalled by specific hardware units tuned to the discriminating properties, it should follow that there exist detectors for the above complex types of information (see Julesz, 1980, 1986).

Inspection of those theories currently shaping cognitive neuropsychological work on vision indicates a fairly wide range of approaches to issues concerning the relations between different levels of theoretical description (although these differences are rarely made explicit). For example, Marr's (1982) account of the processes leading up to the generation of a three-dimensional (3-D) representation of a shape assumes that these processes may be described independently of their neural implementation. Other processing accounts seem to be more intimately linked with the known properties of neural hardware. Most "connectionist" theories of visual object processing at least purport to take seriously implications for the design of a system where complex knowledge is expressed via activity in a set of simple (neurone-like) computational units (see Hinton & Anderson, 1981; Humphreys & Quinlan, this volume; McClelland & Rumelhart,

1986). Some connectionist theories not only allocate separate processing units for specific visual properties of stimuli (such as lines at particular orientations and positions; see Fig. 8, Chapter 3, Humphreys & Quinlan, this volume), they also group units corresponding to properties within a given dimension (such as colour or size) to form a "parameter space", where the value(s) of a stimulus along that dimension is specified (cf. Ballard et al., 1983; Feldman & Ballard, 1982). Such parameter spaces may be considered analogous to areas of the visual cortex selectively tuned to different visual dimensions.

What are the implicationsof these different approaches for the aims of cognitive neuropsychology we outlined earlier? First, consider how we may use evidence drawn from brain damaged patients to assess the different models. Models which maintain a clear independence between descriptions of processing mechanisms and hardware descriptions can only be addressed by information concerning the functional deficits of patients (i.e., by the type of behavioural deficit exhibited and by its relation to other component abilities). This position is akin to that typical of cognitive neuropsychological approaches in other areas, such as reading mentioned earlier. Models in which processing mechanisms are tied to the properties and locations of specific cortical areas may similarly be addressed by functional evidence. However, in addition, such models are also open to evaluation by evidence concerning the site and extent of damage. For instance, consider the possibility that a patient continues to exhibit colour constancy following selective ablation of area V4. This result would be difficult to accommodate for a theory which posited a colour-processing system explicitly modelled on our knowledge of the properties of cells in V4, and which maintained that colour-constancy could *only* be achieved using that colour-processing system. A theory positing a colour-processing system which does not have a one-to-one relationship with area V4 would not, of course, be similarly damaged.

Accounts of brain damaged patients in terms of these different approaches will also differ. Models assuming independent algorithm-level and hardware-level descriptions account for behavioural deficits in patients in terms of patterns of dysfunction in (abstracted) processing components. Models assuming some explicit relations between the levels of description may additionally take on board information about the *nature* of the brain damage. Again, this may be illustrated by reference to theories positing that a given ability reflects patterns of activation across representations tuned to specific properties of stimuli (the connectionist accounts discussed by Humphreys & Quinlan, Chapter 3; the cascade model discussed by Riddoch & Humphreys, Chapter 4). Such theories may (eventually) offer different accounts of a particular deficit according to whether the deficit is due to a single selective lesion, due to a pattern of disseminated lesions (cf.

Campion, Chapter 7) or due to a reduced density of connections within a neuronal network (cf. Marin, Chapter 9). Taken to their furthest conclusion, such theories may even return to the approach of classifying patients according to the nature (i.e. the type, extent, and site) of their brain damage, at least where our knowledge of the nature of the brain damage and its relation to behaviour is sufficiently precise. Campion, Chapter 7, argues for this approach to classifying patients with visual processing deficits following carbon monoxide poisoning.

Whichever approach is adopted, we believe it important to realise that models can differ both in terms of their processing mechanisms and in terms of their assumptions concerning how the hypothesised processing mechanisms relate to the hardware of the system. The kinds of inferences we make will depend on the assumed processing—hardware relations.

2.3. Processing Modules

The assumption that information processing is *modular*, in the sense that it is thought to comprise of a set of functionally independent processes, is one that is clearly of fundamental importance to cognitive neuropsychological approaches to behaviour (see Coltheart,1985). Such an assumption is at the heart of accounts of brain damaged patients in terms of a pattern of intact and impaired component abilities (see Funnell, Chapter 8). A principle of modularity has also been espoused by workers in computer vision (Marr, 1976; Stevens, Chapter 2). In the latter context, workers have suggested that breaking a large computation up into a series of separate modules is useful because a small change to one process will not have consequences on others. By specifying a complex behaviour in terms of a series of separate processing modules, direct links between computer vision theories and theories of human behaviour seem to be facilitated.

However, it is relevant to point out that concepts of modularity can differ. One view, outlined by Funnell (Chapter 8), maintains that the principle of modularity relates to the knowledge requirements and processes demanded by different tasks, not to the tasks themselves. When this approach is applied to brain damaged subjects, we would expect that damage could selectively affect certain types of knowledge or certain processes. Two tasks will dissociate only to the extent that they tap the same damaged or intact processing modules.

It is also possible to outline a rather different interpretation of modularity, apparent amongst at least some computer vision researchers. For instance, Stevens (Chapter 2) considers the view that any two computations may be thought of as being modular to the extent that they can be performed independently of one another. One implication of this view is that two tasks may be considered modular even though both tasks require the same type of process. Stevens cites the example of surface interpolation. Our ability to see a smooth surface at a different depth to its background when presented with a random-dot stereogram (Julesz, 1971) requires the interpolation of this surface between corresponding points in the left and right retinal images. Also, our ability to derive 3-D form information from motion requires the interpolation of a smooth surface between points and edges in the image where velocity profiles can be computed. It is possible that two-surface interpolation procedures are instantiated in two different modules: One concerned with deriving 3-D form information by stereopsis and one concerned with deriving 3-D form information from motion. The job of such modules would be to make available (independently), 3-D form descriptions from different types of stimulus information. Such descriptions would then be combined via a further, subsequent process. The implications of this second view of modularity for understanding neurological deficits in performance are quite different to the implications of the first. Here, we would expect brain damage to selectively affect abilities such as the computation of 3-D form from stereo information, or even a process such as surface interpolation in stereopsis. However, extensive damage to the "stereopsis module" may nevertheless leave the "form from motion module" (including its surface interpolation component) intact.

Present knowledge of the modules mediating visual object processing is probably insufficient to decide between these two views. Indeed, it may even be that the type of modularity governing early visual processing differs from that governing "higher-order" processes such as recognition and identification. The implications of the differing views of modularity should, however, be borne in mind when considering the kinds of approaches taken when investigating selective visual processing disorders.

2.4. Interactions between Modules

In discussing the principle of modularity, Marr (1982) notes that this principle "does not forbid weak interactions between different modules". The problem here from a behavioural point of view is in defining the extent and nature of any interactions. At one extreme we might presume that processing is organised in a series of discrete stages, with information being made available to each subsequent stage only following the resolution of processing at an earlier stage. Such discrete stages can be described as being strongly modular, in the sense that each processing stage is immune from other stages (e.g., from the influence of partial information from earlier stages or from information fed forward from later stages). At another extreme, one could imagine a system in which no processing stage is immune from the influence of any other. This can be said of "interactive activation" models of information processing, in which partial information is transmitted between processing stages and in which later stages feed forward to constrain earlier stages (McClelland & Rumelhart, 1986). Such models are only weakly modular. For instance, brain damage could selectively isolate an earlier process from a later process, even though in normality the processes would interact (see Patterson & Morton, 1985, for a similar distinction concerning models of visual word pronunciation).

Again, models differ in terms of whether they take a relatively strong or weak view on this topic. Marr's (1982) view is characteristically strong; the connectionist models discussed by Humphreys and Quinlan and the cascade models of picture naming discussed by Riddoch and Humphreys (both in this volume) are relatively weak. Different accounts of brain damaged patients may follow from the contrasting assumptions about modularity. For instance, a strongly modular account of picture naming might hold that the structural characteristics of objects are processed fully before later information about, say, an object's name is contacted. According to this account, a patient who makes visual errors in naming pictures would be thought to have a problem in processes up to the stage of accessing structural knowledge about objects. An account assuming only weak modularity (e.g., the cascade model; Riddoch & Humphreys, Chapter 4) would not necessarily take the same position, since stages subsequent to that involving access to structural knowledge about objects could be affected by partially activated structural information. A patient could make visual errors due to problems in these later stages (see Riddoch & Humphreys, 1987, for a more detailed discussion).

Additionally, the inferences we make about normal processes, using evidence from patients, are influenced by assumptions about modularity. In a strongly modular system, selective damage to one process would leave any functionally independent processes intact. In a weakly modular system this may not occur, since a problem in one process could constrain the operation of others. Such a conclusion is possible whether one's account is pitched at an algorithm-level description or at a description at the level of the hardware. Sergent (Chapter 5) is concerned with the functions of the left and right cerebral hemispheres in object perception (a hardware-level issue). She argues that the capabilities of the left and the right hemisphere to process high and low spatial frequency information may differ. For example, the right hemisphere may preferentially operate on lower spatial frequencies than the left. Following unilateral right hemisphere damage, a patient may fail on a task *not* because the processes required for performance are functionally lateralised in the right hemisphere (e.g., the processes required to match objects across viewpoints; cf. Warrington, 1982; see also Humphreys & Quinlan, Chapter 3), but because right hemisphere damage changes the quality of the information available to the left hemisphere. In normality, task performance may be critically dependent on the co-activation of information in both hemispheres. In this case, we would be wise to be cautious when using single pieces of evidence from brain damaged patients to infer the localisation of one behavioural function either within a single processing module or neural structure. For instance, our conclusions about the nature of any processing module or its anatomical locus would be bolstered by converging evidence that a deficit was functionally localised: by using tasks tapping other processing stages, by examining the temporal characteristics of processing in more detail, or by simulation.

2.5. Positive Attributes

The problems involved in taking a cognitive neuropsychological approach to visual object processing thus concern issues about the kinds of description that are most appropriate for explaining behaviour, about the relations between the different descriptions, about the kinds of processes which serve as the functional modules within the processing system, and about the relations between modules. Overall, it seems likely that visual object processing will best be understood by detailed examination of different kinds of description and of the contrasting questions which arise. As our knowledge about performance expressed at these different levels increases, we may hope for increasing convergence between such apparently contrasting fields of study as computer vision, experimental psychology, and neurophysiology. The possibility of constraints between these different fields represents one of the most exciting areas of future development, and one of the strengths of the cognitive neuropsychological approach.

One of the probable consequences of developments in the field is that we will produce more detailed models of the component processes involved in different tasks. Such models in turn produce more detailed predictions of the kinds of performance dysfunction which may follow brain damage. Disorders specific to visual object processing are typically classed within the syndrome of visual agnosia, of which two forms are distinguished: apperceptive agnosia, thought to pertain to the perceptual representation of the visual world, and associative agnosia, thought to pertain to the association of perceptual information with world knowledge (see Kertesz, Chapter 6). However, as our knowledge of visual object processing from other areas grows, it seems increasingly unlikely that a simple two-stage account of processing and its breakdown will suffice. The initial "nosological" distinction between apperceptive and association stages (cf. Marin, Chapter 9) will fractionate, to provide a more precise account of the similarities and differences between patients. By bringing together work from different research fields, we hope to indicate the ways in which new distinctions about visual object processing in general are developing (e.g. Stevens, Humphreys & Quinlan, Sergent, Riddoch & Humphreys, Funnell, this volume), and the ways in which such distinctions are being applied to understanding agnosia (e.g., Kertesz, Marin, Humphreys & Riddoch, this volume, Chapter 10). The utility of the multi-stage view which appears on the horizon (see Kertesz, Humphreys & Riddoch, this volume) can only be judged in time, in terms of how well it accounts for patients and of how useful its distinctions are for accounting for normal performance. In the meantime, it may serve as a fresh focus for work in the area.

3. THE BOOK

The book is divided into two sections. In the first section, the chapters approach visual object processing from a consideration of which processes may *need* to be adopted either to develop an intelligent artificial visual system or to explain normal performance.

Stevens (Chapter 2) discusses object processing from the perspective of computer vision. He outlines the kinds of assumptions adopted by workers in this field concerning functional modularity and the implementation of the knowledge into procedural rules within the modules (such as "rigidity" assumptions in deriving 3-D form information from motion). He goes on to consider some of the implications of computer vision for understanding both normal vision and its breakdown following brain damage.

The following chapters by Humphreys and Quinlan (Chapter 3) and by Riddoch and Humphreys (Chapter 4) focus on particular operations in visual object processing: Object constancy and the processes involved in accessing stored structural, semantic and name information about objects. Humphreys and Quinlan's chapter draws on work from a number of fields, such as computer vision, experimental cognitive psychology, animal vision, and neurologically impaired human vision. After considering the kinds of logical problems which constrain theories of object constancy, evidence concerning the mechanisms involved is reviewed. Humphreys and Quinlan propose that the problems of object constancy are not solved in any single way by the visual system, but that different solutions are adopted depending on the kinds of information available and the uses to which that information must be put. They suggest that future research would prosper by de-emphasising general purpose solutions to constancy and by considering in more detail stimulus and task constraints.

Riddoch and Humphreys (Chapter 4) are concerned with the higher-order processes involved in accessing stored knowledge for picture naming. Various accounts of picture naming in normal observers are outlined, and a framework is developed which holds that picture naming operates in cascade. The cascade model is then applied to account for different forms of picture naming disorder in patients. This chapter provides an example of a "weakly modular" account of visual object processing (see Section 2.4 above), and it attempts to explain both why such an account might be needed and its implications for understanding neurologically impaired patients.

The final chapter in this section of the book, by Sergent (Chapter 5), focuses primarily on the anatomical localisation of processing mechanisms in the left and right cerebral hemispheres. However, in attempting to do this, Sergent draws on evidence from normal observers and animals in addition to brain damaged humans. It again provides an illuminating example of how we may look to evidence from seemingly different areas to further our understanding of vision. Necessarily, the chapter highlights the issue of face perception, since considerably more detailed work on hemispheric differences in face perception has been conducted than on such differences in object perception (particularly in terms of developing the kinds of process models necessary to explain both abilities). Nevertheless, many of the lessons to be learned are the same, since faces are perhaps but one extreme example of objects which require accurate and integrated visual information for recognition to occur (see Diamond & Carey, 1986). The importance of viewing normal performance as the product of interactions between different processes is emphasised (see Section 2.4).

The second section of the book deals with the types of visual object processing disorder which may occur in human subjects after brain damage. Kertesz (Chapter 6) outlines the historical background of work in this area. He describes which behavioural deficits are typically labelled as apperceptive or associative agnosia, or as other forms of visual object processing disorder such as optic aphasia; he considers the relations between these disorders and some associated deficits (such as colour and face perception, word recognition, etc.); and he considers the utility of a two-stage account of agnosia (see earlier). Kertesz's review provides a useful introduction to agnosia from a clinical perspective.

Campion (Chapter 7) focuses on the visual processing disorder typically labelled as apperceptive agnosia. His particular concern is with how psychological constructs (such as "perceptual representation") should be operationally defined to help understand the deficits in such patients, and on whether distinctions between "sensory" and "perceptual" processes are useful in this respect. He discusses how, in at least some instances, it might be useful to group patients according to the type of neurological damage sustained, rather than on the basis of higher-order constructs. Insights might then be gained by considering how the neurological damage constrains information processing. This approach stresses how "hardware-level" descriptions can further our understanding of the processing mechanisms mediating task performance.

Funnell (Chapter 8) discusses more central deficits in visual object processing, particularly those concerned with the involvement of semantic knowledge. She outlines a novel approach which uses evidence from word matching, naming, and comprehension tasks with patients to address the issue of the nature of the semantic information mediating both these tasks and visual object processing. The relations between our stored knowledge of different properties of objects (such as sensory and functional knowledge) are also considered, using data drawn from the ratings of normal subjects. Views of the nature of the semantic system are clearly important for understanding central deficits in visual object processing. Funnell argues that the semantic representations of objects differ in terms of the types and number of attributes which are specified, and that the loss of particular types of attribute may be important in understanding certain types of dysfunction.

Central deficits in visual object processing are also of concern to Marin (Chapter 9). He deals with the physiological changes to the brain which occur in various forms of dementia, and with how such changes may precipitate deficits in object recognition and naming. Of particular interest is the fact that dementia is often consequent on quite different physiological changes to those observed in patients with brain lesions following head injury, stroke or tumour. The question is raised whether accounts of the processing deficits sustained also need to reflect these physiological differences (see Section 2.2). Irrespective of whether one is sensitive to such hardware-level effects, cases of dementia can provide examples of remarkably spared islets of ability amongst otherwise gross behavioural disturbances; and it seems likely that work with such cases will be increasingly important for understanding the breakdown of what are, in normality, highly-interactive processes.

In the final chapter we (Humphreys & Riddoch) attempt to examine in detail some of the implications for classifying visual agnosia in terms of a multi-stage theory of visual object processing. An expanded classification scheme is outlined to account for documented cases of agnosia, and to predict further ways in which object processing might break down. The aim is to provide a more flexible classification scheme which enjoys a better fit with theories of normal vision and which can be used predictively. Consideration is also given to the relations between different behavioural deficits and different types and sites of lesion.

We hope that the differing fields drawn upon in this volume will attract readers from contrasting backgrounds and that each will find something of interest, not only from within their own field. We also hope that the approach adopted illustrates some of the ways in which we may, in future, cross the boundaries of different disciplines to gain a fuller understanding of human behaviour.

REFERENCES

Ballard, D. H., Hinton, G. E., & Sejnowski, T. J. (1983). Parallel visual computation. *Nature*, *306*, 21–26.

Beck, J. (1967). Perceptual grouping produced by line figures. *Perceptual & Psychophysics*, *1*, 371–394.

Beck, J. (1982). Texture segregation. In J. Beck (Ed.), *Organization and representation in perception*. Hillsdale, N.J.: Lawrence Erlbaum Associates Inc.

Coltheart, M. (1984). Editorial in *Cognitive Neuropsychology*, *1*, 1–8.

Coltheart, M. (1985). Cognitive neuropsychology and the study of reading. In M. I. Posner and O. S. M. Marin (Eds.), *Attention and performance*, Vol. XI. Hillsdale, N.J. Lawrence Erlbaum Associates Inc.

Cowey, A. (1985). Aspects of cortical organization related to selective attention and selective impairments of visual perception. In M.I. Posner and O.S.M. Marin (Eds.), *Attention and performance*, Vol. XI. Hillsdale, N.J.: Lawrence Erlbaum Associates Inc.

Desimone, R., Schein, S. J., Moran, J., & Ungerleider, L. G. (1985). Contour, color and shape analysis beyond the striate cortex. *Vision Research*, *25*, 441–452.

Diamond, R. & Carey, S. (1986). Why faces are and are not special: An effect of expertise. *Journal of Experimental Psychology: General*, *115*, 107–117.

Feldman, J. A. & Ballard, D. H. (1982). Connectionist models and their properties. *Cognitive Science*, *6*, 205–254.

Hinton, G. E. & Anderson, J. A. (1981). *Parallel models of associative memory*. Hillsdale, N.J.: Lawrence Erlbaum Associates Inc.

Hubel, D. H. & Wiesel, T. N. (1968). Receptive fields and functional architecture of monkey striate cortex. *Journal of Physiology, 195*, 215–243.

Julesz, B. (1971). *Foundations of cylopean perception*. Chicago: University of Chicago Press.

Julesz, B. (1980). Spatial nonlinearities in the instantaneous perception of textures with identical power spectra. *Philosophical Transactions of the Royal Society, London, B290*, 83–94.

Julesz, B. (1981). Textons, the elements of texture perception and their interaction. *Nature*, *290*, 91–97.

Julesz, B. (1986). Texton gradients: The texton theory revisited. *Biological Cybernetics*, *54*, 245–251.

Land, E. H. (1977). The retinex theory of color vision. *Scientific American*, *237*, 108–128.

Marr, D. (1976). Early processing of visual information. *Philosophical Transactions of the Royal Society, London, B275*, 483–524.

Marr,D. (1979). Representing and computing visual information. In P. H. Winston and R.H. Brown (Eds.), *Artificial intelligence: An MIT perspective*. London: MIT Press.

Marr, D. (1980). Visual information processing: The structure and creation of visual representations. *Philosophical Transactions of the Royal Society, London, B290*, 199–218.

Marr, D. (1982). *Vision*. San Francisco: W. H. Freeman.

Marr, D. & Nishihara, H. K. (1978). Representation and recognition of the spatial organization of three-dimensional shapes. *Proceedings of the Royal Society, London, B200*, 269–294.

McLelland, J. L. & Rumelhart, D. E. (1986). *Parallel distributed processing: Explorations in the microstructure of cognition, Vol. 2: Psychological and biological models*. London: MIT Press.

Mehler, J., Morton, J., & Jusczyk, P. W. (1984). On reducing language to biology. *Cognitive Neuropsychology*, *1*, 83–116.

Patterson, K. E. & Morton, J. (1985). From orthography to phonology: An attempt at an old interpretation. In K. E. Patterson, J. C. Marshall, and M. Coltheart (Eds.), *Surface dyslexia: Neuropsychological and cognitive studies of phonological reading*. London: Lawrence Erlbaum Associates Ltd.

Quinlan, P. T. & Humphreys, G. W. (1987). Visual search for targets defined by combinations of color, shape, and size: An examination of the task constraints on feature and conjunction searches. *Perception & Pyschophysics*, *41*, 455–472.

Riddoch, M. J. & Humphreys, G. W. (1987). Visual object processing in optic aphasia: A case of semantic access agnosia. *Cognitive Neuropsychology*, *4*, 131–186.

Sutherland, N. S. (1979). The representationof three-dimensional objects. *Nature*, *278*, 395–398.

Treisman, A. & Gelade, G. A. (1980). A feature integration theory of attention. *Cognitive Psychology*, *12*, 97–136.

Treisman, A. & Paterson, R. (1984). Emergent features, attention and object perception. *Journal of Experimental Psychology: Human Perception and Performance*, *10*, 12–31.

Treisman, A. & Souther, J. (1985) Search asymmetry: A diagnostic for preattentive processing of separable features. *Journal of Experimental Psychology: General*, *114*, 285–310.

Warrington, E. K. (1982). Neuropsychological studies of object recognition. *Philosophical Transactions of the Royal Society, London*, *298*, 15–33.

Zeki, S. M. (1980). The representation of colours in the cerebral cortex. *Nature*, *284*, 412–418.

Zeki, S. M. (1983). Color coding in the cerebral cortex: The responses of wavelength-selective and color-coded cells in monkey visual cortex to changes in wavelength composition. *Neuroscience*, *9*, 767–781.

2 Visual Object Perception from a Computational Perspective

Kent A. Stevens
Department of Computer and Information Science, University of Oregon, Eugene, Oregon 97403, U.S.A.

1. INTRODUCTION

David Marr introduced a computational approach towards the study of biological information processing, which stresses that a complex system such as the visual system is feasibly understood only across several levels of abstraction (Marr, 1982; Marr & Poggio, 1977). The suggestion is that no single level of description, be it behavioural, psychophysical, computational, or neurophysiological, can adequately describe both function and implementation with sufficient detail and scope to allow the necessary breadth of understanding.

The necessity for multiple levels of description is accepted in computer science without question. When designing or analysing a complex information processing system one attends either to questions of *what* the requirements, goals, and tasks of the system are, or to questions of *how* the system achieves these goals, such as what the algorithms are and how the data are organised.[1] One shifts between these two levels of description often

[1]An algorithm, as defined in computer science, is the formal specification of a particular computation. Informally, it is a sequence of step-by-step instructions or commands which, if interpreted by some processor, would result in the achievement of some computation. An algorithm is expressed by means of a language having an agreed-upon set of constructs for referring to data structures, operations on data structures, and constructs for controlling the execution of these operations. In principle, one can define parallel as well as sequential algorithms, for a variety of types of processing mechanism ranging from analogue to digital

without regard for a third, more detailed level, that of the actual hardware on which the algorithms run and the data reside. These three levels of description are rather distinct in computer science, and each has its appropriate use and limitations. It is simply not feasible to describe a complex computation in terms of events at the level of the hardware. The technical language and formal principles that are relevant at the level of the digital hardware are neither appropriate nor relevant at the level of algorithm and program, and vice versa. Descriptions of computations are best made via a technical language and a set of formal principles concerned with algorithms, data structures, and other relevant abstractions.

It would be theoretically possible to describe the precise pattern of hardware events arising within a computer during, say, the computation of a least squares fit algorithm. The determinism of the digital computer allows, with considerable tedium, the complete specification of its detailed behaviour down to the most elemental state transitions within its electronic components. However, consider working upwards, inferring what the processor is doing, what function it is performing, purely on the basis of the observed hardware event. It is not merely a matter of the overwhelming complexity which makes this not feasible, it is the inappropriateness of the technical language for other than the description of local events.

Different languages have been developed for describing computations at different levels of specificity. Of course, computer science is a synthetic science involved with the development and study of computational machinery as it can be humanly conceived and understood. One might argue that limitations in our ability to conceive of and understand complex systems fairly forces one to attend exclusively to either the higher (algorithmic) level or the lower (implementation) level. Be that as it may, one might also argue that computer science has found a fundamental principle of computation (a law perhaps as fundamental as entropy or the conservation laws in physics), namely, that one can describe a computation independently of how it is implemented, or equivalently, that there are arbitrarily many equivalent implementations of a given computation. This

(discrete state). When one forwards a particular algorithm one suggests a particular recipe for how the computation proceeds and in what form the data to be manipulated are represented. There are infinitely many equivalent algorithms for achieving any given computation (consider how many ways one could rewrite a computer program which would not effect its external behaviour). The choice of algorithm depends, in part, on issues of how the given primitive representations and functions are implemented—the machinery at hand. It also depends on design goals such as fault tolerance or "graceful degradation" of behaviour as input is impoverished, time and space efficiency, the immediacy with which the output of the computation is provided to subsequent computations, and so forth (Marr, 1982, p. 106). Thus, when discussing a computation at the level of algorithm one uses rather specific notions of data structure and the operations that transform input into output.

principle, established by Turing and others earlier in this century, has provided the underpinnings for the formal description of computations.

Marr suggests that there is no fundamental reason why this principle does not apply equally to biological information processing, and to vision in particular. That is, vision is achieved by processes that extract and manipulate visual information. These computations, while certainly not implemented in the same manner as those performed in silicon technology, are computations nonetheless. Furthermore, being computations, they are amenable to a formal description.

One question, then, is what advantage is gained by describing human vision formally as computations? Another question is whether that formal description is really able to be divorced from the biology, or whether it is a nicety of computer science applied to computers, but not of computer science applied to organisms. I think that the answers to both are to be found in the computational work that has been performed in the last decade or so. The purpose of this chapter is to indicate the utility of this approach and to demonstrate where the extensions of these results will take us.

2. MODULARITY IN VISION

If vision is to be characterised in terms of information processing problems, how do we determine what any specific problem is in order to study it? Consider colour perception, stereopsis (the creation of depth information from the disparities between the images in the left and right eyes) and the extraction of three-dimensional (3-D) information from motion, all of which have clear computational goals. In principle, one could imagine an independent solution to each, and behaviourally, there appears to be substantial independence of function.

The dogmatic view of functional modularity would be that if two computations are theoretically orthogonal (i.e. logically able to be performed independently), they should be treated as distinct even though they may share many common underlying mechanisms. For example, the perception of colour seems orthogonal to the problem of determining the direction of motion in the retinal image. Consider then the colour-contingent motion and after-effect. One defers the question of how or why such couplings occur until later, when questions of visual mechanism are examined.

A reasonable sceptic might regard this approach as dangerously simplistic. How can we trust our intuitions as to what computational problems are distinct and which are inherently interrelated, and how can we tell which visual phenomena reflect the visual algorithms and which are merely due to "implementation details"? More generally, how can we tell whether our decomposition of vision into modules reflects that which nature chose? The still more sceptical might further suggest that it is misguided to imagine any modular decomposition of vision, that vision can be understood only by embracing its complexity and interactions as a whole. I would remind them that we have already developed computer systems the complexity of which defy understanding except in terms of levels of abstraction (ignoring the hardware when thinking of the functionality, and vice versa) and only very locally (considering only a very narrow aspect of the system under the simplifying assumption that there are no important dependencies on global states of the system that are not already reflected by local parameters). Of course, we return to the fact that computer systems are artefacts that are intentionally made with a high degree of strict modularity—we cannot make complicated systems otherwise.

Marr (1982, p. 102), however, suggests that nature has also adopted the *principle of modular design,* primarily because if the components of a system are not made as independent of one another as the individual tasks allow, a small change to one component will have undesired consequences elsewhere. A system that is not modular would be difficult to improve or extend; evolution presumably favours a functionally modular design.

Functional modularity does not mean strict segregation of function at the neural level, however. Actual segregation or isolation of processes, in fact, has its disadvantages, primarily poor economy of design and the problem of communicating functionally useful information among processes. If two problems are interrelated (such that the solution to one partly constrains the solution to the other), it would be disadvantageous to isolate them. Moreover, just as evolution favours functional modularity, it probably is limited in how literally the modularity can be extended. That is, it would seem improbable that evolution would extend the capabilities of a visual system by implementing the new perceptual ability with neural structures that are strictly isolated from the neural mechanisms that preceded it. More likely would be either the duplication or subdivision of existing cortical structures in order to perform some new, ecologically advantageous, computation on existing internal information structures (see, for example, Livingstone and Hubel, 1984, where they suggest that new functional architecture to support colour vision was introduced into the centre of the hypercolumns found in striate cortex). As a consequence, the new functional architecture would not only be intimately tied with the earlier architecture, it would probably incorporate facilitatory interactions between related processes in an *ad hoc* and case-by-case manner. I would doubt that evolution adheres to strict design standards for adding new functional capabilities; it is probably governed primarily by the particular problems at hand.

For example, consider the problem of combining the 3-D information delivered simultaneously by stereopsis and motion. Both motion and stereopsis have limitations in the quality of the 3-D information they can deliver individually. In fact, they are complementary so that the results of each process can be combined to provide information that is otherwise ambiguous (Richards, 1985; Waxman & Ullman, 1985). It is not known, however, whether the combining of motion and stereopsis is achieved at a later stage of depth processing, with no "cross-talk" between the two processes that deliver depth information, or concurrently by more intimate interaction between the two. Since there are, in addition to motion and stereopsis, several additional sources of 3-D information, it would seem easier to imagine a computational architecture for combining 3-D information that minimises interactions between or among the contributing "modules". As to what global architecture is incorporated in human vision is still largely a matter of speculation. Most of the insight has been gained at the level of the brain's "microarchitecture", as it were, the processing achieved by individual neural units selective to, for example, motion or stereo disparity.

3. SURVEY OF COMPUTATIONAL PROBLEMS

In the following we discuss several problems central to spatial perception: stereopsis, the 3-D interpretation of motion, the interpolation or "filling in" of smooth surfaces, the description of surface shape, the 3-D interpretation of contours and texture gradients, and very briefly sketch the processing that might follow the perception of visible surfaces. In examining a variety of information processing problems such as these one can discern a recurring theme in this type of work—one of discovering the physical (or geometrical) constraints that allow the solution to a given visual problem, postulating the method by which the constraints are incorporated into some computation, making explicit various aspects of how the data are represented and processed, and eventually accounting not only for psychophysical results but tying these suggestions to particular neuorophysiological mechanisms. It is a relatively recent idea to attempt to bridge between computationally motivated theories and clinical findings. After the following survey we will close on that note.

3.1. The Matching Problem in Stereopsis

A particularly clear problem is presented by the matching problem in stereopsis, namely the determination of the correspondence between left and right images in order that the angular disparity between corresponding elements may be registered. Each image point in the one eye might correspond to any of a range of image points in the other eye, depending on where the point projects when viewed from the perspective of the other eye. This has also been termed the false-targets problem. For instance, given an image with 4 points in the left eye and 4 points in the right eye, there are 16 possible matchings, only 4 of which are correct, the remaining 12 being false targets. How is the correct matching established over a rich, detailed image where false targets abound?

Various proposals could be made as to the image features that are brought into correspondence—intensity points, segments of edges or lines, and more complicated features involving colour, contrast magnitude, and so forth. For example, one might propose local correlation of the intensity values to estimate the stereo disparity in each vicinity. However, is the computational problem of stereopsis being addressed appropriately in such proposals? Does intensity-value correlation solve the underlying computational problem? Empirically, correlation of individual pixels (intensity samples) has generally proven inadequate. The problem lies in the appropriateness of the tokens that one seeks to match across left and right images. Simply put, there is no reason to expect a pixel-to-pixel correspondence across images. In contrast, Marr and Poggio (1977) recast the computational problem of stereo matching more as one of matching corresponding physical surface features, or at least, of matching elements in the image that have a more reliable tie to surface features than mere pixels. One consequence of this view was to rethink the basis for the matching computation and to derive three constraints on the matching problem. One is the *continuity* constraint. Because the visual world is dominated by smooth, opaque surfaces, stereo disparity varies smoothly almost everywhere, because the distance to the visible surfaces varies continuously except at surface boundaries. Note that it is precisely at surface boundaries where the correlation approach would fail. Additionally, Marr and Poggio recognised two additional constraints on the matching problem—*compatibility*, which means that the descriptive elements in each eye must be compatible with being adjacent views of the same physical features (hence the contrast signs must match, and edges must match edges, etc.), and *uniqueness*, which means that the correspondence must be one-to-one almost everywhere (the exceptions occurring along occlusion boundaries).

Marr (1982, p. 114) reflects on these constraints and suggests the following *fundamental assumption of stereopsis*. If a correspondence is established between physically meaningful primitives extracted from left and right images of a scene that contains a sufficient amount of detail, and if the correspondence satisfys the three matching constraints, then that correspondence is physically correct (and it follows that the correspondence is unique). Marr suggests that these three constraints are sufficient to solve the stereo matching problem. Identifying, justifying, and demonstrating the sufficiency of such a set constraints is the central activity of deriving a computational theory. We will see other examples momentarily. Note that while the constraints seem reasonable and plausible it is not clear that much headway has been made on the problem at hand, namely explaining how the visual system solves the stereo matching problem. After all, one must get back to worrying about matching corresponding items in the two images, and terms such as "physically meaningful" do not immediately suggest particular matching primitives. In fact, it is when one attempts to become more specific that one inevitably goes "down" a level of abstraction, down to the level of algorithm. Marr and Poggio have examined two quite different algorithms for stereopsis (Marr, 1982), and Mayhew and Frisby (1981) independently proposed similar, highly plausible algorithms *vis-à-vis* human stereopsis. The insight that produced these computational theories of human stereopsis came from thinking about the underlying physical constraints that might, in principle, admit a solution.

It should be pointed out that a variety of computational theories for matching have been proposed, each based on a different combination of constraints. Mayhew (1982) describes five constraints that are more or less independent and which can lead to different matching schemes having different performances. The constraints are: (1) the opacity constraint; (2) the epipolar constraint, that a plane passing through the optical centres of the eyes projects to a straight line in each eye, leading to strategies for searching along particular loci for matches; (3) figural continuity, that edges of surfaces and surface markings are spatially continuous; (4) an object in a given point in space will project to luminance changes in the two eyes with similar descriptions; and (5) the ordering constraint, wherein the stereo projection almost always preserves the ordering of luminance changes along corresponding paths. Mayhew (1982) then shows how different combinations of these constraints have been incorporated in different theories and discusses the relative power of these constraints (in enforcing particular matches or excluding certain matches locally).

A computer implementation can be made of a particular algorithm which embodies a given set of these matching constraints, and its behaviour examined when given digitised images of stereo pairs. It is possible to digitise the image with sufficiently fine resolution and broad dynamic range to match the granularity and range of the retinal receptors, then filter the digital image by local lateral-inhibition operators that model retinal ganglion X-cells. The receptive field of these operators is modelled as a difference of Gaussian distributions (see Marr, 1982; Marr & Hildreth, 1980; Wilson & Giese, 1977). With an implemented model of the early intensity processing and for the specific image features of tokens that are matched between left and right images, one can implement and test a given stereo matching algorithm. The performance of the algorithm can be compared with human vision across a wide range of visual stimuli, from random dot stereograms to natural images. The "psychophysics" of a computer implementation of a stereo matching theory is rather difficult to interpret. If the implementation utterly fails to achieve the same stereo correspondence as do humans in viewing a particular stereo pair one can surmise that the two methods differ in some combination of the matching constraints or the matching tokens, (for example, Mayhew and Frisby, 1981, devised an ingenious stereo pair that tested a detailed prediction regarding the stereo matching tokens incorporated in human vision). It is more difficult to interpret the behaviour of an implemented theory when it is reasonably close to human behaviour but deviates consistently and significantly. One interpretation of the performance disparity is that the human visual system embodies a close, but not exact, engineering approximation to the process laid out in the given theory. That is, the theory is correct but does not capture all the implementation details. The alternative explanation is that one does not yet have the right theory, of course. There have been several stereopsis implementations by different investigators, each based on similar but slightly different combinations of computational constraints. The evolution of theories has led to increasingly close matches of predictions of the known psychophysics of stereopsis, but a conclusive demonstration of the validity of a given theory solely on the basis of similarity of behaviour has remained illusive.

The basic problem of stereopsis, recall, is determining the correct match between the two images, so that stereo disparity may be computed. There are subsequent computational problems associated with the interpretation of the disparity information, foremost being the computation of distance from disparity (see Mayhew & Longuet-Higgins, 1982). Another problem, which has been considered primarily in the context of stereopsis, but which likely has wider scope, concerns the interpolation or reconstruction of a smooth surface between the points where stereopsis is able to provide depth information. In a sparse random dot stereogram, for instance, once the stereogram is fused, the points appear in space to lie on an apparently continuous surface that exists between the dots, as if the dots were embedded in a transparent sheet. Because interpolation phenomena can be seen also in surfaces depicted by motion sequences, we will return to it as a computational problem in its own right, after considering problems involved in the perception of space from motion. This interweaving of computational problems is commonplace and probably inherent to the nature of vision, and while it makes it difficult to develop clearly demarcated theories, it is possibly unavoidable. Let us turn to the next topic of our survey, the 3-D interpretation of motion across the retinal image.

3.2. Motion Interpretation Problems

The stereo matching problem was one of the first computational problems in vision to be addressed in detail. Another computational problem which has recently received at least as much attention concerns the 3-D interpretation of motion. Gibson (1950) wrote of the spatial information provided by motion parallax, and showed that in the instantaneous velocity field cast on the retina there is information about the layout of surfaces relative to the observer. That information has generally been regarded as either distance or local surface orientation. What earlier was regarded as merely motion parallax has been decomposed more recently into many computational problems, depending on whether one is concerned with continuous vs. discrete motion, orthographic[2] vs. perspective projection, and so forth. (For the case of continuous motion in perspective projection see Koenderink & van Doorn, 1976 and Longuet-Higgins & Prazdny, 1980; for continuous motion in orthographic projection see Hoffman, 1982; and for case of discrete motion in orthographic and perspective projection see Ullman, 1979.)

Koenderink and van Doorn's (1976) work demonstrated how the optical velocity field[3] contains information about the spatial distribution of surfaces about an observer as one moves. The local velocity field in the image was shown to be decomposable into quantities that are related to depth, surface orientation, and velocity. Ullman (1979) examined the minimal information from which 3-D structures could be derived, and, for instance, was able to show that three distinct orthographic views of four non-coplanar points in a rigid configuration are sufficient for the recovery of their spatial arrangement, up to a reflection. That is, rigidity of motion results in a unique interpretation under those viewing circumstances. Again, assuming rigidity, Tsai and Huang (1984) have shown that, with certain exceptions, two perspective views of seven points are also sufficient. Various other results have been shown for restricted sorts of motion, such as motion about a planar or fixed axis (Bobick, 1983; Hoffman & Flinchbaugh, 1982), which have relevance to the interpretation of articulated systems such as animals in locomotion.

Rigidity provides the strongest mathematical constraint on the spatial interpretation of motion. In fact, much of the computational work in the last decade has concentrated on the fundamentals of interpreting motion in the abstract, as essentially a mathematical issue. It assumes that motion information is available in some usable form in an image, such as the instantaneous velocity field (retinal angular velocity provided for all visual directions). Whereas Gibson (1950) discussed the wealth of spaital information provided by the velocity field, the information in the idealised optic

[2]Orthographic, or parallel projection is approximated when the variation in distance across a region of a 3-D scene is small relative to the overall distance.

[3]The 2-D array of velocity vectors across the retinal image induced by movement relative to the visual surrounds. The velocity field is presumably computed by motion detectors that deliver information about speed and direction of movement across the retinal image. The velocity field is then expected to be a rich source of information for subsequent 3-D analysis.

array that is incident on the retina is quite difficult to extract or "register". It appears that computing the velocity field poses substantial problems in its own right, problems that certainly were not foreseen prior to recent computational experiments. For instance, the so-called "aperture problem" states that only the velocity component normal to an edge or line segment is locally computable, the component tangent to the edge or line cannot be determined by a motion detection operator having a limited aperture or receptive field (Marr & Ullman, 1981). In actuality perhaps only a rather sparse and perhaps crude approximation to the instantaneous velocity field is neurally determined, which would then pose severe problems on any motion processes that use this velocity information as input. The perceptual processes that seek to make 3-D interpretations must be able to cope with errorful and incomplete velocity information (see, for example, Ullman & Hildreth, 1983).

While progress has been made regarding the measurement and interpretation of motion, the result of the 3-D interpretation, whether represented in terms of depth, surface orientation, or some other form, is still quite obscure. Part of the problem is that we have, as yet, little insight into how spatial information, however extracted, is organised within the human or animal visual system. Some of the issues that must be clarified are: precisely how distance information is encoded, whether distance is made explicit for all visible points across the seen surfaces up to some resolution, how surfaces are described over different scales (for instance, some natural surfaces are smooth on a coarse scale but quite irregular on fine scale, others are smooth in detail but jagged overall). These issues arise when attempting to actually account for the interpretation of motion in natural images, since the irregularities of the seen surfaces result in irregularities in the velocity field, just as smoothness of the surfaces results in smoothness in the velocity field. But the problems of surface description are not restricted to motion interpretation, and that leads us to the next point.

3.3. Surface Interpolation Problems

It was mentioned earlier that stereopsis does not provide stereo disparity information at all points in the binocular image, but only at discrete places such as edges, lines, and points that have been brought into stereo correspondence. The intervening, featureless, regions can only be assumed to lie at similar depths if the surface is assumed to be smooth. To make a particular reconstruction of a smooth surface consistent with the points where the disparity is known is not a problem unique to stereopsis, however. Just as stereopsis brings only certain features into stereo correspondence, motion provides spatial information only at places for which velocity information can be attributed, such as edge and line segments, blobs, and points. Nonetheless, one can derive from a discrete pattern of moving dots the impression of seeing a coherent sheet of dots in 3-D, as if one attributes motion to the intervening regions between such features. To do so requires an assumption of viewing a smooth surface when the dots behave in a coherent manner. The same holds for surfaces suggested by contours, such as shown in Fig. 2.1. The smooth surface is depicted by discrete, separated contours, between which no surface information is explicitly available. The impression of an overall surface under the contours may be attributed to a surface interpolation process.

Some computational attention has been paid to the problem of *surface interpolation,* the process of reconstructing a smooth surface between the discrete places where the surface is known (see, e.g., Grimson, 1981). Two fundamental research concerns are: (1) whether or not the human visual system explicitly interpolates an entire smooth surface in parallel across the image, and if interpolation exists in human vision: (2) to determine the interpolation strategy or strategies. Although it is not certain that explicit interpolation does take place in human vision, it has been assumed so, and work thus far has centred largely on formalising mathematical schemes for surface reconstruction analogous to the engineering practice of determining smoothly faired surfaces. For instance, one can regard the interpolation as a smooth membrane that is stretched over the discrete places where the surface shape is known, then compute that particular surface shape for the membrane that minimised its elastic potential energy. Rather than use a membrane, an alternative approach is to model the surface as a thin plate, which is resistant to flexure and torsion, and which smoothly bends without fractures or creases to conform with the boundary constraints.

Clearly one of the issues that must be dealt with theoretically is how a surface can be described simultaneously as being smooth overall but jagged or irregular in detail, or vice versa. The answer to this might result in different approaches to surface interpolation. One central question, it seems, is to what extent the visual system goes to the effort to explicitly compute multiple surface interpolations at various scales, the alternative being the computation of a surface discription, on demand as it were, for a particular scale of description, and only locally to a given patch of surface.

A complementary problem to the interpolation problem is the discontinuity detection problem. That is, given a collection of discrete spatial points lying on different, spatially separated surfaces, how does one decide where to fit smooth surfaces and where to postulate surface boundaries? What constitutes a discontinuity, such as a crease or step edge between two smooth surfaces clearly depends on the scale one has in mind (e.g., a crumpled, then flattened sheet of aluminum foil presents both smoothness and jaggedness depending on the scale of reference). But consider the presumably simpler problem of deciding, for a given scale, whether or not the surface is creased or smooth at a given point. One approach, for surfaces modelled as thin plates, is to locally measure the "strain" on the surface and explicitly create discontinuities where the strain becomes excessive.

3.4. Describing Visible Surfaces and Objects

Interpolation and the determination of surface creases and boundaries, as well as several other issues such as the description of local surface topography, are issues that span a broad range of surface perception processes. Parsimony would suggest that the solution to these problems are provided by central mechanisms of surface discription that are common to stereopsis, motion, shading, texture, and so forth. Marr (1982) collectively termed the representation and associated processes that manipulate internal descriptions of visible surfaces the $2\frac{1}{2}$-D sketch. The name suggesting that it is a sketch or representation of the salient spatial properties of the seen surfaces, not a full 3-D representation of the objects including the enclosed volumes and portions that are not visible from the particular viewpoint. The $2\frac{1}{2}$-D sketch would achieve the integration of 2-D information from different sources such as stereopsis and motion, resulting in an at least locally consistent description of the surfaces that are visible at a given instant. It would also subserve the description of seen objects for purposes of object recognition, manipulation, and so forth.

The quantitative description of object and surface layout had been central to computer vision efforts (see, Horn, 1977). Questions of 3-D representation arise in a very concrete manner when one seeks to describe viewed objects within a computer so that they might be automatically recognised, or grasped by a manipulator, or navigated around. However, unlike the proposed $2\frac{1}{2}$-D sketch, in computer vision the representation question has concerned description of a single type of 3-D information derived from a single source (typically either shading or stereopsis) and questions of consistency with information generated from other processes, such as motion, have not been addressed. In contrast, from a psychological perspective there has been concern for the integration of visual cues, notably Attneave's (1972, 1982) discussions of viewer-centred[4] local descriptions of surface orientation and depth, and the intimate relationship between the representation of 3-D information and its extraction from

[4] A viewer-centred description is relative to the instantaneous perspective the observer has of the surrounding surfaces. Local surface shape and disposition is described relative to the line of sight to each surface patch, so that if the observer moves relative to the surface all values within the viewer-centred description might be expected to change. While volatile, such a description would be the basis for eventually deriving more stable object-centred descriptions (see discussion of axis-based schemes, p. 30).

images. However, the $2\frac{1}{2}$-D sketch proposal, and perhaps more importantly its theoretical motivation, constitutes the broadest statement of the *purpose* of early vision, namely the processing of image information in order to develop a description of the visible surfaces (Marr, 1982). Vision achieves descriptions of the visual world, and towards that goal the $2\frac{1}{2}$-D sketch would be one of the important representations within which these descriptions would lie.

When phrased in such terms, one also sees clear parallels to Gibson's (1950) theory that the visual system registers spatial information by means of "higher order" variables in the optic array (the interested reader is referred to Ullman, 1980, for an excellent discussion of Gibson's direct perception viewed from this perspective). The major contribution of proposing that early vision culminates in a description of the visible surfaces is probably that it causes one to question precisely what constitutes that description. There are many ways to quantify spatial information that are formally equivalent, but presumably only a few such ways are actually used within the visual system to encode such information. At some point in the course of investigation of surface and object perception these issues will have to be pinned down.

Making precise and specific the nature and structure of the internal representations of surfaces and objects is extraordinarily difficult. The problem is difficult for many reasons, some of which are sketched in the following. First, one faces the thorny issue that there are indeed many equivalent ways of achieving an equivalent description, given that one cannot rule out specialised processes that access and manipulate the information contained in the representation. To illustrate, suppose the visual system has a 2-D buffer containing perceived depth as a function of visual direction (i.e. a depth map), and associated with it, the ability to compute the gradient of depth in a given locality. Since the magnitude and direction of the gradient of depth is straightforwardly related to the local surface orientation (see Stevens, 1983b), by having the ability to compute the gradient at any point one has, in effect, a local surface orientation map for all smooth surface points. Since a depth map facilitates the perception of local surface orientation, how then does one determine whether or not local surface orientation is made explicit within some 2-D buffer or simply computed locally "on demand"? The visual system is likely to be quite robust in its ability to derive different types of spatial inference as required by the visual task at hand. It is still an open question as to what primitive information is stored in a visual buffer and what information is subsequently inferred or computed on that basis.

Depth and local surface orientation constitute but two means for representing surface shape. Other types of 3-D shape primitive can be proposed, such as measures of the local surface curvature (predicates indicating qualitative flatness or perhaps measures of the sign and magnitude of the Gaussian curvature and the principal directions). More extended topographic features such as ridges and troughs, peaks and dips, etc., might be involved in the description of surface shape in human vision. A ridge or trough or an extremum in surface curvature is clearly visually salient, and it is reasonable to suspect that such features of surface shape are explicitly represented. From a computational point of view it is important to ask how a surface shape *should* be described, keeping in mind that the representation of surface shape must subserve certain processing tasks that follow, such as object recognition, manipulation, and navigation.

In the case of object recognition one of the important criteria of a representation (Marr & Nishihara, 1978) is how stable the description is over changes in viewpoint. Clearly the visual system should derive the same conclusion as to an object's identity over as many different viewpoints as possible, with recognition difficulties arising for only particular vantage points where critical features are obscured, such as major axes of elongation or symmetry that are severely foreshortened (see Marr & Nishihara, 1978). Marr and Nishihara (1978) describe a hierarchical representation of objects that is particularly suited for articulated objects such as animals that can be regarded as the composition of parts. In this scheme each part of an object is described in terms of how the cross-section of the part varies as a function of position along its axis (an approach introduced by Binford, 1971). The connectivity among the component parts of an object is then described in terms of how the axes join, the relative sizes of the parts, etc. Marr and Nishihara (1978) observe that such descriptions capture the essence of a broad range of animal shapes, and demonstrate this fact with effective renditions of different animals by pipecleaners. That approach is most effective for describing objects made of connected parts that can themselves be described by axes. More recently, Hoffman (1983) has considered how to decompose a complex surface shape into component parts. The problem can be solved in part by considering the silhouette outline, and identifying the points along the silhouette where the parts intersect (see also Marr, 1977, concerning the interpretation of silhouettes, and the sketch of that work in Section 3.5.). Hoffman (1983; Hoffman & Richards, 1984) also extends these 2-D rules to 3-D, showing that surfaces can often be decomposed along extrema of negative principal curvature into physically meaningful parts. Note that in this scheme an object is described in terms of the intrinsic geometry of its surfaces and not in terms of volumetric primitives such as axes and cross-sections. Both schemes might well be incorporated in human vision, as these researchers demonstrate. Furthermore, the work of Shepard and Metzler (1971) regarding the mental rotation of 3-D shapes strongly suggests that the visual system is able to manipulate in an effectively continuous manner an internal representation of a seen object which captures salient part–whole relations (see Shepard, 1981 for discussion). The connection between this ability and objection perception is not at all clear, unfortunately.

3.5. Interpreting Contours in 3-D

The visual system is quite adept at imposing 3-D interpretations on line drawings, the line-drawn Necker cube being a familiar example. Although there are infinitely many 3-D configurations that might have projected to any given 2-D image, we tend to see a specific configuration in 3-D (and its reversal)—clearly, we impose strong constraints on the 3-D interpretation. It is well established that in viewing such figures we prefer that interpretation which favours regularities, symmetries, parallelisms, coplanarities, etc. Consequently, we tend to see parallelograms and trapezoids as slanted rectangles or squares, trihedral vertices as right trihedral vertices, and so forth (see, e.g., Perkins, 1982; Shepard, 1981; Stevens, 1983a). These tendencies might be indirect consequences of more general *Praegnanz* principles or in some cases they might directly reflect specific perceptual assumptions, (e.g., of perpendicularity). To amplify this point, the *Praegnanz* principle (Koffka, 1935) says that we tend to choose the simplest interpretation, particularly in cases of minimal stimuli, hence given a trapezoid in 2-D we prefer the 3-D interpretation which, in addition to preserving parallelism and symmetry, results in equal length lines and equal angles at the vertices (which implicitly results in 90° angles in 3-D). While there is considerable evidence for *Praegnanz* in our visual interpretations, it does not exclude the possibility that we also drive our interpretations by strongly constraining assumptions that more directly entail perpendicularity and other geometric properties (discussed later). As to whether such geometric assumptions can be rephrased in terms of *Praegnanz* is probably a pursuit of secondary importance. In contrast, of considerable importance from a computational point of view is determining precisely what 3-D interpretation problems exist, what each entails, and what constraint is employed to solve each. It is another matter to study how these various constraints are integrated, that is, by what methods do simultaneous and potentially conflicting constraints force one interpretation over another. Questions of how these constraints might be implemented within some perceptual process can be studied distinctly from the constraints themselves. It is there that issues of *Praegnanz* re-emerge (see, for example, the discussion on "hill-climbing", i.e. the method of gradient ascent, discussed by Attneave, 1982 and various proposed computing architectures such as connectionist models, e.g., Ballard, Hinton, & Sejnowski, 1983; see also Humphreys & Quinlan, this volume, Chapter 3).

In the following, we take the view that we can address the constraints that allow the interpretation of 3-D shape independently of how the constraints are implemented. The computer vision community examined the constraint question in the limited domain of blocks (Waltz, 1975), showing how local configurations of vertices, while individually ambiguous, are mutually constraining so that a global 3-D interpretation can usually be derived, given assumptions of general position (ruling out accidental alignments) and *a priori* assumptions about the restricted domain (right trihedral vertices, planar facets, etc.). Note that the computer vision work is clearly related to the empirical observations by Hochberg (1982) concerning the accumulation of local geometric constraint when viewing a line drawing through a limited aperture.

Consider now the 3-D interpretation of smooth curves. The approach has been to distinguish three physical categories of curve: (1) the bounding, or occluding, contours that comprise the silhouette boundary of a smooth shape (Marr, 1977, 1982); (2) foreshortened texture contours such as the mottled pattern of light and shadow under a tree (Witkin, 1981); and (3) smooth contours that extend across a surface, such as seams, creases, wrinkles, and linear pigmentation markings (Stevens, 1981, 1986). These three, distinctly different categories of contour provide information about surface shape in different ways.

Marr's (1977) work on smooth silhouette boundaries concerns inferring the axis of an object and its shape about that axis, all on the basis of its silhouette shape in the image. Marr uses the term *contour generator* to refer to the 3-D locus of surface points that projects to the (silhouette) contour, and makes three geometrical assumptions about the contour generator that allow the 3-D interpretation: (1) each line of sight from the viewer to the object grazes the object's surface at exactly one point; (2) that nearby points on the contour arise from nearby points on the contour generator; and (3) the contour generator lies wholly in a single plane. It would appear that these assumptions must be held *a priori* to make any concrete inferences about the shape of an object from its boundary. Interested readers are referred to Marr (1982) for continuation of this issue.

What about the contours that lie interior to the silhouette of an object? Of these it is useful to distinguish between contours that follow or reflect the shape of the underlying surface (Fig. 2.1) from those whose shape is

---

[5]That is, the surface texture is random in that the contour curvature is not correlated with the tangent direction.

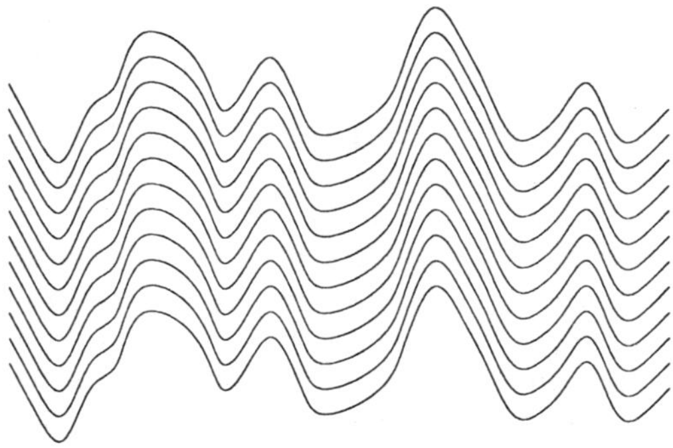

FIG. 2.1. Contours following or reflecting shape of underlying surface.

random, but whose systematic foreshortening reflects the orientation of the approximately planar surface underneath (Fig. 2.2) (Stevens, 1981; Witkin, 1981). With reference to Fig. 2.2, Witkin (1981) has shown that the slant and tilt of a surface patch can be estimated from a measure of the foreshortening of texture contours (there is a lawful relationship between the magnitude of the contour curvature and the orientation of the tangent along the contour), provided the viewer assumes that the texture is isotropic[5] and the surface is approximately planar under the contours. When these assumptions hold, the surface orientation predicted by that computational method corresponds rather well with the apparent surface orientation. Of course, if the surface texture is actually anisotropic in a manner that mimics foreshortening, the method would fail, giving an

FIG. 2.2. Foreshortening of texture contours.

inaccurate estimate of the true surface orientation (and if there were no visual information to the contrary, so would our perception be inaccurate). For example, wood grain often mimics foreshortening, with patterns resembling Fig. 2. One could easily misperceive the spatial orientation of a wooden board viewed monocularly (so stereopsis does not reveal the true orientation) if the physical edges are not visible (whose rectangularity would also indicate the orientation of the board). All one could base the orientation judgement on would be the apparent foreshortening of the wood grain, which would lead to an erroneous impression of a foreshortened, hence slanted, surface. As in the case of interpreting silhouette contours, the assumptions required to make a spatial interpretation of foreshortening in image texture seem unavoidable. The same seems true for the interpretation of surface contours such as those in Fig. 2.1, which we discuss next.

The third type of contour corresponds to a curve that travels across a surface, following the shape of the underlying topography. In strong distinction to the foreshortened contours in Fig. 2.2, which amble across a flat surface, the contours in Fig. 2.1, for example, appear to travel directly in the direction of greatest curvature across the undulating surface (note that they appear perpendicular to the ridges and troughs). They also appear to be planar and to be geodesic (normal sections) of the apparent surface. Most importantly, the image contours define a specific apparent surface in 3-D. A theory for how the visual system constrains the interpretation of these contours was developed by Stevens (1981, 1986). Sufficient constraint on the problem is provided by three assumptions. The first two are assumptions of general position, that neither the viewpoint nor the particular placement of the contours across the surface is misleading. The third assumption is that the contours correspond to lines of principal curvature across the surface. These assumptions not only allow inference of the intrinsic geometry of the surface but estimation of the local surface orientation as well (Stevens, 1981, 1986). In Fig. 2.3 the local surface orientation predicted by the theory is demonstrated. In Fig. 2.3a two points are marked and the direction of the rulings indicated by short line segments. The angle of intersection between the line segment and the tangent to the curve is a foreshortened right angle in each case. In Fig. 2.3b the range of surface tilts consistent with that intersection being perpendicular in 3-D is indicated at each point. The surface normal at each point, as predicted by the computer implementation is shown in Fig. 2.3c, and a series of ellipses are shown in Fig. 2.3d depicting how circular markings on the surface would project according to the theory.

The visual system uses geometric evidence about the shape of the contours to decide how to interpret a contour, whether to treat it as the boundary or silhouette contour of a smooth object, a contour across a

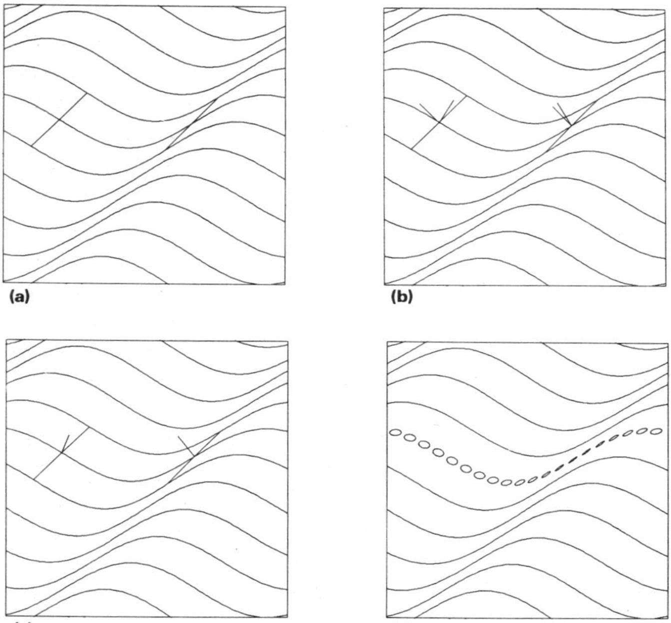

(a) (b) (c) (d)

FIG. 2.3. Local surface orientation.

smooth surface, or a texture contour whose foreshortening reveals the surface orientation of the underlying surface. Bilaterally symmetric pairs of contours are likely to correspond to object boundaries (e.g., see Marr, 1977). Qualitative (i.e., approximate) bilateral symmetry in image contours might be regarded as triggering criteria for their interpretation. Similarly, parallel contours probably correspond to physically parallel curves across an undulating surface. Parallelism, when present, seems to trigger this interpretation (Stevens, 1981). Finally, Witkin (1981) has shown a clear tendency to treat as textures contour curves that display systematic evidence of foreshortening. Each of the three types of contour has a distinct "triggering" condition, partly geometric and partly provided by other deciding evidence. The labelling of a contour (as in a line drawing) seems to be an important first step towards the subsequent analysis of its 3-D shape and its relationship to the underlying surface and object.

4. CONCERNING VISUAL DEFECTS

So far we have outlined the computational underpinnings of various perceptual abilities. That research was pursued under the (generally tacit) expectation that the visual system is modular, solving distinct computational problems by independent processes. The modularity assumption does not rule out interactions across or among modules, particularly where such interactions would provide disambiguation, redundancy, etc. Such interactions have not been spelled out in much detail. Neither have the visual representations that would serve as sources of input or the destinations of output of the various modules—in general, the computational theories are not yet sufficiently predictive. There is an emerging consensus, however, that at the level of surface and object perception many processes appear to deliver complementary types of spatial information and to require similar types of input.

One question to address from a clinical point of view, it would seem, is the validity of the modularity assumption. Operationally, this reduces to asking, for each of a variety of proposed modules, whether one can discover deficits specific to only one purported module. Total loss of one ability with many other abilities remaining intact, of course, points strongly towards modularity for that ability. On the other hand, defects found in two purported modules does not necessarily suggest that they are in fact interdependent, since both might be dependent on input from a third module which is the true site of the defect. The puzzle of how vision is modularised—if at all at the level of surface perception—clearly would require many independent contributions and would be pieced together slowly.

In attempting to be more concrete regarding modularity, I have found few formal tools available to borrow from computer science. Consider a particular module or process responsible for a particular visual ability, and how a defect might arise in that ability. The module taps input information from an earlier representation, delivers output information to a later representation, and operates, presumably, under certain additional control inputs that act as trigger conditions. One immediately sees several obvious ways in which the associated visual defect might arise, being some combination of: the module itself being defective, the input representation failing to provide the required input, the output representation not storing the information provided by the module, or the module not operating merely because it was not activated or triggered by the necessary control input. The cascading of a visual defect due to failure of a triggering condition is quite insidious. Since the consequences might ultimately involve a variety of global and high-level perceptions, it will likely be difficult to isolate a rather focal defect occurring early in the visual pathways (see Humphreys & Riddoch and Sergent, this volume, for further discussion of this point).

Consider the case of a visual agnosic patient, presenting with right homonymous hemianopsia, described in detail in Wapner et al. (1978). Of the various defects and impairments exhibited by this patient, one surprisingly clear-cut defeat was found by Stevens (1983c): The patient was unable

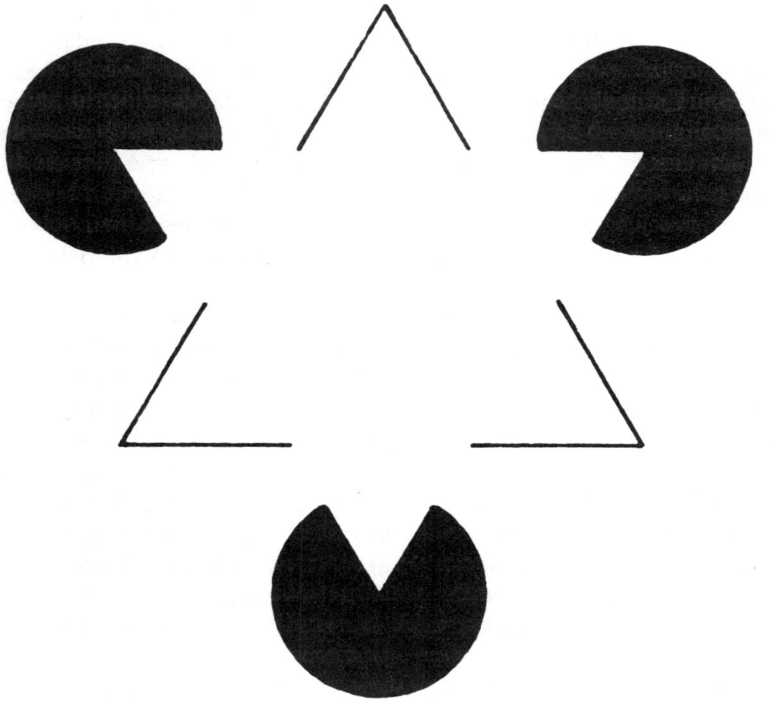

FIG. 2.4. Kaniza's triangle.

to see subjective contours, a defect which likely was a consequence of the patient's simultaneous inability to interpret interposition cues normally. This case might reflect an instance of cascading visual defects. The well-known perceptual phenomenona of subjective contours are generally regarded as constructions (by processes of surface interpolation as discussed earlier), in which an apparent surface is generated to account for indirect evidence of such a surface (see e.g., Coren, 1972; Kaniza, 1976). The usual subjective contour demonstration shows a surface that is apparent only by the disruption or partial obliteration of the background, with cues such as line terminations aligned along the subjective edge, incomplete or partly occluded figures, and so forth (see Fig. 2.4). In such demonstrations one sees illusory contrast across the edges of the apparent surface. A variety of "interposition" or "occlusion" cues seemingly may trigger the perception of an apparent intervening surface bounded by subjective contours.

The patient in question, J.R., had normal eye movement and ocular function, stereopsis, spatial and verbal reasoning, and of particular importance, normal performance on standard illusions such as the Necker cube, Schroeder staircase, reversible craters and blisters, corridor, Ponzo, Müller-Lyer, and Hering, and the naming of basic geometric shapes. It was clear that J.R. could see in depth, and specifically, to see depth edges in random dot stereograms, where the apparent (or subjective) edge is indicated purely by disparity discontinuities. As discussed in Section 3.3, the apparent edge seen in a stereogram is probably the consequence of some processes of smooth surface interpolation or filling in. J.R. was able to see subject edges in stereogram versions of the standard subjective contour demonstrations, but curiously, not in the monocular versions. In the monocular patterns J.R. always provided an accurate, but literal, description of the constituent elements of the pattern, never providing a verbal description in terms of partly obliterated or incomplete figures or any other of a variety of interposition cues. When asked to replicate the figure, important alignments of contour fragments, which suggest partial occlusion by a nearer surface, were not preserved in J.R.'s drawings, although care was taken to replicate other aspects of shape and arrangement. J.R. displayed a clear inability to derive a 3-D interpretation from illustrations that depicted surfaces in front of surfaces, despite an intact ability to interpret figures such as the Schroeder staircase and Necker cube in 3-D. This persistent finding was replicated over a variety of stimuli, leading to the conclusion that J.R. did not see subjective contours because there was no need to. That is, J.R.'s severely impaired processing of interposition seemed to prevent the triggering of later surface perception processes. While the patient had many other visual defects including extensive scotomata, difficulties in visual tracking, and considerably impaired visual object recognition, none of these seemed sufficient to account for the specific inability to see subjective contours as part of a more general defect.

The fact that J.R. made normal 3-D interpretations of line drawings such as the Schroeder staircase suggests that the underlying problem was not one merely of integrating visual information, or simultanagnosia. Moreover, the fact that J.R. saw subjective edges from one source (stereopsis) but not another (monocular evidence of interposition) supports the notion of modularity. This study, unfortunately, was unable to pursue further the question of why J.R. persistently failed to make interpretations involving interposition. Nonetheless, it illustrates the idea of working backwards from a specific defect to determine its antecedents, as predicted by a theory such as Coren's (1972) concerning subjective contours.

More generally, a reasonably specific functional modularity of visual function can be inferred by examining the breadth of processes that have been proposed for various stages of vision. This modularity is implicit in the problems that appear functionally distinct from the point of view of the investigators. The actual decomposition of vision into distinct processes might turn out rather different, but nonetheless, it offers some testable hypotheses.

The discussion thus far has treated vision as a collection of relatively independent processes, each performing some task, and by combinations of parallelism across processes and pipelining of processes feeding processes, the combined processing results in the perception of objects in 3-D. One should not take away the impression, however, that vision is achieved in a purely autonomous and bottom-up manner. Quite to the contrary, it is becoming increasingly clear that vision involves tasks that are inherently sequential and that require directed attention (Treisman, 1977, 1982; Treisman & Gelade, 1980; Ullman, 1984). The role of attention in combining information across "feature maps" and in sorting out geometric relationships among parts of objects is only recently being appreciated. Ullman (1984) points out that one cannot expect any single, fixed collection of visual processes to suffice, the combinatorial complexity of the tasks of vision prohibit it. Instead, Ullman suggests that the visual system builds a collection of base representations (likely related to the feature maps Treisman discusses) then by the execution of "visual routines", generates incremental representations that hold specific information—information that would not be feasible to compute automatically and in parallel across the visual field. These notions are addressing visual processing at the level of algorithm. That is, presuming that the computational theories at the level of constraint and representation are sufficiently precise as to make clear what information is to be extracted, it becomes increasingly valid to address how that information is processed.

5. CONCLUSION

We have surveyed several computational problems, tasks that can be characterised formally as information processing problems, each requiring the application of constraints for their solution. The visual system is an ensemble of mechanisms designed to solve these problems subject to several sorts of constraint, some inherently computational (as discussed), others imposed by restrictions on the types of computations that neural mechanisms can perform, and still others by the restrictions due to the evolution of the cortex (see the discussion of "Continuous transformations" in Humphreys & Quinlan, this volume, Chapter 3). The computational approach delves into the inherent complexity of a given visual task and can reveal strategies for its solution. Just how these strategies are implemented by neural mechanisms, however, does not follow from first principles. There are infinitely many algorithms and implementations of any given computational strategy, and the specific version chosen by the human visual system is a consequence of many non-computational factors. There are limits, therefore, to what might be said about the visual system from a purely computational perspective. Recall the central assumption underlying the computational approach, namely that, to a first approximation, *what* the visual system does can be divorced from *how* it does it. That assumption is based on the belief that computations are entities that can be described independent of their particular implementations—a belief central to theoretical computer science. However, on the other hand, given insight from experimental or clinical psychology about *how* some information is represented (e.g. on the basis of behavioural limits or functional failures), one can become increasingly specific about particular computational architectures. In sum, it is extraordinarily difficult to make sense of a complex information processing system without a theory for what its goals are. The recent development of computational theories for visual processing, such as surveyed here, should provide a useful matrix of ideas towards that end.

In closing, I would like to note that several of the chapters that follow in this volume report studies that offer clear ties between theoretical notions and clinical findings, but they mainly concern visual object recognition, the higher-level visual descriptions of form and function, and their relationships to semantic systems. Given the coverage of these (presumably) later perceptual processes, I chose to emphasise earlier visual processes associated with object perception, namely those that generate the descriptions of the component surfaces of objects. Over the last decade, many computational studies of these processes have been pursued; these emerging theories make reasonably specific predictions that should be testable clinically, in like fashion to later theories of semantic categories. Recalling the range of theoretical explanation (from computational theory at one end to proposals of implementation and specific mechanisms at the other), my expectation is that it will be easier to find clinical evidence that either supports or challenges the fundamental computational underpinnings of these theories (e.g. their purported constraints, and their modular decomposition) than to find clinical evidence regarding their implementation details (e.g. connectionist vs. alternative architectures).

REFERENCES

Attneave, F. (1972). Representation of physical space. In A. W. Melton and E. J. Martin, (Eds.), *Coding processes in human memory*. Washington, D.C.: Winston.

Attneave, F. (1982). Praegnanz and soap bubble systems: a theoretical exploration. In J. Beck (Ed.), *Organization and representation in perception*. Hillsdale, N.J.: Lawrence Erlbaum Associates Inc.

Ballard, D. H., Hinton, G. E., & Sejnowski, T. J. (1983). Parallel visual computation. *Nature, 306,* 21–26.

Binford, T. (1971). Visual perception by computer. *IEEE Conference on Systems and Control,* Miami.

Bobick, A. (1983). A hybrid approach to structure-from-motion. *Proceedings of the ACM Interdisciplinary Workshop on Motion.* Toronto, Canada, April, 91–109.

Coren, S. (1972). Subjective contours and apparent depth. *Psychological Review, 79,* 359–367.

Gibson, J. J. (1950). *The perception of the visual world.* Boston, Mass.: Houghton Mifflin.

Grimson, W. E. L. (1981). *From images to surfaces: A computational study of the human early visual system.* Cambridge, Mass.: MIT Press.

Hochberg, J. (1982). How big is a stimulus? In J.Beck (Ed.), *Organization and representation in memory.* Hillsdale, N.J.: Lawrence Erlbaum Associates Inc.

Hoffman, D. D. (1982). Inferring local surface orientation from motion fields. *Journal of the Optical Society of America, 72 (7),* 888–892.

Hoffman, D. D. (1983). The interpretation of visual illusions. *Scientific American 249, 6,* 154–162.

Hoffman, D. D. & Flinchbaugh, B.E. (1982). The interpretation of biological motion. *Biological Cybernetics, 42,* 195–204.

Hoffman, D. D. & Richards, W. (1984). Parts of recognition. *Cognition, 18,* 65–96.

Horn, B. K. P. (1977). Understanding image intensities. *Artificial Intelligence, 8,* 201–231.

Kaniza, G. (1976). Subjective contours. *Scientific American, 234,* 48–52.

Koenderink, J. J. & van Doorn, A. J. (1976). Local structure of movement parallax of the plane. *Journal of the Optical Society of America, 66,* 717–723.

Koffka, K. (1935). *Principles of Gestalt psychology.* New York: Harcourt, Brace & World.

Livingstone, M. S. & Hubel, D. (1984). Anatomy and physiology of a color system in the primate visual cortex. *Journal of Neuroscience, 4,* 309–356.

Longuet-Higgins, H. C. & Prazdny, K. (1980). The interpretation of a moving retinal image. *Proceedings of the Royal Society, London, B208,* 385–397.

Mayhew, J. E. W. (1982). Stereopsis. In Braddick O. J. and Sleigh A. C. (Eds.), *Physical and biological processing of images.* Berlin: Springer-Verlag.

Mayhew, J. E. W. & Frisby, J. P. (1981). Psychophysical and computational studies towards a theory of human stereopsis. *Artificial Intelligence, 17,* 349–386.

Mayhew, J. E. W. & Longuet-Higgins, H. C. (1982). A computational model of binocular depth perception. *Nature, 297,* 375–378.

Marr, D. (1977). Analysis of occluding contour. *Proceedings of the Royal Society, London, B197,* 41–47.

Marr, D. (1982). *Vision.* San Francisco: W. H. Freeman.

Marr, D. & Hildreth, E. C. (1980) Theory of edge detection. *Proceedings of the Royal Society, London, B207,* 187–217.

Marr, D. & Nishihara, H. K. (1978). Representation and recognition of the spatial organization of three-dimensional shapes. *Proceedings of the Royal Society, London, B200,* 269–294.

Marr, D. & Poggio, T. (1977). From understanding computation to understanding neural circuitry. *Neuroscience Research Progress Bulletin, 15,* 470–488.

Marr, D. & Ullman, S. (1981). Directional selectivity and its use in early visual processing. *Proceedings of the Royal Society, London, B211,* 151–180.

Perkins, D. N. (1982). The perceiver as organizer and geometer. In J. Beck (Ed.), *Organization and representation in perception.* Hillsdale, N.J.: Lawrence Erlbaum Associates Inc.

Richards, W. (1985). Structure from stereo and motion. *Journal of the Optical Society of America, A, 2,* 343–349.

Shepard, R. (1981). Psychophysical complementarity. In Kubovy, M. and Pomerantz, J. R. (Eds.), *Perceptual organization.* Hillsdale, N.J.: Lawrence Erlbaum Associates Inc.

Shepard, R. & Metzler, J. (1971). Mental rotation of three-dimensional objects. *Science, 171,* 701–703.

Stevens, K. A. (1981). The visual interpretation of surface contours. *Artificial Intelligence, 17,* 17–45: 47–74.
Stevens, K. A. (1983a). Tilt (the direction of slant): a neglected psychophysical variable. *Perception & Psychophysics, 33,* 241–250.
Stevens, K. A. (1983b). Slant tilt: The visual encoding of surface orientation. *Biological Cybernetics, 46,* 183–195.
Stevens, K. A. (1983c). Evidence relating subjective contours and interpretations involving interposition. *Perception, 12,* 491–500.
Stevens, K. A. (1986). Inferring shape from contours across surfaces. In A. Pentland (Ed.). *From pixels to predictates: Recent advances in computational and robotic vision,* pp. 93–110.
Treisman, A. (1977). Focused attention in the perception and retrieval of multidimensional stimuli. *Perception & Psychophysics, 22,* 1–11.
Treisman, A. (1982). Perceptual grouping and attention in visual search for features and for objects. *Journal of Experimental Psychology: Human Perception and Performance, 8,* 194.
Treisman, A. & Gelade, G. (1980). A feature integration theory of attention. *Cognitive Psychology 12,* 97–136.
Tsai, R. Y. & Huang, T. S. (1984). Uniqueness and estimation of 3-D motion parameters and surface structures of rigid objects. In S. Ullman and W. Richards (Eds.), *Image understanding, 1984.* Norwood, N.J.: Ablex.
Ullman, S. (1979). *The interpretation of visual motion.* Cambridge, Mass: MIT Press.
Ullman, S. (1980). Against direct perception. *The Behavioral and Brain Sciences, 3,* 373–415.
Ullman, S. (1984). Visual routines. *Cognition, 18,* 97–159.
Ullman, S. & Hildreth, E. (1983). The measurement of visual motion. In O. J. Braddick and A. C. Sleigh, (Eds.), *Physical and biological processing of images.* Berlin: Springer-Verlag.
Waltz, D. (1975). Understanding line drawings of scenes with shadows. In P. H. Winston, (Ed.), *The psychology of computer vision,* pp. 19–91. New York: McGraw-Hill.
Wapner, W. Judd, T., & Gardner, H. (1978). Visual agnosia in an artist. *Cortex, 14,* 243–364.
Waxman, A. M. & Ullman, S. (1985). Surface structure and three-dimensional motion from image flow kinematics. *The International Journal of Robotics Research 4,* 72–94.
Wilson, H. R. & Giese, S. C. (1977) Threshold visibility of frequency gradient patterns. *Vision Research, 17,* 1177–1190.
Witkin, A. (1981). Recovering surface shape and orientation from texture. *Artificial Intelligence, 17,* 17–45.

3 Normal and Pathological Processes in Visual Object Constancy

Glyn W. Humphreys and Philip T. Quinlan
Cognitive Neuropsychology Research Group,
Department of Psychology, Birkbeck College,
University of London, Malet Street, London WC1E 7HX, U.K.

1. INTRODUCTION

In everyday life, we are able to recognise the structure of objects with some facility when we see them from different, even novel, viewpoints. This ability, termed visual object constancy, is established at an early age in human infants. For instance, children as young as 12 weeks old seem able to perceive the equivalence of different views of the same 2-dimensional (2-D) shape (Bower, 1966; A. Caron, R. Caron, & Carlson, 1978, 1979), and infants from about 14 weeks onwards seem able to respond specifically to invariant 3-dimensional (3-D) form information from moving objects (Kellman, 1984). However, such an early-developed and apparently effortless ability masks the fact that, in achieving object constancy, the visual system is solving a far from trivial problem. For instance, whenever there is a change in the position of an object with respect to a viewer there is a corresponding change in any description of the object coded in terms of retinal co-ordinates. To achieve object constancy, the visual system must extract a common object description across the varying viewpoint-dependent, retinally-based descriptions; that is, in some way it must compute the correspondence between the retinal description and the underlying object description. The difficulty is that there are very many retinal descriptions possible for any given object, and therefore very many possible correspondences.

In this chapter we will consider some of the procedures which have been thought to mediate visual object constancy, and we will attempt to evaluate the different accounts in the light of the available data. In fact, analyses of visual object constancy have been undertaken from widely differing approaches, including studies of normal (intact) human vision, studies of individuals with selective neurological impairments, studies of computer vision, and studies of animal vision. Consequently, the topic is one where we may look for convergence between the evidence drawn from the different areas.

In view of the separate lines of work on object constancy, the chapter will contain several subsections. First, we will try to elucidate some of the problems solved by the visual system when we recognise objects from different viewpoints, and we will consider how different accounts of object constancy deal with these problems. We will then discuss some approaches to object constancy in more detail, drawing on work from intact human vision and from studies of computer vision. Subsequently, we will discuss evidence relating to neurologically impaired human vision and animal vision, their relevance to current accounts of object constancy, and the type of questions which need to be addressed by future research.

2. THE PROBLEM OF VISUAL OBJECT CONSTANCY

The changes in any retinally based description of an object which occur once the viewpoint is moved are many and varied. For instance, depending on the relative position of the light source, there may be changes in surface illumination and hue; the size and orientation of the object will be determined by the distance and head position of the viewer, and even the available shape information will change if there is transformation in depth (surfaces will be hidden, new parts may emerge) or if movement behind other objects occurs (producing occlusion). The ability of the visual system to cope with such changes places strong constraints on any theory of visual object recognition.

Most theories assume that visual object recognition is contingent on a mapping of the visual input onto some stored representation specifying the object's structure (a process termed indexing; see Feldman, 1985). The most simple instance of such a mapping process would be for there to be a one-to-one correspondence between the retinal description of an object and its stored representation (e.g., if the stored representation was simply a coded intensity array). Such a mapping process is typically referred to as *template matching* (see Lindsay & Norman, 1977; Neisser, 1967; Pinker, 1984). In a template-matching model, recognition might be achieved on the basis of the best fit between the stimulus and the templates stored in memory.

Now, object constancy is clearly a major hurdle for any template-matching theory since any changes in the retinal description of an object which accompany changes in viewpoint lessen the goodness of fit between the input and the template. Nevertheless, it is possible to modify template-matching accounts to facilitate object constancy, and it turns out that such modifications provide more general insights into how the effects of viewpoint-change might be accommodated by any visual processing theory.

One modification would be to normalise the input prior to matching it with the template. For instance, the effects of distance on the size of a retinal description could be accommodated by embellishing the description with distance information (see Section 3.3). To normalise for transformations within the picture plane (such as rotation and lateral displacement) is less straightforward, as the preferred or canonical orientation is dependent on the particular shape. The canonical orientation for the letter "A" is to have the apex at the top of the shape, whereas the canonical orientation for a "V" has the apex at the bottom. For normalisation to occur, we must posit either that stored knowledge can in some way direct the normalising process or that a canonical orientation can be specified from geometrical properties defined independently of the shape's identity (Sections 3.4.2 and 3.6). However, there is no easy way for normalisation to deal with occlusion or with the changes in shape information due to transformation in depth (where the simple application of depth information to a retinal description will not work).

A rather different way of enabling template matching to cope with viewpoint-change would be to store templates for all possible views of a given object. Recognition across different views might then be achieved by feeding input from the viewpoint-dependent templates into a representation which accepts input from all the templates for a given shape. The massive storage requirements demanded by this approach could be reduced by various means. For instance, templates may exist for only a limited number of ecologically important views (Minsky, 1975). It would also be useful if the same *object* description could be indexed when transformations produce changes in only *some of its local parts*. Here we might envisage separate templates for the local parts of objects which all "feed-in" to a template of the whole object, with there being separate templates for the parts in different views. According to this scheme, object recognition might be based on the activation of a set of hierarchially arranged representations, where descriptions of the local parts are activated prior to activation of the representation of the whole object.

Another account of visual object recognition which assumes the hierarchical representation and processing of object information is *feature detection*. The main difference between feature detection and template-matching concerns the "grain size" of the mapping from the visual input to stored information. The level of mapping in template-matching is typically assumed to be whole shapes (e.g., nameable parts of objects or the objects themselves). The initial level of mapping for feature detection models is from discrete, local geometrical properties ("features"), such as lines and edges of particular width at particular orientations.

In a feature account, whole populations of feature detectors are thought to exist for each location in the input array (e.g., for retinal input, locations could be specified by receptive field positions). The feature detectors respond according to how closely they match the input, and this information is passed on to detectors at increasingly higher-levels of representation including, ultimately, object representations which respond irrespective of the object's position in the input array. For instance, the representation for an "O" may be fed by all detectors which respond to continuous curves in the input; the representation for a "Q" may be fed by all "continuous line detectors" plus those detectors which respond to oblique lines and acute angles (see Lindsay & Norman, 1977; Selfridge, 1959; Selfridge & Neisser, 1960).

However, there are serious problems even with the simple outline we have just given. For instance, a scheme in which object representations are coded in terms of the "on" or "off" state of a set of discrete features (such as continuous curves and oblique lines) would encounter difficulties when presented with objects in different orientations. Consider the responses which may be made to a "Q" rotated 180 degrees within-the-plane (Ỏ). If the "Q" representation is coded in terms of continuous curve and oblique line detectors, then it will respond as much to the rotated Q as to a normally-oriented Q; that is, it will fail to discriminate the change in orientation. Further, if the Q is only rotated 45 degrees then the straight line is then no longer oblique (O-) and so would not activate an oblique line detector. One way to overcome such problems is to specify the spatial relations between the features of an object prior to the indexing process (cf. Minsky & Papert, 1972; Sutherland, 1968, 1973); that is, we may propose that object recognition is based on a *structural description* in which both the parts of the object and their spatial relations are defined (Minsky, 1975; Winston,1975). For instance, a "Q" might be defined both in terms of the presence of a continuous curve and an oblique line and by the information that the line must bisect the bottom of the curve, so enabling a Q to be discriminated from its 180 degree rotated version.

However, identification of the 45 degree rotated Q is more complicated, since the identity of one of the local features (the oblique line) has changed (to a horizontal line). Note, however, that the feature's identity only changes if it is defined in terms of retinal co-ordinates. The identity of the feature may stay constant if it is defined in terms of some other co-ordinate system which is sensitive to the orientation change. A suggestion here (e.g.,

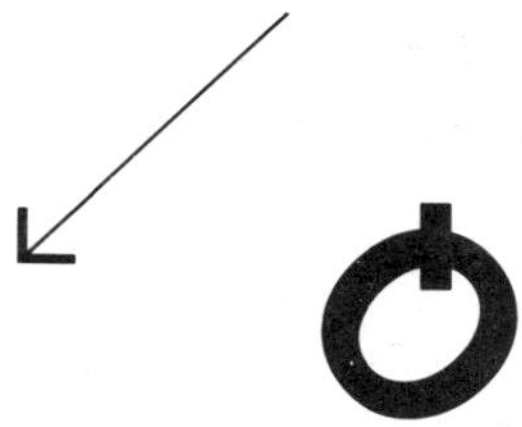

FIG. 3.1. The shape may be identified as a letter Q by describing its structure relative to a reference frame oriented 135 degrees anti-clockwise from the vertical.

Hinton, 1981; Marr, 1982; Marr & Nishihara, 1978) is that the shape information involved in indexing takes the form of a description of the features present, specified relative to a reference frame defined by some characteristic of the whole object or by a salient part (see Fig. 3.1). Such a description will stay constant across different orientations, enabling a common stored description of the object to be accessed (and object constancy to occur). Of course, for such an account to be more than just a description of the problem of object constancy, it must indicate how the reference frame is derived.

Template-matching, feature detection, and structural description accounts all assume that visual object recognition operates on shape information defined by the position of local contours on either a retinal or a non-retinotopic co-ordinate system. A rather different approach is to suggest that visual object recognition is based on an independent analysis of a limited range of spatial frequencies (e.g., Ginsberg, 1971, 1973). *Spatial frequency* accounts assume that early visual processing performs a spatial Fourier analysis, in which the information is broken down according to the change in image intensity in one orientation as a function of sinusoidal variation at a particular frequency (where the frequency refers to the number of bright-dark pattern repetitions over a given unit of space). The component information yielded by this breakdown will specify the degree of brightening and darkening in an image at set spatial intervals along a single direction. The family of components (or Fourier transform) for a given image will indicate two things: the degree of contrast across a range of spatial intervals (or spatial frequencies) and orientations (the amplitude spectrum), and the positions in the image defining the peaks and troughs in the intensity-change function for each component (the phase spectrum). Object recognition may then proceed by matching the Fourier transform of a given image with stored representations containing the Fourier transforms of particular objects.[1]

[1]Cornsweet (1970), Sekuler and Blake (1984), and Weisstein (1980) give more detailed, non-technical introductions to the application of Fourier analysis to vision.

As regards object constancy, the spatial frequency approach has both advantages and disadvantages relative to the approaches discussed hitherto. For instance, the amplitude spectrum for a given object remains approximately the same when the object is shifted to different positions in the visual field, and it is identical for mirror images (though their phase spectrums will differ). Object constancy following position shifts and rotations to a mirror image may therefore be based on the amplitude spectrum for the image. Also, size invariant information may be extracted by a further, relatively straightforward transform (see Cavanagh, 1978, 1981, 1984).

A primary disadvantage is that the Fourier transform for an object cannot be extracted *in isolation* from its contextual scene. Thus, even minor shifts in the position of an object in a scene will precipitate different transforms, even though the amplitude spectrum for the same object shown in isolation will not change (discussed earlier). It is most unlikely that object recognition is so strongly contingent on specific scene contexts that objects cannot be recognised in novel scenes or that familiar objects cannot be recognised in unfamiliar positions in familiar scenes (indeed, see Biederman, 1981; and Biederman, Mezzanotte, & Rabinowitz, 1982, for evidence that this is not the case). For this reason the Fourier transform for a given object does not seem a good candidate for input to the indexing process (see Pinker, 1984, for further discussion of this and other difficulties with the spatial frequency approach). Nevertheless, the spatial frequency argument is important. For instance, information about small, local details in an image will tend to be conveyed by high spatial frequency components, whilst global shape information will tend to be conveyed by low spatial frequency components. Low and high spatial frequencies are thought to be processed independently and in parallel. So the approach emphasises the parallel processing of visual information at different spatial scales. We could relinquish the strict spatial frequency account whilst maintaining that input coded in parallel at these different spatial scales is incorporated into some form of structural description, in which information about intensity changes at different spatial scales is interrelated (e.g. Marr, 1982).

3. APPROACHES TO OBJECT CONSTANCY

We have suggested that the problems set by object constancy constrain different accounts of visual object recognition and allow us to reject at least some simple proposals (e.g. direct template matching onto a single template). In this section, we will consider different approaches to object constancy in more detail. These approaches are derived primarily from work on normal human vision and on computer vision. Although many of the approaches have not been allied to a particular account of object recognition, we will attempt to indicate such relations wherever possible. Also, to illustrate the arguments, we will outline the relevant evidence for studies of normal human vision. Such evidence will then provide the background against which we can evaluate the different theoretical accounts.

3.1. Landmark Features

Probably the simplest way to ensure the correct identification of an object across changes in viewpoint would be to tag it with a unique (landmark) feature which could be identified irrespective of the orientation and distance of the object, (cf. Hochberg & Gellman, 1977). Identification might then proceed via the extraction of the landmark feature whatever the viewpoint (providing, of course, that the feature is visible). Also, it might be possible for a distinctive feature in a novel object to be tagged on first viewing, and for the newly defined landmark then to be matched when the object is later re-presented from a differing viewpoint. The latter proposal would account for our ability to perceive that the structure of a novel object remains constant across viewpoint shifts.

To begin with, though, we should note that we are unable to de-couple elements of form very easily, at least when those elements can be coded into some form of "higher-order" structure. There are numerous examples of this. For instance, detection of a target may be more difficult when it is incorporated within a more global figure than when it is perceptually isolated from the figure, even when the distance between the target and figure elements is controlled (e.g., Printzmetal & Banks, 1977). In tasks where subjects are asked to count the number of dots (Foster, 1978a; Humphreys, Riddoch, & Quinlan, 1985) or lines in a figure (Humphreys, 1983, 1984), performance can be affected by the global figure formed by the dots or the lines, etc. Such data suggest that landmark features are less likely to be single lines or elements in a pattern than some salient local grouping of lines or elements. Grouped local elements may still be termed landmark features provided they are more local than the whole pattern.

There are some results consistent with the landmark feature account. For instance, Hochberg and Gellman (1977) presented subjects with a series of relatively simple, 2-dimensional (2-D) shapes composed of horizontal and vertical line segments. Some of the shapes contained unique features (defined across the set of possible shapes in the experiment). Subjects had to decide whether two simultaneously presented shapes were structurally identical or whether one was a mirror image of the other. The shapes could be in the same or different orientations. For shapes defined by unique (landmark) features there were only minor effects of orientation-change on reaction times (RTs), suggesting that the landmark features could be rapidly identified irrespective of the shape's orientation. Much stronger effects of orientation change were found on the shapes without landmarks.

Landmark effects have also been obtained with more complex 3-D (3-dimensional) stimuli. Yuille and Steiger (1982) presented subjects with 3-D block figures similar to those used in the seminal studies of mental rotation by Shepard and his colleagues (e.g. Shepard & Cooper, 1982; Shepard & Metzler, 1971; see following). On each trial, a pair of figures were simultaneously exposed; half were the same figure, half were mirror images. Subjects had to decide whether the stimuli were identical, and the relative orientations of the stimuli were varied. In a first experiment, some of the subjects were instructed that the critical information distinguishing targets from their mirror images was carried by only a few of the blocks present. The RTs for these subjects were much less affected by the angular disparity between the targets than were those of subjects not given this information. It appears that subjects may selectively attend to landmark features in stimuli, and that, by so doing, the detrimental effects due to orientation transforms of the whole figure are reduced.[2]

However, in both Hochberg and Gellman's (1977) and Yuille and Steiger's (1982) studies, there remained non-negligible effects of orientation-change on RTs even when the stimuli contained landmarks. Thus, although landmark features may lessen rotation effects, they do not seem invariant to viewpoint-change. A question which also arises is whether the observed effects of viewpoint-change are dependent on the tasks. The effects of landmark features may be reduced in object matching tasks, where, depending on the relations between targets and distractors, the mere presence of such features may not carry sufficient information on which to base a response. Nevertheless, landmark features may still be extracted irrespective of the viewpoint, and so they could support performance in more favourable circumstances.

In fact, at least six experiments investigating identification, as opposed to matching, have failed to demonstrate reliable effects of stimulus orientation on RT (Corballis & Nagourney, 1978; Corballis, Zbrodoff, Shetzer, & Butler, 1978; Eley, 1982, 1983; Simion, Bagnara, Roncato, & Umilta, 1982; White, 1980). The null effect of orientation on identification time has been found both with familiar alphanumeric characters (e.g., Corballis et al., 1978) and with novel symbols of varying complexity (Eley, 1982,

[2] Note also that Yuille and Steiger's (1982) results could have occurred because subjects mentally transformed partial object descriptions (rather than transforming the whole figure). If this was the case, then performance could not be said to depend on the *detection* of landmark features, only their transformation.

1983), and so it does not seem confined to overlearned stimuli. The result supports the notion that simple 2-D stimuli can contain landmark features and that such features can support identification.

However, more recently, Jolicouer and Landau (1984) have reported orientation effects on the identification of alphanumeric characters. In this study, individual characters were briefly presented and pattern masked, and the proportion of correct identifications was taken as the dependent variable. Correct identifications decreased linearly as a function of the angle of the characters from the upright (at least up to 180 degree rotations within-the-plane). Jolicoeur and Landau also found that increasing the exposure duration by just 5msec led to relatively large benefits in character identification across the range of orientations, suggesting rapid compensation for the effects of orientation (e.g., assuming that the effects of exposure duration on visual processing are linear, an increased exposure of only 15msec would have been sufficient to eliminate the high error rate found with 180 degree rotated stimuli). It could well be that such small effects of orientation-change are difficult to detect when identification time is the dependent variable (cf. Corballis et al., 1978; Eley, 1982, 1983; Simion et al., 1982).

Jolicoeur and Landau's finding indicates that, when performance is taken to the limit, orientation effects are obtained even on the identification of highly familiar stimuli often presumed to contain landmark features. A question which arises, then, is whether these observed orientation effects resemble those found when subjects seem to use whole-object descriptions for task performance. If they do not, then a case for landmark features can be made, even if the use of these features is affected by orientation information.

3.2. Mental Transformations

One of the most interesting aspects of Jolicoeur and Landau's (1984) finding of orientation effects on character identification is the linear relationship between the angle of departure from the upright and the percentage of correct identifications. There is now a great deal of evidence from studies of object-matching that performance can vary linearly with the magnitude of the shift in the viewpoint between target objects. Such linear relationships have been taken as indicating the operation of an effortful mental transformation process in shape-matching (and perhaps also identification), which is directly analogous to the external manipulation needed to transform one target object into another (e.g., Kosslyn, 1980, 1983; Shepard & Cooper, 1982).

As noted earlier, the seminal work here was conducted by Shepard and Metzler (1971). Using a method later followed by Yuille and Steiger

(1982; discussed earlier), except that subjects were not instructed to attend to parts of the 3-D block figures, Shepard and Metzler found that the time taken to match objects increased linearly as a function of the angular disparity between the different views. Similar results have been found with orientation transforms in-depth and within-the-plane (Shepard & Metzler, 1971), and with size disparities (e.g., Bundensen & Larsen, 1975; Larsen & Bundesen, 1978); and the findings have been replicated with a wide range of stimuli including random polygons (e.g. Cooper, 1975) and alphanumeric characters (Corballis et al., 1978). Size and orientation disparities have also been shown to have additive effects on different-view match times (e.g., with there being a constant increment in the time taken to match objects with orientation and size disparities relative to when only one of these transforms is effected; see Bundesen, Larsen, & Farrell, 1981), suggesting that separate mental transformation processes must be serially applied to compensate for the two forms of disparity. In most cases (e.g., Bundesen & Larsen, 1975; Larsen & Bundesen, 1978), viewpoint shifts produce equivalent, linearly related increases in RTs for both matching and mismatching trials. Such findings indicate that mental transformation affects some early process prior to any identification or matching of the objects. Thus, mental transformations may operate as a normalising process, enabling a common stored object description to be accessed from many viewpoints.

However, other aspects of the data should also be taken into account. For instance, estimates of the rate of mental transformation differ widely both for different stimuli, and for the same stimuli in different tasks. Thus, average transformation rates in object matching tasks for 3-D block figures are about 60deg/sec (Shepard & Metzler, 1971), for alphanumeric characters they are about 360deg/sec (Cooper & Shepard, 1973), and for random polygons they are about 460deg/sec (Cooper, 1975). For alphanumeric characters in an identification task, the compensation rate for the effects of orientation away from the vertical may be as much as 12,000deg/ sec (Jolicoeur & Landau, 1984). These different compensation rates for matching and identification tasks suggest that quite different processes are involved, even when orientation exerts a linear effect on identification (as in Jolicoeur & Landau, 1984). One suggestion is that there is a relatively slow and effortful mental transformation process, which uses whole-object descriptions, and which is effected primarily in object-matching tasks (see Corballis, 1986). In addition, there is a relatively fast-acting, perhaps more automatic, compensatory process which is invoked in identification tasks.

One further qualification should be added. Jolicoeur (1985) has shown similar effects of mis-orientation on the time taken to name (i.e., an identification task) *and* on the time taken to decide whether objects are facing left or right (i.e., a kind of matching task).[3] This was only true when the objects were first seen. The effects of mis-orientation on object identification were considerably lessened (and became nonlinear) when the objects were repeated (even when the same objects were repeated at different orientations); the effects of mis-orientation on left–right decisions were maintained. Thus, the faster-acting compensatory process seems to require some initial familiarisation with the stimuli, and it is most easily invoked by the requirement to identify highly learned stimuli such as alphanumeric characters.

The fact that some compensatory procedures are required even for the identification of familiar stimuli is important. It indicates that our stored knowledge of objects is *not* represented in a form which is indifferent to viewpoint. Rather, some preferred (canonical) viewpoint must be specified (e.g., assuming an upright orientation for alphanumeric characters), along with procedures for accessing this stored description under conditions of viewpoint change. In this respect, it is interesting to note that, with familiar objects, small mis-orientations produce only small (nonlinear) RT increments even in matching tasks which, with larger transformations, produce slow, linear compensations (Cooper & Shepard, 1973; Koriat & Norman, 1985). This suggests that the stored representations of familiar stimuli become "broadly tuned", and so are not affected by small deviations from the canonical view (Koriat & Norman, 1985).

Given the operation of a rapid, compensatory process to handle the effects of orientation-change, we must also question why slower and more effortful mental transformation processes are ever required. One hint of this is given by inspecting the tasks where slow and linear effects of orientation-change are found: namely, in shape matching, and particularly where the shapes are difficult to discriminate (cf. Besner, 1983; Besner & Coltheart, 1976; Jolicoeur & Besner, Note 1). It may be that, in such tasks, subjects cannot rely on information given by more rapidly acting compensatory mechanisms. Possibly, such mechanisms only allow rather inaccurate stimulus descriptions of highly familiar objects, but not to distinguish between highly similar objects in a matching task. It may even be that certain forms of information are not made available by the rapid compensatory mechanisms. Hinton and Parsons (1981) suggest that information about whether parts are on the left or right of an object (the "handedness" of the object) is not coded by such mechanisms (see Section 3.4.1). Discriminations based on such information would clearly require some

[3] Decisions concerning whether a mis-oriented object is facing left or right may require matching the object against some upright frame. Thus, this task can be thought of as a particular version of an object-matching task.

extra process, such as the effortful mental transformation of the object's description.

The data we have discussed so far indicate that orientation and size transforms affect both object identification and matching. They therefore refute the (strong) argument for viewpoint-invariant landmark features. It appears that our stored knowledge of the structure of objects specifies a canonical viewpoint (including size and orientation information), and that costs are involved when an object is transformed relative to the canonical view. Two compensatory mechanisms have been distinguished, one of which is relatively slower acting and more effortful than the other (with compensation rates differing by about a factor of 30). The slow, effortful transformation process seems required to distinguish visually similar target and distractor objects. The faster-acting compensatory process seems to be invoked by familiar stimuli, though it may fail to make certain kinds of information explicit within an object description (e.g., handedness).

We now need to evaluate the types of information used to "drive" the faster-acting compensatory process, which is the more likely mechanism underlying the normal rapid and effortless achievement of object constancy (see Section 1).

3.3. Depth Coding, Orientation Coding, and Normalisation

One long-standing account of object constancy holds that it reflects a rapid normalisation process, operating prior to object recognition. Normalisation is thought to occur by embellishing the retinal description of an object with information about the object's distance and orientation relative to the viewer (e.g., Helmholtz, 1925; also Epstein, 1973; Rock, 1983). Many optical correlates of distances and orientation have been documented, including aerial and linear perspective, binocular disparity, motion parallax, motion perspective, occlusion, and texture. Such optical correlates could be coded to represent the orientation and distance of an object relative to the viewer, and, by applying this information to the retinally-coded (viewpoint-dependent) description, a constant (normalised) object description may be derived.

There is indeed a great deal of evidence demonstrating the importance of distance and orientation information for object constancy. For example, early studies of shape constancy indicated that it varied as a function of both the degree of rotation of an object from the frontal plane and the distance of the object from the viewer (see Epstein & Park, 1963; Koffka, 1935): That is, as objects are rotated further in depth (increasing their distance from the viewer), subjects tend to identify the object in terms of its projected, retinally based description. Presumably such effects occur because depth cues become degraded in such instances. Likewise, shape constancy is considerably better with binocular than monocular viewing (e.g. Epstein & Hatfield, 1978).

Other work suggests that normalisation using depth and orientation cues can be selectively disrupted. In an early study, Leibowitz and Bourne (1956) showed that a circle rotated in depth tended to be matched according to its projected (2-D) shape description when presented for briefer than 100msec, whilst objective (3-D) shape matches were made given longer stimulus presentations. In more detailed studies, Epstein, Hatfield, and Muise (1977) and Epstein and Hatfield (1978) presented a series of ellipses varying in their degree of depth rotation. On each trial one ellipse was tachistoscopically presented and followed by a random noise mask. Subjects had to decide which shape had been presented from amongst a series of comparison shapes. Epstein and his colleagues found that the judged shape of the stimulus tended to shift from its objective (3-D) shape to its projected (2-D) shape as the interval between the stimulus and the mask decreased. On other trials, subjects were asked to judge the orientation of the shape. Here it was found that decreasing the stimulus-mask interval led to increasing under estimation of the degree of depth rotation. Also, the effect of the mask on the perceived orientation of the shape (i.e., whether or not the shape was seen as depth rotated) was proportional to its effect on the perceived shape (i.e., whether the projected or the objective shape was seen). It appears that the mask disrupts the assimilation of orientation information and this in turn produces perception based on retinally coded shape descriptions.

The distinction made by Epstein and his colleagues is between a retinally coded description of an object and a description which has been embellished by depth information. Both descriptions are viewpoint-specific.

A contrasting result has been reported by Ellis and Allport (1985). They showed that a viewpoint-specific description can be selectively disrupted, whilst leaving an object description abstracted across viewpoints relatively intact. Ellis and Allport had subjects match consecutively presented photographs of objects according to whether the objects had the same name. When a "same" response was made, the stimuli could be identical (same object in the same orientation), the same object but rotated 45 degrees in depth, or physically different objects with the same name (e.g., two different types of clock, etc.). Ellis and Allport found that, with short intervals between the stimuli, RTs to identical stimuli were faster than RTs to rotated stimuli, and that RTs to rotated stimuli were in turn faster than those to same-name only stimuli (see also Bartram, 1976). The advantage for the identical over the rotated stimuli decreased as the interval between the stimuli lengthened, while the advantage for the rotated over the same-name stimuli was relatively constant. The advantage for identical stimuli can be attributed to the presence of common viewpoint-specific representations; the advantage for rotated objects (over same-name only objects) can be attributed to the presence of common descriptions abstracted across viewpoints. Ellis and Allport's finding shows that the viewpoint-specific description decays quite rapidly over time. Interestingly, the identical-stimulus advantage with short intervals still occurs when objects are presented at different positions on the screen (i.e., when the objects have different retinal-codings), providing the photographs preserve viewing angle, orientation, and size (Ellis, 1985). This indicates that the indentical-stimulus advantage is based on a description which is viewpoint-specific but *not* retinotopic. The latter distinction mirrors that made by Epstein (aforementioned).

The data we have discussed so far in this section suggest that successively more abstract descriptions can be generated during visual object processing, progressing from a retinally coded description, to a non-retinotopic viewpoint-specific description, to a yet more abstract description which can serve the recognition of an object across differing viewing distances and angles. These different descriptions appear to take successively longer times to generate (Ellis, 1985; Epstein & Hatfield, 1978), though all are generated relatively rapidly (at least when compared with mental transformation estimates; see Section 3.2).

However, other data indicate that the generation of non-retinotopic descriptions may be contingent on the strategies adopted by subjects. A relevant study here has been reported by Epstein and Lovitts (1985). On each trial, subjects received an irregularly contoured shape at one of a number of depth rotations, and on the vertical axis of each shape there was a line of between 5 and 8 black dots. Following a series of 20 trials, the subjects were presented with comparison shapes and they were asked to judge which shapes they had seen earlier. There were two groups of subjects. One group was told the nature of the shape discrimination task at the outset, the other was initially told to judge whether there was an odd or an even number of dots on each shape and they were unaware that shape discriminations would subsequently be required. The first (*shape-directed*) group tended to choose comparison shapes matching the objective shapes of the test stimuli; the second (*dot-directed*) group tended to choose comparison shapes matching the projected (retinal) shapes of the test stimuli (when forced to choose between objective and projected-shape comparison stimuli). This is consistent with the argument that, unless directed to attend to the target shapes, subjects tended only to form retinally coded shape representations; it follows that the coding of more abstract representations requires further steps and that these steps are contingent on subjects attending to shape information.

Unfortunately, it is unlikely that normalisation via the application of depth and orientation information can provide a full account of visual object constancy, as there are instances where distance information does not affect objective shape judgements. Norman (1980) presented subjects with a test square which could be one of five sizes and it could be at one of five distances. Subjects were also presented with a comparison square which fell at the mid-point of the size ranges used in the experiment (i.e., test squares 1 and 2 were smaller, test squares 4 and 5 were larger). Subjects judged whether the test and the comparison square on each trial were the same *objective* size. Norman found that RTs to squares 2 and 4 (i.e., the two nonmatching squares nearest in objective size to the comparison square) were much more strongly affected by the distance of the squares from the viewer than were RTs to squares 1 and 5, and RTs to the smallest square were quite unaffected by distance. From this it appears that distance information is primarily used to compute the objective size of a shape when relatively difficult discriminations are needed (e.g. with squares 2 and 4 in Norman, 1980); for tasks requiring less fine discriminations objective size may be judged directly from stimulus information (i.e., without a prior normalisation process). The shape information mediating the latter judgements could vary from landmark features to descriptions of whole-objects. Whatever the case, the data suggest that there can be direct mapping from retinally coded descriptions to object recognition procedures. Thus normalisation via the application of orientation and distance information is not *necessary* for object constancy to occur, though it may often be the means by which it is achieved.

There are also other problems for the normalisation argument. Perhaps most serious is the failure to provide a detailed mechanism for how constancy via depth-normalisation occurs. While there is much evidence indicating that, at least in the appropriate circumstances, distance information is taken into account in a second computational step following the generation of retinally based description, there is little work on how this is done. The assignment of depth to a retinotopic representation of form is a difficult computational problem (see Feldman, 1985). We need to know the size of the form units involved (cf. Section 3.1), how differences in receptive field size and acuity for foveally and peripherally presented stimuli are accommodated, how such transformations can produce linear relationships as a function of the magnitude of the orientation or size disparity between different views of an object, etc.

Additionally, the embellishment of a retinally based description with depth information will only lead to the generation of a non-retinotopic, viewpoint-specific representation. It does not explain how a description normalised across viewpoints can be achieved. To understand the latter process, we must consider the effects of the structure of objects on visual information processing.

3.4. Axis-based Structural Descriptions

3.4.1. Some Evidence

Consider a finding obtained in our own laboratory (Humphreys, 1983). Subjects were presented with two successive shapes, each of which could be in a number of different orientations. The task was to match shapes according to whether they had the same or a different number of sides, irrespective of their orientations. Two types of shape were used: one type had an unambiguous principal axis (e.g., isosceles triangles), the other had ambiguous principal axes (e.g., squares, which have two possible axes of symmetry—one through the mid-points of the sides, one across the diagonal). Humphreys (experiment 3) found that for both depth and within-plane rotations of squares and isosceles triangles, RTs to match the shapes increased linearly as a function of their angular disparity (i.e., the difference in the angle of rotation of the two views). There was, however, one exception. When squares were rotated 45 degrees within-the-plane, RTs to match the shapes were considerably longer than could be predicted from a linear extrapolation of the RTs found with smaller orientation transforms. This departure from linearity is difficult to explain on the basis of all the accounts we have discussed so far (Sections 3.1–3.3). The strong landmark feature account holds that few effects of orientation change should occur. The mental transformation account would hold that RTs should increase as a function of the angle of transformation, but the effects should not diverge for one particular shape at one particular orientation. The normalisation via depth-coding account fails to explain why such effects should be found with rotation within-the-plane (when no change in depth occurs). Some alternative account is needed. One suggestion is that these effects reflect the structural characteristics of the different shapes, and, most especially, they reflect changes in the internal representation of shapes under transformation conditions. To put this simply, a square rotated 45 degrees within-the-plane may change its internal representation into that of a diamond; this change increases the RT to respond that the shape is the same despite the transformation. An isosceles triangle rotated 45 degrees within-the-plane does not change its internal representation, and so does not generate similar increases in RTs. The internal representation of a square seems contingent on which axis aligns with the vertical, as if the representation took the form of a description of the shape relative to its principal (in this case vertical) axis. A 45 degree within-plane rotation aligns different axes of the square with the vertical (the diagonal as opposed to the mid-side axis). As the descriptions of the shape relative to the diagonal and the mid-sides axes differ, different internal representations are generated. Such effects would not occur with stimuli which

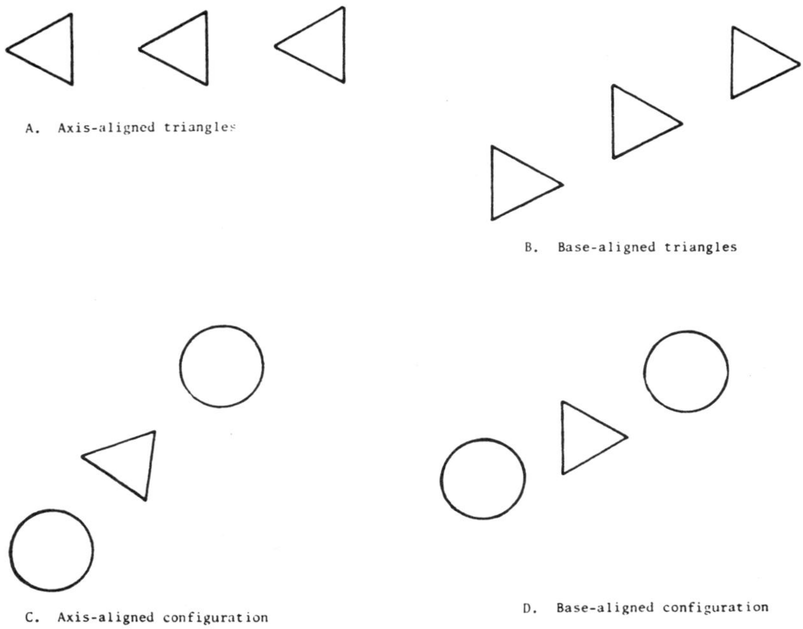

FIG. 3.2. "Axis" and "base" alignment biases in the perceived direction of pointing of equilateral triangles, studied by Palmer (1980).

maintain an unambiguous principal axis under the transformation conditions (such as an isosceles triangle), and so maintain a constant description relative to this axis.

The implication of the above argument is that our internal representation of a shape takes the form of a *structural description*, in which the parts of the shape are defined in relation to its principal axis (see Section 2). For shapes with ambiguous principal axes, the representation of the shape may be determined by its description relative to some extrinsic reference system, such as the gravitational vertical. The principal axis can therefore be thought of as a kind of reference frame, providing the co-ordinate system relative to which the shape is described.

Information about the principal axis of a shape can also be affected by its surrounding context. Palmer (1980) and Palmer and Bucher (1981) presented subjects with shapes such as those shown in Fig. 3.2, and subjects had to decide as quickly as possible whether the central equilateral triangle was pointing up, down, left or right. RTs to decide the triangle's direction of pointing were quicker when the triangle was placed in a configuration whose principal axis was consistent with the required response (cf. Fig.3. 2A) than when the configuration's principal axis was inconsistent with the

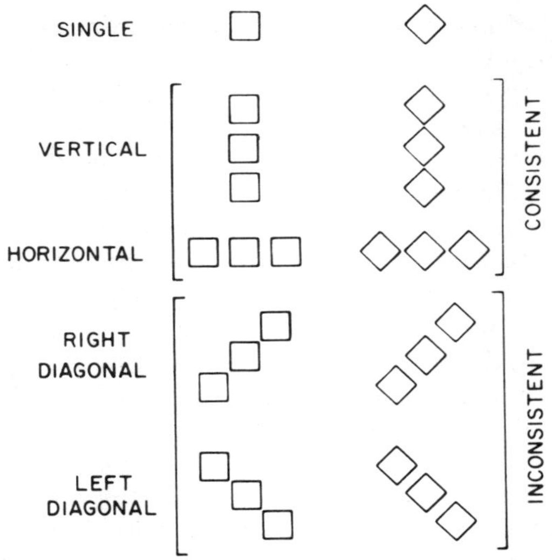

FIG. 3.3. The configural stimuli used by Palmer (1985). Subjects had to identify the central shape in each configuration.

required response (cf. Figs 2B, C, and D). This result occurred both when the target was surrounded by other triangles and when it was surrounded by circles, which indicates that it is the axis of the configuration which produces the bias rather than the presence of biasing axes in individual context members (since circles do not have a principal axis). The result also occurred when the context shapes aligned with an axis of symmetry in the target and when they aligned with one of its sides. When the context aligns with one of the sides, the side appears as the "base" in each figure and the figures are seen pointing in a direction perpendicular to the base (see Fig.3.2). The "base" and "axis" biases indicate that the frame has orthogonal axes, so that a bias can be induced perpendicular to the main orientation of the frame.

Contextual biases do not only affect the perceived direction of pointing of ambiguous shapes, they also affect shape identification. Palmer (1985) presented subjects with either a central square or diamond shape which they had to identify. Note that these shapes contain ambiguous principal axes and so change their structural description according to which axis is deemed the principal (Humphreys, 1983). The central square or diamond could be surrounded by context figures which aligned with either the diagonal or the mid-side axis (see Fig.3.3). There were marked differences in identification times according to whether the contextual shapes aligned with an axis of the target which was consistent or inconsistent with the required response.

What kinds of information determine the principal axis of a shape? Again, relevant work here has been done by Palmer and his colleagues, who have shown that configural biases are influenced by the distances separating the shapes (smaller biases occur with relatively larger distances between the shapes; see Palmer, 1985; Palmer & Bucher, 1981). This suggests that locally-coded information is crucially important (e.g., local inter-element distances). Now, since the configurations typically contain non-elongated elements, there seems to be no obvious mechanism by which locally-derived form information could specify a global property of the configuration, such as its axis of elongation. Information about the relative elongation of the configuration's principal axis would need to be based on a more global analysis where each form is treated as a primitive unit. Such a global analysis should not be so sharply tuned to inter-element distance. The data may therefore be better explained in terms of *local symmetry-detecting mechanisms*. Information about the relative degree of symmetry of different axes may be specified in local form descriptions, and this information may then be compared between form descriptions to give rise to higher-order information concerning the relative degree of symmetry for different axes in the configuration (Palmer, 1982). Symmetry detection is strongly affected by inter-element distance (Julesz, 1971).

Further evidence suggests that the process of assigning a reference frame to a shape is sensitive to low spatial frequency information. Palmer (1985) and Palmer and Bucher (1982) presented single shapes containing internal stripes of various widths (or spatial frequency; see Section 2). Subjects responded either to the direction of pointing of the shape or to its identity (where the identity could change as a function of the principal axis chosen; see Fig.3.4) and the direction of the internal stripes was either consistent or inconsistent with the response. The effects of the stripes increased as they became wider. This spatial frequency effect may be explained in either of two ways: it occurs either because the processing of low spatial frequency information is completed prior to that of high spatial frequency information (e.g., Breitmeyer, 1975), producing a greater bias on responses; or because perceptual reference frames are contingent on low spatial frequency information in a stimulus.[4]

Overall, the data indicate that object recognition can be based on a description of an object's structure relative to a perceptual reference frame. The derivation of the reference frame can be controlled by stimulus information, such as global symmetry derived from local form descriptions and also the low spatial frequency components present. We may account

[4]It is possible for reference frame effects to be influenced by local spatial frequency components of a stimulus because such information becomes available early to a decision process, without them being *contingent* on low spatial frequency information, in the sense that reference frame effects would not occur if low spatial frequency information were filtered from the input.

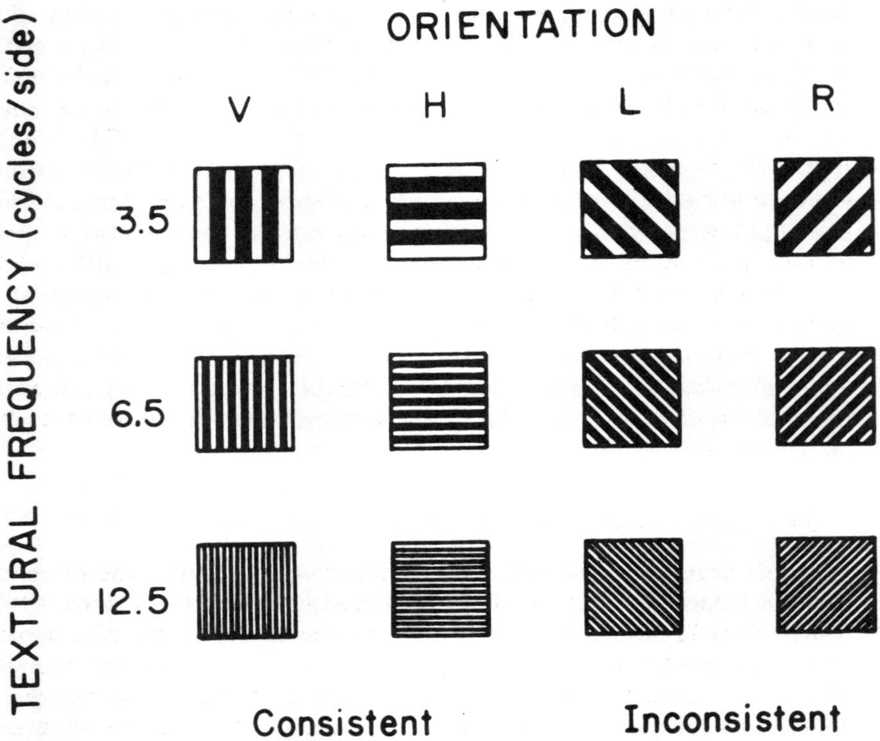

FIG. 3.4. Stimuli containing internal patterns of varying width or spatial frequency, used by Palmer (1985).

for these stimulus-based effects by combining ideas from the structural description and the spatial frequency approaches to object recognition (Section 2). For instance, it may be that the reference frame is derived by integrating information from local spatial regions subsequent to an initial spatial frequency filtering which is itself only computed for small, local areas (cf. Cavanagh,1978). The data of Jolicoeur and Landau (1984) further indicate that, even with familiar objects, some time is taken to compensate for the effects of viewpoint-change on identification performance. The axis-based account would maintain that costs are involved in the time taken to assign the axis of description when an object is shifted from its canonical position.

Other results demonstrate that the "top" position assigned to the perceptual reference frame is crucially important for object recognition. In studies of recognition memory, altering the top and bottom positions of the test object is much more detrimental to performance than altering the positions of the sides (e.g., Rock, 1973; Rock, De Vita, & Barbeito, 1981).

Also, judgements of whether a feature is located at the top or bottom of a rotated object are considerably faster than judgements of whether it is on the right or left (Greene, Plastow, & Braine, 1985). The "top" position for the frame may be based on the position of some salient feature (Braine, 1978) or simply using gravitational information (Rock, 1973, 1983). Left–right directions may only be assigned following the coding of the top-bottom positions of a reference frame (cf. Hinton & Parsons, 1981). Left–right judgements on rotated objects thus require an additional, mental rotation process. Such an argument would help explain why differences between top, bottom, left, and right direction assignments are minimised when objects are upright (since the left–right coding of features will be explicit *only* in upright objects; see Greene et al., 1985), why mirror image judgements are so difficult (Corballis & Beale, 1976), and why evidence for mental rotation most clearly obtains with mirror image judgement tasks e.g. Shepard & Cooper, 1982).

3.4.2. Axis-based Accounts of Object Constancy

Marr's Account. One of the most detailed axis-based accounts of object constancy has been proposed by Marr and his associates (Marr, 1980, 1982; Marr & Nishihara, 1978). Marr proposed that visual object constancy was mediated by the generation of three separate internal descriptions of an object. The first description, termed the *primal sketch*, is thought to represent information about the geometrical distribution and organisation of intensity changes in the image. Surface detail information is made explicit by marking the presence of edges, corners, and "blobs" of various sizes and orientations at specific positions, using a *retinotopic* co-ordinate system. Information for the primal sketch is extracted at a variety of scales by coding intensity changes at different spatial intervals (frequencies), enabling scale-specific marking of surface detail.

The creation of the second description, termed the *2½-D sketch*, involves the specification of depth and orientation information for local surface details using optical correlates such as binocular disparity, texture gradients, etc. (Marr & Poggio, 1977; Stevens, 1981). The 2½-D sketch itself represents information about the relative distance from each surface patch to the viewer, its orientation relative to the line of sight and the presence of discontinuities in the surface (two forms of discontinuity are marked; discontinuity in depth, indicating an edge, and discontinuity in orientation, indicating a ridge).

Both the primal sketch and the 2½-D sketch are *viewpoint-specific*, and in both descriptions information is represented relative to the line of sight (more specifically, the information is represented in terms of retinocentric polar co-ordinates; see Fig. 3.5). Clearly, neither description will allow

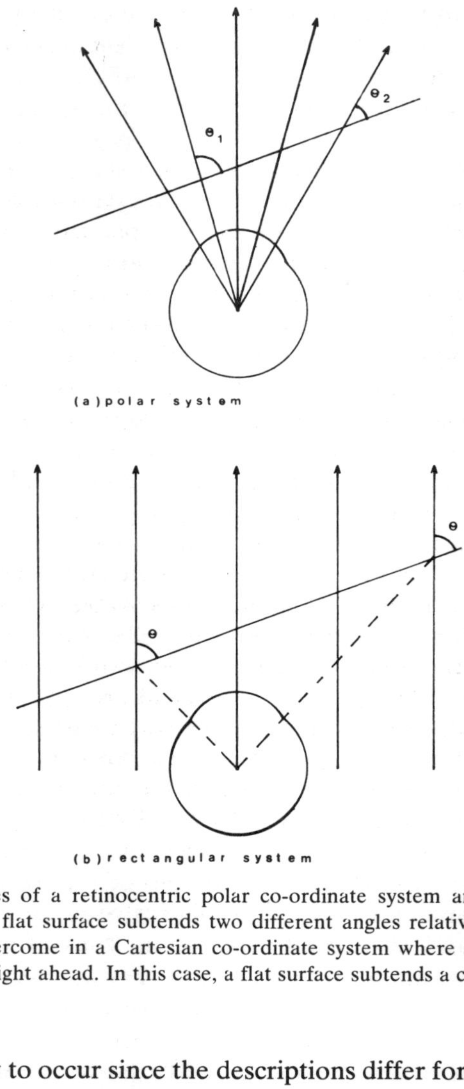

FIG. 3.5. Examples of a retinocentric polar co-ordinate system and of a Cartesian co-ordinate system. A flat surface subtends two different angles relative to the line of sight. This problem is overcome in a Cartesian co-ordinate system where all angles are referred to the direction straight ahead. In this case, a flat surface subtends a constant angle (derived from Marr, 1982).

object constancy to occur since the descriptions differ for different views of objects. Marr (1982) also notes that there are some disadvantages in using polar co-ordinates even for the integration of different forms of depth information, since there are different correlations to the line of sight for different depth cues. Polar co-ordinates also obscure some aspects of surface information. For instance, it is difficult to specify that a surface is flat using polar co-ordinates since the surface orientation will differ in different parts of the visual field (Fig 3.5). Marr therefore suggests that information is converted into a Cartesian co-ordinate system in which surface details are referenced relative to the directions forward, backward, left and right. Note here that a flat surface in different parts of the field would then have the same orientation with respect to the viewer (see Fig.3.5), producing some normalisation for the orientation of objects transformed in depth.

However, even if surface form information is coded in terms of a Cartesian co-ordinate system, the 2½-D sketch would not specify internal object structure (since surface details are coded independently), and the description would change for transformations within-the-plane (translations and rotations). Such a description would not easily serve for object recognition unless many such descriptions for a given object were stored (see Section 2). To bypass this problem, Marr proposed that a third object description is constructed, the *3-D model description*. One crucial difference between the 3-D model description and the description suggested above is that the 3-D model description is defined on a co-ordinate system based on characteristics of the object, and not the viewpoint. Because of this, the 3-D model description will be *viewpoint-independent*; for instance, when an object as a whole is moved, the parts of the object relative to the viewpoint will change but their positions relative to a standard point on the object will remain constant (see Fig. 3.1 for an example of this proposition).

The object-centred co-ordinate system for the 3-D model description is based on the natural axes of the object. The description is formed by first deriving the component axes in an object and then by coding the arrangement of the object's parts with respect to the immediate axis. However, such a description would still be inherently unstable as a change in the location of one axis relative to others in the object would give rise to a different description. Marr and Nishihara (1978) therefore suggested that stability might be introduced if the description for a whole object were itself constructed from a hierarchy of nested descriptions, with each more-local description specifying parts of decreasing size coded relative to its own axis. Marr and Nishihara give the example of the 3-D model description for a human body specifying, at the highest level, the position, orientation, and lengths of the head, arms, torso, and legs (the main sub-axes) relative to the principal axis given by the height of the body. The description of a "part", such as the arm, might then consist of the position, orientation, and lengths of its own sub-axes, such as the upper arm and the fore-arm, etc. (see Fig. 3.6).

The 3-D model description is thus hypothesised to have a modular organisation, with each level of description composed of an arbitrary number of independent descriptions of smaller parts. Thus we can define an object as being a *level of form description* (such as a body or a hand) *articulated relative to a co-ordinate system based on its own principal axis*. Object recognition may be achieved by matching the 3-D model description with

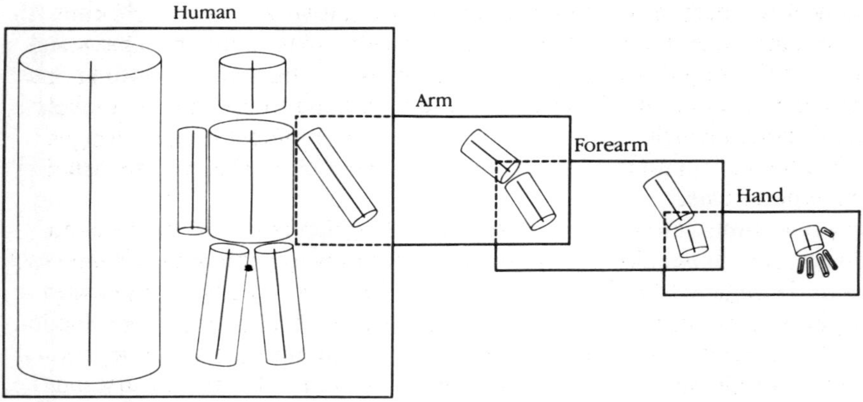

FIG. 3.6. An illustration of the hierarchical shape information in a 3-D model description. Each box corresponds to a 3-D model, with its model axis on the left-hand side of the box and the arrangement of the component axes on the right. Some component axes also have 3-D models associated with them, as indicated by the way the boxes overlap (although, in Marr's scheme the arrangement of each model's component axes should be specified in an object-centred system, not the viewer-centred system shown here) (from Marr, 1982).

a stored description of the object. It follows that, for such matching to occur, stored object descriptions must themselves be modular, being composed of separate representations for local parts organised at increasingly higher levels of description. Recognition might then occur from matching at any level of description, from the gross overall description of the whole object to a local description of a salient part, providing of course that the part uniquely specifies the object.

In such a scheme, those changes in the whole object description produced by movement of local parts will be constrained, as the degrees of freedom for movement of a given part relative to its own principal axis will be considerably less than those for the part relative to the whole object (e.g., the position of a hand may move relatively freely about a torso when compared with its freedom to move relative to its connecting arm). The problem of the representation being unstable following the movement of local parts are thus reduced. However, they are not eliminated. For instance, the position of a hand relative to its connecting arm can still change, constrained by the movements of the wrist. Object recognition based on matching a 3-D model description to a stored object description which specifies an *exact* position for a hand relative to an arm would be disrupted by hand movements. One way around this would be for the stored object description to indicate a range of possible positions for the movement of parts, so that recognition occurs providing the position of the part falls within the range; alternatively, position information for parts might be coded rather coarsely, with only the absolute position of the object's principal axis being coded. Behaviour contingent on the exact location of a local part would then need to operate on a level of description at which that part is represented as an object in its own right (see Quinlan & Humphreys, 1987, for an application of this idea to visual search experiments).

Marr's account can accommodate configural effects on the time taken to identify or to decide the direction of pointing of ambiguous shapes (Palmer, 1980, 1985; Palmer & Bucher, 1981, 1982), as the 3-D model description of ambiguous shapes will change according to the axis about which the description is articulated. Further, by building in the assumption that it takes time and attention to convert a $2\frac{1}{2}$-D sketch onto a Cartesian co-ordinate system, it can accommodate the data indicating selective effects of masking and attention on object constancy (Epstein et al., 1977; Epstein & Lovitts, 1985), and it can account for why a viewpoint-dependent representation may be disrupted separately from a more abstracted, 3-D model description (cf. Ellis & Allport, 1985).

Now, as we pointed out in Section 2, any frame-based account of object constancy needs to specify a mechanism by which a reference frame is derived. According to Marr and Nishihara (1978), the reference frame for a 3-D model description of an object is based on the object's principal axis. There are many ways in which an object's principal axis could be derived. For instance, stored knowledge about the principal axis in different objects might be used to determine the choice. Marr and Nishihara's approach to the problem was to suggest that the visual system would articulate as detailed an object description as possible without the influence of stored knowledge, thereby enabling constancy to occur for novel objects. Accordingly, they suggested that the principal axis would be determined by geometrical characteristics of the object, such as elongation and symmetry. There may also be additional biases towards a vertical axis, consistent with the constraints of gravity, which would apply irrespective of the object's identity (cf. Humphreys, 1983; Palmer, 1980).

Although the derivation of form descriptions at a number of levels of specificity may take place in parallel, action may usually only be directed to one description at a time (cf. Allport, Tipper, & Chmiel, 1985; Duncan, 1984, 1985; Humphreys, 1985). There is therefore a need for some sort of control or attentional mechanism which determines the spatial scale of the description needed to guide behaviour (see Palmer,1982, for a similar suggestion). Thus, descriptions at different scales may mediate visual object processing as a function of the "attentional set" of the observer (cf. Duncan, 1980).

There is some evidence consistent with the above proposal. Humphreys

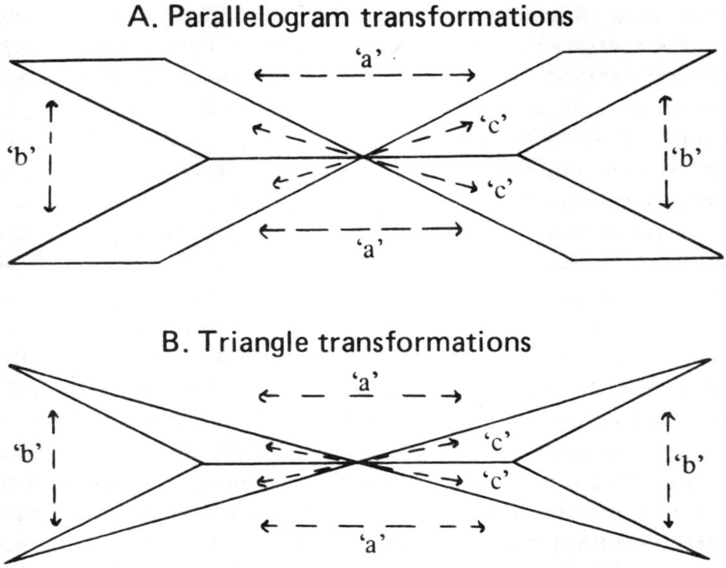

FIG. 3.7. 2-D geometrical shape stimuli used by Humphreys (1984). Each shape could be subjected to any of three orientation transformations. ("a", "b", or "c"). For the present purposes, the important transforms are "c" (which maintains the orientation of the shape's principal axis) and transform "a" (which changes the orientation of the shape's principal axis while leaving a focal feature at the top).

(1984) presented subjects with consecutive shapes, and subjects had to respond according to whether the shape on a given trial had the same form. The shapes were either scalene triangles, with a principal axis of elongation, or elongated parallelograms. On "same-shape" trials, the shapes could either be in the same orientation or they could be orientation transformed. The orientation transforms changed the orientation of the shape's principal axis whilst leaving the "top" feature unchanged (e.g., by a 180 degree rotation in depth) or they changed the location of the "top" feature whilst leaving the orientation of the principal axis the same (see Fig.3.7). Humphreys found that, when subjects could not predict the location of the second shape, RTs were faster when the shape's orientation was constant (transform "c", Fig. 3.7) than when it changed (transform "a"). In fact, RTs in the same-orientation condition were then as fast as RTs when no transformation occurred, consistent with the idea that matching operated using axis-based shape descriptions and that maintaining the axis orientation in some way facilitated computation of the shape's description on its re-presentation. However, quite different effects were found when subjects could predict the location of the second shape. Then, RTs were fastest when no transformation occurred, and there was no difference between the orientation-change and the orientation-constant transformations (Humphreys, 1984, experiment 3). This suggests that subjects only used the global property of the shape's orientation under conditions of spatial uncertainty, so that the orientation effects were eliminated when subjects attended to the location of the features discriminating targets from distractors. It appears that when a task allows subjects to attend selectively to informative parts of an object, subjects use local form descriptions for matching across viewpoints. Under conditions of spatial uncertainty, more global form descriptions are used.

Connectionist Accounts. Marr's work derived from attempts to implement visual object recognition in a computer. Other schemes developed in the field of computer vision also hold that object constancy is achieved by constructing an axis-based description from the image; however, the means by which this occurs are somewhat different to those outlined by Marr. These other schemes may be grouped under the heading of "connectionist" accounts of object constancy. The basic assumption of connectionist accounts is that visual information processing occurs via activity in massively parallel networks of simple computational units (e.g., Ballard, Hinton & Sejnowski, 1983; Feldman, 1985; Feldman & Ballard, 1982; Hinton & Anderson, 1981). Each computational unit simply conveys a single value (which in a biological system, might correspond to the firing rate of a neurone), but, by means of its connections with other units, it can constrain the operation of the network. Information processing constraints are built into a connectionist system by means of excitatory and inhibitory connections between the processing units, so that the excitation of one unit will inhibit activity in other units with which it is inconsistent. Thus, as information consistent with one unit is processed over time, the unit will activate all other units consistent with it whilst concurrently inhibiting all other units, until the system converges on one interpretation of the input (this iterative approach to a self-consistent solution is termed relaxation; see Attneave, 1982; Ballard et al., 1983; see also Humphreys, Riddoch, & Quinlan, in press, and Riddoch & Humphreys, Chapter 4, for an application of the idea to picture recognition and naming).

One sketch of a connectionist account of object constancy has been outlined by Hinton (1981). Hinton posits the existence of two independent sets of processing units which are selectively activated by local features present in the stimulus. One set of units respond to local features which fall at particular locations and at particular orientations on the retina (*retina-based units*). The other set respond to features at given locations and orientations with respect to some object-centred reference frame

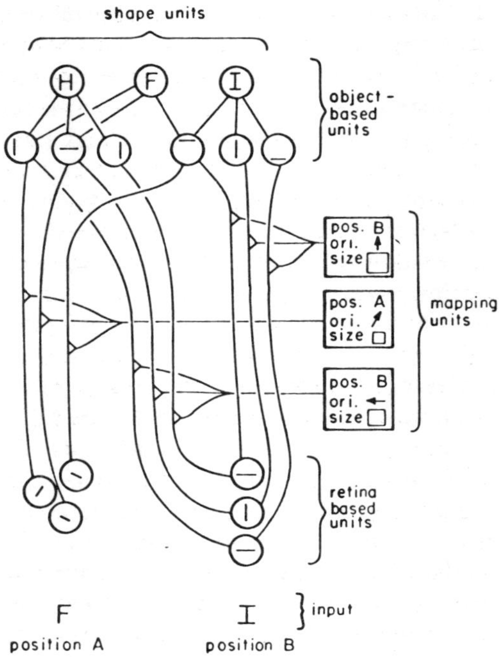

FIG. 3.8. Outline of a connectionist account of pattern recognition. Each mapping unit controls a set of channels from the retina-based units to the object-based units. The triangular symbols represent particular connection rules (from Hinton, 1981).

(*object-based units*). Object-based units may be arranged hierarchically, so that activation of local object-based features in turn activates units corresponding to increasingly larger parts. Such units accept input from many different retina-based units. Activation to retina-based units is transmitted to object-based units via the operation of a separate set of *mapping units* which regulate connections between specific retina-based units and object-based units. These mapping units effectively represent different reference frames for describing an object (see Fig.3.8).

When an object is presented, it will initially activate those retina-based units consistent with it, and activity in retina-based units will then be transmitted to consistent object-based units. However, the degree to which any object-based unit becomes activated will depend on the state of the mapping units as well as those retina-based units to which it is connected. Normally, there may be some pre-existing bias for mapping-units corresponding to a vertical reference frame, which ensures that an object comes to be identified as being vertically oriented (i.e., as an "I" at position B in the example given in Fig.3.8). It is also possible for mappings to be influenced by activity in object-based units (if such activity is transmitted back to consistent mapping units): That is, there may be some "top-down" influence on object constancy. By this latter mechanism, other mappings can determine the object being identified in terms of its description relative to a non-vertical frame (e.g., by imposing a horizontal frame it is possible to identify an "I" as an "H" on its side; see Fig.3.8).

There are some interesting aspects of connectionist accounts. First, only one mapping between retina-based units and object-based units at a time can "win". Such models therefore predict that we may only perceptually identify only one object at a time, though of course partial activation of many object descriptions may occur before the system "relaxes" and a given pattern of activation across the various processing units comes to dominate (see Feldman, 1985; Hinton, 1981). Secondly the approach provides a mechanism for top-down as well as purely data-driven derivation processes in object constancy (see Section 3.6). Thirdly, the notion of massively parallel processing being conducted by simple computational units has clear analogies with information processing in the brain, which contains relatively slow computational units (neurones) with complex parallel connections. The idea that the essential computational work of the system is carried out in parallel by the connections between units, rather than, say, by the serial transmission of symbolic descriptions, may elegantly account for how we carry out complex behaviours in a few hundred milliseconds when the basic computational speed of neurones is itself of the order of milliseconds (see Feldman, 1985; Hinton & Anderson, 1981).

In order for connectionist accounts to accommodate the data we have discussed earlier (Sections 3.1–3.4.1), we need further to assume that mappings are influenced by optical correlates of depth and orientation (see Feldman, 1985), and that mappings can be implemented independently by different levels of form description (as, for instance, when the mapping required to identify the whole object is different from that required for its parts).

3.4.3. There's More to it than Axes

Both Marr's and the connectionist accounts maintain that object constancy is attained via the description of an object's shape relative to a perceptual reference frame. However, we have already noted instances where constancy is based on descriptions of features more local than the whole object, such as when subjects attend to landmark features (Humphreys, 1984; Yuille & Steiger, 1982). It appears that any full account of object constancy will be even more complicated than those we have considered.

The above conclusion is further supported by some work we have recently conducted on shape perception. We were interested in the relations between the properties of elongation and symmetry in the internal representation of shape. Subjects were presented with shapes containing axes of symmetry or of elongation. The *symmetrical* shape had only a principal axis of symmetry; the *elongated* shape had only a principal axis of elongation; the *conjoint* shape had a principal axis of both symmetry and elongation; the *disjoint* shape had two possible principal axes, one of elongation and one of symmetry (see Fig.3.9). The shapes also either had their principal or their minor axis drawn-in (of course, for the disjoint shape this meant that either alternative axis could be drawn-in; see Fig.3.9). Subjects were consecutively presented with two stimuli on a trial. The stimuli could be rotated versions of the same shape ("same" response) or different shapes ("different" response). Rotations always aligned different axes with the vertical, and the axis drawn-in on the first shape could either be maintained in the second shape (axis-constant) or it could be altered (axis-change). For same-responses, the effect of keeping the axis constant differed as a function of the shape. For the conjoint and the symmetrical shapes, RTs were considerably faster when the principal axis was drawn-in and remained constant than in any of the other conditions (rotation 1 in Fig.3.9a and 3.9c). Such a result suggests that these shapes were matched from a description coded relative to their principal axis, and that drawing in the axis facilitated matching. For the disjoint shape, RTs were quicker for both the axis-constant conditions relative to the axis-change conditions (rotations 1 and 2 vs. rotations 3 and 4; Fig. 3.9b), suggesting that *either* the axis of symmetry or the axis of elongation could be used to represent this shape internally.[5] However, there were *no* effects of the orientation of the drawn-in axis on RTs to the elongated shape (see Fig. 3.9d). It is as if the drawn-in axis played no part in the internal description mediating the matching of the elongated shape across the two viewpoints.

In other studies we have shown that subjects must respond to the global outline and the drawn-in axis of the elongated shape as if they were separate items of information: RTs contingent on both the global outline orientation and the axis orientation are much longer than RTs contingent on either alone (cf. Garner, 1974). In contrast, subjects respond to the drawn-in axis of the conjoint shape as if it were part of the overall shape description: RTs contingent on both the global outline orientation and the axis orientation are nearly as fast as RTs to the global outline alone, and tend to be faster than those to the axis alone.

[5] Although the fact that there were only small differences between RTs to the conjoint and the symmetrical shape in this experiment suggests that symmetry was the principal factor underlying the derivation of the conjoint shape's principal axis.

The main implication to be drawn from these data is that axis-based descriptions may *only* be useful for some shapes (in particular, those shapes whose geometrical characteristics yield a good axis). Thus, theories which advocate that object constancy is dependent on such descriptions are only partially correct. For some shapes (such as the elongated shape shown in Fig. 3.9d), axis-based descriptions are *not* used. The kinds of information used for shape matching and identification appear to be highly constrained by the stimulus. For the elongated shape, local feature-coding seems to be used even when more global, axis-based descriptions could be beneficial. Quite the opposite result obtains with the conjoint shape (Fig. 3.9a). As noted earlier, RTs to the orientation of the *axis* in this shape were affected by the orientation of the shape. We have found the latter result even when subjects fixated the location where the axis appears, which ought to maximise the opportunity for its selective encoding. How can we reconcile this result with our earlier claim that we are able to effect some control over the spatial scale of the description mediating object constancy (Section 3.4.2)? One way to do this is to propose that attention does not directly influence the (perceptual) derivation of such descriptions, but rather that it determines the scale of the descriptions mediating a given response. The characteristics of some stimuli mean that performance is constrained to operate at a particular spatial scale. Other stimuli may be described with equal facility at different spatial scales, and the descriptions at the different scales may be equally useful for a given task. For instance, the scalene triangles used by Humphreys (1984) may yield a number of separate descriptions, including that of each local angle and of a more global description of the shape relative to its principal axis. These triangles may be distinguished from the parallelograms used in that study on the basis of either the local angle descriptions or the more global description, and the type of description used for response purposes may depend on whether subjects are able to attend to the local distinguishing features. Our suggestion is that *attention influences the uses to which the products of perceptual processing are put, and not perceptual processing itself.* This suggestion can also be applied to the data of Epstein and Lovitts (1985; see Section 3.3). Epstein and Lovitts argued that subjects failed to generate other than retinally-coded descriptions of objects unless instructed to attend to 3-D shape. Our alternative account would hold that, in fact, more abstract (non-retinotopic) descriptions were generated, but that the test of recognition memory used by Epstein and Lovitts was insensitive to such descriptions. A more suitable empirical test might involve investigating priming effects produced by 3-D shape information (cf. Allport et al., 1985). Of course, it could also be that attention constrains the *type* of description which is generated (i.e., whether it is retinotopic or more abstract), but not its spatial scale.

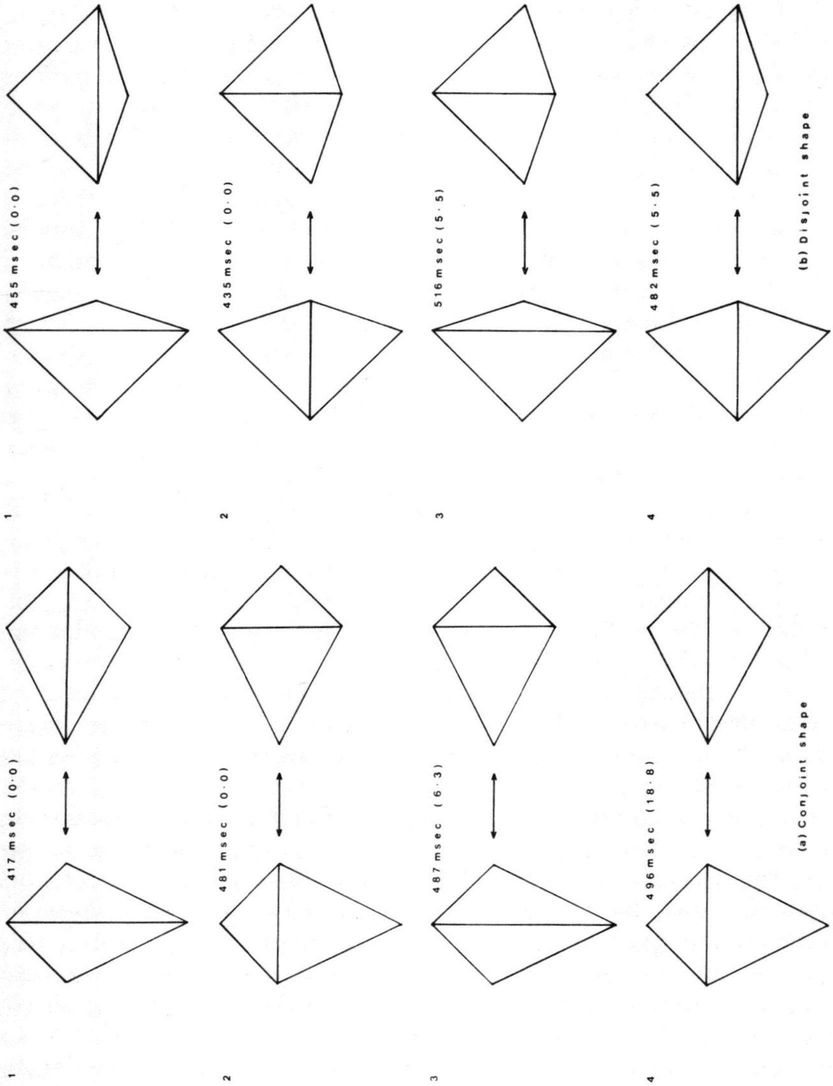
1
417 msec (0·0)
2
481 msec (0·0)
3
487 msec (6·3)
4
496 msec (18·8)
(a) Conjoint shape
1
455 msec (0·0)
2
435 msec (0·0)
3
516 msec (5·5)
4
482 msec (5·5)
(b) Disjoint shape

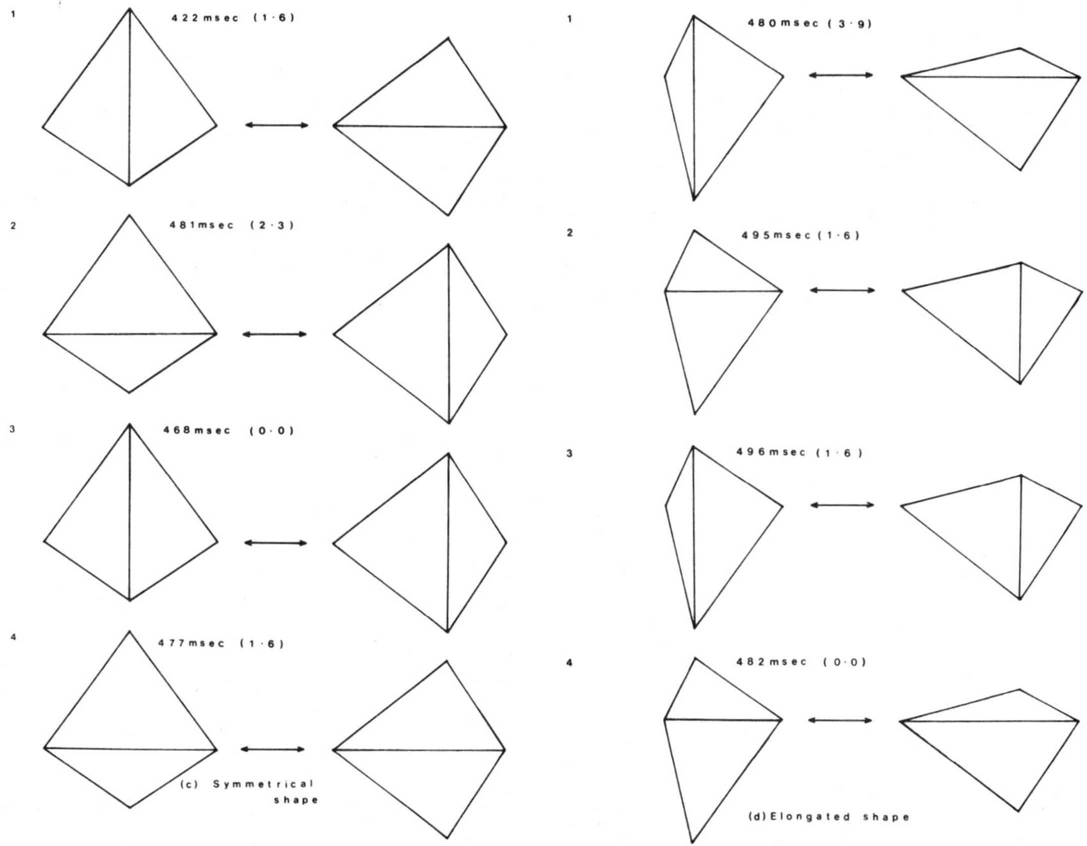

FIG. 3.9. Examples of the conjoint (a), disjoint (b), symmetrical (c), and elongated (d) shapes. Rotations either keep the drawn-in axis constant (1 and 2) or they alter it (3 and 4). Mean correct RTs (msec) and percentage errors made by 8 subjects are given.

3.5. Deriving Continuous Transforms

Axis-based account of object constancy assume that the internal representation of a shape takes the form of a structural description, and that constancy is achieved by generating the same structural description when an object is seen from different viewpoints. It is also important to note some quite different approaches, which assume that the representation of a shape has no internal structure (i.e., there is no specification of the principal axis or of salient parts). This would be the case if shape representations simply approximate the spatial distribution of light intensity on the retina. We now discuss approaches to object constancy which stress that our internal representations of shapes are unstructured, as such approaches appear to contrast quite markedly with those discussed hitherto.

One way to match unstructured representations across viewpoints would be to apply what are termed "continuous transformations", which seek to determine the overlap between the different representations (see Dodwell, 1983; Foster, 1978b; Shepard, 1981, 1984). A continuous transformation is an operation which takes a geometrical object (a point, a line, a figure, etc.) into another object by a series of infinitesimally small, local steps (see Dodwell, 1983). The general idea here is that the visual system applies sets of continuous transformations to incoming information, and that it registers both the retinal position and orientation codings of local forms *and* the invariant information yielded by the transformations. The derivation of this invariant information enables object constancy to occur.

The notion that the visual system responds to invariant information yielded by the continuous transformation of input data was originally proposed by Mach (1906) and by some of the Gestalt psychologists (e.g., Koffka, 1935). Gibson (1950, 1966, 1979) also exploited this notion in his proposal that, given the changes in the optical array consequent on the observer moving around an object or by an object moving relative to the observer (both of which create continuous transformations of the data), the observer is able to extract invariant information which defines the structure of the object. One well-known example of this recovery of structure from motion is Johansson's (1973, 1975) demonstration that a group of moving spots (lights attached to the main joints of a subject) can give a vivid and immediate impression of human movements, even though the spots appear as a random dot array when the subject is stationary (see also Dunker, 1937; Gibson & Gibson, 1957; Green, 1961; Wallach & O'Connell, 1953; for other examples). The importance of this demonstration is its indication that motion alone can be sufficient for the derivation of invariant structural information. In recovering structure from motion it is as if the visual system assumes the existence of rigid objects in the environment, so that "any set of elements undergoing a 2-D transformation which has a unique interpretation as a rigid body moving in space should be interpreted as such a body" (Ullman, 1979).

Dodwell (1982, 1983, 1984) has argued that families of continuous transformations are applied to visual input as a function of the anatomical structure of the visual cortex. The general idea is that the visual system (and in particular, the structure of the cortex) has evolved so that ecologically important transformations (e.g., the rotation, translation, and dilation transformations underlying object constancy) are easily effected by means of comparisons between local representations of form in the cortex. Such comparisons specify the rate of change of orientation information across the local form representations, enabling global properties of the form to be derived. For instance, a global circular form could be represented by an equation such as $dy/dx = -x/y$, which specifies an orientation (dy/dx) for arbitrary x and y locations (see Fig. 3.10). Importantly, the same global description is derived even when the local features have been rotated within-the-plane. Thus the generation of this global description enables constancy to occur across this particular transformation. The suggestion is that interactions between local feature detectors in the cortex have become tuned to registering such transformations. In this way, assumptions about rigidity and other properties of the real physical world may become "hard-wired" into a visual system in which transformations yielding interpretations favouring rigid objects in 3-D space are most easily effected.

However, even armed with the concept of continuous transformations, it remains difficult for theories positing unstructured form representations to

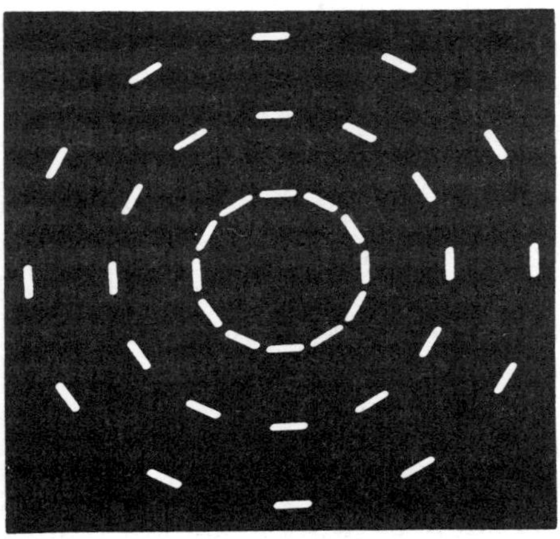

FIG. 3.10. Example of a global circular form defined from continuous local transforms.

account for discontinuities in object constancy which may occur as a function of the structural properties of different objects (e.g., the departures from linearity which obtain when squares are rotated 45 degrees within-the-plane into diamonds; Humphreys, 1983; see Section 3.2). The transformation of each local segment in a square should be equivalent to that of each local segment in an isosceles triangle, when each are rotated 45 degrees within-the-plane. That squares are more difficult to match following this rotation suggests that structural descriptions are derived in shape perception. However, the continuous transformation account and the structural description account are not mutually inconsistent. For instance, it is possible that structural descriptions and continuous transformations are computed independently and in parallel in shape processing.

Shepard (1981, 1984; Shepard & Farrell, 1985) has also proposed that there are certain internal constraints which determine the perception of rigid form. Shepard suggests that, in order to understand the effects of rotation on visual perception, we may consider that objects are internally represented within a 3-D parameter space, which may be modelled by the interior of a sphere. Within this space, each point corresponds to a position of the object in physical space, and the paths connecting two points along the surface of the sphere correspond to possible rigid motions between locations. Thus, when a shape is presented and re-presented internally within its parameter space, the effects of all possible transformations may themselves be implicit in the form of the parameter space.

Shepard's approach predicts that the perception of rigid (apparent) motion between two views of a stationary object will be a function of the length of the path along the surface of the parameter space. As the path lengthens (e.g., as the orientation change between the two views increases) so the critical interval required to see the apparent motion will increase (e.g., Shepard & Judd, 1976). Similarly, the paths of mental transformations when subjects match shapes across different views should correspond to the shortest trajectories between the representations in internal space (with match times increasing linearly as a function of the magnitude of the transformation; see Section 3.2). A virtue of this approach is that it is possible for the parameter space to reflect some of the structural characteristics of the object. A sphere may characterise the parameter space for an asymmetric object (which only maps onto itself following a 360 degree rotation); objects with partial symmetries will give rise to parameter spaces which reflect that smaller rotations will be required for complete correspondences to occur (see Shepard, 1981; Shepard & Farrell, 1985). Consequently, at least some aspects of the effects of object structure on constancy can be accounted for.

Now, while the application of continuous local transforms may be sufficient to derive invariant form information, it is important to note that further processing may be needed before a form can be identified. Consider an example documented by Sumi (1984). Sumi took a film demonstrating Johansson's (1973, 1975) forward-moving light spots (see earlier), inverted it and ran it backwards to subjects who were asked to write down their impressions. Most subjects reported that they saw an upright image of a person walking forwards, but in a very strange manner. This suggests that motion information gave rise to the perception of rigid structure but that the interpretation of the structure was dependent on other factors. For instance, the fact that subjects perceived an upright form suggests that they *interpreted* the structural information in terms of a vertical, upright reference frame (presumably reflecting gravitational constraints). Because subjects described the structural information relative to this frame, they perceived the moving spots as reflecting unfamiliar biological motion (with movements of the actor's knee interpreted as arm movements, etc.).

3.6. Top-Down Effects

With the exception of the connectionist accounts, all of the approaches to object constancy that we have so far discussed have emphasised that constancy is primarily affected by characteristics of the stimulus (or at least of the internal representation determined by the stimulus), and not by the knowledge brought to bear by the observer. It is possible, however, that our stored knowledge plays some role in our processing of objects in different views (see Gregory, 1970; Neisser,1967). It is not difficult to provide illustrative evidence for the latter position. For instance, observers typically find it more difficult to identify objects as the objects are rotated further away from their canonical (prototypical) perspective (see Palmer, Rosch, & Chase, 1981). Providing the observers with perspective information before the object is presented facilitates naming time for those objects rotated furthest (Palmer et al., 1981). Similarly, Humphreys and Riddoch (1984) presented subjects with a series of photographs of common objects rotated in depth to foreshorten their principal axis. The subjects identified only 30% of the foreshortened objects shown in isolation, and usually interpreted the objects in terms of their 2-D projections. However, when the subjects were given three photographs, two of a target (one taken from a canonical view and one from the foreshortened view) and one of a visually similar distractor, they were able to make correct target matches on about 87% of the trials. The latter result suggests that subjects may use the canonical view to derive the correct description of an object presented in an unusual view.

A question which arises is whether top-down influences only become apparent under conditions of extreme distortion, when, effectively, there is insufficient stimulus-driven information for correct perception to occur. Studies which have reported effects of familarity on object constancy (e.g., the effects of using objects of known size and shape) have generally limited the amount of stimulus information available to subjects (e.g., Fitzpatrick, Pasnak, & Tyler, 1982) and the effects of familiarity can be overruled when other distance cues are available (Gogel, Hartman, & Harker 1957). Such data suggest that top-down information at best influences performance when stimulus-driven descriptions are ambiguous. The data reported by Jolicoeur (1985; see Section 3.2) also indicate that top-down information is effective when stimulus-based compensatory processes are relatively slow. He found that the effects of mis-orientation on naming times to line drawings were lessened when the objects were re-presented at different orientations. In this case, information activated by the stimulus helped invoke more rapid compensatory processes. Thus we have a picture in which top-down information can play a role in object constancy. With ambiguous stimuli, top-down information may be *necessary* for constancy to occur (cf. Humphreys & Riddoch, 1984); in other circumstances, it may play a more limited, compensatory role.

It should also be noted that accounts stressing top-down effects on object constancy need to clarify the nature of the information which is effective. For instance, we may distinguish between stored conceptual knowledge about objects and stored knowledge about object structure (see Humphreys et al., 1985; Riddoch & Humphreys, this volume, Chapter 4). It is possible that stored structural knowledge is normally important for object constancy, in the sense that constancy may be more easily achieved for objects with known structures than for novel objects. However, such a result would not necessarily imply the involvement of *semantic* knowledge. To illustrate this point, consider again the results of Jolicoeur (1985; Section 3.2, see also earlier). Although the intervals between the re-presentations of the objects in that study were not strictly controlled, it seems likely that, on average, quite long intervals were involved.[6] As semantic priming effects are known to show rapid decay over time (cf. Gough, Alford, & Holley-Wilcox, 1981; Meyer, Schvaneveldt, & Ruddy, 1975), the effects of repetition observed by Jolicoeur may likely be attributed to the activation of structural rather than semantic information about objects.[7]

[6] For example, in Jolicoeur's (1985) experiment 1, objects were presented in 36 trial blocks and they were then repeated across each successive trial block (the order of presentation within the block being random). Thus the minimum number of intervening items between repititions was 0, the maximum was 35, and the average was 18. There was also a one second interval between trials.

[7] Jolicoeur (1985) himself convincingly argues that the effects are due to the repetition of structural information, and not orientation information, as responses were facilitated to the same objects at new orientations rather than to new objects presented at previously used orientations.

3.7. A Summary: Horses for Courses

We have discussed evidence from normal human subjects concerning various approaches to visual object constancy. Our review suggests that:

1. There is limited evidence for the use of landmark features, though their use may be confined to a few specific circumstances (such as when there is a small set size of possible stimuli, or when subjects are told or are able to attend selectively to the features; Sections 3.1 and 3.4.1).
2. Objects can be matched across viewpoints by some form of mental transformation analogous to that performed on the external object. However, such processes are relatively slow and effortful, and they may only be required for difficult discriminations. With familiar objects, more rapid compensatory processes are invoked (Section 3.2).
3. The effects of depth rotation can be compensated for by embellishing retinotopic descriptions of objects with optical correlates of depth. The non-retinotopic, viewpoint-dependent descriptions so generated can be further distinguished from even more abstract descriptions by the selective effects of variables such as the inter-stimulus interval, and the stimulus exposure duration (Section 3.3).
4. Abstract representations can take the form of descriptions of the parts of the object relative to the reference frame of its principal axis, and such descriptions can be articulated for parts as well as for whole objects. However, axis-based descriptions do not seem to mediate the perception of all shapes; other mechanisms, such as the coding of local part descriptions, can also underly object constancy. The efficacy of different descriptions is dependent both on the characteristics of the stimulus (e.g., whether or not it has a salient principal axis, etc.) and on how attention is allocated to it (Section 3.4).
5. The visual system is able to extract invariant form information when the optical array changes due to motion. The application of continuous transforms across local form elements in stationary patterns can also lead to the derivation of invariant global form descriptions, and the specification of these transformations in the shape's internal representation may enable it to be matched across viewpoints (Section 3.5).
6. Stimulus-driven information alone is sufficient for object constancy to occur, though stored knowledge may influence performance when the stimulus is ambiguous and/or when stimulus-based procedures are relatively slow (Section 3.6).

From the foregoing analysis, it would appear that visual object constancy may be achieved using different types of form description and different information processing mechanisms in different circumstances. When subjects must identify objects from a wide range of alternatives, peformance can be dependent on axis based structural descriptions. Codings of partial object descriptions may be sufficient to support performance when the stimulus alternatives are limited, and feature positions can be predicted. However, contrasting results occur when matching across viewpoint is required. With difficult discriminations, some form of mental transformation is typically carried out. This may be because specification of the left-right direction of features in objects may be useful with difficult discriminations, and such coding may not be explicit in non-upright axis-based descriptions (cf. Hinton & Parsons, 1981). With less difficult discriminations, or when there is motion information, performance may depend on the application of continuous local transformations. Indeed, the information thus derived concerning the local structure of objects under specific transformations may subserve particular types of behaviour, such visuo-motor tracking. However, in cases where the application of orientation information is important (such as identification), then the object needs to be represented relative to a perceptual reference frame (such as its principal axis). Coding continuous transformations and coding axis-based descriptions may even constitute separate modules within the visual processing system (cf. Stevens, this volume Chapter 2).

4. ANIMAL WORK

Our understanding of visual object constancy has been enhanced by work on animals and on neurologically impaired human vision, as well as by the work on normal human vision (Section 3). Of particular interest here are the implications of the former two lines of work for understanding the functional relations between object constancy and information processing tasks such as object identification and recognition, and for understanding how the mechanisms underlying constancy are implemented in the brain. Indeed, since at least some accounts hold that object constancy is dependent on "hard-wired" neuronal structures (e.g., Dodwell, 1983, 1984; Hinton, 1981), we may expect some fairly transparent relations between visual object constancy and brain organisation.

Work with animals has been at the forefront of our understanding of visual pattern processing since the early studies of Hubel and Wiesel (1962). Hubel and Wiesel demonstrated that cells in the primary visual cortex of the cat respond selectively to local features of objects such as edges, line orientations, and angles. This important work converged with the then developing theories of pattern recognition (in particular the Pandemonium model; Selfridge, 1959; Selfridge & Neisser, 1960) to suggest that pattern recognition was based on a hierarchical analysis of visual features. The "local feature" detectors described by Hubel and Wiesel respond to input which falls on specific retinal locations. Since then, at least 8 visual areas preserving retinotopic information have been documented in the posterior cortex of the owl monkey (e.g. Allman & Kaas, 1971; Weller & Kaas, 1985); 11 in the macaque monkey (Van Essen, 1985), and 13 in the cat (Tusa, Palmer, & Rosenquist, 1975). The positions of various visual areas in the posterior cortex of the rhesus monkey are given in Fig. 3.11.

To some extent, these different areas appear to respond selectively to different properties of the input. For instance, single cell recordings in the cortex of the squirrel-monkey have shown that cells in both V1 and V2 respond to retinal disparity; there are a larger proportion of disparity

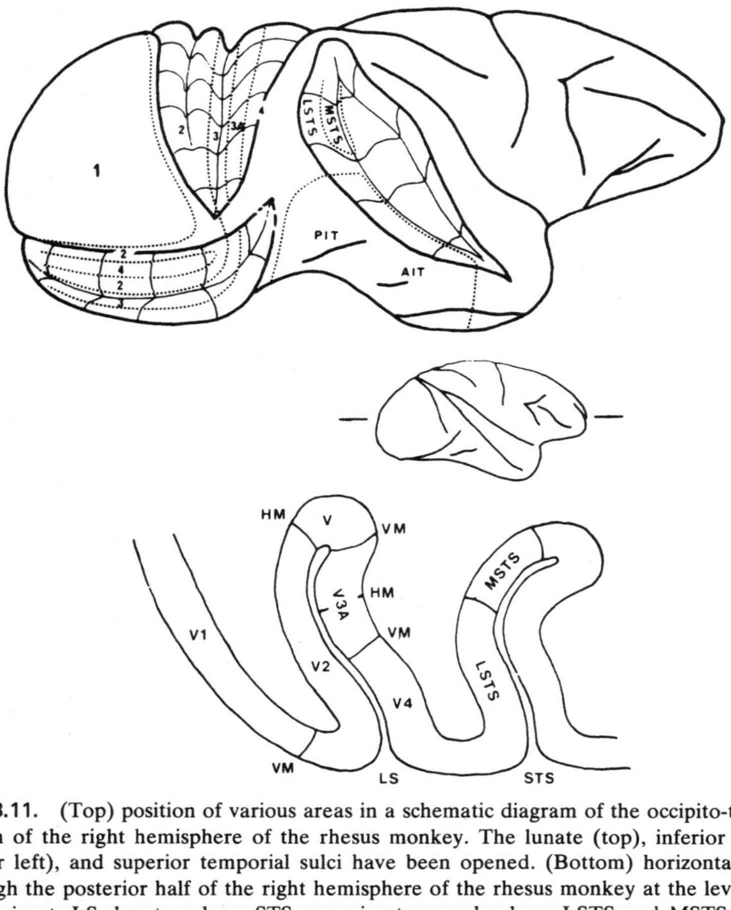

FIG. 3.11. (Top) position of various areas in a schematic diagram of the occipito-temporal region of the right hemisphere of the rhesus monkey. The lunate (top), inferior occipital (lower left), and superior temporal sulci have been opened. (Bottom) horizontal section through the posterior half of the right hemisphere of the rhesus monkey at the level shown in the inset. LS, lunate sulcus; STS, superior temporal sulcus; LSTS and MSTS refer to lateral and medial visual areas in STS; VM, vertical meridian; HM, horizontal meridia (from Cowey, 1979).

responding cells in V2 than in V1, and the cells in V2 seem to respond to larger disparities (Fischer & Poggio, 1979; Poggio & Fischer, 1977). Cells in the STS respond primarily to stimuli moving with particular velocities and in particular directions (Zeki, 1974) and some cells in V4 and the lateral bank of the STS respond selectively to colour (Zeki, 1977, 1980).

One picture which emerges from this work is of separate cortical areas analysing various properties of visual input in parallel, and with each concerned with the position-specific coding of particular visual attributes (e.g., Cowey, 1979, 1981; see also Sergent, this volume Chapter 5). However, it is perhaps more typically the case that cells in each of the different visual areas are tuned to several rather than one attribute. For instance, cells in V4 can be tuned to orientation (Desimone, Schein, Moran, & Ungerleider, 1985) and depth (Felleman & Van Essen, quoted in Van Essen, 1985), in addition to colour. It may be then that each visual area is involved in multiple functions, though the particular functions may differ between areas.

Whatever the case, we might question how such local, retinotopic analyses lead to recognition and identification responses which occur across different viewpoints. At least two different answers to this question can be generated. One possibility is that neurones in the retinotopic visual areas pass information on to further areas which code input across different positions and orientations; this mirrors the case for the coding of successively more abstract object descriptions in object recognition (see Sections 3.3 and 3.4). A second suggestion is that the visual system computes invariance via the application of continuous transforms to the retinotopically coded information (see Section 3.5). These two accounts are not mutually exclusive.

Preliminary evidence for the early computation of continuous transforms in animals comes from the work of Dodwell, Wilkinson, and von Grunau (1983) and Wilkinson and Dodwell (1980). These investigators have shown that patterns illustrating the transformations underlying rotation within-the-plane and dilation (changes due to movement towards or away from the object) are extremely easy for young kittens to discriminate (see Fig. 3.12, p 90 for an example of a pattern illustrating the transformation underlying within-the-plane rotation). For instance, such patterns seem easier for kittens to discriminate than patterns consisting solely of horizontal and vertical lines (Wilkinson & Dodwell, 1980) and than patterns such as checkerboards, triangles, and crosses (Dodwell et al., 1983). It is true that these data by no means demonstrate that the computation of these transformations across retinally coded local elements can generate object constancy in kittens, nor do the data indicate the location of any such computations in the cortex. Nevertheless, they do demonstrate that patterns illustrating certain underlying transformations are very salient, consistent with the notion that the visual system is tuned to registering invariance by detecting such transformations across local feature-detectors (see Section 3.5).

The other account of object constancy, in terms of the hierarchical analysis of successively more abstract form descriptions, also receives support from animal work. For example, in contrast to the visual areas we have so far described, at least one visual area, the inferior temporal lobe, contains no topographical representation of the retina. Cells in the inferior temporal lobe receive convergent input from the other visual areas, they have extremely large receptive fields, which always include the fovea, and many respond to binocular and bilateral input (Gross, Rocha-Miranda, & Bender, 1972). Most interestingly, the responses of such cells to their optimal stimulus are not strongly affected by changes in size, orientation, and colour (Gross & Mishkin, 1977; Gross et al., 1972; Sato, 1981). It may be then, that cells in the inferior temporal lobe support visual object constancy (cf. Gross & Mishkin, 1977).

In addition to demonstrating the relative invariance of the responses made by cells in the inferior temporal lobe to the effect of size, position, and orientation change, single cell recordings have also shown that such cells can manifest remarkable specificity in their responses to particular stimuli. Gross et al. (1972) first demonstrated the selective responses of inferior temporal lobe cells in the macaque monkey to paws. Since then, other studies have shown cells in the upper bank of the anterior STS which respond selectively to various faces (Bruce, Desimone, & Gross, 1981; Perret, Rolls, & Caan, 1982). Some cells have even been shown to respond to particular faces (Perret, Smith, Potter, Mistlin, Head, Milner & Jeeves, 1984) in particular orientations (Perret, Smith, Potter, Mistlin, Head, Milner, & Jeeves,1985). For instance, Perret et al. (1985) reported that some cells responded maximally to full views of a face, others to the face in profile, others to the back of the head, and yet others respond maximally either when the head is rotated down by 45 degrees (revealing the top of the head) or up by 45 degrees (raising the chin). The cells which responded maximally to particular views of the head continued to respond to the preferred view even when there were changes in image size and when the head was rotated 90 degrees within-the-plane, although the latency of their responses was then slower. Finally, yet other cells responded to both full face and profile views.

For our present purposes, the most interesting aspects of the cells documented by Perret et al. (1984, 1985) are that they respond to specific individual stimuli, they show a preference for a limited number of different viewpoints, and they respond to the different viewpoints despite changes in size and within-plane rotations. It is tempting to suggest that such cells are concerned with the stored representations of object descriptions. The implication which follows from this is that at least some stored object descriptions are viewpoint-specific and that such viewpoint-specific representations are also non-retinotopic. However, a degree of caution remains warranted. To state, from single cell recordings, that some cells respond selectively to a given stimulus property should *not* be taken to imply that those cells act as detectors for the property (in the sense that only those cells subserve a psychological detection function). Even given highly selective responses in a given cell, the detection of the stimulus property may still be based on complex interactions between a network of selectively tuned cells (see Van Essen, 1985). Furthermore, demonstrations that cells are selectively tuned to a particular property do not rule out the possibility that the same cells are also tuned to other properties. A final caveat is that cells apparently responding to a complex stimulus property may, in fact, be activated by some rather simpler co-varying attribute. In this respect, we should remember that there is no guarantee that individual cortical cells will be tuned to readily identifiable stimulus properties, particularly if perception is based on interactive cell networks.

Even given the above problems, the single cell recording work still provides intriguing hints concerning the organisation of visual processing in the cortex. Such hints provide the background against which we may interpret lesion studies with animals. For instance, if there are selective visual areas which code depth information and which contain cells which respond to a given input from a number of different viewpoints, we may expect damage to those areas to precipitate deficits in visual object constancy. Certainly, lesions of the different visual areas can produce selective deficits in animal vision. Wilkinson and Cowey (quoted in Cowey, 1981) lesioned the section in V2 concerned with central vision and found large selective decreases in stereo-acuity, although questions about deficits in object constancy remain unanswered. As might be expected, lesions to the inferior temporal lobe have been reported to impair constancy. Humphrey and Weiskrantz (1969) and Ungerleider, Ganz, and Pribram (1977) both noted that inferior temporal lesions impaired size constancy in the monkey, with the animals responding either to the size of the retinal image of the object or to its distance away (i.e., taking no account of the actual image size) but not to some combination of these two forms of information (although see Dean, 1976; for an alternative interpretation). Ungerleider et al. (1977) also reported that lesions of the prestriate cortex produced a rather different impairment in size constancy, in which the animals responded primarily to the retinal image size. More recently, Weiskrantz and Saunders (1984) showed that monkeys with inferior temporal lesions were impaired at both the initial learning of discrimination responses to objects and at generalising their responses to orientation and to size transformed versions of the objects. Monkeys with lesions to the foveal prestriate cortex were less impaired at learning the initial discriminations, although they were also impaired at responding to transformed versions of the objects. The latter results may be interpreted according to a two-stage theory of object constancy involving normalised stored descriptions of objects and processes which enable those descriptions to be accessed from many viewpoints (cf. the connectionist accounts of object-based features and mapping procedures; see 3.4.2). Inferior temporal lobe lesions may distort the stored form descriptions, impairing both the initial learning and subsequent generalisation across transformations. Lesions to the foveal prestriate region may disrupt the processes used in accessing the stored descriptions when objects are placed in new views, so that only generalisation across transformations is impaired, not the initial learning process.

Again however, we should be cautious in using positive evidence from animal work (in this instance, the failure to perform a given task following a particular lesion) to evaluate a theory of human object constancy. For instance, it is typically the case that the inferior-temporal lesioned monkeys are poor at almost all difficult visual learning tasks (see Gross, 1973). Considered in this light, the demonstration that such animals are poor at generalising across viewpoints appears less informative. E. A. Gaffan, Harrison, and D. Gaffan (1986) have also noted that inferior-temporal lesioned monkeys show marked variability when learning to discriminate between different stimuli. Some discriminations are learned very quickly, others extremely slowly. Such a pattern of responses suggests that inferior-temporal lesions do not disrupt the storage of form descriptions *per se* (as some discriminations are rapidly learned). D. Gaffan, Harrison and E. A. Gaffan (1986) propose that inferior-temporal lesions decrease the number of attributes used to discriminate visual objects because the lesions remove cells responding selectively to those attributes. Discriminations dependent on those attributes left intact will occur rapidly; discriminations based on attributes usually indicated by lesioned cells will be difficult to learn. The implication of this proposal is that object discriminations are based on particular combinations of activity in a set of inferior-temporal region neurones, each of which may respond to several attributes.

To summarise, the work with animals again indicates that object constancy can be achieved in rather different ways, probably using rather different neural machinery. There is some (preliminary) data suggesting that continuous transformations can be computed across local feature detectors. Such computations can generate information about pattern invariance across transformations. Other work suggests that recognition across different viewpoints is achieved by relaying information from areas which code information retinotopically to areas indifferent to retinotopic information. In the latter pathway, there are some grounds for distinguishing between the storage of form descriptions and the access processes which must deal with the effects of size, orientation, and position change. The manner in which such changes are accommodated suggests a process which seeks the best fit between the input and a limited number of stored viewpoint-specific, non-retinotopic representations, rather than a process which constructs an explicit viewpoint-independent description prior to indexing (cf. Marr, 1982). The animal work also hints that these stored representations are intimately involved in object constancy, since inferotemporal lesions, apparently affecting the stored representations, can impair constancy, even when the computation of 2-D form and distance information seems intact (e.g., Humphrey & Weiskrantz, 1969).

5. NEUROLOGICAL IMPAIRMENTS OF HUMAN VISION

Cases of brain damage in man are less likely to have the circumscribed lesions found in studies of animals. Nevertheless, cases of selective loss of particular visual processing functions following brain damage have been reported. For instance, damage to the parietal lobe can markedly disrupt the ability to localise visual targets which can still be easily detected (Cole, Schutta, & Warrington, 1962; Holmes, 1918; Ratcliff & Davies-Jones, 1972; Riddoch, 1935). This might be taken to suggest an ability to address stored knowledge of objects without their prior coding in terms of retinal co-ordinates (see Cowey, 1981). However, it may also be that, in such cases, position information is initially registered but that the higher levels of representation which support object detection have unstable position information attached. More fine-grained analyses of such patients need to be conducted to pinpoint the level of representation for which spatial information is lost.

Can patients also be selectively impaired at achieving visual object constancy? De Renzi, Scotti, and Spinnler (1969) first showed that patients who had sustained damage to the right hemisphere could be impaired at matching objects presented in different views. They reported that, relative to left hemisphere damaged patients, patients with right hemisphere lesions and concomitant visual field defects were impaired at matching front-view and profiles of faces. The impairment was not due to the presence of visual field defects alone, since similar effects were not found in left hemisphere damaged patients with similar field defects. Warrington and Taylor (1973) similarly found that right hemisphere damaged patients were poor at identifying photographs of objects taken from unusual views, relative to left hemisphere damaged patients and age-matched control subjects. Furthermore, this deficit was confined to patients with damage to posterior areas of the right hemisphere, a result confirmed by Warrington and Taylor (1978). Indeed, it is not only orientation change which renders object identification difficult for patients with right posterior lesions; Warrington (1982) quotes a study by Warrington and Ackroyd which showed that such patients have difficulty identifying photographs of objects taken in uneven lighting conditions. These results suggest that damage to posterior regions of the right hemisphere in man can bring about marked deficits in identifying objects not presented under prototypical viewing conditions (from a canonical viewpoint and under even lighting conditions; see Palmer et al., 1981). That is, right hemisphere damage may selectively impair visual object constancy (e.g., Warrington,1982).

Warrington and Taylor (1973) also found that *both* right and left hemisphere damaged patients were impaired at identifying enlarged line drawings of objects, relative to when the drawings were approximately life-size when compared with control subjects. From this it would appear that some effects of viewpoint-change are accommodated in the right hemisphere (e.g., orientation and illumination changes) whilst others are accommodated bilaterally (e.g., size). Also, right hemisphere damaged patients are typically impaired on a range of other visual processing tasks, such as matching line orientations and gap size in contours (Warrington & Rabin, 1970), matching the positions of dots in space (Taylor & Warrington, 1973; Warrington & Rabin, 1970), and identifying fragmented figures (Warrington & James, 1967; Warrington & Taylor, 1973; although Warrington & Rabin, 1970, failed to find this). Unfortunately, as these effects have typically been reported in group studies, it is unclear whether the patients who are impaired on tasks requiring the identification of objects under unusual viewing conditions are also impaired at the apparently lower level visual processing tasks.

Single case studies of patients with impairments in identifying and matching objects across different viewpoints have been reported by Humphreys and Riddoch (1984; Riddoch & Humphreys, 1986). Humphreys and Riddoch (1984) presented five brain damaged patients with two types of matching task. In one task, patients had to match a photograph of a common object taken from a prototypical view with a photograph of the same object taken with the object rotated in depth to foreshorten its principal axis (the foreshortened condition). In the other task, patients had to match the prototypical-view photograph with one taken with the object rotated within-the-plane. Objects were rotated within-the-plane to decrease the saliency of their most distinctive feature, whilst the saliency of the object's principal axis remained apparent (the minimal feature condition; see Fig. 3.12). Following each matching response, patients were asked to name the objects. Four right hemisphere damaged patients (D.B., J.L., C.R., and G.S.) were impaired in the foreshortened condition relative to the minimal feature condition.[8] There was a similar trend in the control data, although it was not significant. Another patient (H.J.A.),with a

---

[8] Although patients D.B., J.L., C.R., and G.S. had all sustained right hemisphere damage, we do not wish to stress the locus of that damage here. It is possible that patients with quite different lesions could also manifest similar deficits. The patients in the Humphreys and Riddoch (1984) study were selected because they showed a selective deficit, not because of the site of their lesions. It is the type of functional deficit presented by the patients which is of primary interest. Nevertheless, for ease of exposition, the patients will be grouped under the label "right hemisphere damaged" here.

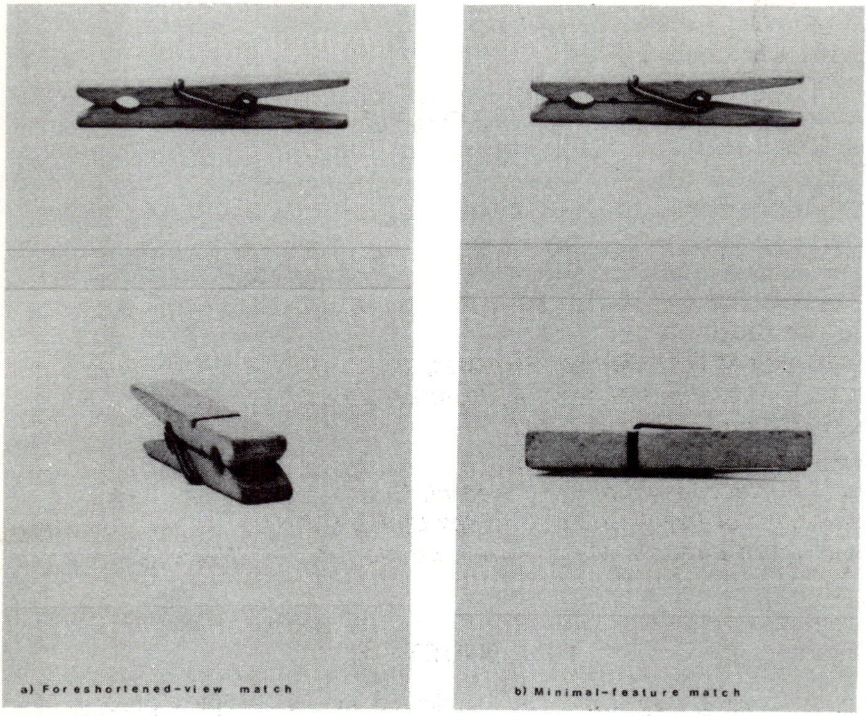

FIG. 3.12. Examples of the foreshortened-view and minimal-feature view transformations used by Humphreys and Riddoch (1984).

bilateral occipital lesion, was impaired in the minimal feature condition relative to the foreshortened condition, when compared with the opposite trend found in the controls. Similar effects were found in the naming data. The right hemisphere damaged patients were all poor at identifying foreshortened relative to prototypical and minimal feature view objects; H.J.A. was poor at naming minimal feature view objects relative to prototypical view objects (see also Riddoch & Humphreys, 1986). Furthermore, each photograph was rated according to the saliency of the chosen distinctive feature in the particular view and the featural goodness of the object when seen from that view. The objects named correctly by the right hemisphere damaged patients tended to be more figurally good than those named incorrectly; feature saliency had no effect on their naming. In contrast, the objects named correctly by H.J.A. tended to have a more salient distinctive feature than those named incorrectly, and figural goodness had no effect on his naming performance.

Humphreys and Riddoch's (1984) results demonstrate that simply causing some form of viewpoint change may not *by itself* be sufficient to impair the matching and identification of patients who have difficulties achieving object constancy; the nature of the change is crucially important. The right hemisphere damaged patients seemed to depend primarily on global form information, and were therefore affected by those gross changes to the global form of the object which occur with foreshortening. Consequently, their naming responses reflected the object's figural goodness. The other patient, H.J.A. seemed to depend on the presence of salient local features for object identification and matching. Consequently, he was relatively poor at minimal feature matches and his naming responses reflected the salience of the object's primary distinctive feature.

The fact that foreshortening disrupted the right hemisphere damaged patients is consistent with the idea that identification and matching across viewpoints was dependent on an axis-based structural description (see Section 3.4), so that performance suffered when the principal axis was made difficult to derive (by foreshortening). Indeed, the naming responses of these patients suggested that they often misidentified foreshortened objects because they failed to perceive that the object was oriented in-depth, and they interpreted the form information as being oriented in-the-plane. That is, the patients failed to derive the principal axis of the objects.

However, other accounts of the above results are possible. For instance, it may be that the right hemisphere damaged patients were affected by any large deviation of an object from its prototypical viewpoint, and that foreshortening tended to produce rather larger deviations from the prototype than the minimal feature transform.[9] In a follow-up study, Riddoch and Humphreys (1986) had the same patients carry out either minimal feature matches or matches in which one view of a target was *both* minimal-feature and size transformed (to three times its size in the prototypical view). Again, naming was required after each matching response. Three of the right hemisphere damaged patients (D.B., J.L., and G.S.) were now impaired in the size transformed condition, relative to when only a minimal feature transform took place. This was not because the patients were impaired at making size transformations *per se*, as the two patients who were tested (D.B. and J.L.) were able to match two prototypical-view objects transformed in size. In this case, the patients were affected by the relatively large deviation from the prototype caused by the combined minimal-feature and size transform, but not by the single transforms alone. Two other aspects of Riddoch and Humphreys's data are also of interest.

[9] Consistent with this argument, the foreshortened-view objects were rated as less familiar than their minimal-feature view counterparts.

One is that the right hemisphere patients were not affected by whether the objects approximated to their real-world size in the photographs: The patients were as likely to name prototypical-view objects correctly when the objects were not their real-world size as when they were, and they were likely to misidentify size and orientation transformed objects irrespective of whether the objects were their real-world size. The other interesting aspect of the data was that the patients often misidentified magnified objects as objects which were larger than the prototypes they were paired with, and reduced objects as objects smaller than the prototypes. This suggests that they used the prototypes as a reference scale for the transformed objects. Thus retinal size was not the crucial factor affecting performance. What was more important was the change in the size and orientation of the transformed object, relative to its prototypical partner. These size and orientation changes are viewpoint-specific, but non-retinotopic—suggesting that identification and matching in these patients involves a direct comparison of a non-retinotopic, viewpoint-specific description with a stored, prototypical-view description. This direct indexing process enables prototypical-view objects to be identified, as well as objects subject to small transformations (perhaps because the stored representations have "broadly tuned" size and orientation parameters; cf. Koriat & Norman, 1985; see Section 3.2).

However, when relatively large transformations occur, some specific mapping procedure may need to be invoked to enable indexing to occur (e.g., using depth information or an axis-based description). At least some patients may be impaired at invoking any mapping procedures following brain damage (e.g., patients D.B., J.L., and G.S. described by Riddoch & Humphreys, 1986). The other right hemisphere damaged patient, C.R., was disrupted by foreshortening but not by the joint size and minimal-feature transformation (Humphreys & Riddoch, 1984; Riddoch & Humphreys, 1986). This suggests that C.R. was impaired at invoking a particular mapping procedure; for example, that using local depth information to derive the principal axis of an object.

The picture which emerges is that patients may be impaired at tasks requiring visual object constancy for quite different reasons. Some patients seem impaired at using any mapping process which enables objects presented under unusual viewing conditions to activate their stored structural representations (e.g., D.B., J.L., and G.S.), whereas other patients seem impaired at using particular mappings (C.R.). Also, other patients (H.J.A.) seem unable to assemble any useful global description of objects and so seem reliant on local feature descriptions for identification and matching across viewpoints; the latter process may be akin to using landmark features (see Section 3.1; see also Humphreys & Riddoch, this volume, Chapter 10).

The data do have some implications for understanding the processes which may normally mediate object constancy. First, since H.J.A. was generally poor at visually identifying objects (even in prototypical views), it seems that landmark features may normally be of little use for object identification. Secondly, our stored structural representations of objects seem to be coded relative to a prototypical viewpoint from which both the object's principal axis and its primary features are salient. The stored representation is not coded for absolute size, but seems to specify the relations between local part and more global information. Thirdly, recognition across different viewpoints seems to involve mapping a non-retinotopic, viewpoint-specific description onto a stored representation, rather than the construction of an explicit, object-centred representation from the stimulus (such as the 3-D model description described by Marr & Nishihara, 1978; see Section 3.4.2). Fourthly, the mapping process may involve coding the object's parts relative to its principal axis, so that foreshortening may produce particular recognition difficulties.

In the light of the argument that some patients can have problems coding the relations between the parts of an object and its principal axis ("the mapping process"), data recently reported by Robertson and Delis (1986) are of interest. They investigated the effects of configurations of the type shown in Fig. 3.2 on judgements of the direction of pointing of central, ambiguous equilateral triangles (see Section 3.4). Patients with right hemisphere damage were found to be *less* affected by the configurations than control subjects, indicating that they were relatively insensitive to the relations between the central triangle and the principal axis of the configuration. Patients with left hemisphere damage were found to be *more* affected by the configurations than the controls. Such patients seemed to be insensitive to the local orientation information in the central shape. Normal object constancy may depend on the integration of the more global (configural) and the more local shape information.

What are the relations between object constancy and our ability to perform other visual processing tasks? H.J.A. (Humphreys & Riddoch, 1984) was able to match objects across at least some different views, whilst being quite unable to identify the object. This might be taken to suggest that some form of object-centred descriptions can be invoked independently of stored knowledge about the object. In fact, evidence from other patients with marked visual object recognition deficits (visual agnosia) who were able to match objects across different views (e.g., Taylor & Warrington, 1971) was one of the factors motivating Marr's (1982; Marr & Nishihara, 1978) proposal that the derivation of a 3-D model description could be solely data-driven (see also Section 3.6). A rather different view is that recognition across different viewpoints is always mediated by some form of stored object-based units (cf. Hinton, 1981). However, the object-based units may be coded at different levels of description. The more local descriptions may be activated by many objects, with only higher levels of descriptions diagnostic of individual objects. In the latter scheme, object constancy may be achieved without knowledge of the object's structural identity when a common pattern of local, object-based features are activated by an object seen in different views. Patients unable to generate an adequate global description of the input will be constrained to use such local descriptions. Indeed, it is a prediction of the latter account that patients who are able to match across viewpoints objects which they show no ability to structurally identify will be using local feature descriptions (e.g., H.J.A., described by Humphreys & Riddoch, 1984; Riddoch & Humphreys, in press).[10]

Humphreys and Riddoch (1984) also examined the ability of some of their patients (J.L., G.S., and H.J.A.) to carry out some lower-level visual processing tasks, such as matching line lengths, line orientations, the positions of gaps in circles, and circle sizes. Two right hemisphere damaged patients, J.L. and G.S., showed no impairments on these tasks relative to slightly younger control subjects. H.J.A. performed normally on the length, orientation, and position discriminations, though he was impaired on the size discriminations. These results indicate that at least some patients can be impaired at achieving visual object constancy despite relatively intact lower-level visual processing. Such cases would arise when brain damage selectively affects the processes mapping viewpoint-specific descriptions onto more abstracted object descriptions, whilst leaving the viewpoint-specific descriptions intact.

Our discussion of work with neurologically impaired patients has tried to show how such work can throw light on the normal mechanisms of object constancy. There is, however, a general assumption underlying the inferences we have made. This is that, in brain damaged patients, we witness the operation of a normal processing system bereft of selective processing component. It follows that the resultant (damaged) system is simply a reduced normal system. The validity of this assumption is in many instances difficult to assess, especially when we consider the variety of strategies used

---

[10] What is meant here by being able to structurally identify an object is something more than being able to name it or being able to make semantic judgements about it; by being able to structurally identify an object we mean that a subject shows evidence of correctly accessing stored structural information specific to that object. Riddoch and Humphreys (in press; see also Humphreys, Riddoch, & Quinlan, in press; Riddoch & Humphreys, Chapter 4, this volume) have reported the case of a patient who, following brain damage, showed intact categorisation of objects on the basis of whether they had familiar forms (in an object-decision task), even though he was impaired at making semantic judgements and at naming visually presented objects. Thus access to stored structural knowledge about objects may co-occur with impaired access to semantic and name information.

by patients when performing what are often quite loosely constrained tasks. It is usually the case that this assumption is simply the best working hypothesis on which to proceed.

Sergent (this volume, Chapter 5) also makes the point that it is possible to reach a rather different conclusion about why right hemisphere damage often produces apparent difficulties in object constancy, than the standard account that the right hemisphere contains the mechanisms enabling constancy to occur (e.g., Warrington, 1982). Sergent proposes that right hemisphere damage produces difficulty in constancy because such damage produces "knock-on" effects on the processing capabilities of the left hemisphere: The left hemisphere may contain mechanisms for constancy, but it is unable to operate normally because right hemisphere damage changes the quality of the information available. Because of such difficulties in interpretation, it may be best always to view evidence from patients in the light of work from other, converging areas. We may have increasing confidence in a particular account of a deficit if it supports work from normal human or from animal vision.

6. SOME CONCLUSIONS

Our aim in this chapter has been to draw together some of the wide body of work from different research areas on visual object constancy. It is, then, quite reassuring to note the degree of convergence from areas as different as computer vision, experimental cognitive psychology, neurophysiology, and clinical neuropsychology. For instance, both single cell neurophysiological recordings from animals (Section 4) and neuropsychological work on brain damaged humans (Section 5) indicate the importance of viewpoint-specific coding in the representation of stored knowledge about object structure. It appears that one solution effected by the visual system to achieve object constancy is to code representations specific to a limited number of viewpoints. Another solution is to normalise the input prior to matching it with stored knowledge of the object. One normalisation process seems to involve the integration of form information with optical correlates of orientation and depth (Section 3.3). In addition, a more abstracted description can be effected by describing the parts of an object relative to its principal axis (Section 3.4). Selective brain lesions can also impair normalisation whilst leaving both viewpoint-specific and stored object descriptions intact (Sections 4 and 5). One suggestion here is that normalisation involves a particular set of neuronal units which enable mapping between viewpoint-specific descriptions and object-based descriptions at increasingly higher levels of form representation to occur, and that these mapping units can be selectively impaired by brain damage (see Section 3.4.2).

Object constancy can be based on different levels of form description, from those specifying only local parts to those specifying the whole object. Thus, in limited circumstances, normal human observers can use landmark features (Section 3.1) and brain damage can enforce dependence on such features in selective cases (Section 5). The coding of visual input at a number of levels of description will also allow some independence in the coding of the local and global characteristics of an object, so that those changes in one characteristic which do not alter the other will not overly disrupt recognition.

Perhaps not surprisingly, the solutions settled on by the visual system to accommodate the effects of viewpoint change resemble those which we earlier suggested would need to be imposed on any theory of visual object recognition (Section 2). It should be noted, however, that no one solution will suffice. The visual system appears to adopt whichever solution best fits the problem at hand. Viewpoints commonly encountered may tend to become encoded in stored descriptions of the particular object, producing relatively broad "tuning" of such representations, and reducing the need for normalisation in such cases. Also, when only a small set of possible stimulus alternatives are used, when the locations of distinctive features can be predicted, or when the shape does not contain a well-defined axis, constancy may depend on more local feature descriptions (Sections 3.1, 3.4.2, and 3.4.3).

Normalisation, when it occurs, can often proceed independently of our stored semantic knowledge about the object, although there is some suggestion that structural knowledge can be applied when the stimulus is ambiguous or when stimulus-based encoding is slow (Section 3.6). Clearly, it makes sense for the visual system to have developed to be relatively immune from any top-down effects, since it would not be computationally efficient if all the procedures invoked to match across viewpoints were specific to particular objects (see also Shepard, 1984). However, this is not to state that normalisation does *not* involve coding viewpoint-specific descriptions onto stored object-based descriptions (as posited by connectionist accounts of object constancy; Section 3.4.2). Indeed, we have interpreted evidence from the effects of lesions to the inferior temporal cortex in animals (Humphrey & Weiskrantz, 1969; Weiskrantz & Saunders, 1984) as supporting the view that stored object-based descriptions may be important for constancy (Section 4). The point here is that the mapping procedures involved will be invoked (at least initially) solely from geometrical properties of the input, and the procedures will be the same for many different objects. Also, the structural identity of an object will only be specified at high levels of form description or by particular patterns of activation across a wide range of local units; constancy will usually be based on correspondences across smaller structural units. Thus, to maintain that stored object-based units are involved in object constancy is not to hold that object *identity* is usually important.

We have also suggested that the types of information used to achieve constancy differ as a function of the task requirements. Whereas an axis-based normalisation process may be useful for object recognition and identification, it may not be necessary when the observer simply needs to keep track of an object as the viewpoint changes. In this case, those (invariant) structural properties yielded by comparisons between local form representations (generating continuous transformations) may be sufficient to support behaviour, though the resultant invariant information may itself need to be interpreted relative to some perceptual reference frame for identification purposes (Section 3.5).

One question for future research concerns the relations between local form comparisons and the application of perceptual reference frames. For instance, it may be that, given pattern information, the visual system carries out comparisons between local form elements to compute correlatory information about rates of orientation change across space. Such comparisons may be effected at increasingly higher levels of form, leading to the derivation of axis-based descriptions (e.g., where such comparisons specify a description which is symmetrical about a particular point or line; see Palmer, 1982; Section 3.4.1). Alternatively, global frame-based descriptions may be applied directly to viewpoint-specific representations, and they emerge *independently* of descriptions based on continuous local-transforms. It may even be that the relations between global frame-based procedures and continuous local transforms could be indicated by studying the effects of neurological damage on the application of continuous local transforms. If frame-based procedures are invoked independently of continuous local transforms, a patient could be poor at deriving the transform whilst showing a good ability to impose global frame-based descriptions. Similarly, a patient may be impaired at generating axis-based descriptions of objects whilst showing intact discrimination of patterns representing different underlying continuous transforms (see Section 3.5). Both of the above predictions follow if the mechanisms computing structural descriptions and those computing continuous transforms constitute separate modules within the visual object processing system.[11]

It also follows that, if the two procedures are not independent, then analogous deficits should be found in deriving both types of information. We may also note that such questions may be more precisely addressed by

[11] Of course, a deficit in the two procedures would need to be separated from a deficit in deriving the different levels of form description to which the same procedure is applied. This could be done by screening out those patients with loss of a selective range of spatial frequency information (i.e., with selective loss of some levels of form description).

the development of more detailed models specifying how continuous local transforms and frame-based descriptions are effected. It is clear that reciprocity between clinical studies and models derived from other areas (such as computer vision and studies of intact human vision) is important for future progress.

ACKNOWLEDGEMENTS

This work was supported by grants from the ESRC to both authors and from the MRC and the SERC to the first author. We should like to thank Rob Ellis and Jane Riddoch for comments on earlier drafts, and David Gaffan for his discussion of some of the animal work.

REFERENCES

Allman, J. M. & Kaas, J. H. (1971). A representation of the visualfield in the caudal third of the middle temporal gyrus of the Owl monkey (*Aotus trivirgatus*). *Brain Research*, *31*, 85–105.

Allport, D. A., Tipper, S. P., & Chmiel, N. R. J. (1985). Perceptual integration and postcategorical filtering. In M. I.Posner and O. S. M. Marin (Eds.), *Attention and performance*, Vol. XI. Hillsdale, N.J.: Lawrence Erlbaum Associates Inc.

Attneave, F. (1982). Pragnanz and soap bubble systems: A theoretical exploration. In J. Beck (Ed.), *Organization and representation in perception*. Hillsdale, N.J.: Lawrence Erlbaum Associates Inc.

Ballard, D. H., Hinton, G. E., & Sejnowski, T. J. (1983). Parallel visual computation. *Nature*, *306*, 21–26.

Bartram, D. J. (1976). Levels of coding in picture-picture comparison tasks. *Memory & Cognition*, *4*, 593–602.

Besner, D. (1983). Visual pattern recognition: Size pre-processing re-examined. *Quarterly Journal of Experimental Psychology*, *35A*, 209–216.

Besner, D. & Coltheart, M. (1976). Mental size scaling examined. *Memory & Cognition*, *4*, 525–531.

Biederman, I. (1981). On the semantics of a scene at a glance. In M. Kubovy and J. R. Pomerantz (Eds.), *Perceptual organization*, Hillsdale, N.J.: Lawrence Erlbaum Associates Inc.

Biederman, I., Mezzanotte, R. J., & Rabinowitz, J. C. (1982). Scene perception: Detecting and judging objects undergoing relational violations. *Cognitive Psychology*, *14*, 143–177.

Bower, T. G. R. (1966). Slant perception and shape constancy in infants. *Science*, *151*, 832–834.

Braine, L. G. (1978). A new slant on orientation perception. *American Psychologist*, *33*, 10–22.

Breitmeyer, B. G. (1975). Simple reaction time as a measure of the temporal response properties of transient and sustained channels. *Vision Research*, *15*, 1411–1412.

Bruce, C. J., Desimone, R., & Gross, C. G. (1981). Visual properties of neurones in a polysensory area in the superior temporal sulcus of the macaque. *Journal of Neurophysiology*, *46*, 369–384.

Bundesen, C. & Larsen, A. (1975). Visual transformation of size. *Journal of Experimental Psychology: Human Perception and Performance*, *1*, 214–220.

Bundesen, C., Larsen, A., & Farrell, J. E. (1981). Mental transformations of size and orientation. In J. Long and A. D. Baddeley (Eds.), *Attention and performance*, Vol. IX, Hillsdale, N.J.: Lawrence Erlbaum Associates Inc.

Caron, A., Caron, R., & Carlson, V. (1978). Do infants see objects or retinal images? Shape constancy revisited. *Infant Behaviour & Development*, *1*, 229–243.

Caron, A., Caron R., & Carlson, V. (1979). Infant perception of the invariant shape of objects varying in slant. *Child Development*, *50*, 716–721.

Cavanagh, P. (1978). Size and position invariance in the visual system. *Perception*, *7*, 167–177.

Cavanagh, P. (1981). Size invariance: A reply to Schwartz. *Perception*, *10*, 469–474.

Cavanagh, P. (1984). Image transforms in the visual system. In P. C. Dodwell & T. Caelli (Eds.), *Figural synthesis*. Hillsdale, N.J.: Lawrence Erlbaum Associates Inc.

Cole, M., Schutta, H. S., & Warrington, E. K. (1962). Visual disorientation in homonymous half-fields. *Neurology*, *12*, 257–263.

Cooper, L. A. (1975). Mental rotation of random two-dimensional shapes. *Cognitive Psychology*, *7*, 20–43.

Cooper, L. A. & Shepard, R. N. (1973). Chronometric studies of the rotation of mental images. In W. G. Chase (Ed.), *Visual information processing*. New York: Academic Press.

Corballis, M. C. (1986). Is mental rotation controlled or automatic? *Memory & Cognition*, *14*, 124–128.

Corballis, M. C. & Beale, I. L. (1976). *The psychology of left and right*. Hillsdale, N.J.: Lawrence Erlbaum Associates Inc.

Corballis, M. C. & Nagourney, B. A. (1978). Latency to categorize disoriented alphanumeric characters as letters and digits. *Canadian Journal of Psychology*, *32*, 186–188.

Corballis, M. C., Zbrodoff, N. J., Shetzer, L. I., & Butler, P. B. (1978). Decisions about identity and orientation of rotated letters and digits. *Memory and Cognition*, *6*, 98–107.

Cornsweet, T. N. (1970). *Visual perception*. New York: Academic Press.

Cowey, A. (1979). Cortical maps and visual perception. The Grindley memorial lecture. *Quarterly Journal of Experimental Psychology*, *31*, 1–17.

Cowey, A. (1981). Sensory and non-sensory visual disorders in man and monkey. *Philosophical Transactions of the Royal Society, London, B298*, 3–13.

Dean, P. (1976). Effects of inferotemporal lesions on the behaviour of monkeys. *Psychological Bulletin*, *83*, 41–71.

De Renzi, E., Scotti, G., & Spinnler, H. (1969). Perceptual and associative disorders of visual recognition. *Neurology*, *19*, 634–642.

Desimone, R., Schein, S. J., Moran, J., & Ungerleider, L. G. (1985). Contour, color and shape analysis beyond the striate cortex. *Vision Research*, *25*, 441–452.

Dodwell, P. C. (1982). Geometrical approaches to visual processing. In D. Ingle, M. Goodale, and R. Mansfield (Eds.), *Analysis of visual behaviour*. Cambridge, Mass.: MIT Press.

Dodwell, P. (1983). The Lie transformation group model of visual perception. *Perception & Psychophysics*, *34*, 1–16.

Dodwell, P. C. (1984). Local and global factors in figural synthesis. In P. C. Dodwell and T. Caelli (Eds.), *Figural synthesis*. Hillsdale, N.J.: Lawrence Erlbaum Associates Inc.

Dodwell, P. C., Wilkinson, D., & von Grunau, M. (1983). Pattern recognition in kittens: Performance on Lie patterns. *Perception*, *12*, 393–410.

Duncan, J. (1980). The demonstration of capacity limitation. *Cognitive Psychology*, *12*, 75–96.

Duncan, J. (1984). Selective attention and the organization of visual information. *Journal of Experimental Psychology: General*, *113*, 501–517.

Duncan, J. (1985). Visual attention. In M. I. Posner and O. S. M. Marin (Eds.), *Attention and performance*, Vol. XI. Hillsdale, N.J.: Lawrence Erlbaum Associates Inc.

Dunker, K. (1937). Induced motion. In W. D. Ellis (Ed.), *A source-book of Gestalt psychology*. London: Routledge and Kegan Paul.

Eley, M. G. (1982). Identifying rotated letter-like symbols. *Memory and Cognition. 10*, 25–32.

Eley, M. G. (1983). Symbol complexity and symbol identification with rotated symbols. *Acta Psychologica, 53*, 27–35.

Ellis, R. (1985). *Levels of representation in vision*. Unpublished D.Phil. thesis, Oxford University.

Ellis, R. & Allport, D. A. (1985). Multiple representations for visual objects: A behavioural study. Paper presented at the Easter Meeting of the *Society for the Study of Artificial Intelligence and Simulation of Behaviour*, (Warwick, 10–12 April 1985).

Epstein, W. (1973). The process of "taking into account" in visual perception. *Perception, 2*, 267–285.

Epstein, W. & Hatfield, G. (1978). Functional equivalence of masking and cue reduction in perception of shape at a slant. *Perception & Psychophysics, 23*, 137–144.

Epstein, W., Hatfield, G., & Muise, G. (1977). Perceived shape at a slant as a function of processing time and processing load. *Journal of Experimental Psychology: Human Perception and Performance, 3*, 473–483.

Epstein, W. & Lovitts, B. E. (1985). Automatic and attentional components in perception of shape-at-a-slant. *Journal of Experimental Psychology: Human Perception and Performance, 11*, 355–366.

Epstein, W. & Park, J. N. (1963). Shape constancy. Functional relationships and theoretical formulations. *Psychological Bulletin, 60*, 265–288.

Feldman, J. A. (1985). Four frames suffice: A provisional model of vision and space. *Behavioural and Brain Sciences, 8*, 265–289.

Feldman, J. A. & Ballard, D. H. (1982). Connectionist models and their properties. *Cognitive Science, 6*, 205–254.

Fischer, B. & Poggio, G. F. (1979). Depth sensitivity of binocular cortical neurons of behaving monkeys. *Proceedings of the Royal Society, London, B204*, 409–414.

Fitzpatrick, V., Pasnak, R., & Tyer, Z. E. (1982). The effect of familiar size at familiar distances. *Perception, 11*, 85–91.

Foster, D. H. (1978a). Visual comparison of random-dot patterns: Evidence concerning a fixed visual association between feature and feature-relations. *Quarterly Journal of Experimental Psychology, 30*, 637–654.

Foster, D. H. (1978b). Visual apparent motion and the calculus of variations. In E. L. J. Leeuwenberg and H. F. J. M. Buffart (Eds.), *Formal theories of visual perception*. Chichester: John Wiley.

Gaffan, D., Harrison, S., & Gaffan, E. A. (1986). Visual identification following inferotemporal ablation in the monkey. *Quarterly Journal of Experimental Psychology, 38B*, 5–30.

Gaffan, E. A., Harrison, S., & Gaffan, D. (1986). Single and concurrent discrimination learning by monkeys after lesions of inferotemporal cortex. *Quarterly Journal of Experimental Psychology, 38B*, 31–52.

Garner, W. (1974). *The processing of information and structure.* Potomac, MD.: Lawrence Erlbaum Associates.

Gibson, J. J. (1950). *The perception of the visual world*. Boston: Houghton Mifflin.

Gibson, J. J. (1966). *The senses considered as perceptual systems.* Boston: Houghton Mifflin.

Gibson, J. J. (1979). *The ecological approach to visual perception* Boston: Houghton Mifflin.

Gibson, J. J. & Gibson, E. J. (1957). Continuous perspective transformations and the perception of rigid motion. *Journal of Experimental Psychology, 54*, 129–138.

Ginsberg, A. P. (1971). Psychological correlates of a model of the human visual system. *Proceedings of the IEEE National Aerospace and Electronics Conference*. 283–290.

Ginsberg, A. P. (1973). Pattern recognition techniques suggested from psychological correlates of a model of the human visual system. *Proceedings of the IEEE National Aerospace and Electronics Conference*, 309–316.

Gogel, W. C., Hartman, B. O., & Harker, G. S. (1957). The retinal size of a familiar object as a determiner of apparent distance. *Psychological Monographs*, *71*, (13, whole no. 442.)

Gough, P. B., Alford, J. A., & Holley-Wilcox, P. (1981). Words and contexts. In O.J.L. Tzeng and H. Singer (Eds.), *Perception of print: Reading research in experimental psychology*. Hillsdale, N.J.: Lawrence Erlbaum Associates Inc.

Green, B. F. (1961). Figure coherence in the kinetic depth effect. *Journal of Experimental Psychology*, *62*, 272–282.

Greene, S. L., Plastow, E., & Braine, L. G. (1985). Judging the location of features of naturalistic and geometric shapes. *Perception & Psychophysics*, *37*, 148–154.

Gregory, R. L. (1970). *The intelligent eye*. London: Weidenfield & Nicholson.

Gross, C. G. (1973). Inferotemporal cortex and vision. In E. Stellar and J. M. Sprague (Eds.), *Progress in physiological psychology*, Vol. 5. New York: Academic Press.

Gross, C. G. & Mishkin, M. (1977). The neural basis of stimulus equivalence across retinal translation. In S. Harnad, R. W. Doty, L. Goldstein, J. Jaynes, and G. Krauthamer (Eds.). *Lateralization in the nervous system*. New York: Academic Press.

Gross, C. G., Rocha-Miranda, C. E., & Bender, D. B. (1972). Visual properties of cells in inferotemporal cortex of the macaque. *Journal of Neurophysiology*, *35*, 96–111.

Helmholtz, H. von. (1925). *Treatise on psychological optics*. Translated from the third German edition (1909–1911) by J. P. Southall (Ed.). Rochester, New York: Optical Society of America.

Hinton, G. E. (1981). A parallel computation that assigns canonical object-based frames of reference. *Proceedings of the International Joint Conference on Artificial Intelligence*, Vancouver, Canada.

Hinton, G. E. & Anderson, J. A. (Eds.) (1981). *Parallel models of associative memory*. Hillsdale, N. J.: Lawrence Erlbaum Associates Inc.

Hinton, G. E. & Parsons, L. M. (1981). Frames of reference and mental imagery. In J. Long and A. D. Baddeley (Eds.), *Attention and performance*, Vol. IX. Hillsdale, N.J.: Lawrence Erlbaum Associates Inc.

Hochberg, J. & Gellman, L. (1977). The effect of landmark features on mental rotation times. *Memory & Cognition*. *5*, 23–26.

Holmes, G. (1918). Disturbances of visual orientation. *British Journal of Ophthalmology*, *2*, 449–468; 506–516.

Hubel, D. H. & Wiesel, T. N. (1962). Receptive fields, binocular interaction and functional architecture in the cat's visual cortex. *Journal of Physiology*, *160*, 106–154.

Humphrey, N. K. & Weiskrantz, L. (1969). Size constancy in monkeys with inferotemporal lesions. *Quarterly Journal of Experimental Psychology*, *21*, 225–238.

Humphreys, G. W. (1983). Reference frames and shape perception. *Cognitive Psychology*, *15*, 151–196.

Humphreys, G. W. (1984). Shape constancy: The effects of changing shape orientation and the effects of changing the position of focal features. *Perception & Psychophysics*, *36*, 50–64.

Humphreys, G. W. (1985). Attention, automaticity and autonomy in visual word processing. In D. Besner, T. G. Waller, and G. E. MacKinnon (Eds.), *Reading research: Advances in theory and practice*, Vol. 5. New York: Academic Press.

Humphreys, G. W. & Riddoch. M. J. (1984). Routes to object constancy: Implications from neurological impairments of object constancy. *Quarterly Journal of Experimental Psychology*, *36A*, 385–415.

Humphreys, G. W., Riddoch, M. J., & Quinlan, P. T. (1985). Interactive processes in perceptual organization: Evidence from visual agnosia. In M. I. Posner and O. S. M. Marin (Eds.), *Attention and performance*, Vol. XI. Hillsdale, N.J.: Lawrence Erlbaum Associates Inc.

Humphreys, G. W., Riddoch, M. J. & Quinlan, P. T. (in press). Cascade processes in picture identification. *Cognitive Neuropsychology.*

Johansson, G. (1973). Visual perception of biological motion and a model for its analysis. *Perception & Psychophysics*, *14*, 201–211.

Johansson, G. (1975). Visual motion perception. *Scientific American*, *232*, 76–88.

Jolicoeur, P. (1985). The time taken to name disoriented natural objects. *Memory & Cognition*, *13*, 289–303.

Jolicoeur, P. & Landau, M. J. (1984). Effects of orientation on the identification of simple visual patterns. *Canadian Journal of Psychology*, *38*, 80–93.

Julesz, B. (1971). *Foundations of cyclopean perception*. Chicago: University of Chicago Press.

Kellman, P. (1984). Perception of three-dimensional form by human infants. *Perception & Psychophysics*, *36*, 353–358.

Koffka, K. (1935). *Principles of Gestalt psychology*. New York: Harcourt, Brace & World.

Koriat, A. & Norman, J. (1985). Mental rotation and visual familiarity. *Perception & Psychophysics*, *37*, 429–439.

Kosslyn, S. M. (1980). *Image and mind*. Cambridge, Mass.: Harvard University Press.

Kosslyn, S. M. (1983). *Ghosts in the mind's machine*. New York: Norton.

Larsen, A. & Bundesen, C. (1978). Size scaling in visual pattern recognition. *Journal of Experimental Psychology: Human Perception and Performance*, *4*, 1–20.

Leibowitz, H. & Bourne, L. (1956). Time and intensity as determiners of perceived shape. *Journal of Experimental Psychology*, *51*, 277–281.

Lindsay, P. H. & Norman, D. A. (1977). *Human information processing: An introduction to psychology*, 2nd edn. New York: Academic Press.

Mach, E. (1906). *The analysis of the sensations*. Chicago: Open Court.

Marr, D. (1980). Visual information processing: The structure and creation of visual representations. *Philosophical Transactions of the Royal Society, London, B290*, 199–218.

Marr, D. (1982). *Vision*. San Fransisco: W. H. Freeman.

Marr, D. & Nishihara, H. K. (1978). Representation and recognition of the spatial organization of three-dimensional objects. *Proceedings of the Royal Society, London*, *B200*, 269–294.

Marr, D. & Poggio, T. (1977). Cooperative computation of stereo depth. *Science*, *194*, 283–287.

Meyer, D. E., Schvaneveldt, R. W., & Ruddy, M. G. (1975). Loci of contextual effects on visual word recognition. In P. M. A. Rabbit and S. Dornic (Eds.). *Attention and performance*, Vol. V. London: Academic Press.

Minsky, M. (1975). A framework for representing knowledge. In P. H. Winston (Ed.), *The psychology of computer vision*. New York: McGraw-Hill.

Minsky, M. & Papert, S. (1972). *Perceptrons*, 2nd edn. Cambridge, Mass.: MIT Press.

Neisser, U. (1967). *Cognitive psychology*. New York: Appleton–Century–Crofts.

Norman, J. (1980). Direct and indirect perception of size. *Perception & Psychophysics*, *28*, 306–314.

Palmer, S. E. (1980). What makes triangles point: Local and global effects in configurations of ambiguous triangles. *Cognitive Psychology*, *12*, 285–305.

Palmer, S. E. (1982). Symmetry, transformation and the structure of the perceptual system. In J. Beck (Ed.), *Organization and representation in perception*. Hillsdale, N.J.: Lawrence Erlbaum Associates Inc.

Palmer, S. E. (1985). The role of symmetry in shape perception. *Acta Psychologia*, *59*, 67–90.

Palmer, S. E. & Bucher, N. M. (1981). Configural effects in perceived pointing of ambiguous triangles. *Journal of Experimental Psychology: Human Perception and Performance*, *7*, 88–114.

Palmer, S. E. & Bucher, N. M. (1982). Textural effects in perceived pointing of ambiguous triangles. *Journal of Experimental Psychology: Human Perception and Performance*, *8*, 693–708.

Palmer, S. E., Rosch, E., & Chase, P. (1981). Canonical perspective and the perception of objects. In J. Long and A. D. Baddeley (Eds.), *Attention and performance*, Vol. IX. Hillsdale, N.J.: Lawrence Erlbaum Associates Inc.

Perret, D. I., Rolls, E. T., & Caan, W. (1982). Visual neurones responsive to faces in the monkey temporal cortex. *Experimental Brain Research*, *47*, 329–342.

Perret, D. I., Smith, P. A. J., Potter, D. D., Mistlin, A. J., Head, A. S., Milner, A. D., & Jeeves, M. A. (1984). Neurones responsive to faces in the temporal cortex: Studies of functional organization, sensitivity to identity and relation to perception. *Human Neurobiology*, *3*, 197–208.

Perret, D. I., Smith, P. A. J., Potter, D. D., Mistlin, A. J. Head, A. S., Milner, A. D., & Jeeves, M. A. (1985). Visual cells in the temporal cortex sensitive to face view and gaze direction. *Proceedings of the Royal Society, London, B223*, 293–317.

Pinker, S. (1984). Visual cognition: An introduction. *Cognition*, *18*, 1–63.

Poggio, G. F. & Fischer, B. (1977). Binocular interaction and depth sensitivity in striate and prestriate cortex of behaving rhesus monkeys. *Journal of Neurophysiology*, *40*, 1392–1405.

Prinzmetal, W. & Banks, W. P. (1977). Good continuation affects visual detection. *Perception & Psychophysics*, *21*, 389–395.

Quinlan, P. T. & Humphreys, G. W. (1987). Visual search for targets defined by combinations of color, shape and size: An examination of the task constraints on feature and conjunction searches. *Perception & Psychophysics*, *41*, 455–472.

Ratcliff, G. & Davies-Jones, G. A. B. (1972). Defective visual localization in focal brain wounds. *Brain*, *95*, 49–60.

Riddoch, G. (1935). Visual disorientation in homonymous half fields. *Brain*, *58*, 376–382.

Riddoch, M. J. & Humphreys, G. W. (1986). Neurological impairments of object constancy: The effects of orientation and size disparities. *Cognitive Neuropsychology*, *3*, 207–224.

Riddoch, M. J. & Humphreys, G. W. (1987). Visual object processing in a case of optic aphasia (semantic access agnosia). *Cognitive Neuropsychology*, *4*, 131–136.

Riddoch, M. J. & Humphreys, G. W. (in press). A case of integrative visual agnosia. *Brain*.

Robertson, L. C. & Delis, D. C. (1986). 'Part-whole' processing in unilateral brain-damaged patients: Dysfunction of hierarchical organization. *Neuropsychologia*, *24*, 363–370.

Rock, I. (1973). *Orientation and form*. New York: Academic Press.

Rock, I. (1983). *The logic of perception*. Cambridge, Mass.: MIT Press.

Rock, I., De Vita, J., & Barbeito, R. (1981). The effect on form perception of change of orientation in the third dimension. *Journal of Experimental Psychology: Human Perception and Performance*, *7*, 719–732.

Sato, S. (1981). Neuronal mechanisms of pattern vision in the inferotemporal cortex of the monkey. In Y. Katsuki, R. Norgren, and M. Sato (Eds.), *Brain mechanisms of sensation*. New York: John Wiley.

Sekuler, R. & Blake, R. (1984) *Perception*. New York: Knopf.

Selfridge,O. G. (1959). Pandemonium: A paradigm for learning. In *Symposium on the Mechanization of Thought Processes*. London: HMSO.

Selfridge,O. G. & Neisser, U. (1960). Pattern recognition by machine. *Scientific American*, *203*, 60–68.

Shepard, R. N. (1981). Psychological complementarity. In M. Kubovy and J. R. Pomerantz (Eds.), *Perceptual organization*. Hillsdale, N. J.: Lawrence Erlbaum Associates Inc.

Shepard, R. N. (1984). Ecological constraints on internal representation: resonant kinematics of perceiving, imagining, thinking and dreaming. *Psychological Review*, *91*, 417–447.

Shephard, R. N. & Cooper, L. A. (1982). *Mental images and their transformations*. Cambridge, Mass.: MIT Press.

Shepard, R. N. & Farrell, J. E. (1985). Representation of the orientation of shapes. *Acta Psychologica*, *59*, 103–121.

Shepard, R. N. & Judd, S. A. (1976). Perceptual illusion of rotation of three-dimensional objects. *Science*, *171*, 701–703.

Shepard, R. N. & Metzler, J. (1971). Mental rotation of three-dimensional objects. *Science*, *191*, 952–954.

Simion, F., Bagnara, S., Roncato, S., & Umilta, C. (1982). Transformation processes upon the visual code. *Perception & Psychophysics*, *31*, 13–25.

Stevens, K. A. (1981). The visual interpretation of surface contours. *Artificial Intelligence*, *17*, 47-74.

Sumi, S. (1984).Upside-down presentation of the Johansson moving light-spot pattern. *Perception*, *13*, 283–286.

Sutherland, N. S. (1968). Outlines of a theory of pattern recognition in animals and man. *Proceedings of the Royal Society, London, B171*, 297–317.

Sutherland, N. S. (1973). Object recognition. In E. C. Carterette & M. P. Friedman (Eds.), *Handbook of perception*, Vol. 3. London: Academic Press.

Taylor, A. M. & Warrington, E. K. (1971). Visual agnosia, a single case report. *Cortex*, *7*, 152–161.

Taylor, A. M. & Warrington, E. K. (1973). Visual discrimination in patients with localised cerebral lesions. *Cortex*, *9*, 82–93.

Tusa, R. J., Palmer, L. A., & Rosenquist, A. C. (1975). The retinoptic organization of the visual cortex in the cat. *Neuroscience Abstracts*, *1*, 52.

Ullman, S. (1979). The interpretation of structure from motion. *Proceedings of the Royal Society, London, B203*, 405–426.

Ungerleider, L. G., Ganz, L., & Pribram, K. H. (1977). Size constancy in rhesus monkeys: Effects of pulvinar, prestriate, and inferotemporal lesions. *Experimental Brain Research*, *27*, 251–269.

Van Essen, D. C. (1985). Functional organization of primate visual cortex. In A. Peters and E. G. Jones (Eds.), *Cerebral cortex, Vol. 3: Visual cortex*. New York: Plenum Press.

Wallach, H. & O'Connell, D. N. (1953). The kinetic depth effect. *Journal of Experimental Psychology*, *45*, 205–217.

Warrington, E. K. (1982). Neuropsychological studies of object recognition. *Philosophical Transactions of the Royal Society, London*, *B298*, 15–33.

Warrington, E. K. & James, M. (1967). Disorders of visual perception in patients with localised cerebral lesions. *Cortex*, *9*, 82–93.

Warrington, E. K. & Rabin, P. (1970). Perceptual matching in patients with localized cerebral lesions. *Neuropschologia*, *8*, 475–487.

Warrington, E. K. & Taylor, A. M. (1973). The contribution of the right parietal lobe to object recognition. *Cortex*, *9*, 152–164.

Warrington, E. K. & Taylor, A. M. (1978). Two categorical stages of object recognition. *Perception*, *7*, 695–705.

Weiskrantz, L. & Saunders, R. C. (1984). Impairments of visual object transforms in monkeys. *Brain*, *107*, 1033–1072.

Weisstein, N. (1980). The joy of Fourier analysis. In C. S. Harris (Ed.), *Visual coding and adaptability*. Hillsdale, N. J.: Lawrence Erlbaum Associates Inc.

Weller, R. E. & Kaas,J. H. (1985). Cortical projections of the dorsolateral visual area in owl monkeys: The prestriate relay to inferotemporal cortex. *Journal of Comparative Neurology*, *234*, 35–59.

White, M. J. (1980). Naming and categorization of tilted alphanumeric characters do not require mental rotation. *Bulletin of the Psychonomic Society*, *15*, 153–156.

Wilkinson, F. W. & Dodwell, P. C. (1980). Young kittens can learn complex visual pattern discriminations. *Nature*, *284*, 258–259.

Winston, P. H. (1975). Learning structural descriptions from examples. In P. H. Winston (Ed.), *The psychology of computer vision*. New York: McGraw-Hill.
Yuille, J. C. & Steiger, J. H. (1982). Nonholistic processing in mental rotation: Some suggestive evidence. *Perception & Psychophysics*, *31*, 201–209.
Zeki, S. M. (1974). Cells responding to changing image size and disparity in the cortex of the rhesus monkey. *Journal of Physiology, London*, *243*, 827–841.
Zeki, S. M. (1977). Colour coding in the superior temporal sulcus of rhesus monkey cortex. *Proceedings of the Royal Society, London*, *B197*, 195–223.
Zeki, S. M. (1980). The representation of colours in the cerebral cortex. *Nature*, *284*, 423–428.

REFERENCE NOTES

1. Jolicoeur, P. & Besner, D. Perceptual comparisons of visual shapes: Size scaling and response bias. Paper submitted to the *Journal of Experimental Psychology: Human Perception and Performance*.

4 Picture Naming

M. Jane Riddoch
Department of Paramedical Sciences,
North East London Polytechnic, Romford Road,
Stratford, London E15 4LZ, U.K.
Glyn W. Humphreys
Cognitive Neuropsychology Research Group,
Department of Psychology, Birkbeck College,
University of London, Malet Street, London WC1E 7HX, U.K.

1. INTRODUCTION

Many processing stages may be implicated in the complex process of picture naming. Models of picture naming aim to specify these component stages. There are two distinct approaches to this problem. One is to investigate the influence on picture naming by normal subjects, of variables which may be assumed to influence particular processes such as the similarity of the picture to other depicted items, or the frequency of occurrence of a particular picture's name. A second is to investigate breakdowns in picture naming following brain damage. A patient may be impaired in the naming of pictures for a variety of reasons; most commonly, patients can be found to have a marked word finding difficulty in normal speech; the same difficulty is apparent in their naming of pictures (Goodglass, 1968; Spreen, Benton, & Van Allen, 1966). Such patients are termed "anomic" and their difficulty is thought to reflect a problem in accessing or using output phonology because they clearly understand the nature of the item (e.g., they know what an item is used for, where it is found, etc.), and, furthermore, they demonstrate a marked frequency effect with relative sparing of high frequency items (Stemberger, 1984). In contrast, patients may be demonstrated with normal speech but with marked impairments in picture naming attributable to deficits in low level perceptual processes (see chapters by Campion, Humphreys & Riddoch, and Kertesz, this volume). Between these two extremes are other patients whose picture naming impairment seems consequent on a deficit in accessing or using more central information concerning stored knowledge of the structure of the object or of associated conceptual information.

The aim of this chapter is to bring investigations of normal and of impaired picture naming together and to provide some indications of underlying mechanisms.

2. STUDIES OF PICTURE NAMING IN NORMAL SUBJECTS

One may speculate as to which representations are necessary in an intact picture naming system. For instance, for picture naming to occur, there may need to be access to stored structural knowledge about the picture (we will term this the structural description system; see also Humphreys & Riddoch, this volume, Chapter 10; Humphreys, Riddoch, & Quinlan, in press); in addition there may need to be access to stored information regarding the use of the item, where it may be found, what items it will be found in association with, etc.; finally, there will need to be access to a stored phonological representation of the object's name.

It seems clear that some of the above representations might be relatively specialised for the processing of pictures whilst others might specify knowledge for stimuli accessed from other modalities. For instance, it seems likely that stored knowledge about the structural characteristics of an object are independent of the stored knowledge about the structural characteristics of words (i.e., their orthographic forms); on the other hand, stored semantic and name information may subserve the processing of words as well as pictures. One way to assess the picture processing system, then, is to compare picture processing with that of words.

Indeed, the data from studies of picture naming in normal subjects suggests that words and pictures may access at least some separate representations of a particular object. Potter and Faulconer (1975) demonstrated that subjects were faster to name a word than they were to name the picture of the item that that word denoted. In contrast, subjects were faster at categorising the picture of an item than they were at categorising the item from its written word form. This at least implies different orders of access to the representations subserving naming and categorisation for pictures and words. Pictures seem to have relatively fast access to a semantic representation and relatively slow access to a phonological (name) representation, whilst words have relatively slow access to a semantic representation and relatively fast access to a phonological representation. This result is consistent with the idea that pictures may only access name information following access to a semantic representation, whilst words may have direct (non-semantic) access to name information (cf. Morton & Patterson, 1980; Schwartz, Marin, & Saffran, 1979). A question which then follows is, are the semantic representations for words and pictures the same? One way to investigate this is to look at priming effects between words and pictures (i.e., where prior presentation of one prime stimulus affects performance on a subsequent target stimulus). Here we may contrast repetition priming effects, which may be based on some form of structural representation of the word or picture (see Monsell, 1985) and priming between associates and between semantically related stimuli, where we may assume the involvement of at least some form of semantic knowledge.[1]

2.1. Priming and Interference Effects

Before embarking on a review of studies investigating priming between words and pictures, a note of caution is warranted. Priming effects are fickle phenomena, sensitive to multiple factors (e.g., Humphreys, Besner, & Quinlan, in press; Monsell, 1985). Consider the effect of repeating a picture on its identification. Repetition effects with clearly presented pictures separated by short intervals are likely to reflect temporary characteristics of episodic memory rather than the underlying architecture of the picture recognition system. To avoid such contamination, at the very least studies need to examine repetition effects only when there are long lags between repetitions (see Monsell, 1985).

When this is done, substantial *within-modality* repetition effects occur for both pictures and words (e.g., Durso & Johnson, 1979; Kirsner, Milech, & Stumfel, 1986; Warren & Morton, 1982). In contrast, *cross-modality* repetition effects between pictures and words seem much weaker, although still obtainable (e.g., Durso & Johnson, 1979; Kirsner et al., 1986; although see Scarborough, Gerade, & Cortese, 1979; Warren & Morton, 1982). The contrast in the magnitude of cross- and within-modality repetition effects between pictures and words is consistent with the idea that (a) pictures and words are recognised using only partially overlapping sets of processes (Kirsner et al., 1986), and (b) that non-overlapping processes include accessing stored knowledge about the structural characteristics of the stimuli. For instance, at least part of the facilitation from long-term repetition priming could be due to persistent activation in the structural representations of the stimuli, which lessens the amount of information required for their subsequent identification (e.g., Warren & Morton, 1982).

[1]Associative and semantic priming effects are typically not differentiated in studies of picture naming (although see Lupker, 1985). However, it is feasible that only priming effects between semantically related items indicate semantic-based knowledge (see Humphreys, 1985).

Whilst long-term cross-modality repetition effects tend to be relatively small, quite substantial associative priming effects have been reported between pictures and words (e.g., measuring naming latency, by Carr, McCauley, Sperber, & Parmalee, 1982, and by Sperber, McCauley, Regain, & Weil, 1979; measuring living/non-living categorisation latencies, by Guenther, Klatzky, & Putnam, 1980; measuring lexical decision times to words, by Vanderwart, 1984). These substantial cross-modality associative priming effects may reflect activation in a common, amodal semantic system subserving the comprehension of both pictures and words. Interestingly, in the studies measuring naming latency, associative priming effects tend to be stronger on picture targets than on word targets (e.g., Carr et al., 1982). This asymmetry may be because access to the semantic system may be *required* to name pictures but not words (see Humphreys & Evett, 1985).

At first sight, studies which seem relevant to the issue of whether picture naming is normally semantically mediated, are those investigating picture-word interference effects. When subjects have to name pictures which have words overlaid (see Fig. 4.1), their naming times are slowed relative to when no words are present (e.g., Rosinski, 1977). This interference is greater when the word denotes an object from the same category as the depicted object, compared with when the picture and the word are unrelated. Lupker (1979) has shown that interference is dependent on the categorical relationship between the stimuli. When the word refers to an associate from a different category to the depicted object, performance does not differ from the unrelated condition (the "hat–head" example, in Fig. 4.1). Also, the interference effect is not influenced either by whether the picture and word are frequent associates within the category (e.g., "chair–table" vs. "dog–beaver", Fig. 4.1), or by whether the stimuli are

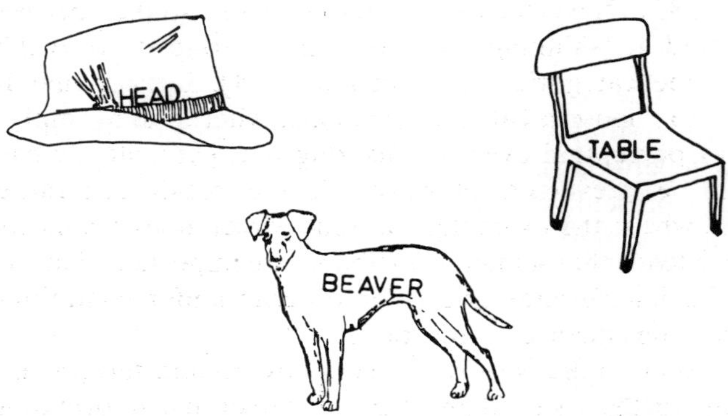

FIG. 4.1. Picture-word interference stimuli (from Lupker, 1979).

typical category members (the "dog–beaver" example again). Thus the effects seem due to the retrieval of category-specific (as opposed to associative) attributes from the word, which influence the naming of the picture. The question is, are these category-specific attributes perceptual or semantic (e.g., concerned with functional relations between the stimuli)?

In a subsequent study, Lupker and Katz (1981) had subjects decide whether or not the pictures were of dogs. On negative trials, the pictures could correspond either to other animals or to objects from other categories. Lupker and Katz proposed that subjects should make the dog/not-dog decision purely on the basis of perceptual features (e.g., the presence of four legs, a head, and a tail, etc.). If picture-word interference reflects response competition between the names generated to the word and the picture, it should be eliminated in this task. However, Lupker and Katz found that words corresponding to the names of other animals continued to disrupt verification times to the pictures of dogs (on positive trials). On negative trials, pictures of other animals were rejected more slowly than those of objects from other categories, and the word "dog" selectively affected reaction times (RTs) to the pictures of other animals. These results suggest that category-specific picture-word interference effects are not simply due to response competition between the picture and the word. Rather, they seem to stem from the retrieval of perceptual attributes about the object corresponding to the word, which influences the perceptual classification and identification of the picture. When the picture and word correspond to different objects with similar perceptual attributes, verification times are slowed to the picture.

According to the last study, the category-specific attributes which seem important for picture-word matching are perceptual and not semantic in nature: a bleak conclusion, since it suggests that the data are, after all, not relevant to the issue of semantic mediation during picture naming (see also Lupker, 1985). Nevertheless, we mention the studies because there are other grounds for thinking that perceptual-overlap effects will be particular only to some categories (see Section 2.3.4). Lupker and Katz (1981) happened to choose a category (animals) where the exemplars have high degrees of perceptual overlap, ensuring that perceptually-based interference will be prevalent. However, if the result generalises to other categories where the examplars are not perceptually similar, we can have more confidence that semantic attributes are important. This would be true even if the interference effects only occur under conditions of picture naming and not picture verification.

We mention Lupker's work on picture-word interference also because it is relevant to the issue of the *type* of perceptual information mediating picture identification. We discuss this issue next.

2.2. Object Form Knowledge

We have suggested that picture identification requires access to structural representations which differ from the structural representations mediating word recognition (e.g., orthographic input logogens; cf. Morton & Patterson, 1980). Picture naming may, in addition, require access to semantic information. The perceptual information mediating picture identification will correspond to that required to access the appropriate structural representation. Thus, the issue of the perceptual information involved cannot be divorced from questions concerning the nature of the stored structural representations.

Morton has called the structural representation of a picture a "pictogen"; this is thought to be analagous to an orthographic input logogen in word identification, and to correspond to an abstract representation which is activated by all objects with the same name. Thus, different exemplars of an object having the same name will give rise to long-term repetition effects (Warren & Morton, 1982).

However, the notion that pictogens only exist at the level at which different objects have the same name can probably be rejected on both logical and empirical grounds. The logical argument is that it is possible to recognise (access the appropriate semantics for) specific objects; for later representations to be specific, a specific entry point needs to exist.

Empirical evidence can be drawn from a number of sources. For instance, Bartram (1974) asked subjects to name photographs of objects over a number of blocks of trials. Over the different blocks stimuli could be:

1. Identical repeats of an earlier item.
2. A repeat of an earlier item which had been photographed from a different view.
3. A target with the same name as an earlier item with which it was physically dissimilar.
4. A target which was both physically different and with a different name to earlier items.

Bartram found that RTs to targets in conditions (1), (2), and (3) were faster than RTs in condition (4). Further, facilitation was greatest for identical targets, less for items repeated in a different view and least for physically different targets with the same name as an earlier item. This suggests that objects repeated in different views produce priming over and above those effects due to repetition of the name. Quite similar effects in a task where subjects had to match objects on the basis of whether they had the same name have been reported by R. Ellis (1985; Ellis & Allport, 1985). This result is consistent with the view that structural representations exist, separate from semantic and phonological representations of objects, and that these representations can be primed irrespective of the viewpoint of the stimulus.

Kelter, Grötzbach, Freiheit, Höhle, Wutzig, and Diesch (1984) used a different procedure. Of most relevance to our present concern were two groups of subjects who had to categorise the same pairs of consecutively presented pictures but using different criteria. Group 1 responded "same" if the two pictures were physically identical. Group 2 responded "same" if the two pictures had the same name (e.g., if they were two types of chair, an office chair and a kitchen chair). Included in other pairings were pictures of the same object but in different views, where they were objects from the same category (e.g. a bed and a chair), and where they were unrelated objects. Objects from the same category and unrelated objects were always assigned to the "different" response category. Pairings of the same object in different views, and of objects with the same name, were assigned to the "different" category for the physical-identity group (Group 1) and to the "same" response category for the name-identity group (Group 2). Of most interest were the effects of the various picture-pairings on "different" responses. For Group 1, different-views of the same object were rejected more slowly than any other pairings. There was no difference between the same-name, the same-category, and the unrelated picture-pairings. Again, correspondence of an object-description across the different-views seems important here, and this correspondence is difficult to ignore even when subjects have only to match for physical identity. In contrast, for Group 2, objects from the same-category were rejected more slowly than unrelated objects. This suggests that, when judging for name identity (or for physical correspondences at the name level), subjects find it difficult to ignore semantic relations between objects. This does not mean that name-level judgements can only be made on the basis of semantic information (e.g., semantic information might be activated prior to the completion of access to "pictogen" representations, see Section 2.3.4), although it is consistent with the suggestion. What is clear is that we can draw a distinction between structural representations common to individual objects in different views, and any structural representations common to different objects having the same name.

A rather different approach to defining the structural representations of objects has been taken in the field of computer vision. In particular, Marr and Nishihara (1978) have suggested that knowledge of object form or an object's structural description (e.g., the object's parts specified relative to its major axis, see Humphreys & Quinlan, this volume, Chapter 3, for further details) is stored in a "catalogue" in a hierarchical manner, according to the precision of information carried by a particular structural description (see Fig. 4.2). The top level of description would contain the

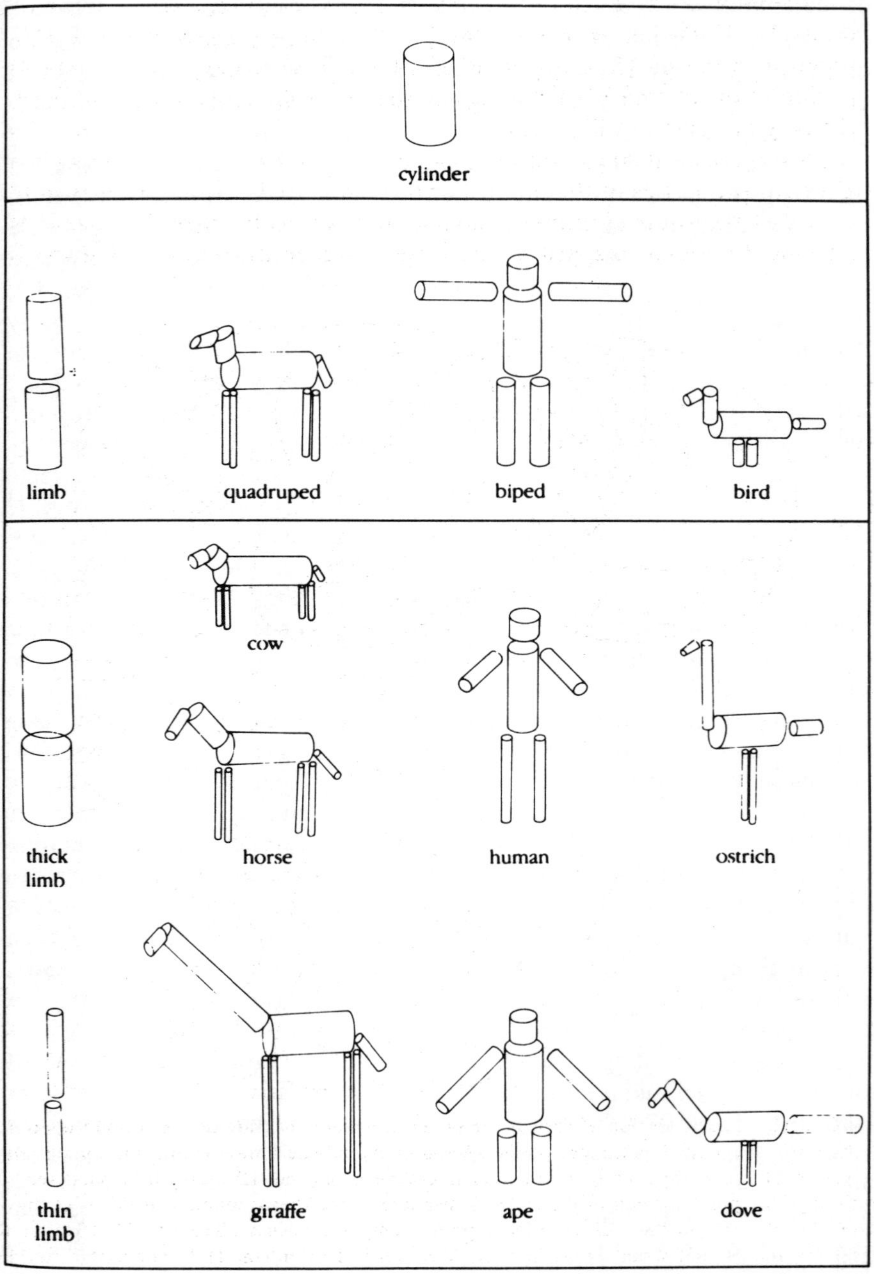

FIG. 4.2. Hierarchical structural descriptions (from Marr, 1982).

most undifferentiated information: a three-dimensional model without component decomposition (e.g., an animal rather than a mammal, man, or bird). At the next level, coarse information about lengths and orientations of parts of the object is available, allowing differentiation between, say, an animal and a bird. At the final level, the description is precise enough to distinguish between, for example, horse, cow, and giraffe shapes. This theory strongly suggests that recognition may proceed differently for different objects; in particular, objects from some categories will have more overlap with their coarse level descriptions than will objects from other categories. Indeed, it is difficult to conceptualise what a coarse level description corresponding to some categories will be (e.g. what would be a description corresponding to furniture?). For some categories then, exemplars may have only one entry within a catalogue of stored structural descriptions.

A point to note here is that no allowance is made within this theory for recognition of a particular item; one's own particular pet dog, for example. This must add another level to the catalogue account.

2.3. Semantic Representations

2.3.1. Prototypes

The type of form description(s) accessed by a particular object may also determine the type of semantic information which may be accessed when objects are identified. For instance, if a given object initially activates a coarse structural description then it seems likely that coarse (superordinate) semantic information would initially be accessed during object identification. A number of views have been offered on the nature of semantic involvement in object identification. Rosch (1975) has argued that object identification is mediated by access to semantic information, and that access to semantics is based on a specific level of form description. She has proposed that, in semantic memory, items may be coded in terms of prototypes of the most characteristic members of the category. Factors which may be influential in determining a categorical prototype are common perceptual attributes, common motor movements, similarity in shape and identifiability of averaged shapes of category members. She suggests that semantic memory can be categorised at three different levels of description. The superordinate category is defined by function (e.g., fruit is for eating), basic level items have the largest number of perceptual attributes in common with other exemplars of the category (e.g., apple, orange, and pear would all be independent base level representations), while the subordinate level involves the differentiation of base level items according to the specific exemplar (e.g., Coxes Orange Pippin apple vs. Red Worcester apple). Entry into the semantic system is via the base level. Roschs' work suggests that objects are first recognised and classified as members of their basic category; for instance a Siamese cat would first be recognised as a cat before it would be classified as a Siamese cat (Rosch, 1975; Rosch, Mervis, Gray, Johnson, & Boyes-Bream, 1976). The superiority of the basic level may be because labels of items are learned first at the basic level, because items represented at the basic level are more familiar or because the basic name may be the preferred label of two equally frequently used words (Murphy & Smith, 1982). As with Marr's catalogue, it is clear that not all categories are equivalent using Rosch's classification scheme. Thus "birds" as a category, are represented in semantic memory at the basic level ("animal" being the superordinate level), particular birds have specific representations at the subordinate level. "Animals", on the other hand, do have specific representations at the basic level (deer, horse, cow, etc.) even though these representations still tend to be characterised by a high degree of perceptual overlap (cf. Marr & Nishihara, 1978). Items of furniture also have specific representations at the base level (chair, table, wardrobe), though the specific representations here have little perceptual overlap.

A similar problem exists for Rosch's theory as has been described for Marr's theory. Namely, in order to recognise a specific object (e.g., a specific type of dog, or, even more particularly, one's own dog) a specific entry point needs to exist. It is therefore difficult to account for how we ever identify stimuli at a subordinate level, if their semantic descriptions can *only* be accessed at the basic level. A more reasonable suggestion is that semantic information can be addressed at either the superordinate, basic, or subordinate levels, but that addressing the different levels operates over different time courses. Basic level effects may dominate object classification tasks because semantic descriptions at the base level are often the first to be activated; other levels of description may be activated in parallel but more slowly.

However, even this account runs into difficulty. Consider the experiment of Lupker and Katz (1981) which we discussed earlier. They found picture-word interference effects from the names of other animals on the time taken to verify pictures of a dog, and corresponding interference from the word "dog" on the time taken to reject pictures of other animals as "not dogs". How could such effects occur if access to base level is completed prior to access to category information? Since information about "dogs" is specified at a base level, category level information should not affect performance. This suggests that access to higher level (category) and base level information can take place concurrently, and that category information can affect access to more specific structural and semantic information about objects.

Other evidence damaging to Rosch's position has been reported by

Jolicoeur, Gluck, and Kosslyn (1984). They had subjects produce the first name that came to mind when they were presented with pictures corresponding either to typical or to atypical members of their category (e.g., for the category bird, a robin would be a typical member and a penguin an atypical member). They found that typical members were named at the base level ("robin" → "bird"), whilst atypical members were named at a subordinate level (e.g. "penguin" → "penguin"). Jolicoeur et al. (1984) argue that, for object identification to occur, the item must contact semantic memory at what they call "the entry point level". This level corresponds to the basic level for many objects; however, for very distinctive or atypical exemplars of a base level category, the object's entry point into semantic memory is defined at a subordinate level.

2.3.2. The "Perceptual Model"

A contrasting point of view to that of Rosch is put by Murphy and Smith (1982). They propose a "perceptual model" in order to account for the tendency for subjects to name pictorial items at the base level rather than the superordinate or subordinate levels (i.e., base level superiority). According to this model, naming depends on the type of perceptual representation accessed by an object. At the basic level, objects have many perceptual attributes in common, so there may exist a single base level representation for many objects. At the superordinate level, objects have fewer perceptual attributes in common and so it is less likely that a single perceptual representation for a superordinate class exists (although see Marr & Nishihara, 1978). The advantage of base level information over superordinate information occurs because objects initially access *perceptual* representations at the base level. Murphy and Smith's account is again based on a simple picture naming experiment. Prior to the presentation of a picture (e.g., a chair) subjects would be given auditorily the category name (e.g., furniture). In order to conceptualise superordinate knowledge such as "furniture", Murphy and Smith suggest that subjects must activate two (or more) perceptual representations such as "chair", "bed", etc. If a picture of a bed is presented it will be compared with all the activated perceptual representations rather than just "bed" in order to determine whether it may be categorised as "furniture". On the other hand, at the base level, there is a single perceptual representation; if the name of this perceptual representation is given prior to a picture, it will correspond more closely to the depicted item. Thus extra features will be required to match with superordinate knowledge. Similarly, Murphy and Smith claim that typical category exemplars should be faster to categorise than atypical category exemplars because the former share more perceptual features with the category than do the latter (see Smith, Shoben, & Rips, 1974).

Consistent with these claims, objects are matched more quickly with base level than with superordinate names, and typical category members are verified faster than atypical members

Murphy and Smith (1982) further supported their account in the following way. They designed 14 hierarchically organised categories of novel tools. The categories resembled natural superordinate, basic, and subordinate categories in that superordinates had only one attribute (that of function) common to their members, basic level category members shared many perceptual attributes in common while subordinate category members had only one attribute (in addition to basic level attributes) common to their members. Each item in the hierarchy of categories was given a nonsense syllable as a name. Subjects had to learn the names. Whatever the learning order, subordinate > basic > superordinate or superordinate > basic > subordinate, basic level superiority was still manifest in the test situation. Murphy and Smith argue that base level superiority does not hinge on position in a hierarchical semantic structure, or on category frequency, conjoint name frequency (preferred name given the choice of both category name and object name), number of categories per level or number of instances in a category. Rather, they hold that picture naming is dependent on a variable operating on a pre-semantic representation; that is, a representation concerned with the structural characteristics of objects. Indeed, we may even suppose that, in some instances, objects may be named directly from the structural (pre-semantic) representation as the existence of such representations is thought to be the primary determinant of object naming (see Section 3). It is important to emphasise, however, that Murphy and Smith's results may be as artificial as the novel items that they constructed.

2.3.3. The Semantic Mediation Account

One further account of access to semantic and name information in picture naming has been proposed by Jolicoeur et al. (1984). In contrast to Murphy and Smith, Jolicoeur et al. maintain that the primary factor determining picture naming times is the "entry point" for gaining access to semantic information. In contrast to Rosch, Jolicoeur et al. maintain that not all objects will have the same entry point to semantics; rather, typical category members are thought to enter at the base level while atypical category members are thought to enter at the subordinate level. Clearly, Jolicoeur et al.'s data suggest that not all objects gain access to name information in the same way and the relations between a given object and other members of its category are primarily important for naming typical category exemplars. The question here is how is typicality defined? Could it be that typical category members share many perceptual features in common, while atypical category members do not have many features in common with other items from the category? If this is so then the differences between Jolicoeur et al.'s position and that of Murphy and Smith disappear: both accounts must then hold that naming is strongly dependent on perceptual distinctiveness.

However, perceptual distinctiveness is by no means the only factor affecting picture naming time, and therefore neither Jolicoeur et al.'s nor Murphy and Smith's accounts can provide a full explanation of picture naming. For instance, for at least some categories of object there seem to be independent effects of perceptual distinctiveness and prototypicality on picture naming (see Section 2.3.4). This suggests that prototypicality reflects the overlap of semantic characteristics between an object and other members of its category (and not just the overlap of perceptual attributes), and that these semantic characteristics can influence picture naming latency. Further, word frequency is known to have strong effects on the speed of object naming (Oldfield, 1966) although these effects disappear when subjects have to determine whether two successively presented pictures are physically the same or different (Bartram, 1976; Wingfield, 1978). The latter result suggests that frequency effects are primarily confined to name retrieval, and therefore that the name retrieval stage also has strong effects on picture naming reaction times.

To explicate these differing effects of perceptual distinctiveness, prototypicality and name frequency on picture naming, we have turned to a new account of picture naming.

2.3.4. The Cascade Model

Recently (Humphreys et al., in press), have proposed that at least three discrete representations are contacted when a picture is named. First, a representation specifying the structural properties of the object; second, a representation concerned with knowledge about the functional and associative characteristics of objects; and third, a representation concerned with output phonology. Factors such as perceptual distinctiveness, non-perceptual aspects of prototypicality and name frequency will operate at different stages in the naming process. Perceptual distinctiveness will influence access to the structural description system; prototypicality will influence access to semantic knowledge; and name frequency will affect access to output phonology. Most importantly, we propose that the stages involved in picture naming do *not* operate discretely; that is information is not transmitted from one stage to the next only after the completion of processing at each stage. Instead, processing conforms to a class of models which hold that different processing stages can be initiated in parallel, prior to the completion of any given stage (e.g., McClelland, 1979; Meyer,

Yantis, Osman, & Smith, 1985; Miller, 1982). One particularly strong instance of this class of models is a *cascade* model, which holds that information is transmitted continuously between the processing stages following the initiation of any one stage. We have suggested that, in normal picture naming, information is transmitted in cascade between the structural description, the semantic, and the phonological systems.

Evidence supporting the cascade account was demonstrated in a simple experiment examining naming times to pictures from different categories (Humphreys et al., in press). Pictures came from categories classed as having structurally similar exemplars (e.g., animals, fruit, vegetables, etc.) and from categories classed as having structurally distinct exemplars (e.g., furniture, tools, clothing, etc.). The frequency of the object names was varied orthogonally with the structural similarity factor. We found that items classed as structurally similar were slower to name than structurally distinct items; thus a picture of an airplane was named faster than the picture of a cow. Further, there were different effects of name frequency on the naming of the two classes of stimuli. Name frequency had little effect on naming times to objects from structurally similar categories; the picture of a cow was named no faster than that of a gorilla, despite the name "cow" having a higher frequency of occurrence. In contrast, name frequency exerted a strong influence on naming times to objects from structurally distinct categories; thus, an airplane was named faster than a helicopter, consistent with the higher frequency of occurrence of its name. This pattern of interaction between two factors, perceptual distinctiveness and name frequency, which ought to influence different stages in picture naming, is what might be expected from a cascade account. For instance, the cascade account maintains that, once processing has started in the structural description system, the semantic and phonological systems can also be activated. Items which are perceptually similar to other items will activate the structural descriptions of those items; similarly, as well as activating its own semantic representation, an item will activate the semantic representations of items from the same category and the semantic representations of perceptually similar items (because their stored structural descriptions have been activated). Following on from this, phonological information specifying the names of the target object plus those of its structural and semantic "neighbours" can be activated. This all means that the system will initially be very "noisy", with the representations of several items at the structural, semantic, and phonological levels being activated. In order for the processing system to achieve a stable state, inhibitory as well as excitatory interactions may be assumed between representations. That is, activation of a given representation will inhibit activation in other candidate representations. Accordingly, as further visual processing of the target item occurs, inhibition of perceptually and/or semantically similar items will spread through the system until the target item can be unambiguously named. Items which are not perceptually similar to other items will activate other structural descriptions less, and their processing will therefore proceed in a much more direct manner. Further, since the system is assumed to operate in cascade, then the time taken to resolve processing at the structural and/or the semantic level will influence the operation of a variable affecting later processing stages (such as name frequency). In particular, when there is relatively rapid access to structural and semantic information (e.g., with clearly presented, structurally distinct objects) there will be quite strong effects of late-acting variables (such as name frequency). Correspondingly, there will be weak effects of late-acting variables when there is relatively slow access to structural and semantic information because there will then be more time for late representations to be partially activated, reducing differences which may exist a priori in the activation levels of those representations (Humphreys et al., in press). A framework illustrating the cascade model is given in Fig. 4.3.

In addition to collecting naming latencies to the pictures, we also correlated the naming times for each picture with various measures, including (a) the frequency of occurrence of the picture's name, (b) ratings of the prototypicality of the object as a member of its category, and (c) a measure of the picture's structural similarity relative to other members of

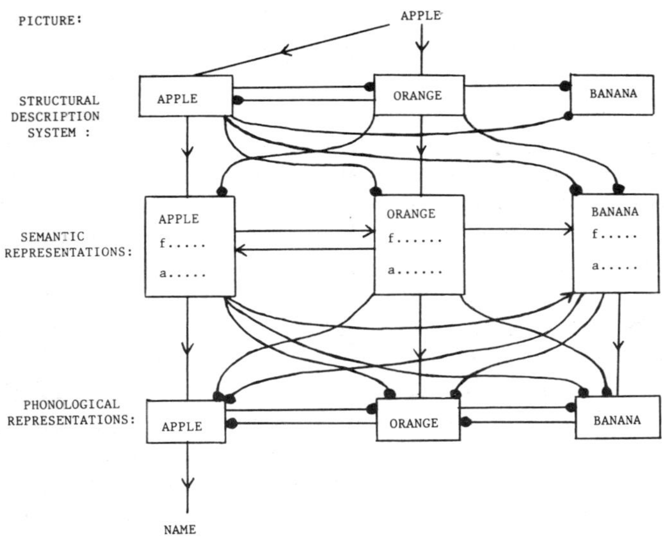

FIG. 4.3. Processing framework illustrating the cascade model of picture naming, and the responses of the system to a picture of an apple. —→— denote facilitatory process; ——• denotes inhibitory processes; f . . . refers to functional attributes of objects; a . . . refers to associative attributes.

its category (based on the degree of overlap between the contours of the picture and those of other pictures from its category given in Snodgrass and Vanderwart's, 1980, norms). Quite different patterns of correlation emerged for the structurally similar and the structurally distinct objects. For the *structurally similar* objects, there were reliable and independent correlations between naming RTs and both the structural similarity and the prototypicality measures; there were no correlations with their name frequency. Items low in structural similarity were named faster than those high in structural similarity; thus a giraffe, which has low levels of structural similarity relative to other animals, was named faster than a cow, which has a high level of within-category similarity. Also, prototypical items (such as a cat, rated a prototypical animal) tended to be named faster than less typical members of their categories (such as a bear). The effects of structural similarity and prototypicality contributed separately to naming times, consistent with there being strong and independent contributions of structural and semantic factors to the naming of objects from structurally similar categories. For the *structurally distinct* objects, there was only a reliable correlation between naming time and name frequency. There were no independent correlations with either of the structural similarity or the prototypicality measures. Thus, for objects from categories with structurally distinct exemplars, neither the degree of within-category structural similarity nor the prototypicality of the item as a member of its category strongly affects performance.

How do we explain the category-specific effects of these different variables? One possibility is that, for categories with structurally similar exemplars, there may exist some form of superordinate structural description which specifies the structural characteristics common to category exemplars. We may think of such descriptions as being akin to the undifferentiated (category level) descriptions posited by Marr and Nishihara (1978). Objects from such categories will activate the superordinate description in addition to their own descriptions, and activation of the superordinate description may lead to the activation of the descriptions for many category exemplars. Such widespread activation will give rise to strong structural similarity effects. In contrast, superordinate descriptions may not exist for categories where the exemplars have distinctive structures (see Section 2.2). Consequently, there is less likelihood that other category exemplars will be activated following the presentation of a given object, and the degree of structural similarity between category exemplars will have little effect on naming. Also, because of this difference in the number of structural "neighbours" which are activated, there will also be differences in the number of semantic "neighbours" called-up by objects in structurally similar and structurally distinct categories. Thus the naming of exemplars from different categories of objects will tend to be subject to different degrees of semantic mediation: The naming of objects from structurally similar categories will show stronger effects of semantic mediation than the naming of objects from structurally distinct categories (see Humphreys et al., in press).

There are also other ways to conceptualise these category-specific effects. For instance, instead of thinking of there being one representation corresponding to every object we have encountered, we could envisage that information about each object is distributed across a set of parallel representations, and this could be so for each of the levels we have specified (i.e., the structural, the semantic, and the phonological). In such a distributed system, the representation of a particular object would correspond to the instantiation of a specific pattern of activation across the distributed representations (e.g., Hinton & Anderson, 1981; McClelland & Rumelhart, 1985, 1986; see the discussion of "connectionist models", in Humphreys & Quinlan, this volume, Chapter 3). Further, those units which are consistently co-activated together will come to have strong interconnections, whilst there will only be weak interconnections between units which are co-activated infrequently (see McClelland & Rumelhart, 1985). This will mean that there will be strong interconnections between the processing units within the structural description system which represent objects from structurally similar categories, and weak interconnections between units representing objects from structurally distinct categories. Indeed, for the structurally distinct categories the "within-category" interconnections may be no stronger than those across categories, since the "parts" of structurally distinct objects may be common to many objects from different categories (e.g., "long handles" are common to tools, kitchen implements, office equipment, etc.). In contrast, the "parts" of structurally similar objects have a stronger tendency to occur only within their category (e.g., feathered wings and beaks in birds; a head, four legs, and a tail in animals; six legs and antennae in insects, etc.). As a consequence, there will be greater activation for the structural "neighbours" of structurally similar than of structurally distinct objects. And if, for the structurally distinct objects, the co-activation across categories is as great as that within-category, then measures of within-category structural similarity will have little bearing on performance (as indeed we found; see Humphreys et al., in press). Essentially, the distributed memory approach translates the idea of a hierarchically-organised structural description system into predictions based on the magnitude and "breadth" of co-activation across processing units corresponding to "part" information for different exemplars. We have discussed the approach in some detail because it turns out to be a useful way of thinking about how picture recognition and naming breaks down after brain damage.

Whether we adopt a distributed or a localised, single unit approach, the cascade model does make the strong prediction that performance will vary as a function of the different types of information which are picked up over time, during the course of picture naming. For instance, global form information may initially exert a stronger influence on decision-making than local detail (cf. Navon, 1977; see Sergent, this volume, Chapter 5). This global form information may selectively affect different levels of representation within the structural description system. In a system with localised units, coarse levels of description will initially be activated prior to descriptions corresponding to particular objects. In a distributed system, units common to many category members will be activated prior to those distinguishing between category members (at least where there is a relatively strong commonality of "parts" within the category). Naming responses will be affected by the degree of overlap between an object and this initial information. For the most part, the descriptions most strongly activated by the initial, global information will conform to what Rosch termed the base level representation (see earlier), so producing a bias towards base level naming (see Rosch et al., 1976). The overlap idea, however, also provides a natural explanation for Jolicoeur et al.'s (1984) finding that atypical category exemplars are given subordinate names faster. For instance, if atypical category exemplars differ in their global shape from other category members, they will not be so affected by the early global form information.

Different predictions are made about picture categorisation. Let us assume that higher order (category level) structural descriptions exist for some categories (specifically, categories with structurally similar exemplars). It follows that, for objects from these categories, picture categorisation may be based upon the activation of those category level descriptions. This should not be possible for objects from categories which do not support a category level structural description (specifically, categories with structurally distinct exemplars). For such objects, categorisation would need to be based on access to semantic information. Thus category-specific effects should emerge in picture categorisation tasks. Pictures from categories with structurally similar exemplars should be easier to categorise than pictures of objects from structurally distinct exemplars, as the former pictures can be categorised on the basis of structural rather than semantic information.

We have tested this last prediction using the frequency-matched stimuli of Humphreys et al. (in press, experiment 1). Subjects were given a choice of two category labels prior to the presentation of each item, and they had to name the correct category label as quickly as possible following the items presentation. Pictures of structurally similar items were categorised more quickly than pictures of structurally distinct items (652msec vs. 772 msec), and there were no effects of picture name-frequency. The categorisation latencies were also correlated with ratings of typicality of each exemplar as a member of its superordinate category. There was a strong correlation between item typicality and categorisation time for *structurally distinct* objects, confirming that typical exemplars tend to be categorised relative to their superordinate category label more quickly than atypical exemplars (cf. Smith, Shoben, & Rips, 1974). However, there was no sign of a positive correlation between the two measures for structurally similar objects. The correlations between picture categorisation latencies and item typicality contrast strongly with those obtained between picture naming latencies and item typicality. For pictures of *structurally distinct* objects, item typicality correlates with categorisation time but not with naming time; for pictures of *structurally similar* objects item typicality correlated with naming time but not categorisation time (see Table 4.1).

The data for *structurally distinct* objects suggest that item typicality primarily determines the time taken to access semantic information concerning an exemplar's category; thus, typicality correlated with categorisation time. Typicality does not correlate with naming latencies to pictures of *structurally distinct* objects because the naming of such objects is not strongly influenced by semantic information. It also follows that typicality does not correlate with categorisation latencies to pictures of *structurally similar* objects because categorisation of these objects is based on structural rather than semantic information; and, as the naming of *structurally similar* objects is strongly influenced by semantic information, the naming latencies for such objects will correlate with item typicality.[2]

Further corroboration for the above arguments is provided by data on the time taken to categorise words corresponding to the above picture names. *Word categorisation* correlated with prototypicality, for both the

---

[2]Although we have argued here that item typicality affects semantic-access time, we do not wish to suggest that this is the only locus of typicality effects. Ratings of item typicality may reflect structural similarity between category exemplars in addition to the exemplar's relation to the category label (cf. Murphy & Brownell, 1985; Murphy & Smith, 1982; Rosch et al., 1976). It may therefore be possible to observe typicality effects on categorisation times to exemplars from structurally similar categories when the exemplars are chosen to have atypical structures relative to other category members (e.g., Murphy & Brownell, 1985). In our study, exemplars were selected by category membership and no attempt was made to include items with atypical structures within the class of structurally similar items. Thus those structurally similar exemplars rated as atypical in our study (e.g., giraffe and kangaroo, which were both rated as atypical animals, presumably on the basis of semantic information), still tended to share general structural characteristics with other category members (e.g., head, body, legs). Such items could be classified using structural information, and there would be no resultant correlation between categorisation times and rated typicality. In this respect it seems that item typicality defined in terms of the structural properties of objects will not have a normal distribution within categories with structurally similar exemplars; many of the exemplars will have typical structures and there will be only a few atypical exemplars.

TABLE 4.1
Correlations Between RTs and Ratings of Item Prototypicality in Naming and Categorisation Tasks

	Picture Naming	*Picture Categorisation*
Objects from structurally similar categories	$r = 0.494$* significant	$r = 0.146$ not significant
Objects from structurally distinct categories	$r = -0.05$ not significant	$r = 0.647$** significant

*$P < 0.01$; **$P < 0.001$.

structurally distinct and the structurally similar objects, indicating semantic mediation of the decisions in both cases. Also, correlations between RTs to the stimuli in the different tasks gave the pattern shown in Table 4.2. For *structurally distinct* items, word categorisation correlated with picture categorisation but not with picture naming. This is consistent with the argument for semantic effects on the categorisation of such pictures but not on their naming. For *structurally similar* items, word categorisation correlated with picture naming but not with picture categorisation. This is consistent with the argument for semantic effects on the naming of such pictures but not on their categorisation.

TABLE 4.2
Correlations Between Picture Categorisation, Picture Naming, Word Categorisation, and Word-naming Tasks

	Structurally Distinct	*Structurally Similar*
Picture categorisation and picture naming	0.304*	0.401**
Picture categorisation and word categorisation	0.519**	0.194
Picture categorisation and word naming	0.247	0.005
Picture naming and word categorisation	−0.03	0.471**
Picture naming and word naming	0.507**	0.165
Word categorisation and word naming	0.082	0.05

Note: Items are from structurally distinct and structually similar categories.

*Denotes a correlation reliable at the 0.05 level.

**Denotes a correlation reliable at the 0.01 level.

Finally, it is of interest that categorisation times to pictures of structurally distinct items were faster than those to words corresponding to the same objects (772msec vs. 1030msec). The size of this difference was, if anything, larger than that between RTs to pictures and words corresponding to structurally similar objects (652msec vs. 878msec).[3] It appears that fast categorisation times to pictures do not solely reflect structural factors, since fast times are found with both structurally distinct and structurally similar objects (although see Snodgrass & McCullough, 1986). An alternative account of such fast times is that pictures correspond more closely to the underlying semantic descriptions of objects than do words.

3. DATA FROM BRAIN DAMAGED SUBJECTS

The first part of this chapter has introduced the theory that picture naming involves accessing stored structural, semantic, and name information, and that these access processes operate in cascade. An attempt will now be made to use the model in order to accommodate the data obtained from brain damaged subjects.

The cascade model maintains that, in order to name a picture, brain damaged subjects must be able to:

1. Generate an adequate perceptual representation of a picture and use this information to access stored knowledge of object form.
2. Access at least some conceptual knowledge about the picture (although this may depend on the category of the object; see earlier).
3. Access the picture's phonological label.

It is generally believed that (3) must proceed from (2), although Ratcliff and Newcombe (1982) have argued in favour of a non-semantic route to picture naming. It is proposed that this route acts as a stabiliser for the semantic system, and Ratcliff and Newcombe illustrate this argument by reference to the syndrome of optic aphasia—where patients have a deficit specific to naming visually presented objects, and yet they appear to show intact recognition because they may often make correct gestures to the objects misnamed (Freund, 1889; Lhermitte & Beauvois, 1973). Ratcliff and Newcombe suggest that in cases of optic aphasia the non-semantic route to naming is damaged, with the result being that the semantic system becomes unstable and the patients fail to name visually presented objects.

---

[3]Faster categorisation times to structurally similar than to structurally distinct objects were found with both pictures and words. This suggests that the difference in categorisation times to stimuli from the two classes can reflect other than structural factors, such as item prototypicality. Structurally similar objects were rated as more prototypical, relative to their superordinate category label, than structurally distinct objects (see Humphreys et al., in press).

Recognition remains intact, however, as is demonstrated by the patients' ability to gesture the use of an item that they cannot name. There are problems with this suggestion. For instance, if specific gestures reflect access to semantic knowledge, it is not clear why specific names could not also be addressed from this knowledge (see Beauvois & Saillant, 1985). To uphold the dual-route position, we must maintain either that gestures reflect non-specific semantic knowledge (see Funnell, this volume, Chapter 8; Ratcliff & Newcombe, 1982) or that they reflect access to other (non-semantic) stored knowledge (see Riddoch & Humphreys, 1987, for evidence on this point). The most important prediction made by the dual-route model is that, given such a functional architecture, it should be possible to demonstrate patients able to name objects and pictures via the non-semantic route when they have sustained impairments to semantic knowledge (see, for example, Shallice, 1987). We know of only one paper which has been in any way convincing in reporting results supporting this conclusion. Kremin (in press) reported data from two left hemisphere damaged patients who showed preserved object naming, but who were impaired at matching pictures of objects from the same category. This pattern of poor category-matching along with good naming is what might be expected if picture naming can operate via a direct route when semantic access is impaired. However, we should note that the category matching task used by Kremin was quite complicated (five target pictures had to be matched with five candidates, with each candidate assigned to a target because of their category relationship). Patients could have failed this task because of its abstract and complex nature, relative to picture naming—in which case, their semantic knowledge about the depicted objects could be spared. Indeed, Kremin specifically reports that the patients were not agnosic, so they presumably had no problems in dealing with visually presented objects in everyday life. It is difficult to reconcile such an ability to cope with visually presented objects in everyday life with the patients' having impaired access to semantic knowledge. Until stronger evidence is found, it is more parsimonious to maintain that a single (semantically mediated) route subserves object and picture naming. Also, we should note that the cascade model of picture naming will, in the limit, approximate to a dual-route model because of its assumption that the naming of some objects will be more determined by semantic knowledge than others (see Section 2.3.4). In effect, the naming of objects from categories with structurally distinct exemplars will be little affected by semantic information.

If the idea of a non-semantic route to picture naming subserving all pictures is not tenable, then, as is suggested by most current models of picture recognition, the semantic system must be accessed before a picture can be named. If an impairment exists within the semantic system, both picture naming and picture comprehension should be impaired. That is, as well as being unable to name the picture, the patient should show little knowledge of what the item may be used for, where it may be found, what it is associated with, etc. Further, according to the cascade model, we should expect the problem to be more severe for some classes of objects than others (in particular, for objects from categories with structurally similar exemplars rather than objects from categories with structurally distinct exemplars).

In addition to problems due to impaired semantic knowledge, we also predict problems in picture naming will arise because of either (a) deficits in accessing the structural description system, (b) deficits in accessing semantics from structural knowledge, or (c) deficits in accessing phonology from the semantic system. And, if we need to draw on information from the structural description system in order to draw objects from memory or to give definitions concerning the perceptual characteristics of objects (e.g. Riddoch & Humphreys, 1987), patients with impaired structural knowledge will also be poor at drawing and defining objects.

This framework allows us to account for a broad range of processing problems.

3.1. Impairments to the Structural Description System

Until recently, few investigators examined whether patients with picture naming problems had good access to structural knowledge about the objects they failed to name. In part, this was because information processing models did not make explicit the contrast between structural and semantic knowledge about objects. It was also because appropriate tasks had not been devised to tap the structural description system selectively. One such task is the object decision task, where subjects have to decide whether a given picture portrays a real or a "constructed" object. We have developed a version of this task in which the distractor objects are created by interchanging the features of objects from the same category. This produces distractors which are highly similar to their real counterparts (see Fig. 4.4). Subjects find it difficult to reject these distractors on the basis of their general physical structure, and we suggest that such object decisions

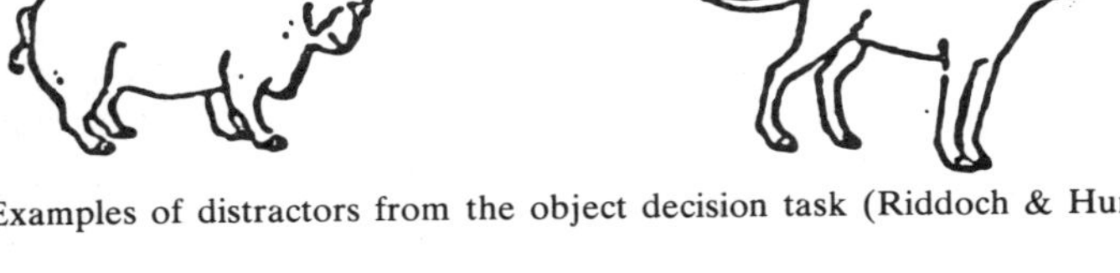

FIG. 4.4. Examples of distractors from the object decision task (Riddoch & Humphreys, 1987).

can only be made with reference to stored structural knowledge concerning particular objects. Interestingly, under conditions where normal subjects manifest associative priming between pairs of pictures in a picture naming task (Humphreys et al., in press, experiment 2), they can show no sign of associative priming in object decision (Humphreys & Riddoch, Note 1). This suggests the independence of structural and semantic (associative) knowledge in normal object processing.

One patient with a particular problem in object decision tasks has been reported by Sartori and Job (in press). Their patient was severely impaired at naming pictures of animate objects (e.g., animals and vegetables). This deficit was accompanied by a variety of other problems. On object decision tasks he tended to classify distractors as real objects. When asked to give definitions of objects he would "graft" erroneous features onto them (e.g., he described an oyster as having four legs). Furthermore, when subsequently given his erroneous definitions, he often accepted them as being correct. Thus, the patient was good at accepting the appropriate structural information about an object as correct, but poor at rejecting inappropriate information. This pattern of performance fits most comfortably with the distributed processing account of the structural description system. For instance, within a distributed system, inappropriate "parts" might be grafted onto objects because of "cross-talk" between strongly interconnected processing units. This cross-talk could arise from noisy interactions within the structural description system (Section 2.3.4). Consequently, activity within the structural description system might never reach a stable state, impairing object naming. This problem would naturally be worse with objects from categories which share common parts (and so have strongly interconnected processing units) than with objects from categories with few common parts. In addition, it would also be characteristic of the patient's definitions, when the definitions draw on structural information about the objects (cf. Riddoch & Humphreys, 1987; Riddoch, Humphreys, Coltheart, & Funnell, in press).

Job and Sartori's patient suffered brain damage due to a herpes viral infection. Warrington and Shallice (1984) have recently reported quite similar data on other patients with a history of herpes simplex encephalitis. Warrington and Shallice studied two patients in most detail (J.B.R. and S.B.Y.). Both patients were densely amnesic, word production was relatively intact while visual object identification and word comprehension were impaired. In both patients, knowledge of inanimate objects was spared relative to knowledge about living things and food. The problem was apparent with naming pictures of objects, naming an object from a verbal description, miming the use of an object and picture/word match tasks. Warrington and Shallice argue that these findings provide compelling evidence for the categorical organisation of semantic memory. That is, that semantic information pertinent to animate objects (living things, food, etc.) is stored independently of semantic information about inanimate objects, and so it can be selectively affected by brain damage. However, some of the data provided by J.B.R. and S.B.Y. do not fit this idea. For instance, in a verbal definitions task J.B.R. demonstrated preserved knowledge of weather and land-formation exemplars, but poor knowledge about different cloths and precious stones. These preserved and impaired instances do not conform to the inanimate/animate distinction. An alternative suggestion is that animate objects, and possibly also objects such as cloths and precious stones, are defined on the basis of their perceptual features, whereas other types of object are defined on the basis of their function (see Warrington & Shallice, 1984). Patients with impaired perceptual knowledge would accordingly have particular difficulty defining animate objects. This impairment could be due either to the complete ablation of some units within the structural description system, or to increased "noise" levels across the system: In either case, this could produce a category-specific deficit in naming as well as defining animate objects (because object naming will also require access to the structural description system and because animate objects tend to produce higher levels of interaction even in the normal system; see Section 2.3.4).

The patients we have discussed hitherto have all tended to have problems with a number of categories of animate object (including animals, food, flowers, etc.). Hart, Berndt, and Caramazza (1985) have reported a patient, M.D., who seemed to show a consistent impairment in naming only fruits and vegetables. This problem was again observed both in object naming and in naming to definition, and M.D. had some difficulty in categorising pictures of fruits and vegetables (categorising some vegetables as fruit, etc.). However, M.D. had good knowledge about the category, size, shape, texture, and colour of these stimuli when their names were read aloud.

M.D.'s case is interesting because, when he is given their names, he appears to have intact knowledge about the objects which he otherwise finds hard to identify. Unfortunately, Hart et al. (1985) provide insufficient data to assess whether this knowledge is retained at the structural or the semantic level, or both. In this respect it would be interesting to examine M.D.'s ability to perform an object decision task using fruits and vegetables, to test the intactness of structural knowledge. If we assume that he has both intact structural and semantic knowledge, then M.D.'s performance suggests that name retrieval processes are category-specific. For instance, there might be transmission lines from the semantic to the phonological system which are devoted specifically to fruits and vegetables. As we have already discussed, the cascade model does predict some category-specific problems in retrieving the names of objects if there are generally increased "noise" levels within the structural and semantic systems, with any problems being most pronounced for objects from categories with structurally similar exemplars. This could account for a patient being impaired at naming fruits and vegetables, but such an impairment should be accompanied by problems in naming other structurally similar objects. In the limit, the problem should be confined to objects which have the closest "clustering" of structural features—conforming to Rosch's base level representation. That is, patients might find it hard to differentiate objects which can all be assigned to the same base level of representation (e.g., different birds, flowers, or insects). Different fruits and different vegetables are not assigned the same base level representations (although there will be quite high levels of overlap between the different stimuli), and so they ought to be *less* difficult than these other objects. However, before we conclude that a general problem (such as increased "noise" levels) could not account for M.D.'s behaviour, we should also note that rigorous testing of these other categories did not take place. It remains possible that his problem lay within the structural description system (generating poor object naming and naming fruits and vegetables to definitions which tap this system). His good performance when given the object names could then stem from intact semantic knowledge.

Interestingly, Bub, Black, Hampson, and Kertesz (in press) have recently reported data on a patient whose problem does seem to be confined to retrieving specific information about objects which can be assigned the same base level representation. Their patient, M.P., was a severe global aphasic who was almost completely unable to name pictures or objects. She was very poor at categorising words and showed no semantic priming between words although she was relatively good at word naming (Bub, Cancelliere, & Kertesz, 1985). Nonetheless, she appeared to have some ability to recognise pictures, as her picture-word matching was above chance. Bub et al. argue that M.P. matches a picture to a word by identifying the picture, retrieving the label and then judging whether the word and the picture are assigned similar names. This hypothesis is supported by the fact that M.P. was capable of rhyme judgements between pictures and words (scoring about 80% correct). However, she was affected by phonological and by semantic confusibility. For example, in one task, M.P. was required to judge whether a simultaneously presented word and a picture referred to the same concept; on the negative trials the accompanying word was either neutral, phonologically similar or semantically similar to the target. She made 21% errors with a phonologically related distractor and 45% errors with a semantically related distractor (chance being 50% correct). This suggests that M.P. was far from perfect at accessing either full semantic or name information from pictures. If this were the case, then her relatively good rhyme judgements may be attributed to an ability to use the phonological description derived from the word to select between partial phonological descriptions derived from the picture.

M.P.'s difficulty in distinguishing between semantically related items was more apparent with some categories than others (in particular, birds, dogs, and flowers rather than musical instruments, tools, and fruits/vegetables). Bub et al. (in press) interpret these data in terms of the notion that recognition proceeds via access to base level representations (cf. Rosch, 1975). It is argued that M.P. can access semantics using base but not other levels of representation. Accordingly, she can access correct semantics for objects which are represented individually at the base level (e.g., vegetables, tools, etc.) but not those without individual base level representations (e.g., types of birds, types of dogs, etc.).

There are, however, problems with the above interpretation of M.P.'s data. First, the entry point to the semantic system cannot exist solely at the base level because we can access specific semantic knowledge about objects without individual base level representations (Section 2.3.4). Also, normal subjects do not show a base level advantage for all objects (e.g., with atypical subordinates; Jolicoeur et al., 1984). The cascade model holds that base level effects are a by-product of high levels of structural similarity between particular objects, and, in the distributed processing version of the model, the effects will stem from strong patterns of co-activation between processing units common to different objects with similar structures. In normality, atypical category exemplars may have sufficiently distinctive features to inhibit these patterns of co-activation, reducing any base level effects. It is of some interest, then, that Bub et al's patient did not find picture-word matching to a typical members of base level categories any easier than to typical category members. Unlike normal subjects, she was *not* sensitive to item typicality. One interpretation of the result is that the normal inhibitory processes did not occur, producing a dominance for base level terms in name retrieval. If her matching and picture-categorisation performance were highly dependent on (even partial) name retrieval, she should manifest a strong base level bias. If we are correct in this supposition, then M.P.'s performance emphasises the importance of inhibitory processes in normal picture naming.

3.2. From Structure To Semantics

Our conclusions concerning patients such as M.D. (Hart et al., 1985) and M.P. (Bub et al., in press) have had to be limited because no tests were administered to assess whether structural knowledge could be accessed normally. We (Riddoch & Humphreys, 1987) have been able to test this in a patient, J.B., who shows some similarity to the above patients. J.B. was poor at object naming and at matching associatively related objects from vision. This suggests some problem in accessing semantic knowledge from vision. In contrast, he was perfectly capable of naming an object from a definition of its function, and of matching associatively related objects when given their names. There seemed to be no impairment of semantic knowledge *per se*. J.B. was also able to perform difficult object decision tasks at a normal level (e.g., he could reject distractors such as those shown in Fig. 4.4 as not being real objects). His structural knowledge seemed to be intact. It follows that J.B.'s problem occured in accessing the semantic system following intact access to the structural description system.

Two other results were of interest. First, his ability to match a picture with its name was poor only if the picture was surrounded by distractors which were visually and semantically similar to target (e.g., a cow, surrounded by a pig, a horse, and a donkey). It was not strongly affected by distractors which were semantically but not visually related. Secondly, he found it more difficult to name objects from categories with structurally similar exemplars than to name objects from categories with more distinctive exemplars. These last two results both suggest that the process of accessing the semantic system from vision is influenced by the structural similarity between an object and its "neighbours", as would be expected if this access process operates in cascade.

The cascade model can also account for a rather different pattern of results reported by Howard and Orchard-Lisle (1984). Their patient, J.C.U., was a global aphasic with severe impairment at naming stimuli presented in all modalities. Her comprehension was limited and spontaneous speech was restricted to a few recurrent utterances. Her picture naming was markedly facilitated by the use of the correct phonemic cue. However, when given a co-ordinate cue (e.g., the initial phoneme of the name of an object which was a semantic co-ordinate of the target item), her naming of the target picture was not facilitated and she made a large number of semantic errors (32/102) and the number of "no responses" was doubled. She also tended to accept her semantic errors as correct, while this was not the case for other error types (e.g., she accepted 55% of her semantic paraphasias, compared to only 7% of word paraphasias). Interestingly, when the same experiment was repeated using words rather than pictures, a co-ordinate cue did not result in a large number of semantic errors.

Unfortunately, the evidence concerning J.C.U.'s access to semantic information from pictures is equivocal. She performed well on a picture association test which required the use of specific semantic information to make an association between the stimulus and a target (e.g., matching the picture of an eskimo to a picture of a house or of an igloo). She did not perform as well on a picture categorisation test where she had to match a target picture to one of two others on the basis of rather more general semantic information (e.g., an elephant with a giraffe or a dog).

Two interpretations of J.C.U.'s performance are therefore possible. One is that she has an impoverished semantic representation of a picture (e.g., Howard & Orchard-Lisle, 1984), and that she has insufficient semantic information to distinguish between a particular object and its closest semantic co-ordinates. An alternative account is that J.C.U. has a problem in accessing phonological information from a semantic description, although the semantic description is itself relatively intact.

The first interpretation assumes that J.C.U. makes semantic errors because of an incomplete semantic description. In order to explain the increased errors which occurred with the initial phonemic cue of a semantic co-ordinate, this account must further assume that there is feedback from the phonological lexicon to the semantic system, leading to the selection of an incorrect semantic entry (see A.W. Ellis, 1985). The second interpretation assumes that J.C.U.'s semantic errors reflect inaccurate addressing of the phonological lexicon from a reasonably complete semantic description. The increase in semantic errors from cueing the co-ordinate would then stem from the increased probability of incorrect selection of an output entry. We must also explain why J.C.U. accepted her incorrect semantic errors. The semantic-deficit hypothesis posits that J.C.U. takes as correct the semantic description currently most available (whether this is from cueing or from the picture). The output-deficit hypothesis either assumes the same position (e.g., if there is feedback from phonology to semantics, then the accepted phonological representation may also re-activate its own semantic description), or it posits that J.C.U. takes as correct the phonological description currently most available. We may note here that Howard and Orchard-Lisle themselves reject the possibility of J.C.U. having an output impairment because there is little evidence in the normal population of such output errors in spontaneous speech. However, this ignores the fact that normally any inappropriate phonological representations which may become activated by feed-forward from the semantic system (if information transmission is operating continuously) will rapidly become inhibited. Also there is evidence of the feed-forward of information from the semantic to the phonological system in normal subjects, witness the structural similarity × name frequency interaction observed by Humphreys et al. (in press; see Section 2.3.4).

3.3. From Semantics to Phonology

Impaired picture naming may still occur even though the semantic system is adjudged to be intact and can be accessed normally. This is commonly thought to be the case for many aphasic patients who give partial descriptions of objects (circumlocutions) when they are unable to retrieve the correct name. One interesting factor is that aphasic subgroups demonstrate a remarkable degree of similarity in the distribution of different types of naming errors. Kohn and Goodglass (1985) examined Broca's aphasics, Wernicke's aphasics, conduction aphasics, frontal anomics, and posterior anomics. Semantic errors (including superordinates, co-ordinates, contextual associates, or materials from which the target was made) were prominent for all aphasic subgroups, comprising 36% of total errors. There was no significant difference between the groups for the production of semantic errors. Phonemic errors (these contained significant phonological elements of the target word such as the initial consonant cluster or stressed syllable) were also prominent, comprising 33% of total errors. The conduction aphasics were responsible for the largest number of phonemic errors.

Butterworth, Howard, and McLoughlin (1984) included Broca's, Wernicke's, conduction, and anomic aphasics within their experimental group. Here, 66·7% of the total errors were classed as semantically related word paraphasias. This group included co-ordinate, superordinate, co/superordinate, part, description/use, and associate word responses. Phonological paraphasias comprised 7·3% of the total errors. Again, the number of semantic paraphasias was not found to be related to any particular diagnostic group while phonemic errors were most likely to be associated with Wernicke's and conduction aphasics.

We have discussed cases where the semantic access process seems to be affected by the visual similarity between objects, consistent with the cascade model of picture naming. The cascade model also holds that activation in the semantic representations will be transmitted to the phonological lexicon of all candidate objects prior to phonological access being completed. Therefore the activation of phonological labels of objects semantically related to a given target should be reflected in the naming errors for patients whose problem is specifically an output problem (i.e., for patients who clearly recognise a pictorial item and can indicate how it might be used, where it might be found, etc., indicating intact access to semantic information).

We should not assume, therefore, that semantic errors reflect only partial access to semantic information; this possibility must be tested directly. One way to do this is to ask the patient to perform picture-word matching. Typically, patients who make semantic naming errors have no difficulty in picture-word matches when the distractor items are drawn from a different semantic category relative to the target item (Butterworth et al., 1984); however, if the distractor items are drawn from the same semantic category as the target item, errors are made (Gainotti, 1976). Furthermore, patients whose characteristic naming error is semantically related to the target give a high rate of semantic pointing errors (Gainotti, Miceli, Callagirone, Silveri, & Masullo, 1981). It should be noted, however, that despite a relationship between semantic pointing errors and naming failure, aphasic patients are as likely to name pictures on which they have made a semantic pointing error as those on which they have made none (Butterworth et al., 1984).

These data may be taken to indicate a semantic deficit in aphasic patients; that is, picture-word matching is poor with semantic distractors because subjects have an incomplete semantic description of the target object. This deficit could contribute to their naming deficit. However, another explanation is possible which holds that the patient's problem resides within the phonological lexicon. It may be that activation in the phonological lexicon of at least some patients never reaches a stable state, with the result that there is simultaneous activation of the target name plus phonologically and semantically similar item names. If responses in the picture-word task are based on the phonological representations of the objects, the activation of the names of many objects from the same semantic field may result in incorrect pointing when the distractor items are semantically similar to the target.

Alternatively, Butterworth et al. (1984) argue that the data may best be explained by postulating a lesion within a "semantic lexicon". This is an additional representation linking the phonological description of an object to its semantic representation. A lesion here could add noise to the system, disrupting both output from the semantic representation to the phonological description, and input to the semantic system from auditory words (when a pointing task is used; Butterworth et al., 1984; Gainotti, 1976; Gainotti et al., 1981). Such a "noisy" system would also lead to inconsistent performance, so that incorrect pointing to a picture paired with semantic distractors may occur together with correct picture naming.

Howard, Patterson, Franklin, Orchard-Lisle, and Morton (1985) also support the notion that semantic errors in naming do not implicate an impaired semantic representation. They describe two groups of aphasic subjects with differential performance on the picture association test used by Howard and Orchard-Lisle (1984, see Section 3.2). These patients were asked to name pictures of common objects, and, after their initial naming response they were asked to perform a picture-word matching task (with semantically related distractors) prior to renaming the pictures. The benefit of the picture-word match task on renaming was as great for those patients who performed normally on the picture association test as it was for those who did not; also, the effects of the picture-word matching task were relatively long lasting (being found up to 24 hours later), unlike phonemic cueing effects. Howard et al. (1985) argue that the facilitation from picture-word matching must occur post-semantically since it occurred equally for unsuccessful and successful patients in the picture association test.[4] However, the effect also does not appear to have its locus within the phonological lexicon, given its different time course relative to phonemic cueing. Howard et al. therefore suggest that the locus of the facilitation is within a further system, the semantic lexicon (discussed earlier).

Over a series of experiments, the tasks found to produce effective long-term facilitation of picture naming by Howard et al. (1985) were:

1. Pointing and naming a target item from an array of unrelated distractors.
2. Pointing to a target item in an array of unrelated distractors.
3. Making a semantic judgement about the item (for example, "does the cow eat grass?").
4. A written word/picture match condition.

Facilitators that were effective in the short term only were: (1) repetition of the target name; (2) rhyme judgements; and (3) rhyme cues.

Thus, the effective long-term facilitators were those tasks which emphasised semantic processing in comprehension; facilitators which provide subjects with information about the phonological characteristics of a picture name were only temporally effective. We may note here that the types of facilitator used by Howard et al. resemble tasks used in depth of processing experiments. Many studies have shown that different levels of stimulus analysis produce quite different memory performances and, in particular, that semantic processing tasks produce better memory performance than "shallow" processing tasks such as rhyme judgements (see Craik & Lockhart, 1972). It could well be, then, that tasks which induce "deep" processing in patients provide long-term picture-naming facilitation by enabling subjects to tag output lexicon entries. Indeed, for the patients used in Howard et al.'s study the mean probability of correct naming was the same whether the distractors in the picture-word match task were semantically related or not, unlike the patients reported by Butterworth et al. (1984), Gainotti (1976), and Gainotti et al. (1981). This emphasises that the patients used in Howard et al.'s study may have had a purely output problem with facilitation having its effect on the retrieval of output phonology.

Interestingly, Howard et al. (1985) also demonstrated that an associate word is an ineffective facilitator of picture naming in aphasic patients (both with long- and short-term cueing). They offer two explanations of this

[4] The assumption here is that patients who are poor at the picture-association task fail to achieve an adequate semantic representation of the picture (Howard & Orchard-Lisle, 1984). If picture-word matching facilitates naming due to semantic activation it would selectively benefit those patients with inadequate semantic representations of the pictures.

result: either inhibition may occur from the elements of meaning that distinguish the associate and the target, so performance is not boosted; or the semantic information accessed by both the target and its associate is not sufficient to specify the difference between the two stimuli. According to the cascade model of picture naming, the name codes of items which are phonologically similar and of items which are semantically similar will be activated in conjunction with the activation of the target name. The correct name will only be selected when sufficient evidence has accumulated within the system to inhibit other activated name codes. For patients with an output naming problem, interactions between the semantic and phonological systems may be weak, giving rise to naming errors. Moreover, such errors will tend to be either phonologically or semantically related to the target object (Butterworth et al., 1984; Kohn & Goodglass, 1985). An associate prime will not facilitate target naming because it will primarily strengthen its own activation within the system, thereby providing more competition for the target.

The cascade model can also account for the findings of Podraza and Darley (1977). In their study, aphasic patients were given a word (or a series of words) prior to a picture which they were to name. Relative to when no cue was given, they found that picture naming was enhanced when the pre-stimulation cue was phonemically related to the target, when it was an incomplete sentence which could be completed by the picture name (i.e., a semantic cue specific to the target) or when it was a series of three unrelated words containing the target name. However, naming was significantly *impaired* if the pre-stimulation cue was a word associatively related to the target word. This suggests that inhibition between elements of meaning in the semantic system is not the cause of the lack of facilitation from associative cueing (see Howard et al., 1984), since elements of meaning should also be activated by the sentence. The reason the sentence works is probably because it provides semantic information specific to the target (and the target's name), thus overriding other output competition.

4. CONCLUSIONS

A possible framework to account for picture naming has been put forward. It has been argued that, following low level perceptual processing (e.g., the segmentation of figure from its background, the integration of local and global form descriptions, etc.) at least three distinct representations must be accessed prior to the naming of a picture; these are a stored structural description (the object form), a semantic representation, and stored phonology. Further, we have suggested that access to these representations operates continuously (i.e., in cascade) following activation of object form knowledge. We believe that the cascade model provides a broad framework which can at present accommodate data from both normal picture naming (Section 2.3.4) and from patients with acquired brain damage (Section 3), without the need either to posit direct connections between structural descriptions and stored phonology for objects or to posit the existence of additional representations (such as a semantic lexicon). Two of the most important consequences of adopting a cascade framework for picture naming are that it provides an explicit account of why picture naming differs from naming responses to stimuli presented in other modalities (such as words), and of why category-specific effects occur in the naming of particular objects (whether reflected in the differential sensitivity of normal response latencies to variables such as structural similarity and name frequency, or in the selective breakdowns following brain damage). Future studies will need to pay close attention to the characteristics of individual stimuli, and of the relations between stimuli, in order to analyse the picture naming system.

ACKNOWLEDGEMENTS

The work reported in this chapter was supported by grants from the Chest, Heart and Stroke Association and from the MRC to both authors, and by a grant from the ESRC to the second author. We would like to thank Elaine Funnell for comments on an earlier draft of the chapter, Max Coltheart for discussion of the work, and Philip Quinlan for his comments and for carrying out the correlational analyses.

REFERENCES

Bartram, D. J. (1974). The role of visual and semantic codes in picture naming. *Cognitive Psychology, 6,* 325–356

Bartram, D. J. (1976). Levels of coding in picture-picture comparison tasks. *Memory and Cognition, 4,* 593-602.

Beauvois, M.-F. & Saillant, B. (1985). Optic aphasia for colours and colour agnosia: A distinction between visual and visuo-verbal impairments in the processing of colours. *Cognitive Neuropsychology, 2,* 1–48.

Bub, D., Black, S., Hampson, E., & Kertesz, A. (in press). Semantic encoding from pictures and words: Some neuropsychological observations. *Cognitive Neuropsychology.*

Bub, D., Cancelliere, A., & Kertesz, A. (1985). Whole-word and analytic translation of spelling to sound in a non-semantic reader. In K. E. Patterson, J. C. Marshall, and M. Coltheart (Eds.), *Surface dyslexia: Neuropsychological and cognitive studies of phonological reading*. London: Lawrence Erlbaum Associates Ltd.

Butterworth, B., Howard, D. & McLoughlin, P. (1984). The semantic deficit in aphasia: The relationship between semantic errors in auditory comprehension and picture naming. *Neuropsychologia, 22,* 409–426.

Carr, T. H., McCauley, C., Sperber, R. D., & Parmalee, C. M. (1982). Words, pictures and priming: On semantic activation, conscious identification and the automaticity of information processing. *Journal of Experimental Psychology: Human Perception and Performance, 8,* 757–777.

Craik, F. I. M. & Lockhart, R. S. (1972). Levels of processing: A framework for memory research. *Journal of Verbal Learning and Verbal Behaviour, 11,* 671–684

Durso, F. T. & Johnson, M. K. (1979). Facilitation in naming and categorising repeated pictures and words. *Journal of Experimental Psychology: Human Learning and Memory, 5,* 449–459.

Ellis, A. W. (1985). The production of spoken words: A cognitive neuropsychological perspective. In A. W. Ellis (Ed.), *Progress in the psychology of language,* Vol. 2. Hillsdale, N.J.: Lawrence Erlbaum Associates Inc.

Ellis, R. (1985). *Levels of representation in vision.* Unpublished doctoral dissertation, University of Oxford.

Ellis, R. & Allport, D. A. (1985). Multiple representations for visual objects: A behavioural study. Paper presented at the *Easter Meeting of the Society for the Study of Artificial Intelligence and Simulation of Behaviour,* (Warwick, 10–12 April).

Freund, C. S. (1889). Über optische Aphasie und Seelenblindheit. *Archiv für Psychiatrie und Nervenkrankheiten, 20*, 276–297.

Gainotti, G. (1976). The relationship between the semantic impairment in comprehension and naming in aphasic patients. *British Journal of Disorders of Communication, 11,* 77–81.

Gainotti, G., Micelli, G., Caltagirone, C., Silveri, M. C., & Masullo, C. (1981). The relationship between type of naming error and semantic-lexical discrimination in aphasic patients. *Cortex, 17,* 401–410.

Goodglass, H. (1968). Studies in the grammar of aphasics. In S. Rosenberg and J. Koplin (Eds.), *Developments in applied psycholinguistics.* New York: Macmillan.

Guenther, R. K., Klatsky, R. L., & Putnam, W. (1980). Commonalities and differences in semantic decisions about pictures and words. *Journal of Verbal Learning and Verbal Behaviour, 19,* 54–74.

Hart, J., Berndt, R. S., & Caramazza, A. (1985). Category-specific naming deficit following cerebral infarction. *Nature, 316,* 439–440.

Hinton, G. E. & Anderson, J. A. (1981). *Parallel models of associative memory.* Hillsdale, N.J.: Lawrence Erlbraum Associates Inc.

Howard, D. & Orchard-Lisle, V. (1984). On the origin of semantic errors in naming: Evidence from a case of a global aphasic. *Cognitive Neuropsychology, 1,* 163–190.

Howard, D., Patterson, K., Franklin, S., Orchard-Lisle, V., & Morton, J. (1985). The facilitation of picture naming in aphasia. *Cognitive Neuropsychology*, *2*, 49–80.

Humphreys, G. W. (1985). Attention, automaticity and autonomy in visual word processing. In D. Besner, T. G. Waller, and G. MacKinnon (Eds.), *Reading research: Advances in theory and in practice,* Vol.5. New York: Academic Press.

Humphreys, G. W. & Evett, L. J. (1985). Are there independent lexical and non-lexical routes in word processing? An evaluation of the dual route theory of reading. *The Behavioural and Brain Sciences*, *8*, 689–740.

Humphreys, G. W., Besner, D., & Quinlan, P. T. (in press). Event perception and the word repetition effect. *Journal of Experimental Psychology: General.*

Humphreys, G. W., Riddoch, M. J., & Quinlan, P. T. (in press). Cascade processes in picture identification. *Cognitive Neuropsychology*,

Jolicoeur, P., Gluck, M. A., & Kosslyn, S. M. (1984). Pictures and names: Making the connection. *Cognitive Psychology, 16,* 243–275.

Kelter, S., Grötzbach, H., Freiheit, R., Höhle, B., Wutzig, G., & Diesch, E. (1984). Object identification: The mental representation of physical and conceptual attributes. *Memory and Cognition, 12,* 123–133.

Kirsner, K., Milech, D., & Stumpfel, V. (1986). Word and picture identification: Is representational parsimony possible? *Memory and Cognition, 14,* 398–408.

Kohn, S. E., & Goodglass, H. (1985). Picture naming in aphasia. *Brain and Language, 24,* 266–283.

Kremin. H. (in press). Spared naming without comprehension. *Journal of Neurolinguistics.*

Lhermitte, F. & Beauvois, M.-F. (1973). A visual-speech disconnection syndrome. Report on a case with optic aphasia, agnosic alexia and colour agnosia. *Brain*, *96*, 695–714.

Lupker, S. J. (1979). The semantic nature of response competition in the picture-word interference task. *Memory and Cognition, 7,* 485–495.

Lupker, S. J. (1985). Relatedness effects in word and picture naming: Parallels, differences, and structural implications. In A. W. Ellis (Ed.), *Progress in the psychology of language,* Vol. 2. Hillsdale, N.J.: Lawrence Erlbaum Associates Inc.

Lupker, S. J. & Katz, A. N. (1981). Input, decision and response factors in picture-word interference. *Journal of Experimental Psychology: Human Learning and Memory, 7,* 269–282.

Marr, D. (1982). *Vision.* San Francisco: W. H. Freeman.

Marr, D., & Nishihara, H. K. (1978). Representation and recognition of the spatial organisation of three dimensional shapes. *Proceedings of the Royal Society, London, B200,* 269–294.

McClelland, J. L. (1979). On the time relations of mental processes: An examination of systems of processes in cascade. *Psychological Review, 86,* 287–330.

McClelland, J. L. & Rumelhart, D. E. (1985). Distributed memory and the representation of general and specific information. *Journal of Experimental Psychology: General, 114,* 159–188.

Meyer, D. E., Yantis, S., Osman, A. M., & Smith, J. E. K. (1985). Temporal properties of human information processing: Tests of discrete versus continuous models. *Cognitive Psychology, 17,* 445–518.

Miller, J. (1982). Divided attention: Evidence for coactivation with redundant signals. *Cognitive Psychology, 14,* 247–279.

Monsell, S. (1985). Repetition and the lexicon. In A. W. Ellis (Ed.), *Progress in the psychology of language,* Vol. 2. Hillsdale, N.J.: Lawrence Erlbaum Associates Inc.

Morton, J. & Patterson, K. E. (1980). A new attempt at an interpretation, or an attempt at a new interpretation. In M. Coltheart, K. E. Patterson, and J. C. Marshall (Eds.), *Deep dyslexia.* London: Routledge and Kegan Paul.

Murphy, G. L. & Smith, E. E. (1982). Basic level superiority in picture categorization. *Journal of Verbal Learning and Verbal Behaviour, 21,* 1–20.

Murphy, G. L. & Brownell, H. H. (1985). Category differentiation in object recognition: Typicality constraints on the basic category advantage. *Journal of Experimental Psychology: Learning Memory and Cognition,11,* 70–84.

Navon, D. (1977). Forest before trees: The precedence of global tectures in visual perception. *Cognitive Psychology*, *9*, 353–385.

Oldfield, R. C. (1966). Things, words and the brain. *Quarterly Journal of Experimental Psychology, 18,* 340–353.

Podraza, B. L. & Darley, F. L. (1977). Effect of auditory pre-stimulation on naming in aphasia. *Journal of Speech and Hearing Research, 20,* 669–683.

Potter, M. C. & Faulconer, B. (1975). Time to understand pictures and words. *Nature, 253,* 437–438.

Ratcliff, G. & Newcombe, F. (1982). Object recognition: Some deductions from clinical evidence. In A. W. Ellis (Ed.), *Normality and pathology in cognitive functions*. London: Academic Press.

Riddoch, M. J. & Humphreys, G. W. (1987). Visual object processing in a case of optic aphasia (semantic access agnosia). *Cognitive Neuropsychology*, *4*, 131–186.

Riddoch, M. J., Humphreys, G. W., Coltheart, M., & Funnell, E. (in press). Semantic system or systems? Neuropsychological evidence re-examined. *Cognitive Neuropsychology.*

Rosch, E., Mervis, C. B., Gray, W. D., Johnson, D. M., & Boyes-Bream, P. (1976). Basic objects in natural categories. *Cognitive Psychology, 8,* 382–439.

Rosinski, R. R. (1977). Picture-word interference is semantically based. *Child Development, 48,* 643–647.
Sartori, G. & Job, R. (in press). The oyster with four legs: A neuropsychological study of the interaction of visual and semantic information. *Cognitive Neuropsychology,*
Scarborough, D. L., Gerard, L., & Cortese, C. (1979). Accessing lexical memory: The transfer of word repetition effects across task and modality. *Memory and Cognition, 7,* 3–12.
Schwartz, M. F., Marin, O. S. M., & Saffran, E. M. (1979). Dissociations of language function in dementia: A case study. *Brain and Language, 7,* 277–306.
Shallice, T. (1987). Impairments of semantic processing: Multiple dissociations. In M. Coltheart, R. Job, and G. Sartori (Eds.). *The cognitive neuropsychology of language.* London: Lawrence Erlbaum Associates Ltd.
Smith, E. E., Shoben, E. J., & Rips, L. J. (1974). Structure and process in semantic memory: A featural model for semantic decision. *Psychological Review, 81,* 214–241.
Snodgrass, J. G. & McCullough, B. (1986). The role of visual similarity in picture categorization. *Journal of Experimental Psychology: Learning, Memory and Cognition, 12,* 147–154.
Snodgrass, J. G. & Vanderwart, M. A. (1980). Standardized set of 260 pictures: Norms of name agreement, usage agreement, familiarity and visual complexity. *Journal of Experimental Psychology: Human Learning and Memory, 6,* 174–215.
Sperber, R. D., McCauley, C., Ragain, R., & Weil, C. (1979). Semantic priming effects on picture and word processing. *Memory and Cognition, 7,* 339–345.
Spreen, O., Benton, A. L., & Van Allen, M. W. (1966). Dissociation of visual and tactile naming in amnesic aphasia. *Neurology, Minneap., 16,* 807–814.
Stemberger, J. P. (1984). Structural errors in normal and agrammatic speech. *Cognitive Neuropsychology, 1,* 281–313.
Vanderwart, M. (1984). Priming by pictures in lexical decision. *Journal of Verbal Learning and Verbal Behaviour, 23,* 67–83.
Warren, C. E. J. & Morton, J. (1982). The effects of priming on picture recognition. *British Journal of Psychology, 73,* 117–130.
Warrington, E. K. & Shallice, T. (1984). Category specific semantic impairments. *Brain, 107,* 829–854.
Wingfield, A. (1968). Effects of frequency on identification and naming of objects. *American Journal of Psychology, 81,* 226–234.

REFERENCE NOTE

1. Humphreys, G. W. & Riddoch, M. J. *Processes in normal object recognition and naming.* Paper presented to the Fifth Cognitive Nueropsychology Workshop, Bressanone, N. Italy, January 1987.

5 Information Processing and Laterality Effects for Object and Face Perception

Justine Sergent
Department of Neurology, McGill University,
Montreal Neurological Institute, 3801 University Street,
Montreal PQ, H3A 2B4, Canada

1. INTRODUCTION

Human information processing capacities are the product of a highly adaptive and versatile nervous system that provides individuals with various alternative means for representing, and operating on, information about the world. This versatility and adaptivity can be partly attributed to the conformation of the brain whose two hemispheres are not functional duplicates of one another but are endowed with their own specific skills, thus increasing the brain's processing capacities while avoiding potential conflicts that would result from promiscuity. Evidence for such a functional hemispheric asymmetry has accumulated for more than a century through the study of neurological patients with damage to one or the other hemisphere, and it has recently been supplemented by research on neurologically intact subjects through the use of techniques allowing an initial segregation of the input to one side or the other of the brain. One such technique is based on lateral tachistoscopic presentation and takes advantage of the anatomical organisation of the visual system whereby the left hemiretinae of both eyes project to the left hemisphere and the right hemiretinae to the right hemisphere. By restricting stimuli to only one visual field, one may determine which of the hemispheres must initiate cerebral processing, and by observing the manner in which responses to various types of stimuli differ for right and left visual field presentations, one may make inferences about the functional asymmetry of the two hemispheres. The general validity and reliability of this technique have been suggested by its capacity to produce results in broad agreement with findings from unilaterally brain damaged patients as well as to discriminate group-performance of left- and right-handed subjects who typically differ in their respective cerebral organisation (e.g., Corballis, 1983). The relative ease with which tachistoscopic experiments can be implemented, together with the view that knowledge becomes more secure through the convergence of differing lines of evidence, has thus contributed to making visual laterality studies one important source of information about functional cerebral asymmetry.

However, the use of lateral tachistoscopic presentation of information as a means of investigating hemispheric specialisation of functions is confronted with a series of difficulties pertaining not only to the technique itself but also to the very problem under study, that of the localisation of functions in the brain. Some of these difficulties are worth pointing out, and they can arise (1) from stimulating the retina for a very brief time in areas of reduced acuity; (2) from the numerous factors that can influence the amplitude and the direction of perceptual asymmetries, some of which may not be directly related to cerebral asymmetry (see Hellige & Sergent, 1986); (3) from a lack of reliable methods for determining whether an observed pattern of visual-field asymmetry reflects unequal hemispheric efficiency or interhemispheric transfer to the "specialised" hemisphere ("direct access' or "callosal relay" interpretations, see Zaidel, 1983), which precludes unequivocal identification of the respective contribution of the hemispheres to a given performance; and (4) from the absence of direct correspondence between anatomical structures and psychological functions. In addition, it is probably fair to say that visual laterality studies in normals have not shown much sophistication in specifying the component operations involved in the realisation of a particular function, which would be necessary to characterise the nature of hemispheric specialisation and the modalities of hemispheric co-operation. Results are often interpreted as if the lateral tachistoscopic presentation created a functional "split-brain", with information being processed exclusively by the hemisphere that receives it, except in conditions where a verbal response has to be produced after left-visual-field presentation. This approach may in fact derive from the clinical tradition in neurology whereby psychological and cognitive functions shown to be impaired in behavioural tests are assumed to be localised in the area that is damaged. Interpretations of findings from normal and neurological subjects are thus made on the ground that only one hemisphere is effectively involved in the realisation of a task and that, in normal subjects, transfer takes place only when the hemisphere has exhausted its processing resources, implying that the two hemispheres cannot be at work simultaneously. Such an assumption rests on an over-simplification of the functioning of the brain, and there is ample evidence that the two hemispheres are engaged in the processing of information, even after unilateral stimulation (e.g., Gevins, 1983; Risberg, Halsey, Wills, & Wilson, 1975).

In spite of these difficulties and of our ignorance regarding most of the functioning of the brain, research on cerebral lateralisation of functions has been very active and productive, and much information is available that sheds some light on the processing efficiency of the cerebral hemispheres. The present chapter addresses certain aspects of this issue, and examines the respective contribution of the hemispheres to the operations underlying object perception. The approach adopted here will be mainly concerned with defining some of the conditions that determine the processing efficiency of the hemispheres, as a function of the information that is made available by the sensory system and that needs to be processed to achieve optimal performance. After discussing some of the factors that have to be taken into account in such an approach, empirical data from studies with normal subjects will be examined and compared with those obtained from brain damaged patients.

1.1. Objects and Faces

A preliminary remark is necessary at the outset concerning the choice made here, due to the scarcity of laterality studies using common objects as stimuli, to discuss the problem of object perception by drawing on findings from research on face perception and recognition. There are indeed experimental and clinical findings suggesting that different mechanisms may underlie face and object recognition, which has led to the view that faces constitute a special class of stimuli (e.g., Carey, 1981; Yin, 1978). For example, when subjects are required to remember objects of various categories within the same experiment, they are more proficient with faces than with any other category (Freedman & Haber, 1974), and with known faces than with unknown faces (Klatsky & Forrest, 1984). This may indicate that our long experience with faces has enabled us to access consistent dimensions that facilitate perception and memory, more so than with any other object. In addition, the findings by Yin (1969, 1970) that recognition of faces suffers more than recognition of other objects from inversion, and that damage to the right or the left cerebral hemisphere differentially affects recognition of upright and inverted faces, have been interpreted as an indication that there exists in the brain a specific area that is uniquely devoted to the processing of faces. This suggestion has found support in clinical evidence of a dissociation, in some patients, between object agnosia and prosopagnosia (Hécaen, 1981; Meadows, 1974).

None of these findings, however, appears to be sufficiently compelling to postulate that faces, considered as visual objects (independently of facial expression of emotion), are treated in a manner qualitatively different from that involved in processing other visual objects. Certainly, there are few, if any, other categories of objects that have so high intra-class similarity while carrying with them such personal, social, affective, and communicative importance that we need pay as much attention to them as we do to faces. In this sense, faces are the most familiar objects with which we are confronted, and they may therefore be processed more efficiently. However, experimental findings suggesting a dissociation between faces and other objects lack robustness. For example, Toyama (1975) failed to replicate Yin's (1969) finding when a different set of face stimuli was used, as did Bruyer (1983) with respect to Yin's (1970) report of a double dissociation of object category and cerebral hemisphere. In addition, post-mortem anatomical evidence of bilateral cerebral damage in all patients suffering from prosopagnosia (e.g., Meadows, 1974) is difficult to reconcile with the view that a unique cortical area localised in the right hemisphere is devoted to the processing of faces. More telling is the finding that some prosopagnosics who, by hobby or professional obligation, had become highly familiar with a particular class of objects characterised by a high intra-class similarity (such as furniture, cows, birds, cars), were also defective at recognising these objects (e.g., Assal, Favre, & Anderes, 1984; Bornstein, Skroka, & Munitz, 1969; Meadows, 1974). Thus, there does not seem to be any fundamental qualitative difference between faces and other classes of objects in the way they are visually processed, when familiarity and high intra-class similarity are ruled out as distinctive variables (see Sergent, in press). It remains that, as social animals, humans need to discriminate between members of the group, and the face may prove the most effective and reliable cue for this purpose. To the extent that the brain shapes its processing capacities as a function of the individual's needs (discussed later), highly efficient mechanisms for discriminating and recognising faces may have evolved in the human brain. However, this high efficiency, even if mainly restricted to faces in most people, potentially applies to the processing of any class of object that carries special importance and relevance for an individual.

2. INFORMATION PROCESSING

Most research on the cerebral lateralisation of functions has been concerned with specifying what characterises, and differentiates, the respective modes of functioning of the two hemispheres. Following the primary interest of clinical neurologists in behavioural deficits as a function of the side of the lesion, experimental neuropsychologists emphasised the processing characteristics of the tasks required from the subjects and described the specialisations of the hemispheres in terms of processing dichotomies that could encompass the various operations mediated by each side of the brain (e.g., verbal/visuo-spatial and analytic/holistic dichotomies). Such specialisations for diametrically opposite functions probably overstress the differences between the two hemispheres at the expense of their numerous similarities. In fact, it seems that the anatomical and organisational requirements for subserving these opposite functions in the hemispheres would be so different that it may hardly be conceivable that the brain can still be an essentially symmetrical structure with basically the same organisation on both sides. The difference between the hemispheres must therefore be rather subtle and at levels that would not impose drastically different structures to underlie the specialised mechanisms on each side.

One such possible level may be concerned with the descriptions of information as they are elaborated in the two hemispheres, and with the respective capacity of the hemispheres to operate on the various attributes of these descriptions. Although this is only one among several levels at which hemispheric specialisation may manifest itself, it offers the possibility to consider functional asymmetry in information processing by examining some of the conditions that lead to the implementation of particular operations. It may in fact be difficult to determine how information is treated unless one specifies what this information is, and, as pointed out by Garner (1970, p. 350): "too often has the nature of the input been ignored, with the consequence of incorrect assessment of the nature of information processing at worst, or an inadequate picture at best". An examination of the information to be processed may thus provide some indications regarding hemispheric processing efficiency while allowing a description of the input in terms congruent with both the physical properties of the external object and its neural representations.

2.1. Nature of Information

While models of human information processing usually concentrate on the operations carried out by the organism, there are reasons to believe that the incoming information is more than an initial stimulation that would trigger a series of operations irrespective of its properties, and that it is, in fact, one of the most important variables in determining the particular processes that can be implemented. Two characteristics of "information" may thus be worth considering.

The spatiotemporal pattern of luminous energy that impinges on the retina provides the brain with information about external objects in the form of electrical and chemical neuronal codes. The initial operations carried out by the visual system can be theoretically understood as a decomposition of the pattern of intensities into spatial sinusoids of different frequency, amplitude, and position at all possible orientations (Shapley & Lennie, 1985), leading to representations of the object that do not correspond to usual verbal descriptions but that preserve the structural and relational properties of the components of the object (see Cavanagh, 1978). These representations carry information about shape, and it is this information that the brain processes, not energy *per se*. However, the latter contributes to the quality and composition of the descriptions of the incoming information, and is therefore an important parameter in the processes underlying object perception, especially when the experimental situations involve viewing conditions unlike those typical of normal situations. In this sense, the energy dimension of visual information may prove a critical factor since it determines what is initially encoded by the visual system.

In a second, and literal sense, information is what puts form into, or gives shape to, the receiving organism, and this is typically the case of the brain whose shaping and development are largely dependent on stimulation from the external world through sensory receptors the function of which is to provide relevant descriptions for guiding behaviour. There is considerable evidence of detrimental, and sometimes irreversible, effects of visual sensory deprivation in young animals and humans (e.g., Colombo, 1982), which may also result in a profound reduction in cortical space devoted to visual processing which is taken over by other sensory modalities (Hyvärinen, Hyvärinen, & Linnankoski, 1981). It is thus through external stimulation that neural cells realise their potentialities and become selectively sensitive to relevant attributes of the visual world. These attributes consist of basic physical components of the stimulus conveyed in the array of light intensities and constitute the units into which information is initially decomposed. This ontogenetic "tuning up" of the sensory system leads to an internalisation of the lawfulness and constraints of the external world and thus permits some veridical perception.

If such an acquired selective sensitivity of visual cells reflects a basic property of neural processing, one may assume that the shaping of cerebral structures underlying cognition beyond the striate cortex is governed by rules similar to, although likely more complex than, those involved in determining the particular sensitivity of visual neurones to the physical attributes of the input. For example, our visual dealing with the external world always exposes us to specific instances of objects, and even the same instance seldom appears under exactly the same conditions; yet we are able to detect recurrences among such objects, despite variations in local stimulus energies, and thus to recognise or categorise them. Classifications and categorisations are learned methods of putting regularities into the diversity, variety, and changes of environmental stimulation, but, phenomenologically, only individual objects are real and visible. It is from a viewer-centred representation that the invariant features of an object, that make it a member of a learned category, must be recognised. Such invariants are conveyed in the particular pattern of intensity variations, and their extraction depends on the sensitivity of neural cells to the specific attributes of the descriptions of the incoming information. Repeated exposures to multiple instances of a class may thus lead to a modification of the composition, structure, and synaptic organisation of the neuronal system, updating as well as diversifying the frame of reference within which the received information is operated on. In this sense, the "stored" information is not simply used as a comparison with the incoming information from which categorisation, and meaning, can be achieved, but it is reactivated (literally, re-presented) more or less faithfully and thoroughly depending on the particular pattern of electrical and chemical events that carry the information and on the congruence between this pattern and previous occurrences (see Humphreys & Quinlan, Chapter 3, Section 3.4.2, this volume, for detailed discussion). The brain is thus functioning as a reactive recipient of information, and the efficiency and versatility of the processes underlying perception, recognition, and categorisation of objects may depend on the sensitivity of its structures to the particular attributes of the incoming information that could be made available by the sensory system, at least until the invariant physical properties have been extracted.

2.2. Some Implications

Although considering information processing in terms of a selective sensitivity of neural cells to attributes of the input that allows a reactivation of stored information addresses only one aspect of the problem, it may provide the opportunity to examine some of the conditions required for the implementation of efficient perceptual operations in the two hemispheres. Three factors may be worth considering in this respect. First, a description of the input in terms of attributes that correspond to the breaking down of luminous energy in early visual processing may allow a better specification of, and control over, the information that is actually operated on than would descriptions based on abstract categories. For instance, a face is still the same face whatever the conditions under which it is presented (e.g., 40 or 1000msec), but its composition in terms of physical attributes that can be resolved by the visual system varies with a change in viewing conditions, which in turn determines the descriptions of the representations on which cognitive operations are initially carried out. As noted by Marr (1982), how information is represented can considerably influence the type of operation that can be implemented, and a differential sensitivity of the hemispheres to the attributes of incoming information may constiute a possible basis for their functional asymmetry. Such a differential sensitivity of hemispheric systems would be consistent with the basic uniformity in structure throughout the brain (e.g., Mountcastle, 1979; Powell, 1981) while making possible the implementation of different processes in the two hemispheres as a result of qualitatively different representations on which each hemisphere would operate.

Secondly, such a concern with descriptions of stimuli may prove particularly necessary when one considers that most investigations into the asymmetrical functioning of the brain involve some limitations on the contents of the incoming information. In normal subjects, this directly derives from the stimulation of retinal areas of reduced acuity for a very brief duration, which induces "abnormal" perception. Retinal areas that have not evolved for fine object perception are stimulated, and a large part of the visual pathways that usually convey the information to which subjects attend is made inoperative. As the near totality of occipital areas are retinotopically organised (e.g., Van Essen, 1985), a considerable part of the visual cortex that normally underlies visual perception is left inactive in lateral tachistoscopic studies. This has important implications for the descriptions of the incoming information as they are elaborated and represented under these particular viewing conditions, because the information extracted and transmitted by the visual system is deprived of some of its normal attributes and does not correspond in all its characteristics to the information that the brain is used to dealing with. Because neural cells are selectively sensitive to narrow bands of spatial-frequency bandwidths, not only in the striate cortex (Shapley & Lennie, 1985), but beyond (Gross, Desimone, Albright, & Schwartz, 1984; Pollen, Nagler, Daugman, Kronauer, & Cavanagh, 1984), the processing structures that have adapted to operating on detailed and high-resolution representations provided by the fovea must operate, following lateral tachistoscopic presentations, on representations stripped of their high-frequency components that the retinal periphery cannot resolve. As will be discussed later, there is also evidence of a deficit in the spatiotemporal integration of the incoming information in patients suffering from posterior cortical lesions, indicating that the representations of the object that can be elaborated in a damaged brain do not contain all the characteristics that can be resolved by an intact brain in normal viewing conditions.

A third factor that motivates an examination of information processing in the cerebral hemispheres, in terms of descriptions of the incoming information, is the fact that there is no guarantee that the brain divides its functions according to categories that correspond to our psychological concepts and vocabulary. There is no one-to-one mapping of psychological functions onto anatomical structures, and, except for speech production, there does not seem to exist any cognitive function that would be the exclusive domain of one hemisphere. This is clearly suggested by results of research from brain damaged patients. For example, Hécaen and Albert (1978, p. 200) have indicated that: "when quantitative analyses of visual recognition defects are done, we find that, whatever the type of drawn, pictured or written stimulus, and whatever the lateralization or intrahemispheric localization of lesion, performances are always impaired in brain-damaged subjects by comparison with normal persons". To consider behavioural performance as a function of the side of the lesion is thus unlikely to reveal the site of a particular psychological function, especially when group performance, evaluated in terms of quantitative results, is used to measure hemispheric processing efficiency. This does not mean, however, that the two hemispheres contribute equally to the realisation of a given function, and the same behavioural deficit may result from different lesions, but the identification of the respective contribution of the hemispheres to performance requires a decomposition of a function into its subcomponent processes. Even then, there is no guarantee that such a decomposition would correspond to the various stages through which information is operated on in the brain.

Emphasis on the information to be processed rather than on the actual processes that underlie a specific function might be regarded as an easy and unproductive way out of the difficulties inherent in addressing the problem of hemispheric processing efficiency. Not only is the identification of operations the clue to an understanding of functional specialisation, but one also quickly loses track of the actual contents of the representations as processing unfolds beyond the striate cortex. Nonetheless, it may be argued that a valid understanding of operations that unfold over time and space necessitates, as a prerequisite, that the early stages of processing be described and that any possible contribution of these processes to observed deficits be ruled out before the cause of impairment be attributed to later stages. As pointed out by Lloyd Morgan (1894), one should never seek to explain a psychological fact by a mechanism at a higher level if it can be explained by one at a lower level. In fact, before recognition, categorisation or interpretation of a perceived object can occur and influence perception, bottom-up and stimulus-bound processes must first achieve preliminary perception, and it is on these processes, their properties, their influence on subsequent operations, and their possible disruption that the remainder of this chapter will dwell, first by considering some characteristics of early visual processing.

3. SOME PROPERTIES OF THE VISUAL SYSTEM AND THEIR IMPLICATIONS

In this section, some conclusions from recent research on the properties and organisation of the mammalian visual system will be briefly outlined along with their implications for object perception. The presentation will be selective and will concentrate on the substance of current knowledge in this area (see Desimone, Schein, Moran, & Ungerleider, 1985; Mansfield, 1982; Merzenich & Kaas, 1981; Van Essen, 1985).

3.1. Cerebral Processing of Visual Information

One basic property of the visual system is its capacity to provide the brain with redundant information about scenes and objects. During the initial decomposition of the visual input into its spatial components, each point of the visual field is encoded several times through orientation- and size-tuned filters corresponding to receptive fields of different sizes. This makes available for processing several descriptions of an object in slightly different representations (e.g., Mansfield, 1982; see also Humphreys & Quinlan, Section 2, Chapter 3, this volume). In addition, the visual system integrates stimulus energy over time such that the various descriptions of a stimulus are not available simultaneously: Low spatial frequencies are extracted and transmitted faster while high spatial frequencies require longer energy summation (Lennie, 1980). A multitude of factors influence this initial extraction process, some related to the stimulus (e.g., size, spatial organisation, contrast), others associated with the viewing conditions (e.g., exposure duration, lighting conditions, foveal or peripheral viewing, masking), and still others related to the receiving organism (e.g., integrity of the visual system, contrast sensitivity).

For a large part, visual processing is conducted in parallel. Information is transmitted through independent pathways (Rodieck, 1979), some of which bypass the striate cortex (Babb, Wilson, & Crandall, 1982; Fries, 1981) or reach extrastriate areas after a relay in subcortical structures (Stone, Dreher, & Leventhal, 1979). This suggests that the striate cortex is not the only cortical recipient of information from the retina and that the elaboration of representations involves various regions of the brain operating to some extent in a simultaneous manner. Other evidence of parallel processing is indicated by the large number of cortical maps of the retina throughout the occipital lobe (Van Essen, 1985). Although these different areas appear to perform specific processing of component-segregated information (e.g., Zeki, 1983), none seems to be specialised for one single type of operation (Desimone et al., 1985). A large part of the occipital cortex thus appears to be devoted to what is called "sensory" processing, and connections between these different zones follow a pattern linking structures with similar receptive fields (Weller & Kaas, 1983), which suggests that few, if any, "associations" can be achieved in this part of the brain (see Sergent, 1984a).

Probably one of the most important properties for understanding deficits following brain damage is the interactive and distributed nature of brain functioning, at least within modalities. As noted by Mountcastle (1979, p.21): "the brain is a complex of widely and reciprocally interconnected systems, and the dynamic interplay of neural activity within and between these systems is the very essence of brain function". Given these interactions and the simultaneous activation of various cerebral structures in the realisation of a given function, damage to one area is unlikely to be without repercussion on other areas within an interconnected system. Indeed, it has been suggested that the secondary changes in the brain which are induced by a lesion, both directly (necrosis, degeneration) and indirectly (transneuronal degeneration, regeneration and sprouting, vascular disruption, diaschisis), may comprise the more significant changes which can account for alteration of behaviour following a lesion (e.g., Schoenfeld & Hamilton, 1977). As a consequence, the destruction of one component of this system produces symptoms that depend not only on the processes normally carried out by the damaged area but also on changes in other components with which it is connected.

3.2. Some Implications

The elaboration of the various descriptions of a stimulus provided by early filtering is a temporal process that provides the brain with progressively refined information, and this can be succinctly illustrated with the stimuli shown in Fig. 5.1. These four stimuli represent the same face with increasing spatial-frequency contents, and they may correspond to some of the stages through which the microgenesis of perception unfolds (cf. Flavell & Draguns, 1957; Sergent, 1986a). The information conveyed in these representations makes explicit certain attributes of the object that are not equally useful for different operations, and higher frequencies may be respectively required for a face detection (is the stimulus a face or not?), a male/female categorisation, and a face identification. Whereas Stimulus 1 would provide the necessary information for a face detection, it would not contain all the relevant information for a decision about the sex of the face, let alone its identity. Thus, different spatial frequencies convey different information about an object and their relevance for information processing depends on the nature of the operations to be performed.

It has been suggested, however, that low spatial frequencies carry most of the relevant information for object recognition (Ginsburg, 1978), and this was recently confirmed by Sergent (1985) using faces similar to Stimulus 2, presented in such a way that spatial frequencies above 2 cycles per degree were filtered out. Subjects familiar with the individuals whose face was presented had no difficulty identifying all 16 of them, which may be consistent with the view that high frequencies convey redundant information that would be of no use for identification, as proposed by Ginsburg

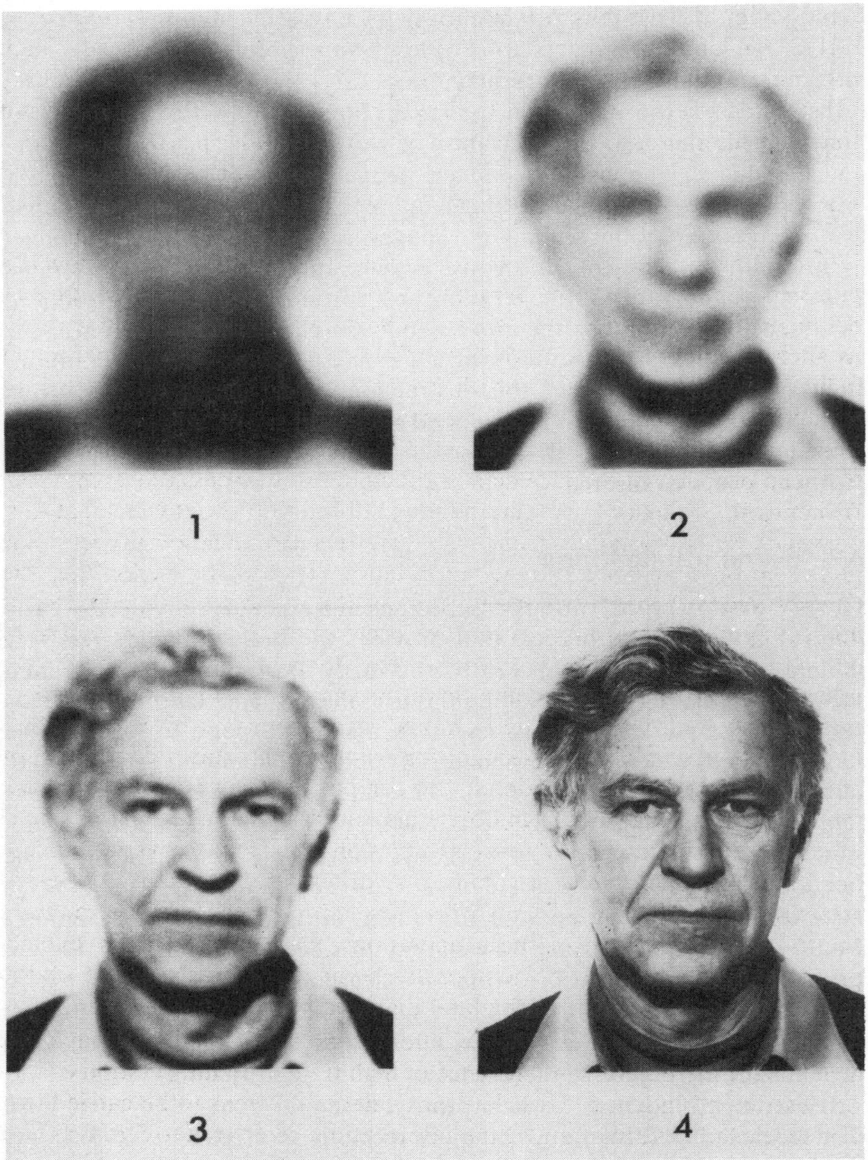

FIG. 5.1. Four representations of a face with increasing spatial frequency contents (expressed in cycles per face width): Stimulus (1) 2.2; (2) 6.2; (3) 12.4; (4) original face.

(1978). Yet, it is obvious that much more information about this particular face is contained in Stimulus 4 than in Stimulus 2, indicating that high frequencies convey information about the face that does not entirely overlap with that contained in the low frequencies, and therefore are not simply redundant. Several points may be worth considering in this respect.

3.2.1. Interaction of Input and Task Factors

Even though Stimulus 2 can be readily identified by those who know the person whom it depicts (see Sergent, 1985), the uniqueness of this face as belonging to a specific individual cannot be derived from the facial features as such, as they are too blurred uniquely to characterise this particular individual. Identification must therefore be achieved on the basis of attributes conveying the particular configuration of the face which emerges from the inter-relationships among the component features, and which is the main property of the face made explicit in this low-pass representation. By contrast, Stimulus 4 contains detailed information about facial features, conveyed by high spatial frequencies, and the identification process may then rely on this more refined information. It must be noted that the configurational property of the face is not lost in Stimulus 4; component and configurational properties co-exist and constitute alternative means of carrying out the identification process. However, although these different representations may individually serve the purpose of identification, they may not be conjointly operated on, and, as pointed out by P. M. Milner (1974), the very process of recognising wholes necessitates discarding, or at least attenuating, information about component parts (failure to extract the configural properties of an object may underlie impaired performance at tasks requiring integrated form information (see Humphreys & Quinlan, Section 5.3, Chapter 3, this volume). A differential sensitivity of neural structures to particular contents of representations may then be required for the implementation of these operations, leading to spatially distinct processes that may also be temporally asynchronous as a result of the different integration time of low and high spatial frequencies.

Whereas low frequencies convey information about the basic shape and structure of the object, the relevance of high frequency information cannot be determined independent of the particular operations to be carried out. For example, Stimulus 4 adds little information, compared to Stimulus 2, if one is to decide whether it is a male or a female face, but it does with respect to age, identity, and specific shape of facial features. In this sense, the degree of redundancy in information processing depends on the type of task and may also vary across subjects depending on the use they have learned to make of the multiple representations that can be derived from an object, and on the integrity of the visual processing structures. A recent study by Fiorentini, Maffei, and Sandini (1983) may illustrate the role of task demands. They found that high-pass faces were more accurately identified than low-pass faces, and they concluded that, contrary to Ginsburg's (1978) claim, high frequencies do not convey redundant information and are in fact more important than low-frequencies for object recognition. However, this conclusion fails to take account of the different task requirements involved in Fiorentini et al.'s and in Ginsburg's studies. The former had their subjects identify each face by names that they had learned to associate to the faces before the experiment while Ginsburg's suggestions relied on observations based on performance in matching tasks, independent of identification (that is, has this particular face been presented earlier?). There is evidence that matching faces does not demand as high resolution requirements as identifying faces (see Sergent, 1983, for a discussion of this issue), and the conclusions drawn from these two studies must be considered in relation to the particular demands of the tasks.

These different resolution requirements as a function of task demands have recently been illustrated in an experiment (Sergent, 1985, experiment 2) showing an interaction between task (identification vs. male/female categorisation) and spatial-frequency content (low-pass vs. broad-pass): Low-pass filtering was less detrimental to the categorisation than to the identification, suggesting that the relevance of spatial-frequency contents for optimal processing efficiency cannot be determined in the absolute but depends on the particular task requirements (see also Humphreys & Quinlan, Section 3.7, Chapter 3, this volume).

3.2.2. Additional Contributing Factors

This problem is further complicated by the choice of faces or objects that compose the stimulus set (e.g., set size, degree of similarity among the various instances of the set, familiar or unfamiliar faces, etc., see Sergent, 1986b). Resolution demands may increase with an increase in the number of stimuli in a set, depending on the time allotted to become familiar with them, and the within-set similarity may influence the level of resolution required for efficient performance. Unfortunately, these variables do not readily lend themselves to objective measurement and therefore to control. Nonetheless, it is worth noting that Fiorentini et al. (1983) used "9 faces of soldiers", all males of about the same age and with the same hairstyle, and their conclusion about the role of high frequencies in face recognition might have been somewhat different had they used a more heterogeneous set of faces (see Hellige, Corwin, & Johnson, 1984, for an illustration of this point). What seems to be established, however, is that performance is affected by manipulation of these variables, and that the processing of the same faces may vary in speed, as well as in hemispheric involvement, depending on their similarity to the faces with which they are paired in matching tasks (e.g., Patterson & Bradshaw, 1975; Sergent, 1982a).

In addition to these variables, and interacting with them, are two factors that selectively disrupt the high-frequency contents of a visual representation, either because of some experimental manipulations or due to some decay to which high frequencies are more vulnerable. For example, the use of black-and-white photographs, in which the various shades of gray reduce the contrast of the component features, is more detrimental to the resolution of high than low spatial frequencies (e.g., compared to line drawings of faces made of black lines on a white background). This vulnerability of high frequencies is also manifest when stimulus presentation is shorter than the duration necessary for complete energy summation, when the retinal periphery is stimulated, or when a mask interferes with the integration of information. Thus specifying the objective composition of a stimulus is not sufficient to infer the descriptions from which processing unfolds, and it is necessary to take into account the various factors that influence the elaboration of object representations in the brain.

It is also the case that the representations of faces decay with time, and this decay does not affect equally all attributes (e.g. Walker-Smith, 1978). Although little research has been conducted on this particular issue, there are some indications that the memory of a face is represented essentially as a function of the low frequencies, at least in the type of experimental conditions prevailing in matching tasks using unfamiliar faces (Harvey & Sinclair, 1985). If one assumes, as suggested earlier, that there must be some congruence and common attributes between the stored and incoming information for a reactivation of memory representations, low frequencies may become of critical importance in the processing of such unfamiliar faces. Millward and O'Toole (1985) have recently shown an imperfect transfer of facial information between high-pass and low-pass faces in a matching task, which suggests that even if high frequencies are available for processing, they may not be entirely useful for comparison with memory representations, because the latter are deprived of such high frequencies.

3.2.3. *Effects of Cerebral Damage on Visual Perception*

A final factor worth considering is specific to brain damaged patients and concerns the deficits in elementary visual functions that may result from posterior brain lesion. This question was highly debated in the 1950s but was put aside and considered of no critical importance after it was suggested that sensory deficits were not a determinant factor in visual object agnosia. Re-examination of this issue, however, suggests that the problem is far from being settled, not only with respect to visual agnosia (e.g., Bender & Feldman, 1972; Critchley, 1964; Teuber, 1978) but also to perceptual impairments in unilaterally brain damaged patients (e.g., Sergent, 1984a; Sergent & Lorber, 1983). In fact, because of the complex interconnections and interactions between the numerous cortical areas involved in visual processing, destruction of one or several of these areas may disrupt the functioning of "intact" areas to which they are connected.

Given the redundancy inherent in the visual system, sensory deficits may remain unnoticed unless a thorough examination is carried out, and visual acuity alone is not sufficient for such a purpose, especially as it does not specify the effect of contrast on the power of spatial resolution. Bodis-Wollner (1972, 1976) has shown that brain damage could result in defective contrast sensitivity, without affecting Snellen acuity, and this may prove important for perception of faces and objects. For instance, Benton and Gordon (1971) have indicated a significant positive correlation between facial recognition and the ability to discriminate patterns of shading. In addition, changing the illumination of a face, which modifies the contrast between the various facial features and introduces shadowed areas not initially present, contributes to decreased recognition in normal subjects (e.g., Goldstein & Chance, 1981). If some modifications in the physical characteristics of a stimulus produce disturbances in object recognition, the capacity of patients to process such characteristics alone should be assessed to determine the source of their deficits.

Evidence for sensory deficits following brain damage was reported by Bay (1953) who indicated that the spatiotemporal characteristics of perception and the constancy of visual objects were the first to be disturbed, despite normal visual acuity and normal visual field. Ettlinger (1956) also found that unilaterally brain damaged non-agnosic patients had sensory deficits of comparable magnitude to those of agnosic patients, and he pointed out (p. 306): "We are thus able to confirm Bay's finding that bilateral visual discrimination defects follow unilateral cerebral lesions". (See Campion and Humphreys & Riddoch, this volume; Sergent, 1984a; Sergent & Lorber, 1983, for further discussion). Strangely enough, Ettlinger's (1956) results have since been used as evidence against sensory deficits in unilaterally brain damaged patients and as an argument to dispense with an examination of elementary visual functions in perceptual studies with neurological patients. For example, Warrington and Taylor (1978), discussing deficits by right-hemisphere damaged patients in categorising objects presented in an unconventional view, stated (p. 701): "It has been repeatedly shown that recognition deficits at this (perceptual categorisation) level are not a trivial consequence of visuosensory defects of impairment of discrimination *per se* and such factors will not be further considered (Ettlinger, 1956) . . .". Actually, there has yet been no study in which visuo-sensory capacities *and* object categorisation or recognition performance were thoroughly examined in the same group of patients. What Ettlinger's study clearly showed, however, is that unilaterally brain damaged patients display sensory impairments when appropriate tests are used, and some of Ettlinger's patients who had marked sensory impairments suffered from the same lesion (e.g. right temporal) as those patients who typically are defective in object categorisation (Warrington & Taylor, 1978) and in face recognition (Milner, 1968).

It may therefore appear that investigations into perceptual capacities of neurological patients that fail to examine elementary visual functions run the risk of missing one contributing factor to observed deficits. This is not to suggest that sensory distrubances are sufficient to explain perceptual impairments but to point out that the representations on which cognitive operations are carried out are deprived of attributes that might be relevant for efficient recognition or categorisation. The main problem is then to determine which attributes are the most vulnerable, whether elementary visual function degrades in a systematic manner, and what would be appropriate tests for these purposes. There is, at present, little empirical evidence on which to rely to answer these questions. Bodis-Wollner (1976, p. 309) has indicated that: "psychophysical measurements of the detectability of sinusoidal gratings (contrast sensitivity functions) established that in the majority of patients detection of high frequencies suffers most". However, there exist cases with deficits in the intermediate or the low frequency range (e.g., Ginsburg, 1978; Regan, 1982). In addition, although contrast sensitivity functions provide a more comprehensive measure of visual efficiency than does a standard acuity score, it is a measure of threshold perception susceptible to be affected by any small but varying noise, whereas the visual system is obviously designed to work in the supra-threshold domain. The capacity to detect non-uniformity in the visual field is no guarantee of an absence of perceptual distortion and provides little indication about more complex aspects of perception. In fact, detection and recognition do not implicate the same sensory capacities (e.g., Johnson, Keltner, & Balestrery, 1978) and each is related to different brain events (Parasuraman & Beatty, 1980). Nonetheless, deficits in detection point to a reduction in the capacity to encode physical characteristics of the input, which gives rise to representations of the external world stripped of some of their components.

3.3. Conclusion

The foregoing discussion suggests that neither research on normal subjects nor findings from unilaterally brain damaged patients allow direct inferences about the processing competences of the intact brain operating in normal conditions. The lateral tachistoscopic presentation creates functional sensory deficits whereas a cortical lesion disrupts the spatiotemporal integration of the incoming information, which results in both cases, in representations unlike those elaborated in normal viewing conditions by an intact brain. Some of the attributes that normally composed the representations of objects may thus be distorted or missing, and the descriptions of information thus made available may not match the specific sensitivity of the cells usually involved in visual cognitive processing. Independent of the processes underlying categorisation, recognition, or identification of the input, limitations are imposed on the quality of the visual representations that the brain can generate. These limitations will affect processing, but differentially so depending on the resolution demands of the tasks. One important question for the study of functional hemispheric specialisation is therefore to determine whether the two hemispheres accommodate themselves equally well to such limitations: If they do, comparison of performance between visual fields of presentation or between sides of lesion can proceed fairly directly while taking into account the presence of sensory deficits; if they do not, asymmetric performance may reflect a differential capacity of the hemispheres to deal with degraded information, over and above differential hemispheric processing competence, and this would have to be considered in making inferences about the respective contribution of the hemispheres to a given function.

4. HEMISPHERIC PROCESSING ASYMMETRY

The critical role of the right hemisphere (RH) in object recognition and categorisation is now well established (e.g., Hécaen & Albert, 1978), but the nature of this contribution remains somewhat elusive. Complete disruption of these functions is observed only after bilateral brain injury (Hécaen, 1981; Meadows, 1974; Rubens, 1979), and there are examples of impaired face recognition following damage restricted to the left hemisphere (LH). Clearly, the integrity of the whole brain and the joint participation of the two hemispheres are necessary for optimal functioning, which leads one to ask why a right-sided lesion is generally more disruptive to visual object and face recognition than a left-sided lesion, and what is the contribution of the RH that makes it more critical to performance than the LH.

It seems that one of the currently fashionable explanations put forward to account for the unequal contribution of the hemispheres, suggesting an analytic/holistic processing dichotomy (e.g., Bradshaw & Nettleton, 1981), can be ruled out at the outset. Support for this view is based on *ad hoc* accounts of findings that could lend themselves equally well to opposite interpretations (Sergent, 1984b). One typical illustration of this approach is the suggestion that the ability to form a Gestalt from incomplete information is a RH function, on the basis of Nebes' (1972) finding of RH superiority at judging from which circle an arc was taken from. As pointed out by Marshall (1981, p. 73): "had the data gone the other way, we can be sure that the task would have been described as implicating the ability to decompose circles into their constituent arcs (an analytic operation)". In one of the few experiments with normal subjects in which the concepts of analytic and holistic processing were operationalised in terms of rules governing the combination of component features of multi-dimensional stimuli (Takane & Sergent, 1983), Sergent (1984c) found qualitatively similar configurational processes underlying the comparison of faces presented in the right or the left visual field, despite hemispheric asymmetry in processing efficiency. Similarly, Humphreys and Riddoch (1984) showed that RH damaged patients achieved object constancy primarily by utilising the global properties of objects while the availability of distinctive features was of little help to these patients for categorising objects. This finding is in direct contradiction with predictions based on the analytic/holistic dichotomy, according to which RH damaged patients should have available LH processes specifying local details rather than the global properties of the object. Thus, the analytic/holistic processing dichotomy does not appear reliable for predicting the pattern of laterality effects in unilaterally brain damaged patients or in normal subjects. This is not to say that these processes cannot characterise perceptual operations, but to point out that each hemisphere has the capacity to subserve these processes.

4.1. Some Evidence in Normal Subjects

The limited heuristic value of hemisphere processing dichotomies probably arises from the absence of consideration of the information to be processed and of the joint participation of the hemispheres, which such dichotomies cannot explain. Two important and related properties characterising the RH seem to emerge from findings with normal subjects. One is its lower threshold for activation, and thus its capacity to operate more efficiently than the LH at low stimulus energy level; the other, which follows from the former, is its capacity to operate better than the LH on low-frequency information, and thus to contribute more than the LH to tasks for which the low frequencies contain the relevant information. Several sources of evidence support these suggestions. For example, in newborn infants, the RH seems to be the only hemisphere activated by light flashes (Crowell, Jones, Kapunia, & Nakagawa, 1973), and it displays a greater sensitivity to the relatively low spatial frequencies that can be resolved by the visual system early in life (Lewis, Maurer, & Kay, 1978). To the extent that the RH develops earlier than the LH (e.g., Geschwind, 1984), and that visual cells become selectively sensitive to narrow bands of spatial frequency in the first months of life, the limited resolving power of the eyes during this period may provide the brain with essentially low-frequency information to which the RH may become selectively sensitive while the "lagging" LH may establish its selective sensitivity later, when higher levels of resolution can be achieved in the visual system. Although such a scenario is admittedly speculative, it is consistent with our current knowledge about the development of the visual system.

Laterality research in normal adults also supports the view of an earlier engagement of the RH in cognitive operations. For example, Hellige (1980; O'Boyle & Hellige, 1982) observed that visual information was encoded faster when initially presented in the left than in the right visual field, especially when some form of degradation was involved, and Sergent (1982b; Sergent & Lorber, 1983; see also Underwood & Whitfield, 1985) found that a reduction in stimulus energy was more detrimental to the LH than to the RH. Thus, a greater tolerance of the RH to low energy levels, along with a greater sensitivity to low frequencies, may give this hemisphere a critical role in early cognitive operations because the level of resolution of visual representations develops over time and is initially a function of the low frequencies. As long as task demands do not require the processing of high frequencies, the RH may prove adequate to carry out the necessary operations. However, even if processing would benefit from operating on high frequencies, the RH may still prove critical when information is presented in such a way that high frequencies cannot be reliably resolved. Only when high frequencies are both available and required for processing will the contribution of the LH become apparent, which does not mean, however, that the RH has not contributed to early stages of processing. In fact, the earlier engagement of the RH in processing may provide the LH with a framework within which to perform its more refined operations, and the two hemispheres may thus operate on different attributes of the same information, which confers to each hemisphere limitations and predispositions in the type of operations that can be efficiently implemented.

Many empirical findings in object and face perception can be interpreted along these lines, provided the numerous variables that determine the quality of the representations and the resolution demands of the tasks are taken into account (see Sergent, 1986b, for a detailed review). There is, in fact, no single factor sufficient to account for an observed pattern of hemispheric asymmetry, and, although an interpretation relying on spatial-frequency contents may provide some homogeneity and coherence in an apparently disparate set of findings, it must be noted that the effects of all the factors involved in early processing are not easily specified in terms of spatial frequencies and sometimes cannot even be. Nonetheless, it seems to be the case that studies on face and object recognition in which experimental variables combine to determine representations containing essentially low frequencies yield a RH advantage. This is best illustrated by recognition accuracy studies, with brief exposure of black-and-white photographs, and a delayed matching between target and test presentations (see Sergent, 1983). On the other hand, the use of highly similar line-drawing faces, either well learned or simultaneously presented for a relatively long exposure duration, all factors contributing to making high frequencies available and required for processing, typically result in a LH superiority (Fairweather, Brizzolara, Tabossi, & Umiltà, 1978; Patterson & Bradshaw, 1975; Sergent, 1982a, 1984c). The most direct support for this view was recently provided in an experiment in which both the spatial frequencies and the resolution demands were manipulated (Sergent, 1985): Face identification resulted in a LH superiority when high-resolution faces were presented, but in a RH advantage with low-pass faces; by contrast, no hemisphere difference was apparent when high resolution faces had to be classed into a male or female category whereas a RH superiority prevailed in the same task with low-pass faces. The balance of hemisphere involvement in these tasks is thus determined by the contents of the representations as well as by the relevance of these contents for the particular operations to be implemented, suggesting a dynamic interplay between the two hemispheres.

4.2. Convergence of Results in Normal and Neurological Subjects

Whereas research on normal subjects is characterised by considerable diversity in methodology as well as in results, experiments on unilaterally brain damaged patients show less variety and consistently demonstrate impaired performance after right-sided injury. The generally greater reliance on findings from the latter than from the former has contributed to the views that the RH is specialised for face and object perception and to discarding evidence from normal subjects that does not conform with neurological results. It seems, however, that trying to understand the sources of divergence between the findings from the two populations may prove fruitful, and that specifying the conditions that lead, in normal subjects, to the same pattern of laterality effect as that observed in RH damaged patients may provide some clues to mechanisms underlying impaired visual recognition and categorisation.

Even if correlations between a specific deficit and the side of a lesion are important in a clinical context, they provide little information concerning the mechanisms that bring such a deficit to the fore. Despite our knowledge of the interactive and distributed nature of brain function, it is still difficult to resist attributing to the damaged area the psychological functions found to be impaired in behavioural tests. As discussed earlier, any damage within cortical areas involved in visual processing has detrimental effects on the remaining components, specifically the spatiotemporal integration of the incoming information, and it is therefore necessary to determine whether the particular representations generated in the presence of brain damage are still compatible with the sensitivity of the structures not invaded by the lesion. Evidence from normal subjects that the RH plays a critical role in the processing of degraded information suggests that a right-sided lesion deprives the brain of a structure crucial in dealing with this information. This may also be inferred from the results reported by Kobayashi, Mukuno, Ishikawa, and Takashi (1985) showing that the contrast sensitivity function of patients with right posterior lesion was significantly impaired compared with LH and control subjects. Such a finding may be interpreted as an indication that the intact LH in a damaged brain requires higher contrast than the intact RH for the detection of stimuli, and therefore that the LH is at a disadvantage compared with the RH, independent of cognitive operations.

One consequence of this impairment is that the LH in a damaged brain has to operate on representations that do not correspond to those it has adapted to deal with. For example, one of the most robust findings in laterality studies with normal subjects is the superiority of the LH in identifying letters and words (e.g., Corballis, 1983), and, considering only the side of the lesion, one should not expect RH damaged patients to be impaired in such a task. This is not the case, however, and Dorff, Minski, and Mishkin (1965) observed that a right temporal lesion produced impairment in both the contralateral and ipsilateral visual fields while a left-sided injury affected performance only on the contralateral visual field. Similarly, Rosenthal and Fedio (1975) reported that, for the identification of three-letter words, the RH damaged group required significantly longer exposure in both visual fields than the LH damaged and the control groups. Thus, while patients with left-sided damage appear capable of performance as good as normals, a right lesion produces deficits in tasks for which the LH, in an intact brain, is consistently superior to the RH. This suggests that the deficit displayed by RH damaged patients is not due to the loss of critical cortical components *per se*, but to the secondary changes produced by the RH lesion that modify the quality of the representations which can no longer efficiently reactivate the neural structures normally involved in the realisation of a given function. In other words, an intact hemisphere in a damaged brain cannot operate as it does in an intact brain.

Considered in this context impairments in face recognition (e.g., Milner, 1968) and in object categorisation (e.g., Humphreys & Riddoch, 1984; Warrington & Taylor, 1978) by RH damaged patients may not necessarily reflect an inherent incapacity of the LH to carry out the required processes.

Instead, such impairments may result from an inability of the LH to process the particular information made available which lacks some of the attributes that this hemisphere needs to operate efficiently. Sergent and Lorber (1983) carried out a study with normal subjects in an attempt to examine the validity of this suggestion. They used a categorisation task with four animals as stimuli each of which could vary in size, orientation, or both. In a condition allowing high resolution of the stimuli, no hemispheric difference was observed; when both exposure duration and luminance were reduced in a subsequent experiment, a significant RH superiority obtained. In as much as this reduction in stimulus energy is grossly comparable to some of the sensory deficits resulting from brain damage, Sergent and Lorber's (1983) results may indicate that the LH is effectively at a disadvantage when the information to be processed lacks its normal redundancy and is stripped of its high frequencies.

Most research with faces in neurological patients has been carried out with black-and white photographs in delayed matching tasks, and those are some of the conditions that have been found to contribute to a RH superiority in normal subjects (Sergent, 1986b). It is also the case that the examination of categorisation of objects presented in an unconventional view uses black-and-white photographs often containing shadows the border of which creates high-frequency information irrelevant for recognition and categorisation. In addition, as noted by Humphreys and Riddoch (1984), the particular patterns of shading on these unconventional views of objects convey depth cues that RH damaged patients fail to utilise, which also may contribute to their deficits. Impairments in object categorisation may in fact result from the fact that most of the available and relevant information is contained in the low-frequency range to which the RH is normally preferentially sensitive. Thus, the RH lesion not only destroys structures that would be necessary to operate on such information but also produces disruption in the remaining structures that impairs the efficient extraction of higher frequencies that the LH would need in order to carry out its operations. Although neurological evidence points to a critical role of the RH in these processes, it does not allow any strong conclusion regarding the competences of the LH unless the secondary changes resulting from brain damage are taken into account.

5. CONCLUSION

The task of characterising the respective contribution of the cerebral hemispheres to the processes underlying object perception is certainly not an easy one, and the present chapter has barely touched the essential heart of the problem. A cognitive neuropsychological approach is necessarily multi-dimensional and must co-ordinate the various levels at which human information processing operates, but the contact between psychological functions and the anatomical structures that subserve them is rather tenuous. Indeed, whereas "the phenomena of interest to cognitive psychologists can be explained without using physical or biological terms, that is, without reference to structural material properties of the organism" (Pylyshyn, 1984), the structural and dynamic properties of neural substrata of behaviour are inescapable considerations for neuropsychologists. Cognitive neuropsychology is therefore inherently confronted with the problem that its object of study, and the level and nature of its explanatory account of behaviour, are diverse and multiple, which requires a stand that, even if implicit, determines in a fundamental way how the problem of cognition is addressed.

The approach adopted here has consisted in reducing the degree of freedom of a cognitive explanation to a minimum constrained by our current knowledge of cerebral properties, and this is admittedly a severe restriction as our understanding of brain mechanisms, especially those underlying the most human aspects of cognition, is extremely limited. Nothing has been suggested here concerning accumulated knowledge of the perceiver about objects and faces, and the influence of top-down processes on the pick-up of information has not even been alluded to. In fact, the present account is an over-simplification of the complexities of cerebral processing and concern for a parsimonious explanation does not do justice to the multitude of variables and components interacting in the emergence of object perception. Indeed, the main thesis of this chapter regarding laterality effects could be formulated in very few sentences: (1) the LH and the RH preferentially operate on high and low spatial frequencies, respectively; (2) a brain lesion or a lateral tachistoscopic presentation creates sensory deficits in the form of a greater disruption of high than low frequencies; (3) therefore, the LH is put at a disadvantage when (2) occurs.

Fortunately, this approach offers the possibility to take into consideration a series of factors that are usually left aside in neuropsychological research, and it compels us to specify each variable involved in the experimental process and to determine its effects on the processing organism. By doing so, one may come to realise that how information is represented, depending on procedural factors or on brain damage, and as a function of the relevance of attributes for processing, is not a trivial matter but constrains in specific ways the implementation of operations and determines the respective involvement of the cerebral hemispheres in the realisation of the processes. In addition, a neuropsychological approach cannot make the economy of disregarding the basic properties of brain, its interactive and distributed nature, and the implications of such properties for understanding its functioning when one of its components has been destroyed. Conceiving the brain as an aggregate of modules perpetuates the tradition of attributing definite cognitive functions to specific areas and, even if some functional localisation characterises cerebral organisation, it cannot override the complex pattern of interconnections between cortical areas. Certainly, our conceptions of the working of the brain, even when not explicit, are powerful in determining the formulation of the problem, the experimental approach, and the interpretation of the outcomes. Although the present approach is concerned with only one portion of the preliminary operations underlying object perception, it may prove a significant, albeit small, step in our asymptotic progress toward a better understanding of brain-behaviour relationships.

REFERENCES

Assal, G., Favre, C., & Anderes, J. P. (1984). Non-reconnaissance d'animaux familiers chez un paysan. *Revue Neurologique*, *140*, 580–584.

Babb, T. L., Wilson, C. L., & Crandall, P. H. (1982). Asymmetry and ventral course of the human geniculostriate pathway as determined by hippocampal visual evoked potentials and subsequent visual field defects after temporal lobectomy. *Experimental Brain Research, 47*, 317–328.

Bay, E. (1953). Disturbances of visual perception and their examination. *Brain, 76*, 515–551.

Bender, M. B. & Feldman, M. (1972). The so-called "visual agnosia". *Brain, 95*, 173–186.

Benton, A. L. & Gordon, M. (1971). Correlates of facial recognition. *Transactions of the American Neurological Association, 96*, 91–96.

Bodis-Wollner, I. (1972). Visual acuity and contrast sensitivity in patients with cerebral lesion. *Science, 178*, 769–771.

Bodis-Wollner, I. (1976). Vulnerability of spatial frequency channels in cerebral lesions. *Nature, 261*, 309–311.

Bornstein, B., Skroka, H., & Monitz, H. (1969). Prosopagnosia with animal face agnosia. *Cortex, 5*, 164–169.

Bradshaw, J. L. & Nettleton, N. C. (1981). The nature of hemispheric specialization in man. *The Behavioral and Brain Sciences, 4*, 51–91.

Bruyer, R. (1983). *Le visage et l'expression faciale*. Bruxelles: Pierre Mardaga.

Carey, S. (1981). The development of face perception. In G. Davies, H. Ellis, and J. Shepherd (Eds.), *Perceiving and remembering faces.* London: Academic Press.

Cavanagh, P. (1978). Size and position invariance in the visual system. *Perception, 7*, 167–177.

Colombo, J. (1982). The critical period concept: Research, methodology, and theoretical issues. *Psychological Bulletin, 91*, 260–275.

Corballis, M. C. (1983). *Human laterality*. New York: Academic Press.

Critchley, M. (1964). The problem of visual agnosia. *Journal of Neurological Sciences, 1*, 274–290.

Crowell, D. H., Jones, R. H., Kapunia, L. E., & Nakagawa, J. K. (1973). Unilateral cortical activity in newborn infants: An early index of cerebral dominance? *Science, 80*, 205–208.

Desimone, R., Schein, S. J., Moran, J., & Ungerleider, L. G. (1985). Contour, color, and shape analysis beyond the striate cortex. *Vision Research, 25*, 441–452.

Dorff, J. E., Minski, A. F., & Mishkin, M. (1965). Effects of unilateral temporal lobe removals on tachistoscopic recognition in the left and right visual fields. *Neuropsychologia*, *3*, 39–51.

Ettlinger, G. (1956). Sensory deficits in visual agnosia. *Journal of Neurology, Neurosurgery, and Psychiatry, 19*, 297–308.

Fairweather, H., Brizzolara, D., Tabossi, P., & Umiltà, C. (1982). Functional cerebral localization: Dichotomy or plurality? *Cortex, 18*, 51–66.

Fiorentini, A., Maffei, L., & Sandini, G. (1983). The role of high spatial frequencies in face perception. *Perception, 12*, 195–201.

Flavell, J. & Draguns, J. (1957). A microgenetic approach to perception and thought. *Psychological Bulletin, 54*, 197–217.

Freedman, J. & Harber, R. N. (1974). One reason why we rarely forget faces. *Bulletin of the Psychonomic Society, 3*, 107–109.

Fries, W. (1981). The projection from the lateral geniculate nucleus to the prestriate cortex of the macaque monkey. *Proceedings of the Royal Society, London, B213*, 73–80.

Garner, W. R. (1970). The stimulus in information processing. *American Psychologist, 25*, 350–358.

Geschwind, N. (1984). Cerebral dominance in biological perspective. *Neurospsychologia, 22*, 675–683.

Gevins, A. S. (1983). Brain potential (BP) evidence for lateralization of higher cognitive functions. In J. B. Hellige (Ed.), *Cerebral hemisphere asymmetry: Method, theory, and application.* New York, Praeger.

Ginsburg, A. (1978). Visual information processing based on spatial filters constrained by biological data. (Report No 78–129, Volumes I & II). Aerospace Medical Research Laboratory, OH: Wright-Patterson Air Force Base.

Goldstein, A, G. & Chance, J. E. (1981). Laboratory studies of face recognition. In G. Davies, H. Ellis, and J. Shepherd (Eds.), *Perceiving and remembering faces*. London: Academic Press.

Gross, C. G., Desimone, R., Albright, T. D., & Schwartz, E. L. (1984). Inferior temporal cortex as a visual integration area. In F. Reinoso-Suarez and C. Ajmone-Marsan (Eds.), *Cortical integration: Basic archicortical, and cortical association levels of neural integration.* New York: Raven Press.

Harvey, L. O. Jr. & Sinclair, G. P. (1985). On the quality of visual imagery. *Investigative Ophtalmology & Visual Science, 26*, 281.

Hécaen, H. (1981). Neuropsychology of face recognition. In G. Davies, H. Ellis, and J. Shepherd (Eds.), *Perceiving and rembembering faces.* London: Academic Press.

Hécaen, H. & Albert, M. L. (1978). *Human neuropsychology*. New York: John Wiley.

Hellige, J. B. (1980). Effect of perceptual quality and visual fields of probe stimulus presentation on memory search for letters. *Journal of Experimental Psychology: Human Perception and Performance, 6*, 639–651.

Hellige, J. B., Corwin, W. H., & Johnson, J. E. (1984). Effects of perceptual quality on the processing of human faces presented in the left and the right cerebral hemispheres. *Journal of Experimental Psychology: Human Perception and Performance, 10*, 90–107.

Hellige, J. B. & Sergent, J. (1986). Role of task factors in visual-field asymmetries. *Brain and Cognition, 5*, 200–223.

Hyvärinen, J., Hyvärinen, L., & Linnankoski, I. (1981). Modification of parietal association cortex and functional blindness after binocular deprivation in young monkeys. *Experimental Brain Reseach, 42*, 1–8.

Humphreys, G. W. & Riddoch, M. J. (1984). Routes to object constancy: Implications for neurological impairments of object constancy. *Quarterly Journal of Experimental Psychology, 36A*, 385–415.

Johnson, C. A., Keltner, J. L., & Balestrery, F. (1978). Effects of target size and eccentricity on visual detection and recognition. *Vision Research, 18*, 1217–1222.

Klatsky, R. L. & Forrest, F. H. (1984). Recognizing familiar and unfamiliar faces. *Memory and Cognition, 14*, 60–70.

Kobayashi, S., Mukuno, K., Ishikawa, S., & Takashi, Y. (1985). Hemispheric lateralization of spatial contrast sensitivity. *Annals of Neurology, 17*, 141–145.

Lennie, P. (1980). Parallel visual pathways: A review. *Vision Research, 20*, 561–594.

Lewis, T. L., Maurer, D., & Kay, D. (1978). Newborn's central vision: Whole or holes? *Journal of Experimental Child Psychology, 26*, 193–203.

Mansfield, R. J. W. (1982). Role of the striate cortex in pattern perception in primates. In D. J. Ingle, M. A. Goodale, and R. J. W. Mansfield (Eds.), *Analysis of visual behaviour*, pp. 443–482. Cambridge, Mass.: MIT Press.

Marr, D. (1982). *Vision*. San Francisco: W. H. Freeman.

Marshall, J. C. (1981). Hemispheric specialization: What, how, and why. *Behavioral and Brain Sciences, 4*, 72–73.

Meadows, J. C. (1974). The anatomical basis of prosopagnosia. *Journal of Neurology, Neurosurgery, and Psychiatry, 37*, 489–501.

Merzenich, M. M. & Kass, J. H. (1980). Principles of organization of sensory-perceptual systems in mammals. *Progress in Psychobiology and Physiological Psychology, 9*, 1–42.

Millward, R. & O'Toole, A (1985). *Recognition memory transfer between spatial-frequency analyzed faces*. Paper presented at the NATO workshop on *Aspects of Face Processing*, Aberdeen, Scotland.

Milner, B. (1968). Visual recognition and recall after right temporal lobe excision. *Neuropsychologia, 6*, 191–209.

Milner, P. M. (1974). A model for visual shape recognition. *Psychological Review, 81*, 521–535.

Morgan, L. (1894). *An introduction to comparative psychology*. London: W. Scott.

Mountcastle, V. B. (1979). An organizing principle for cerebral function: The unit module and the distributed system. In F. O. Schmitt and F. G. Worden (Eds.), *The neurosciences: Fourth study program*. Cambridge, Mass.: MIT Press.

Nebes, R. D. (1972). Dominance of the minor hemisphere in commissurotomized man on a test of figural unification. *Brain, 96*, 633–638.

O'Boyle, M. W. & Hellige, J. B. (1982). Hemispheric asymmetry, early visual processing, and serial memory comparison. *Brain and Cognition, 1*, 222–243.

Parasuraman, R. & Beatty, J. (1980). Brain events underlying the detection and recognition of weak sensory signals. *Science, 210*, 80–83.

Patterson, K. E. & Bradshaw, J. L. (1975). Differential hemispheric mediation of nonverbal visual stimuli. *Journal of Experimental Psychology: Human Perception and Performance, 1*, 246–252.

Pollen, D. A., Nagler, M., Daugman, J., Kronauer, R., & Cavanagh, P. (1984). Use of Gabor elementary functions to probe receptive field substructure of posterior inferotemporal neurons in the owl monkey. *Vision Research, 24*, 233–241.

Powell, T. P. S. (1981). Certain aspects of the intrinsic organization of the cerebral cortex. In. O. Pompeiano and C. Ajmone-Marsan (Eds.), *Brain mechanisms of perceptual awareness and purposeful behavior*. New York: Raven Press.

Pylyshyn, Z. (1984). *Computation and cognition. Toward a foundation for cognitive science.* Cambridge, Mass.: MIT Press.

Regan, D. (1982). Visual information channeling in normal and disordered vision. *Psychological Review, 89*, 407–444.

Risberg, J., Halsey, J. H. Wills, E. L., & Wilson, B. M. (1975). Hemispheric specialization in normal man studied by bilateral measurements of the regional cerebral blood flow. *Brain, 98*, 511–524.

Rodieck, R. W. (1979). Visual pathways. *Annual Review of Neurosciences, 2*, 193–225.

Rosenthal, L. S. & Fedio, P. (1975). Recognition thresholds in the central and lateral visual fields following temporal lobectomy. *Cortex, 11*, 217–227.

Rubens, A. B. (1979). Agnosia. In K. M. Heilman and E. Valenstein (Eds.), *Clinical neuropsychology*. New York: Oxford University Press.

Schoenfeld, T. A. & Hamilton, L.W. (1977). Secondary brain changes following lesion: A new paradigm for lesion experimentation. *Physiology & Behavior, 18*, 951–967.

Sergent, J. (1982a). About face: Left-hemisphere involvement in processing physiognomies. *Journal of Experimental Psychology: Human Perception and Performance, 8*, 1–14.

Sergent, J. (1982b). Theroretical and methodological consequences of variations in exposure duration in visual laterality studies. *Perception & Psychophysics, 31*, 451–461.

Sergent, J. (1983). The role of the input in visual field asymmetries. *Psychological Bulletin, 93*, 481–512.

Sergent, J. (1984a). Inferences from unilateral brain damage about normal hemispheric functions in visual pattern recognition. *Psychological Bulletin, 96*, 99–115.

Sergent, J. (1984b). Requiem for the analytic/holistic processing dichotomy. Paper presented at the *International Neuropsychological Society Meeting*, Aachen, Germany.

Sergent, J. (1984c). Configural processing of faces in the left and the right cerebral hemispheres. *Journal of Experimental Psychology: Human Perception and Performance, 10* 554–572.

Sergent, J. (1985). Influence of input and task factors on hemispheric involvement in face processing. *Journal of Experimental Psychology: Human Perception and Performance, 11*, 846–861.

Sergent, J. (1986a). Microgenesis of face perception. In H. Ellis, M. A. Jeeves, F. Newcombe, and A. W. Young (Eds.), *Aspects of face perception*. Dordrecht, The Netherlands: Martinus Nijhoff.

Sergent, J. (1986b). Methodological constraints on neuropsychological studies of face perception in normals. In R. Bruyer (Ed.), *The Neuropsychology of face perception and facial expression*. Hillsdale, NJ: Lawerence Erlbaum Associates Inc.

Sergent, J. (in press). Face perception: Underlying processes and hemispheric contribution. In G. Denes, C. Semenza, P. Bisiacchi, and E. Andreewski (Eds.), *Perspectives in cognitive neuropsychology*. Hillsdale, NJ: Lawrence Erlbaum Associaties Inc.

Sergent, J. & Lorber, E. (1983). Perceptual categorization in the cerebral hemispheres. *Brain and Cognition, 2*, 39–54.

Shapley, R. & Lennie, P. (1985). Spatial frequency analysis in the visual system. *Annual Review of Neuroscience, 8*, 547–583.

Stone, J., Dreher, B., & Leventhal, A. (1979). Hierarchical and parallel mechanisms in the organization of visual cortex. *Brain Research Review, 1*, 345–394.

Takane, Y. & Sergent, J. (1983). Multidimensional models for reaction times and same-different judgments. *Psychometrika, 48*, 393–423.

Teuber, H.-L. (1978). The brain and human behavior. In R. Held. H. W. Leibowitz, and H.-L Teuber (Eds.), *Handbook of Sensory Physiology, Vol. 8: Perception*, pp. 879–920. New York: Springer-Verlag.

Toyama, J. S. (1975). *The effect or orientation on the recognition of faces: A reply to Yin.* Unpublished doctoral dissertation, University of Waterloo, Canada.

Van Essen, D. C. (1985). Functional organization of primate visual cortex. In A. Peters and E. G. Jones (Eds.), *Cerebral cortex, Vol 3: Visual cortex*, pp. 259–329. New York: Plenum Press.

Underwood, G. & Whitfield, A. (1985). Right hemisphere interactions in picture-word processing. *Brain and Cognition, 4*, 273–286.

Walker-Smith, G. J. (1978). The effects of delay and exposure duration in a face recognition task. *Perception & Psychophysics, 24*, 63–70.

Warrington, E. K. & Taylor, A. M. (1978). Two categorical stages of object recognition. *Perception, 7*, 695–705.

Weller, R. E. & Kaas, J. H. (1983). Retinotopic patterns of connections of area 17 with visual areas V-II and MT in macaque monkeys. *Journal of Comparative Neurology, 220*, 252–279.

Yin, R. (1969). Looking at upside-down faces. *Journal of Experimental Psychology, 81*, 141–145.

Yin, R. (1970). Face recognition by brain-injured patients: A dissociable ability? *Neuropsychologia*, *8*, 395–402.

Yin, R. (1978). Face perception: A review of experiments with infants, normal adults and brain-injured persons. In R. Held, H. W. Leibowitz, and H.-L. Teuber (Eds.), *Handbook of sensory physiology, Vol. 8: Perception*. New York: Springer-Verlag.

Zaidel, E. (1983). Disconnection syndrome as a model for laterality effects in the normal brain. In J. B. Hellige (Ed.), *Cerebral hemisphere asymmetry: Method, theory and application*. New York: Praeger.

Zeki, S. (1983). The distribution of wavelength and orientation selective cells in different areas of monkey visual cortex. *Proceedings of the Royal Society, London, B217*, 449–470.

6 The Clinical Spectrum and Localisation of Visual Agnosia

Andrew Kertesz
Clinical Neurology Department, St. Joseph's Hospital, 268 Grosvenor Street, London, Ontario N6A 4V2, Canada

1. INTRODUCTION

The aim of this chapter is to provide a broad overview of the clinical picture of visual agnosia, and its relation to other visual processing disorders. From this picture, I propose a multi-stage account of visual object recognition which helps to structure the various clinical aspects of agnosia, and to provide a framework for the cases discussed in the following chapters.

Visual disturbance of apparently high level perceptual processes was first demonstrated experimentally by Munk (1881) who published the results of partial occipital cortical ablation in dogs. These animals could obviously see, avoid objects, and look at new stimuli, but behaved as if they did not recognise them. They did not jump back when threatened with a stick, did not recognise food, water, fire, or their masters. Munk called this mind blindness ("*Seelenblindheit*"). Subsequently, the occipital lobectomies of Kluver (1936) could not exactly replicate these findings but bilateral temporal lobectomies by Kluver and Bucy (1937) produced a similar disturbance. Their rhesus monkeys showed no recognition of objects but they reached for them and put them all in their mouth, even live snakes that otherwise terrified them.

Lissauer (1889) proposed the distinction between apperceptive and associative mind blindness on theoretical and clinical grounds. He postulated a two-stage theory of recognition, consisting of apperception and association. The apperceptive variety is characterised by poor copying and matching together with intact elementary visual sensations. In the associative variety, copying and matching are relatively preserved, but the patient is unable to name an object or indicate recognition by other means. Lissauer's case can be classified as an associative agnosic because he could copy, although he himself stated that pure cases are unlikely to occur. The patient had no problems identifying objects by palpation or through auditory clues. Although Lissauer made a point to describe the many intact mental functions of his patient, namely his co-operation, insight, and orientation, he also described some memory loss which later gave rise to the criticism that his patient was demented.

Agnosia, a term attributed to Freud (1891), is usually defined as a failure of recognition with intact perception and language. Visual object agnosia is usually diagnosed clinically if a patient shows no recognition of an object when presented visually, but will do so immediately when he or she is allowed to touch it or hear its characteristic sound. Visual agnosia is probably the most striking and common prototype agnosia, although agnosia is also described for other categories of stimuli, such as auditory verbal agnosia or auditory agnosia for environmental sounds, or tactile agnosia for objects. In this chapter only visual agnosia is discussed, although conceptual similarities apply to the other modalities as well. The concept of agnosia has not always been accepted for several reasons. One of the major sources of controversy is the unusual nature of verbal responses and compensatory behaviour which is seen in many of these cases and led to the attacks on the famous case of Goldstein and Gelb (1918) by Poppelreuter, Lange, Jung, and Bay. Some of these critics considered the syndrome a perceptual deficit associated with general mental impairment (Poppelreuter, 1917; Bay 1953; Bender & Feldman, 1972), or even hysteria (Lange, 1936; Jung, 1949).

2. VARIETIES OF VISUAL AGNOSIA

2.1. Apperceptive Visual Agnosia

The apperceptive process is conceived as the next step beyond the elementary or peripheral aspects of perception (see Fig. 6.1) although its limits have never been well defined. To some psychologists and clinicians, it represents an integration of basic perceptual elements into a meaningful whole. There are several questions raised by the concept, such as what constitutes an elementary level of perception, at what rate and extent the integration occurs, how much the associative processes contribute to the accuracy and speed of integration, and whether this process is separable temporally or neurally from other cognitive operations necessary for

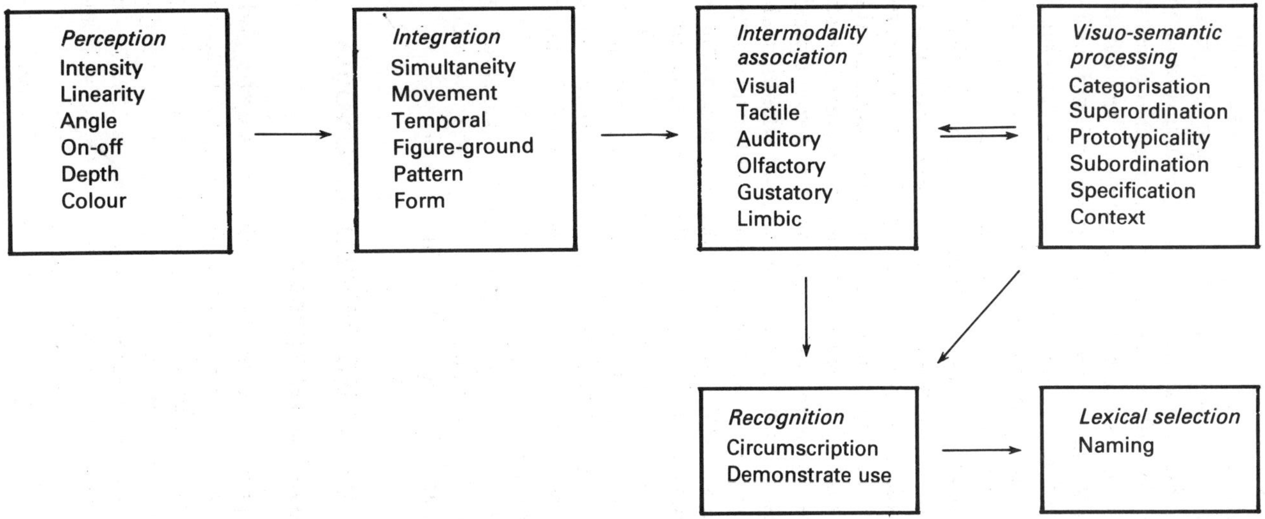

FIG. 6.1. Visual recognition.

recognition (see Humphreys & Quinlan and Humphreys & Riddoch, this volume).

The diagnosis of apperceptive visual agnosia should be restricted to patients who fail to recognise visual stimuli because of a processing deficit that is beyond elementary visual perception, but not due to associative deficit alone. These patients cannot copy or match shapes or objects to sample, and usually they cannot point to objects named. Elementary visual sensory processing, such as visual acuity, should be normal by definition. However, the testing of visual acuity, for instance, represents a difficulty because these patients cannot always recognise the targets. Nevertheless, if only a limited choice, such as the opening on the letter "E", or discrimination between two shapes, such as a diamond and a circle are used, relatively intact visual acuity can be demonstrated. Optokinetic nystagmus, luminance and wavelength discrimination may be intact (Efron, 1968), but flicker fusion and adaptation to light may be impaired. Visual fields show a concentric, irregular shrinking or spiralling inwards (Fig. 6.2) when retested, representing adaptation to repeated stimuli (Kertesz, 1979). These features, in fact, provided the main arguments for Bay (1953) that elementary perception is always impaired, but Ettlinger (1956) found that such deficits often occur without visual agnosia even though generalised mental impairment may be present. Furthermore, bilateral field defects,

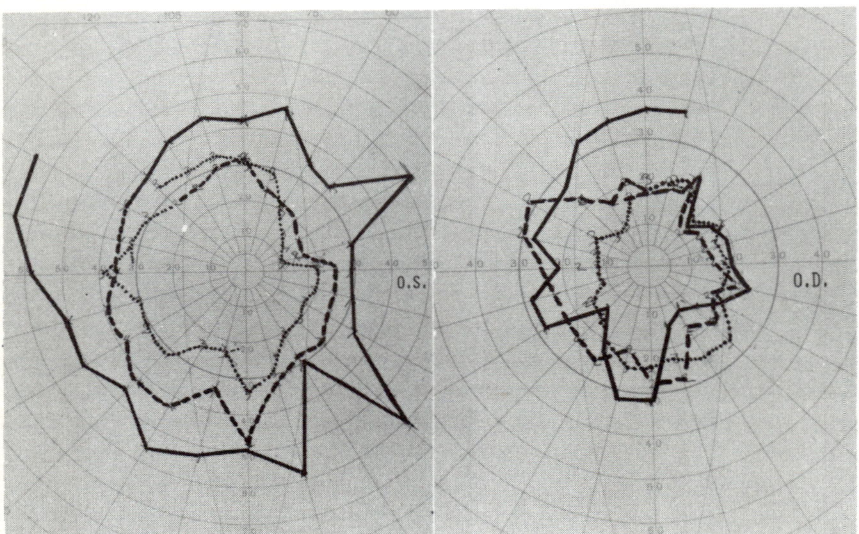

FIG. 6.2. Visual field impairment in a patient with visual agnosia. The left field (O.S.) was tested first. The diminishing circles on repeated testing indicate adaptation to the stimuli (Kertesz, 1979).

often with only macular sparing, do not result in visual agnosia. There is no consensus as to what constitutes an adequate clinical assessment of visual perception but the commonly used tests and the usual results are summarised in Table 6.1.

A specific form of apperceptive agnosia was described as visual form agnosia or failure of shape discrimination by Benson and Greenberg (1969). Their case suffered carbon monoxide poisoning and had a severe form of agnosia, including prosopagnosia and alexia, inability to match or copy but clearly preserved colour recognition and discrimination of luminance, wavelength, and moving light. Details of his psychophysiological testing was reported by Efron (1968). Similar cases in the literature are infrequent, and perhaps the cases of Adler (1944), Goldstein and Gelb (1918), and Landis, Graves, Benson, and Hebben (1982) belong to this category.

TABLE 6.1
Clinical Assessment of Visual Perception

Usually Normal Results	*Usually Impaired Performance*
Visual acuity	Flicker fusion
Optokinetic nystagmus	Light adaptation
Wavelength discrimination	Visual field adaptation
Luminance discrimination	Matrix completion (Raven's)
Length discrimination	Line tracing (Geneva)
Size discrimination	Masked object matching
Depth perception	Embedded figures
Elementary shape matching*	Incomplete pictures
Nonsense shape matching*	Category matching
Object matching*	Foreshortened view presentation
Copying objects*	Minimal features presentation

*May be impaired in apperceptive visual agnosia.

2.2. Associative Visual Agnosia

The classification of associative defects implies that perception and some integration of perceptual elements have taken place, but either the intermodality association or the visuo-semantic identification of the integrated pattern is faulty (Fig. 6.1). These patients can copy drawings, but cannot name or recognise what they have done and cannot answer multiple choice questions about the stimuli. Misidentifications often indicate semantic similarities, indicating that perception is accomplished, but the pattern is mismatched or mislabelled, or the appropriate association, be it verbal or nonverbal, cannot be evoked (Hécaen, Goldblum, Masure, & Ramier, 1974; Ferro & Santos, 1984). These patients often improve when auditory stimuli are supplied for the visual task (as in object–word matching); this suggests that visual characteristics of objects can be evoked from auditory input. This is not usually the case with apperceptive variety. Indeed, relatively good object–word matching may be considered indicative of associative agnosia, because, if no perception takes place (as is supposed to be the case in apperceptive agnosia), identification should not be possible, even with auditory cues.

As noted earlier, associative agnosia is characterised by good copying and visual matching. Together with this, there should be poor recognition, as shown by tests of function-matching, requiring the categorical matching of visually dissimilar stimuli from the same semantic category (e.g., Warrington & Taylor, 1978). As function-matches do not require naming, poor performance cannot be attributed to impaired name retrieval. Recognition may also be more difficult when transformation of the image or completion is required. Objects presented at an unusual angle or masked drawings may be particularly difficult, as may the identification of line drawings as opposed to real objects (e.g., Kertesz, 1979). This suggests some effect of "perceptual" variables on recognition. Also, in at least one case, salient features were more important in visual recognition than the principal axis of an object, in contrast to some right hemisphere damaged controls who did poorly with foreshortened objects with altered principal axis (Humphreys & Riddoch, 1984). None of these aspects of performance are characteristic of aphasia (Kertesz, 1979). Tactile, auditory, and olfactory cues are eagerly sought by the patients who often recognise objects or people by their characteristic noise or odour, and some are observed trying to touch everything in front of them. Combining details of pictures by enumerating them and verbalising components often lead to guessing and recognition, and patients seem to find themselves doing this unconsciously. Anticipation and context improve recognition, and the emotional or limbic significance of the target play an important role. Confabulatory responses, semantic and morphological confusions, as well as perseveration are sometimes prominent.

Hécaen et al. (1974) considered visual agnosia a deficit in categorisation in the sense of Goldstein's failure of abstraction. (i.e., a failure in abstracting the identity of objects, beyond the given visual information). Various forms of categorisation can also be separated (see Humphreys & Riddoch, this volume, Chapter 10, for more details). For instance, Riddoch and Humphreys, this volume, Chapter 4, have also shown that their patient, J. B., while not being able to recognise or show associative knowledge of objects could, however, categorise stimuli as real or not, indicating that categorising the familiar structure of objects is separate from any semantic categorisation.

2.3. Optic Aphasia

There is a related syndrome that is often called "optic aphasia" (Freund, 1889) in which visual naming and auditory-visual matching are impaired just like in visual agnosia. However, when multiple choice questions about the stimulus are asked and appropriately answered or the use of the unnamed object is demonstrated by the patient, recognition may be inferred. Unfortunately, this aspect of behaviour is not documented frequently and testing is not usually quantitative. Most clinicians consider optic aphasia a mild form of associative visual agnosia, often occurring in the recovery phase from visual agnosia.

Some accounts of optic aphasia resemble the account of visual agnosia as a modality specific naming deficit given by Geschwind (1965). The speech and language process is disconnected from the visual input and only receives partial information. This results in a characteristic confabulatory behaviour. The association of colour agnosia and alexia without agraphia is in favour of the disconnection hypothesis because both colour identification and recubing may depend on direct links between vision and language processes in the brain. Nevertheless, it should be pointed out that, at times, the visual fields are normal and colour agnosia, as well as alexia may be absent. Visual field defects are decreed to be important here as signalling the deficit in the visual processing regions in the brain.

Verbalisation interferes with performance in some optic aphasic patients. For instance, one patient misnamed objects, but silent object use demonstration (the patient was instructed to keep his tongue between his teeth) was followed by correct naming. Beauvois (1982) pointed out that the performance of such patients can be influenced by altering the emphasis on visual or verbal strategies. She also noted that verbalisation interferes with performance especially in the associative variety of visual agnosia. The term "optic aphasia" is used by Beauvois to separate those cases with modality specific naming deficit and verbal interference from patients whose deficits are not modality-specific. In aphasic naming deficits, all modalities are affected approximately evenly (Spreen, Benton, & Van Allen, 1966; Goodglass, Barton & Kaplan, 1968). There are exceptions to this rule, but to what extent is a matter of uncertainty, depending on how much of the difference is accepted as significant. Spreen et al. (1966) found that 2 out of 21 of their aphasics had two standard deviations more visual naming deficit than in the tactile modality. No evidence was presented concerning visual recognition.

There is only limited uniformity among clinicians as to how the above terms are used. What some would call "optic aphasia", others call "visual agnosia". Even the crucial tests are not agreed upon at times; what one author considers an important distinguishing element, is missing from another's description. Table 6.2 summarises what, I believe, are the most important discriminant features of these syndromes. Many case descriptions fall between these varieties and the case has been made for a dual apperceptive and associative deficit of recognition (Kertesz, 1979). Adler (1944) introduced her detailed presentation of a victim of the infamous Coconut Grove fire by stating "no two patients suffering from the disorder, visual agnosia, have identical derangements of function", and issues concerning the fractionation of agnosia are taken up by Humphreys and Riddoch (this volume, Chapter 10).

TABLE 6.2
Differentiation of Visual Agnosia

	Apperceptive	*Associative*	*Optic Asphasia*
Object naming	−	−	−
Point to named object	−	±	±
Copy	−	+	+
Draw from memory	+	±	±
Match identical objects	−	+	+
Match categories	−	−	+
Pantomime use	−	−	+
Circumscribe	−	−	±
Name from description	+	±	±

− = failure; + = spared; ± = partial or variable performance.

3. AGNOSIA AND CORTICAL BLINDNESS

Visual agnosia may be distinguished from cortical and cerebral blindness. The term "cortical blindness" indicates selective involvement of the occipital cortex and cerebral blindness indicates complete blindness from more anterior lesions elsewhere in the brain. Cortical blindness is different from visual agnosia, in that the patient complains of blindness, although light reflex and variable perception of light and motion can be demonstrated. There is usually loss of reflex lid closure to bright illumination and threatening gestures. The patient behaves for practical purposes as if he were blind. The relationship between cortical blindness and visual evoked responses (VER) remains confusing. Initial studies suggested the disappearance of VER which recovered parallel with clinical recovery, but subsequent studies, such as Bodis-Wollner, Atkin, Raab, and Wolkstein (1977), and Spehlmann, Gross, Ho, Leestma, and Norcross (1977) reported the persistence of VER in blind subjects with extensive bilateral destruction of cortical visual and association areas. Optokinetic nystagmus (OKN) is often used to differentiate between patients with true cortical blindness and those with functional blindess. The slow component of OKN is related to a conscious pursuit movement and it is absent in patients with cortical blindness. However, there is evidence that so-called passive OKN, which is related to the movement of contrasts in the visual field may be preserved, even in considerable destruction of these visual areas and degeneration of the lateral geniculate bodies (Ter Braack, Schenk, & van Vliet, 1971). OKN is also reported to have been preserved in several cases of visual agnosia, as described in some detail by Gloning, Gloning, and Hoff (1968). Transient cortical blindness is a common clinical experience, but the symptom rarely persists for sufficient documentation, unless the deficit is severe, in which case it tends to be persisting.

4. ASSOCIATED DEFICITS

Visual agnosia can be associated with right hemianopia, alexia without agraphia, colour agnosia, and prosopagnosia, although every one of these have been described independently and in various combinations (see Humphreys & Riddoch, this volume, Chapter 10). Colour agnosia, prosopagnosia, simultanagnosia, and agnosic alexia have all been considered at one time or another as distinct varieties of visual agnosia, but when visual agnosia for objects is present, the others are usually associated with it. The frequent association of these syndromes suggests a common mechanism of processing deficit, such as visuo-verbal disconnection. However, the variability in their co-occurence has been used to argue against a disconnection mechanism and in favour of distinct, dissociable, modular processing. Their association may be related to the anatomical proximity of structures subserving the visual aspects of the functions. Only a few cases of visual agnosia have been seen without alexia, colour agnosia, or prosopagnosia. On the other hand, there are many cases of prosopagnosia or pure alexia without visual agnosia. Other conditions, such as tactile agnosia, are described in association, but if conceptual clarity is to be maintained, they should be regarded as an exception to the rule that only stimuli in the visual modality are affected.

4.1. Colour Deficits

Achromatopsia is a loss of colour sense which is at times described in one visual field only. These patients are unable to name and match colour stimuli and complain of everything appearing either gray or colourless. Lesions of the inferomedial occipital cortex, especially the lingual and the fusiform gyrus, have been responsible for this syndrome (Meadows, 1974), which is a more elementary form of colour disturbance than colour anomia.

In colour anomia, purely visual tasks, such as colour sorting, and purely verbal tasks, such as associating colours with objects verbally, are normal. These patients, however, have a two-way disturbance of associating colour names with colours; that is, they also make errors in choosing the right colour on auditory stimulation. This symptom often accompanies pure alexia (Geschwind & Fusillo, 1966). The lesion is often a left occipital infarction with involvement of the corpus callosum. Colour anomia is the most common colour disturbance that accompanies visual object agnosia. Unfortunately the term "colour agnosia" is, at times, used to describe both achromatopsia and colour anomia. To complicate matters further "colour aphasia" is used for some cases of visuo-verbal disconnections for colours. Patients with colour aphasia fail on tasks that require both visual and verbal strategies (Beauvois & Saillant, 1985).

4.2. Alexia

Characteristically, alexia without agraphia or "pure alexia" accompanies visual agnosia. This is usually a verbal or word-form alexia also called "letter-by-letter reading" or "spelling dyslexia". The patient can recognise individual letters but not the pattern of the word as a whole. The meaning of the word is deciphered laboriously by integrating the sound or the name of the letters, but longer words often fail because of short-term memory limitations of phoneme–grapheme decoding or because of erroneous guessing. Writing to dictation or spontaneously is relatively well preserved, although spelling errors are often recorded and copying is much worse, often impossible. At times, writing is more severely involved and alexia and agraphia are recorded.

A few exceptional instances of visual agnosia have been recorded where reading was preserved (Gomori & Hawryluk, 1983; Levine, 1978; Mack & Boller, 1977; Newcombe & Ratcliff, 1974). Two of these were left-handed patients with left hemianopsia. In some cases, the preserved reading may be related to the preservation of either the more lateral, occipitoparietal tracts or the splenium or both (Albert, Soffer, Silverberg, & Reches, 1979).

4.3. Prosopagnosia

Failure to recognise familial faces, or prosopagnosia, have been noted in every instance of visual agnosia where this was tested or paid attention to, although there are some case descriptions where facial recognition was not even mentioned. The matching and recognition of unfamiliar but previously presented faces or facial memory are somewhat differing functions and have been described in a variety of conditions most often with right hemisphere damage (Benton & van Allen, 1972). Prosopagnosia, on the other hand, can occur without visual agnosia, and the published case reports suggest that bilateral inferior calcarine region infarction is most often the underlying lesion (Damasio & Damasio, 1983).

The recognition of a specific member of a visually distinct member of a class, other than faces, may also be impaired. A patient may not recognise his own car, although he may say it is a car and be able to describe its parts; a farmer may not recognise his cows (Bornstein, Sroka, & Munitz, 1969) or an electrician may be unable to recognise the patterns of blueprints, indicating difficulty with the recognition of the whole and its special meaning (see Sergent, this volume, Chapter 5, for further discussion of the relations between deficits in face recognition and deficits in object processing).

4.4. Confabulation

Sometimes, a striking feature of visual agnosia is the presence of apparently confabulatory responses to visual stimulation. A pen might be reported as a stick, and a ball as a lightbulb, etc. The problem is in distinguishing whether such responses are confabulations or visual confusions. Other cases appear to have predominantly semantic errors and the semantically related responses are perhaps more characteristic of associative agnosia. In these instances, categorisation of the structural characteristics of objects appears to take place, but the final outcome is an inappropriate semantic association. This also appears to be a cardinal feature of optic aphasia where the visuo-verbal process is thought to be specifically impaired. The confabulatory responses are, at times, in striking discrepancy from coexisting recognition indicated by pantomime (Lhermitte & Beauvois, 1973).

Often the confabulatory responses are related to previous stimuli and appear to be perseverations. These can be verbal perseverations, in which the patient uses bits and pieces of the previous conversation, or perseveration of a previously seen stimulus which seems to recur in response to subsequently presented items. One of the more peculiar forms of perseveration is when a correct response to the item appears with a delay after two or three intervening stimuli or even later (Table 6.3). This has been observed to occur even when initially no recognition has taken place (Kertesz, 1979). Although the response appears to be a preserveration to a previous item, it also represents delayed recognition in some instances. Occasionally the correct drawing of a currently viewed item is accompanied by a verbal perseveration of a previous response (Rubens & Benson, 1971; Lhermitte & Beauvois, 1973).

Apperceptive agnosic patients may use extensive verbalisation to

TABLE 6.3
Confabulatory Responses to Objects and Pictures

Object Stimulus	*Response*
Knife	Scissors (F)
Eraser	Suitcase
Paper clip	Eraser (P)
Screwdriver	Toothbrush
Key	Eraser (P)
Pipe	Pen (F)
Lightbulb	Ball (F)
Spoon	"H" (P)
Tape	Key Chain (F)
Pictures	
Key	Box (P)
Knife	Comb (F)
Watch	Beehive
Dog	Combcase (P)

The responses to stimuli in our case of visual agnosia (Kertesz, 1979) classified as F = form confusions: P = perseverative response, those not classified are bizarre with undetermined origin.

describe stimuli, such as the case of Goldstein and Gelb (1918), who would describe the letter "D" as a bowl or a half moon. A very good example of confabulatory responses that are verbally codified mental images was published by Landis et al. (1982) whose patient could only draw objects through an assembly of verbally encoded individual elements, a strategy similar to the one he used for individual letters. Some of the verbalisations lead to recognition as subjects are able to listen to their own verbal description of the details or parts of the objects and they are able to integrate it verbally rather than visually. This process may be additionally helped by contextual cues.

At times, the confabulatory response incorporates the correct response in a peculiarly augmented, semantically related or, at times, morphologically related description. For instance, the response to a picture of a snail is "a lion with a snail in front of its nose" (Landis et al., 1982). The augmentations often represent a previously occurring stimulus. The patient uses semantic approximations to the target and the verbal cues may lead to recognition and covert response. When another patient was shown a beach scene, she would first respond "a lawn with hydro poles on it"; "it also could be a lake. I see boats—these could be vessels with hydro poles on them, unless it is, you know, what are those things sticking out from sailing ships?" (Kertesz, 1979). This semantic "*conduit d'approche*" or semantic approximation is a feature of many of the case descriptions. The instability of the responses is further demonstrated when some of the patients carried on guessing even after their correct responses were reached, or expressed doubts about what they saw (Adler, 1944). Some of the responses are entirely bizarre and cannot be related to any previous visual or verbal stimulus. They seem to represent a disconnected visual process from verbal association that seem to run on by themselves, unchecked by visual matching or feedback.

4.5. Loss of Visual Imagery

Visual imagery and dreaming may also be lost in visual agnosia. This has been reported by Charcot (1883), Wilbrand (1892), and Brain (1941), suggesting that dreams lack visual components. Adler's (1944) patient had impaired visualisation, (she described birds as having four legs) but subsequently was able to describe rooms where she had been. Generation of images is dependent on visual memories, and it is likely that visuo-verbal cognitive processes are closely linked to visual imagery. Drawing from memory also utilises internal visualisation and imagery, but it is complicated by the perceptual input from what is already drawn on the paper and motor constructional processes that may be functionally independent but concurrently impaired.

4.6. Amnestic Syndrome

Memory losses can also be associated with agnosia. Such loss are often misinterpreted as dementia, although agnosic patients may have a specific, severe amnestic syndrome which is substantially different from the diffuse dementia of degenerative disease. Visual agnosia has also been viewed as a selective loss of visual meories (Ross, 1980). This is another way of expressing the influence of stored visual information on perceptual processing. Often the memory loss in visual agnosia extends to auditory material, however, such as paired associate learning or story recall. The amnestic syndrome, although frequent, is not universal in visual agnosia. There are numerous case descriptions reporting normal memory, although few contain information about the tests carried out. Impaired visual or verbal memory may reflect a more anterior extension of the lesions involving the hippocampal and medial temporal regions.

4.7. Anton's Syndrome and Subjective Visual Experiences

Patients with visual agnosia have a variable amount of visual complaints and insight into their deficit. At times this is specific, such as in the case of Levine (1978) who said "everything changes", or "objects disappear"

(Tyler, 1968) but others, such as ours (Kertesz, 1979), actually deny that anything is wrong, even when specifically asked. This particular patient, however, often went through the "spectacles ceremony" so aptly described by Critchley (1953). When confronted with a visual task she would ask for her glasses and then discussed why they did not seem to function, showing a lack of insight or anosognosia for her visual agnosia. This is similar to denial of cortical blindness or "Anton's syndrome". This behaviour is compatible with the notion that primary sensory data continue to activate the remaining intact brain, generating visual sensory awareness in the absence of conscious, insightful appreciation of the deficit. The variable degree of neglect of the deficit, or even its denial, may be related to the amount of right hemispheric (nondominant) thalamocortical involvement, which plays a role in producing hemispatial neglect.

4.8. Balint's Syndrome

The syndrome described by Balint (1909) can also co-occur with agnosia. In this syndrome there is an impairment of: (1) ocular fixation, (2) directing gaze and search, and (3) past pointing visually presented stimuli (termed "optic ataxia and psychic paralysis of gaze" by Balint). Tyler (1968) investigated the eye movements in a case of Balint's syndrome and visual agnosia with an eye camera. Normal patterns of visual fixation were observed for small saccades, but long saccades connecting parts of the picture were absent. The localisation and visual awareness of objects in space are independent of their recognition to some extent, but they are often facilitated by it. Patients with visual agnosia can often reach for an object accurately, although when this is also impaired, "optic ataxia" is the term used for "past pointing". Eye movements play an important role in visual perception (Holmes & Horrax, 1919; Michel, Jeannerod, & Devic, 1965). Eye camera studies show that adults fixate longer on informative or meaningful details of a picture (Mackworth & Bruner, 1970). It appears that recognition is facilitated by the integration of perceptual and oculomotor processes. This suggests that visual perception involves the simultaneous processing of new input with "top-down" information indicating informative spatial regions.

Balint's original case also had visual agnosia, but he paid particular attention to the disturbance of ocular fixation and search, and the clinical phenomenon of pointing past the target. It seems that all cases of Balint's syndrome, in fact, were associated with visual agnosia, even though this is not the case the other way around.

4.9. Static Agnosia

Goldstein and Gelb's (1918) case developed extraordinary compensatory strategies, such as tracing the object with fingers and head movements.

Botez, Serbanescu, and Vernea (1964) recognised, as other have observed, that sometimes the performance could be improved by moving the objects, but the patients were agnosic when the object remained static, and he called this "static object agnosia" (see Campion, this volume, Chapter 7, for further documentation of this). Botez postulated that this represented a dissociated impairment of the geniculostriate visual system from the intact tectopulvinar visual system, which doubles back from the collicular region to the cortex, and this second visual system allows the perception of movements to facilitate the recognition of objects. A case with apperceptive and associative features showed significant improvement on moving the objects, head turning and finger tracing at a distance suggesting that kinesthetic clues play an important role in recognition, at least in some of these patients (Kertesz, 1979). Another case report of striking kinesthetic mediation was published by Landis et al. (1982).

4.10. Simultanagnosia

It is commonly observed that patients with visual agnosia can recognise some details, but not the whole picture simultaneously. This was designated "simultanagnosia" by Wolpert (1924). Luria (1959) interpreted visual agnosia as a defect of simultaneous perception or a breakdown of complex serial feature analysis for processing a picture or pattern. In other cases, however, patients can eventually recognise objects by gradually shifting their attention from detail to detail (e.g., Kinsbourne & Warrington, 1963; Landis et al., 1982). The lack of simultaneous perception *per se* is unlikely to account for agnosia, unless it also produces difficulties in figure–ground discrimination (e.g., Goldstein & Gelb, 1918).

5. THE LESIONS PRODUCING VISUAL AGNOSIA

The anatomical localisation of lesions in visual agnosia is clearly occipital, but controversy exists concerning the anterior extent and bilaterality needed for the full syndrome. Hahn (1895) autopsied Lissauer's case and found a left occipital and splenial lesion. Nielsen (1937) reviewed 13 autopsied cases from the literature and concluded that unilateral involvement is sufficient to produce the syndrome, although inadequate case reports and inclusion of tumour material make this material difficult to interpret. There are several modern post-mortem cases that were reasonably well described in life and they all had bilateral inferior occipitotemporal lesions. Lhermitte, Chain, Escourolle, Ducarne, and Pillon (1972) had a case with infarcts in the right hippocampus, fusiform and lingual gyri, the cortex and subcortical area of the left fusiform gyrus, and an older lesion in the left angular gyrus. Benson, Segarra, and Albert (1974) described lesions in the cortex and subcortical white matter of the left fusiform and hippocampal gyri, as well as in the white matter of the right fusiform gyrus and ventral splenium. Albert et al. (1979) described infarcts in the white matter of the right hippocampal and lingual gyri, and the left fusiform and lingual gyri. The case of Mack and Boller (1977) had CT scan evidence of an infarct in the left posterior cerebral artery territory, and in the right inferior occipital and occipitotemporal region. Levine's (1978) case had a right occipital lobe removal for a tumour which extended bilaterally. A recent case of associative visual agnosia (Ferro & Santos, 1984) had only a left occipital lesion with involvement of the posterior radiations of the corpus callosum on the CT scan; however, the severe amnesia suggests that he may have had histological damage contralaterally. There are other cases with unilateral involvement on the CT scan. Our patient was in a decerebrate state after trauma, and probably compressed both posterior cerebral arteries through tentorial herniation, although a CT lesion was definite only in the left occipital lobe (Kertesz, 1979). A right frontal lesion was also present which was not considered necessary for the deficit. A similar post-traumatic case with prosopagnosia and bilateral CT abnormality was presented recently by Gomori and Hawryluk (1983).

From a general clinical viewpoint, we can state that the lesions associated with severe visual agnosia are usually bilateral occipital lesions with disconnection of the visual areas from speech and the limbic system (see Humphreys & Riddoch, this volume, Chapter 10 for further discussion on this). The inferior temporal region has extensive connections with the occipital lobes and has an important role in the categorical perception of stimuli by evoking visual memories. Inferior temporal neurones distinguish and retain relevant features of visual stimuli in animal experiments (Fuster & Jervey, 1981). In primates this region plays an important role in the categorisation of visual stimuli (Wilson & DeBauche 1981). Single unit studies of this region showed very large receptive fields, yet very selective activity (Gross, Roch-Miranda, & Bender, 1972; see also Humphreys & Quinlan, Chapter 3, this volume). Striatal lesions alone produce hemianopsia but not visual agnosia. Even some of these are shown to have "blind sight" (Weiskrantz, Warrington, Sanders, & Marshall, 1974). Tunnel vision with macular sparing is occasionally seen in bilateral striatal lesions, but this by itself does not cause visual agnosia. Striatal ablation in animals produced a loss of recognition of still objects but visuo-spatial orientation remained (Denny-Brown & Chambers, 1976). Bilateral ablation of striatal cortex in monkeys did not prevent the learning of some visual discriminations (Pasik & Pasik, 1971). Almost all human cases have more than a restricted area-17 destruction in the autopsied reports.

Diffuse degenerative disease can also produce visual agnosia and these cases are often described without hemianopia, indicating that complete striatal lesions are not necessary. Very few autopsy studies were done in the posterior degenerations of Heidenhahn, but in a few instances spongioform degenerations were found. Unilateral lesions with posterior callosal involvement (splenium) may be sufficient to produce the syndrome as evidenced from the many cases with right hemianopsia only. However, autopsy confirmation of this is still meagre. The etiology is often posterior cerebral artery infarction, and this tends to be bilateral in the severely affected cases that come to autopsy. Trauma is also a common etiology, either by contusion of brain or probably more commonly by producing herniation of the brainstem with subsequent compression of the posterior cerebral arteries at the level of the tentorium. Carbon monoxide poisoning or diffuse anoxia have also been described as an etiology, causing diffuse watershed area destruction in bilateral parieto-occipital regions, especially in cases of apperceptive visual agnosia and Balint's syndrome. Some of the variability of the clinical syndromes and presentations may be related to the variability of the structures affected (see Humphreys & Riddoch, this volume, Chapter 10).

6. THE FUNCTIONS OF VISUAL RECOGNITION

The question naturally arises, what do we learn about normal visual function in general by analysing the cases of central visual disturbances? Is there sufficient evidence to support a two-stage theory of visual recognition as it is assumed by classical descriptions or alternatively is there evidence for multiple stages in recognition? These questions are also taken up by Humphreys and Riddoch (this volume, Chapter 10). For the present, I wish to propose a multi-stage, rather than a two-stage, model of visual processing (Fig. 6.1). This model can then guide the further reviews of agnosic patients which are presented in the following chapters.

Evidence from studies of elementary perception (Marr, 1982) indicates that the first stage of perception concerns coding the intensity of light, linearity, angle depth, colour, and the on/off nature of the stimulus. There is ample evidence in the literature that this stage is intact in visual agnosia even in the apperceptive variety (Benson & Greenberg, 1969; Efron, 1968; Ettlinger, 1956). The next stage consists of the integration of the elementary aspects of stimuli and considers the simultaneity of features, their temporal relationship, possible movement, the spatial pattern, the figure ground relationships, and the overall form. There is evidence that this stage is greatly influenced by previous visual memories and limbic associations, as well as intermodality associations. For instance, what determines the figure ground relationship depends greatly on which stimulus is selected to have biological relevance to the individual and will achieve prominence in visual perception. This in turn depends partially on phylogenetically inborn as well as acquired or learned visuo-limbic experiences. Integration of a stimulus, which requires appropriate scanning of the complex visual pattern, is probably simultaneous and reciprocal to a great extent with the next stage which is intermodality association and matching of the stimulus with previous memories.

Impairment of the integrative aspects of visual perception is the major feature of apperceptive agnosia, as both clinical and experimental studies indicate. The close association of simultanagnosia, the recurring disturbance of figure ground discrimination, form agnosia, and static agnosia indicate that some of the components may be consistently affected, but others may occur in isolation. In fact, isolated colour agnosia and form agnosia indicate that some of the impairment occurs specifically at early stages of integration before intermodality association takes place. Therefore, one has to conclude that the visual integration stage is, indeed, an identifiable process and leads to the formation of percept which is a necessary prerequisite for forming further associations. The notion of a percept, therefore, has intrinsic psychological and clinical validity.

The stage of intermodality association allows the perceived and visually integrated stimuli to be matched to visual memories and from there to tactile, auditory olfactory, gustatory, and limbic mechanisms that reinforce and selectively influence the visual association. These other mechanisms may, in turn, feedback to influence the formation of the percept. Given such feedback processes, it is not surprising that matching tasks and other integrative components of visual perception may be defective in cases with primarily "associative" problems. This, in fact, supports the notion that in most instances of predominantly associative agnosia, apperceptive functions are also involved, implying a dual deficit. Nevertheless, some degree of modularity seems likely, as associative and apperceptive functions can be separately impaired.

In the case of associative agnosia, intermodality matching and its association with the integrative stage is weakened or disconnected from semantic specification. It is possible that when this route is disconnected, so that only partially integrated visual input is allowed to reach semantic specification, recognition cannot take place even with an intact semantic field. There is supportive evidence from the nature of confabulatory responses that inadequate information reaches the process of semantic specification in associative agnosia. Reinforcement of intermodality associations, such as providing auditory stimuli, increases the success of semantic categorisation and results in appropriate lexical selection and response.

The next stage, which is lexical selection, is accomplished before the usually elicited responses can be obtained, such as naming an object presented, or writing its name, or indicating its category or to answer questions about it. However, lexical selection is not an absolute prerequisite for recognition as has been demonstrated in cases of optic aphasia where, in fact, recognition may take place as evidenced by circumlocution or demonstrating the use of the object. Indeed, optic aphasia implicates a process of lexical selection beyond the stage of semantic specification. Impaired lexical selection may not be entirely specific for the visually presented stimuli, so that patients often have tactile agnosia, which may not be emphasised in discussions on optic aphasia as a separate entity. This, indeed, brings out the issue that the problem with lexical selection may go beyond modalities. However, there are cases where the visual modality is particularly affected, suggesting that lexical selection in these patients is predominantly impaired on visual stimuli. There are several possibilities explaining these differences. Individuals have different cerebral organisation or different structures may be involved in a selective impairment of lexical selection through a visual route. An alternate explanation is that intermodality associations are so weakened that the process of reaching lexical selection from semantic specification is unstable and unable to achieve a direct visuo-verbal connection (see Riddoch & Humphreys, this volume, Chapter 4).

The clinically demonstrable varieties of visual agnosia are suitable to experimental manipulation to some extent. A word of warning is in order, however. These patients often show a fluctuating disturbance and recovery often takes place precluding consistent experimentation through a lengthy period of time. Many of the case reports in the literature ignore associated disturbances in favour of selective experiments, supporting a certain point of view. Many of the so-called specific impairments between stages could be explained by alternative mechanisms if appropriate control studies were used. Nevertheless, a multi-stage theory of recognition which involves perceptual processes and their integration and association with stored memories is a valid model in considering visuo-semantic specification and visuo-verbal association

In summary, the clinical syndromes of visual agnosia overlap to a considerable extent, but they are sufficiently distinct to suggest a five-stage model of visual recognition that includes perception, perceptual integration, multimodality matching, visuo-semantic categorisation, and lexical selection. Most syndromes involve at least one and some, all the stages.

REFERENCES

Adler, A. (1944). Disintegration and restoration of optic recognition in visual agnosia. *Archives of Neurology and Psychiatry, 51*, 243–259.

Albert, M. L. Soffer, D., Silverberg, R., & Reches, A. (1979). The anatomic basis of visual agnosia. *Neurology (Minneap.), 29*, 876–879.

Balint, R. (1909). Seelenlahmung des "Schauens": optische Ataxie, räumliche Störung der Aufmerksamkeit. *Monatsschrift für Psychiatrie und Neurologie*, *25*, 51–81.

Bay, E. (1953). Disturbances of visual perception and their examination. *Brain, 76*, 515–550.

Beauvois, M.-F. (1982). Optic aphasia: A process of interaction between vision and language. *Philosophical Transactions of the Royal Society, London*, *B298*, 35–47.
Beauvois, M.-F. & Saillant, B. (1985). Optic aphasia for colours and colour agnosia: A distinction between visual and visuo-verbal impairments in the processing of colours. *Cognitive Neuropsychology, 2*, 1–48.
Bender, M. B. & Feldman, M. (1972). The so-called "visual agnosias". *Brain, 95*, 173–186.
Benson, D. F. & Greenberg, J. P. (1969). Visual form agnosia. *Archives of Neurology*, *20*, 82–89.
Benson, D. F., Segarra, J., & Albert, M. L. (1974). Visual agnosia-prosopagnosia. *Archives of Neurology, 30*, 307–310.
Benton, A. L. & van Allen, M. W. (1972). Prosopagnosia and facial discrimination. *Journal of the Neurological Sciences, 15*, 167–172.
Bodis-Wollner, I., Atkin, A., Raab, E., & Wolstein, M. (1977). Visual association cortex and vision in man: Pattern-evoked occipital potentials in a blind boy. *Science, 198*, 629–630.
Bornstein, B., Sroka, H., & Munitz, H. (1969). Prosopagnosia with animal face agnosia. *Cortex, 5*, 164–169.
Botez, M. I., Serbanescu, T., & Vernea, I. (1964). Visual static agnosia with special reference to literal agnosic alexia. *Neurology, 14*, 1101–1111.
Brain, W. R. (1941). Visual object-agnosia with special references to the Gestalt theory. *Brain, 64*, 43–62.
Charcot, J. M. (1883). Un cas de suppression brusque et isolée de la vision mentale des signes et des objets (formes et couleurs). *Progrès médical*, *11*, 568–571.
Critichley, M. (1953). *The parietal lobes*. London: Edward Arnold.
Damasio, A. R. & Damasio, H. (1983). Localization of lesions in achromatopsia and prosopagnosia. In A. Kertesz (Ed.) *Localization in neuropsychology*. New York: Academic Press.
Denny-Brown, D. & Chambers, R. A. (1976). Physiological aspects of visual perception. I: Functional aspects of visual cortex. *Archives of Neurology, 33*, 219–227.
Efron, R. (1968). What is perception? *Boston Studies in Philosophy of Science, 4*, 137–173.
Ettlinger, G. (1956). Sensory deficits in visual agnosia. *Journal of Neurology, Neurosurgery and Psychiatry*, *19*, 297–307.
Ferro, J. M. & Santos, M. E. (1984). Associative visual agnosia: A case study. *Cortex, 20*, 121–134.
Freud, S. (1891). *Zur Auffassung der Aphasien: Eine kritische Studie*. Vienna: Franz Deuticke.
Freund, C. S. (1889). Über optische Aphasie und Seelenblindheit. *Archiv für Psychiatrie und Nervenkrankheiten, 20*, 276–297.
Fuster J. M. & Jervey, J. P. (1981). Inferotemporal neurons distinguish and retain behaviorally relevant features of visual stimuli. *Science, 212*, 952–954.
Geschwind, N. (1965). Disconnexion syndromes in animals and man. *Brain, 88*, 585–644.
Geschwind, N. & Fusillo, M. (1966). Color-naming defects in association with alexia. *Archives of Neurology, 15*, 137–146.
Gloning, L, Gloning, K., & Hoff, H. (1968). *Neuropsychological symptoms and syndromes in lesions of the occipital lobe and the adjacent areas*. Paris: Gauthier–Villars.
Goldstein, K. & Gelb, A. (1918). Psychologische Analysen hirnpathologischer Fall auf Grund von Untersuchungen Hirnverletzter. *Zeitschrift für die gesamte Neurologie und Psychiatrie, 41*, 1–142.
Gomori, A. J. & Hawryluk, G. A. (1983). Visual agnosia without Alexia. *Neurology, 33*, (Suppl. 2), 203.
Goodglass, H., Barton, M., & Kaplan, E. (1968). Sensory modality and object comprehension in aphasia. *Brain and Language, 11*, 488–496.

Gross, C. G., Roch-Miranda, C. E., & Bender, D. B. (1972). Visual properties of neurons in inferotemporal cortex of the macaque monkey. *Journal of Neurophysiology, 35*, 96–111.

Hahn, E. (1895). Pathologisch-anatomische Untersuchung des Lissauer'schen Falles von Seelenblindheit. *Psychiatrische Klink Breslau, 21*, 109–119.

Hécaen, H., Goldblum, M. C., Masure, M. C., & Ramier, A. M. (1974). Une nouvelle observation d'agnosie d'objet. Deficit de l'association où de la catégorisation specifique de la modalité visuelle? *Neuropsychologia, 12*, 447–464.

Holmes, G. & Horrax, G. (1919). Disturbances of spatial orientation and visual attention with loss of stereoscopic vision. *Archives of Neurology and Psychiatry, 1*, 385–407.

Humphreys, G. W. & Riddoch, M. J. (1984). Routes to object constancy: Implications from neurological impairments of object constancy. *Quarterly Journal of Experimental Psychology, 36A*, 385–415.

Jung, C. (1949). Über eine Nachuntersuchung des Falles Schn. von Goldstein und Gelb. *Psychiatrie, Neurologie und Medizinische Psychologie, 1*, 353–362.

Kertesz, A. (1979). Visual agnosia: The dual deficit of perception and recognition. *Cortex, 15*, 403–419.

Kinsbourne, N. & Warrington, E. K. (1963). A study of visual perseveration. *Journal of Neurology Neurosurgery and Psychiatry, 26*, 468–475.

Kluver, H. (1936). An analysis of the effects of the removal of the occipital lobes in monkeys. *Journal of Psychology, 2*, 49–61.

Kluver, H. & Bucy, P. C. (1937). "Psychic blindness" and other symptoms following bilateral temporal lobectomy in rhesus monkeys. *American Journal of Physiologia, 119*, 352.

Landis, T., Graves, R., Benson, D. F., & Hebben, N. (1982). Visual recognition through kinaesthetic mediation. *Psychological Medicine, 12*, 515–431.

Lange, J. (1936). Agnosien und Apraxien. In O. Bumke and O. Foerster (Eds.), *Handbuch der Neurologie*, pp. 807–880. Berlin: Springer-Verlag.

Levine, D. N. (1978). Prosopagnosia and visual object agnosia: A behavioral study. *Brain and Language, 5*, 341–365.

Lhermitte, F., Chain, F., Escourolle, R., Ducarne, B., & Pillon, B. (1972). Etude anatomo-clinique d'un cas de prosopagnosie. *Revue Neurologique, 126*, 329–346.

Lissauer, H. (1889). Ein Fall von Seelenblindheit nebst einem Beitrage zur Theorie derselben. *Archiv für Psychiatrie und Nervenkrankheiten, 21*, 222–270.

Luria, A. R. (1959). Disorders of simultaneous perception in a case of bilateral occipito-parietal brain injury. *Brain, 83*, 437–439.

Mack, J. L. & Boller, F. (1977). Associative visual agnosia and its related deficits: The role of the minor hemisphere in assigning meaning to visual perceptions. *Neuropsychologia, 15*, 345–351.

Mackworth, N. H. & Bruner, J. S. (1970). How adults and children search and recognise pictures. *Human Development, 13*, 149–177.

Marr, D. (1982). *Vision.* San Francisco: W. H. Freeman.

Meadows, J. C. (1974). Disturbed perception of colors associated with localized cerebral lesions. *Brain, 97*, 615–632.

Michel, F., Jeannerod, M., & Devic, M. (1965). Trouble de l'orientation visuelle dans les trois dimensions de l'espace (à propos d'un cas anatomique). *Cortex, 1*, 441–446.

Munk, H. (1881). *Ueber die Funktionen der Grosshirnrinde.* Gesammelte Mitteilungen aus den Jahren 1877–1880. Berlin: Hirschwald.

Newcombe, F. & Ratcliff, G. (1974). Agnosia: A disorder of object recognition. In F. Michel and B. Schott (Eds.), *Les syndromes de disconnexion calleuse chez l'homme*. Lyon: Colloque International.

Nielsen, J. M. (1937). Unilateral cerebral dominance as related to mind blindness. *Archives of Neurology and Psychiatry 38*, 108–135.

Pasik, T. & Pasik, P. (1971). The visual world of monkeys deprived of striate cortex. Effective stimulus parameters and the importance of the accessory optic system. *Vision Research Supplement, 3*, 419–435.

Poppelreuter, W. (1917). *Die psychischen Störungen durch Kopfschuss, Vol. 1: Die Störungen der niederen und höheren Sehleistungen durch Verletzungen des Occipitalhirns*. Leipzig: L. Voss.

Ross, E. D. (1980). Sensory-specific and fractional disorders of recent memory in man, I: Isolated loss of visual recent memory. *Archives of Neurology, 37*, 193–200.

Rubens, A. B. & Benson, D. F. (1971). Associative visual agnosia. *Archives of Neurology, 24*, 304–316.

Spehlmann, R., Gross, R. A., Ho., S. U., Leestma, J. E., & Norcross, K. A. (1977). Visual evoked potentials and postmortem findings in a case of cortical blindness. *Annals of Neurology, 2*, 531–534.

Spreen, O., Benton, A. L., & Van Allen, M. W. (1966). Dissociation of visual and tactile naming in amnesic aphasia. *Neurology, 16*, 807–814.

Ter Braak, J. W. G., Schenk, V. W. D., & van Vliet, A. G. M. (1971). Visual reactions in a case of long-lasting cortical blindness. *Journal of Neurology, Neurosurgery and Psychiatry, 34*, 140–147.

Tyler, H. R. (1968). Abnormalities of perception with defective eye movements (Balint's syndrome). *Cortex, 4*, 154–171.

Warrington, E. K. & Taylor, A. M. (1978). Two categorical stages of object recognition. *Perception, 7*, 695–705.

Weiskrantz, L., Warrington, E. K. Sanders, M. D., & Marshall, J. (1974). Visual capacity in the hemianopic field following a restricted occipital ablation. *Brain, 97*, 709–728.

Wilbrand, H. (1892). Ein Fall von Seelenblindheit und Hemianopsie mit Sectionbefund. *Deutsche Zeitschrift für Nervenheilkunde, 2*, 361–387.

Wilson, M. & DeBauche, B. A. (1981). Inferotemporal cortex and categorical perception of visual stimuli by monkeys. *Neuropsychologia, 19*, 29–41.

Wolpert, I. (1924). Die Simultanagosie: Störung der Gesamtauffassung. *Zeitschrift für die gesamte Neurologie and Psychiatrie, 93*, 397–415.

7 Apperceptive Agnosia: The Specification and Description of Constructs

John Campion*
Ergonomics Unit, Department of Psychology,
University College London, Gower Street, London WC1E 6BT, U.K.

1. INTRODUCTION

The objectives of this chapter are three-fold. First, to examine critically some of the terms used to describe agnosias. Secondly, to propose a theory of one type of agnosia. Thirdly, to test this theory against two cases presented in the literature.

A major problem in neuropsychology, as in psychology in general, is not only the generation of concepts which aid our understanding of the systems we examine, but the generation of a language appropriate for describing them. Consider, for example, the traditional definition of agnosia as "seeing without recognition". The common language use here suggests that such a condition is not unusual. We very often see things (perhaps once familiar faces) that we fail to recognise. However, in the technical clinical sense these terms mean that patients with agnosia fail to recognise objects that people normally recognise, while performance in clinical sensory tests, such as acuity and brightness discrimination remain within normal limits. The various classificatory schemes traditionally used to provide a further specification within this general class of patients reflect the clustering of the disorders as they present themselves in clinical examination (e.g. Nielsen, 1937; Kertesz, this volume, Chapter 6). A major distinction suggested by Lissauer (1889), and one which is the focus of this chapter, was between associative agnosia, in which the percept is intact but the associations for its recognition are not formed, and apperceptive agnosia, in which the percept itself is degraded. The criterion traditionally used to distinguish between these two classes of agnosia is the

---

*Presently at the Behavioural Science Division, Admiralty Research Establishment, Queens Road, Teddington, Middlesex.

ability to copy drawn figures. The associative agnosic succeeds in such a test whereas the apperceptive agnosic fails.

It can be seen then, that the class of patients traditionally defined as apperceptive agnosics sit between two classes of test, sensory tests which admit them to the class of agnosics, and perceptual tests which restrict them to the class of apperceptives. Difficulties arise, however, when attempts are made to convert this classification based on performance in two sets of *tests* into one based on two sets of *functions*. Thus, simply through the use of language, apperceptive agnosia comes to be underpinned by two notions—that of the *sensory function* and that of the *apperceptive function*. It will be argued in this chapter that a failure to consider the true status of these terms has led to a misleading view of agnosia.

2. A NEUROPSYCHOLOGICAL FRAMEWORK FOR VISION

All neuropsychological research is contained within a meta-theoretical framework comprising a description of brain structure, a description of brain function, and some mapping between the two. We can discern three approaches to designing such a framework which are sometimes explicit and are sometimes only implicit in the respective research strategies. They can be described as: (1) direct mapping approach (DMA); (2) function only approach (FOA); (3) levels of description approach (LDA).

Direct mapping can be regarded as the mainstream or traditional approach and may be illustrated by the work of Warrington (1982). In this case brain structures are described in terms of gross anatomy, and putative function terms are mapped directly onto these descriptions. Thus, in the case of Warrington (1982) there are three structure terms—visual cortex, right posterior cortex, and left posterior cortex. The directly mapped function terms are, respectively, visual analysis, perceptual categorisation, and semantic categorisation, also referred to as three "stages in object recognition". A similar approach is adopted by Kertesz (this volume, Chapter 6) who posits five stages in visual recognition.

Direct mapping is criticised by Mehler, Morton, and Jusczyk (1984) who are major proponents of FOA. An important point made by these authors is that, although it is an assumption of neuropsychology that brain physiology is related to mental activity, we cannot specify the constraints between psychological processes and their neurophysiological substrate. The authors also make an important distinction between research activities which attempt to establish a mapping between psychological functions and brain structures, and those which merely use data from brain damaged patients to establish psychological explanations independent of the knowledge of the brain structures damaged.

The authors take their view to be similar to that of Marr (1982), the main proponent of LDA (see also Stevens, this volume, Chapter 2). Marr holds that an information processing device (a computer or a brain), in order to be fully understood, requires explanations at three different levels—computation, algorithm, and hardware. Each level, though, would be regarded as independent of the others.

In this chapter I wish to argue a position which is broadly in agreement with both FOA and LDA, but is more general. Both these approaches import an a priori view of brain systems which could be misleading in the field of neuropsychology, where we are dealing with systems that are damaged in random and complex fashions. In particular, I suggest there are two problems with the concept of levels of description in neuropsychology. First, the number of levels required is not clear; and, secondly the technical language required for describing concepts at a given level is not well developed. The claim of Mehler et al. (1984) is that as psychological accounts are cast at a different level and serve different purposes than brain structure accounts, the latter cannot be held to constrain the former. Now, this could be true if we were only after psychological accounts, but this does not seem to be the case with the issues confronting us in the neuropsychology of vision. What we are after are functional accounts which aid our understanding of the brain processes subserving visual perception, given the nature of brain damage typically found in clinical patients. This is rather a different problem because it means that our accounts are constrained by the nature of the brain damage and the observations of behaviour we can make in relation to this. So it seems that, contrary to the view of Mehler et al. (1984), brain structure accounts do constrain our functional accounts in the sense that structural accounts should capture those aspects of the damage causing the functional change, and functional accounts should be expressed at a level which captures the effects of the damage. Now, in one sense of course, this is done whenever brain damaged subjects and normal subjects are compared at some task, but what seems to cause confusion is the use of non-technical language unable to specify concepts with sufficient precision to tie them to a particular level.

Consider the problem of defining apperceptive agnosia in terms of a notion such as "sensory function" (or "elementary perceptual function" to use the term of Humphreys & Riddoch, this volume, Chapter 10). It is not so much that these terms make assumptions about the organisation of perceptual processing (cf. Humphreys & Riddoch, this volume), but that these terms should not be used in a way which forces them to be seen as having consequences at the perceptual processing level. It seems that these terms, underpinned as they are by observations on a particular set of tests, should only be used to carry "weight" at a level appropriate to these empirical underpinnings, and I suggest that this be referred to as the *task level*. Many of the difficulties which have arisen in the interpretation of agnosias can be understood as failures to make distinctions between task and function level descriptions and one of the symptoms of this failure is that, for a given function term, it has proved difficult for workers to agree on what constitutes an "instance" of it. The effects of this will be made clear in the following section which examines in some detail the notion of "sensory loss" and how this has been used in understanding agnosia.

3. SENSORY LOSS THEORY AND AGNOSIA

3.1. Bay's Theory

A defining attribute of agnosia has been the intactness of sensory function, and traditional debate has centred around whether agnosics are *really* sensorily intact or whether agnosia results from undetected sensory function deficits. The problem thus presents itself as an *empirical* question: "Have adequate tests of sensory function been carried out?" However, the view here is that the problem should present itself as an *analytical* question: "How should performance on a sensory test be employed in a functional account of agnosia".

A major proponent of the "sensory loss" theory was Bay (1953). Bay's theory rested upon the observation that, with a sophisticated battery of sensory tests (particularly those involving temporal parameters such as flicker and fading time), it could be shown that (p. 534): ". . . there does not exist a single case of agnosia without elevated sensory disorders and without mental deterioration". Bay concluded: "There is neither a specific gnostic function nor a specific disorder of this function. Such apparently gnostic activities and disorders as completion phenomena, hemianopic inattention, Gestalt dissolution, and so on, are due to disorders of the so-called primary sensory functions or to general psychological qualities which are not confined to a certain sensory sphere but are necessary for sensory perceptions independent of the sense organ and of the import of the perception". The important contribution made by Bay lay in his demonstration that the definition and extent of visual dysfunction depended critically on the sort of tests employed to investigate it, but he failed to appreciate that physiological and psychological terms refer to different levels of description rather than to different stages in processing. This led him to state that: "As the delimitation of physiological components of perceptions is arbitrary and in contrast to unbiased introspection, agnosia can only be defined per *exclusionem*, namely, as an impairment in the recognition of perceptions without corresponding disorders of the elementary sensory functions and without general mental disability". This statement shows how a poor analytical structuring of the problem (maintaining a single level of description with a consequent enforced arbitrary division of stages) leads to an intractable empirical problem, that of detecting the complete exclusion of deficit in putative sensory functions.

Sensory tests such as those involving acuity, brightness, and colour discrimination are commonly regarded as "primary" or "basic", the implication being that such tests tap functions which are the "building blocks" of higher-level perceptual functions. However, given the integrative functions which must be necessary to produce, for example, complex colour discriminations in terms of hue, saturation, and brightness, it is not clear that such processes are in any sense more basic than those involved in form discrimination. What is important about sensory tests, when contrasted with perceptual tests, is that they involve tasks which do not require the subject to make judgements based on the configural properties of stimuli. The problem seems to be that we require at least two levels of description here: the specification of visual functions found to be sensitive to brain deficits expressed at the level of the perceptual task; and the specification of the relationship between such task descriptions and the brain functions underlying the deficit. The failure to appreciate the need for different levels of description led Bay to his base his claim for a sensory basis to agnosia solely on showing the co-extension of agnosia and defective performance in his tests. This exposed him to an unjustified refutation of his theory, discussed in the following section.

3.2. Ettlinger's Refutation

Perhaps the most influential challenge to the sensory loss theory has come from Ettlinger (1956). His findings are widely taken to provide a definitive demonstration that agnosia is not necessarily related to sensory loss. It is therefore worth considering the logic of his argument in some detail, so that we can see the misleading conclusions which can arise from the use of constructs lacking sufficient precision.

Ettlinger studied 30 patients falling into 3 categories of sensory loss:

1. No field defect or sensory loss.
2. Field defect but no perceptual loss.
3. Field defect and perceptual loss.

Their sensory visual capacities were measured using 6 indices of performance:

1. Tachistoscopic acuity (TA).
2. Flicker fusion (FF).
3. Brightness discrimination (BD).

4. Acuity for small objects (AC).
5. Apparent movement perception (AM).
6. Local adaption (LA).

From these was derived for each patient a Mean Efficiency Index (MEI).

Ettlinger rejected sensory loss theory on the grounds that low MEI was not co-extensive with agnosia. Thus, there were patients with grossly impaired MEIs who did not suffer from agnosia and there were agnosics who did not have grossly impaired MEIs. We should note that Ettlinger (1956, p. 306) admits that: "No true case of visual object agnosia in the classical sense of the term is included in our series. In the one case of prosopagnosia (Case 23), moreover, the overall efficient index was undoubtedly low". This evidence which could be taken to support Bay is dismissed on the grounds that: ". . . three patients in our series (Cases 19, 24 and 26) gave evidence of an even greater reduction in sensory efficiency without the least trace of prosopagnosia. It is also noteworthy that one patient (Case 18) gave no evidence of visual agnosia at a time when fluctuating alterations of sensory function were present over the entire visual field".

The major weakness in Ettlinger's argument arises from the lack of any means of relating, at the task level, performance in his tests to performance in Bay's and from the lack of any means of judging whether the tests tap the complete set of sensory functions which might be defective in agnosia. These points can be illustrated by reference to Ettlinger's treatment of prosopagnosia.

The logic of Ettlinger's argument may be stated as follows:

1. There are 4 patients.
2. A patient is characterised by:
   (a) Perceptual category disorder (P or not P) according to whether he has prosopagnosia or not.
   (b) Sensory efficiency score (SE) between 1 and 100.
3. One patient is P and has low SE.
4. Hypothesis: low SE causes P.
5. But: 3 patients are not P and have low SE.
6. Therefore: low SE does not cause P.

The three patients who have low SE without agnosia are used as negative instances to refute the proposition that low SE causes prosopagnosia. It is thus implied that low SE is not a *sufficient* condition for prosopagnosia (see Fig. 7.1).

Ettlinger then goes further to claim that because three other patients have visuo-spatial agnosia without a low SE, this is further evidence that low SE does not cause agnosia. From this, it is implied that low SE is not a *necessary* condition for visuo-spatial agnosia (see Fig. 7.1). By concluding

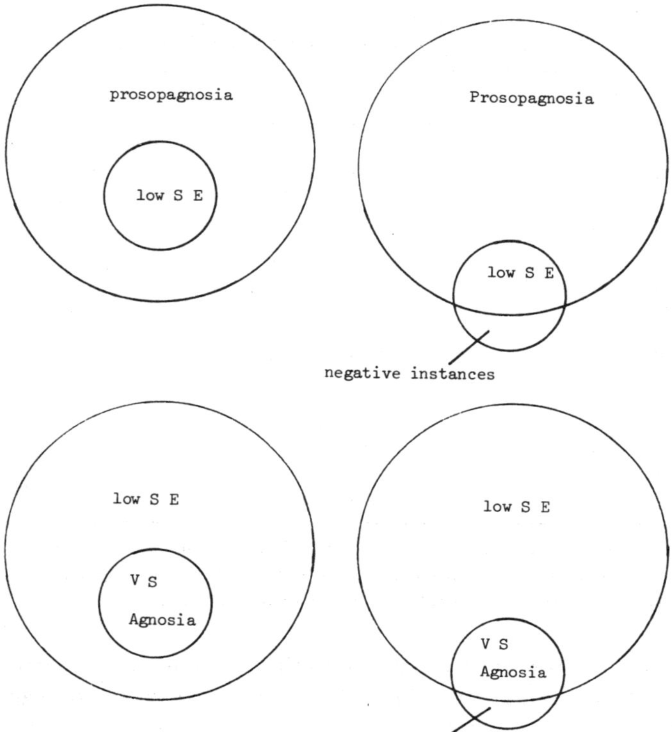

FIG. 7.1. The propositions of Ettlinger's (1956) argument expressed as logical classes. His study was intended to test the theory that all agnosias are caused by sensory deficits (low SE). There were two classes of agnosic patient suffering from prosopagnosia and visual spatial (VS) agnosia, respectively. The reasoning used to refute the theory can be expressed as two propositions represented by the upper and lower pairs of diagrams, respectively. The upper pair of diagrams represent the proposition that all patients having a low SE should suffer from agnosia and its refutation by the negative instances of some low SE patients who did not suffer from agnosia. The lower pair of diagrams represent the proposition that all patients suffering from agnosia should have a low SE and its refutation by the negative instances of some agnosic patients not having a low SE. The discussion in the text shows why the reasoning was false—not because of a failure in logic but the status of the constructs was such that the logical operations failed to reflect relations in the real world of brain damage and patient behaviour.

that: "We cannot, however, find confirmation of his view that such defects play an appreciable part in the generation of visual agnosias", Ettlinger rejects the proposition that low SE is both necessary and sufficient to cause agnosia.

This is unwarranted because Bay's claim was merely that sensory functions in *general* are responsible for all agnosias. The relationship between such functions, a particular set of tests and a particular type of agnosia were left unspecified. From the analysis and data that Bay produced, all that could be predicted is a strong association between a given battery of tests and agnosia in general.

Let me illustrate by argument by examining the patients of Ettlinger's described above. Clinical and SE details of each patient are provided from Ettlinger in Table 7.1. Mean SE is low with respect to the normal value and is similar across patients, whereas scores on particular tests vary widely across patients, who are thus discriminated, not by their mean scores, but by their score profiles.

Performance on the tests used by Ettlinger could be due to a variety of factors. However, let us assume that prosopagnosia is due to a deficit causing the visual system to respond poorly to luminance change, perhaps because of impairment to a particular class of cells. This may be described as the function level deficit underlying prosopagnosia. However, let us also suppose that performance in a particular brightness discrimination test depends on at least two factors: a general (functional level) sensitivity to brightness and the size of the stimulated visual field. Performance on the brightness discrimination test would constitute a task level account of a patient's capacities. It is thus possible to identify both a *function-level* description, of general brightness discrimination capacity, and a *task-level* description of the measured brightness discrimination capacity. If we term the general brightness discrimination capacity *BD*, and the measured capacity *BD′*, we can express the relationship between the two as:

$$\mathrm{BD}' = f\,(BD)$$

where f is a weighting coefficient between 0 and 1 reflecting the size and location of any field defect. A value of f of 1 would indicate intact fields, and a value of 0 would indicate total blindness.

Now suppose that f had a value of 0.9 for Ettlinger's prosopagnosic patient (S23), because he had only a small central field defect. Let us also suppose that for some of the non-prosopagnosic patients (e.g., patients S19, S24, and S26) f had a value of 0.2, because they had larger, more peripheral field defects. *BD′* for each patient, taken from Table 7.1, is 42 (S23), 21 (S19), 42 (S24), and 37 (S26). One might infer from the *BD′* data alone that the three non-prosopagnosic patients had lower brightness discrimination capacity than the prosopagnosic patient, and, therefore, prosopagnosia is not due to a "sensory" disturbance in brightness discrimination. However, given our assumed weighting functions, the function level of brightness discrimination in the patients (i.e., *BD*) would be 46 (S23), 105 (S19), 206 (S24), and 185 (S26). The latter result would of course be entirely consistent with the argument for a "sensory" disturbance underlying prosopagnosia. Obviously this example is hypothetical, but it illustrates that if performance in a test is determined by factors additional to those underlying the functional level deficit, then

TABLE 7.1
Sensory Loss: Four Patients Taken From Ettlinger (1956)

Age	*Diagnosis*	*Field Defect*	*Perceptual Disorder*
Case 19			
27	Suprasellar meningioma; right subtotal frontal lobotomy	Bitemporal constriction	None

BD	FF	AC	LA	TA	AM	*Total*
21	13	47	167	17	50	*35*

Age	*Diagnosis*	*Field Defect*	*Perceptual Disorder*
Case 23			
52	Bilateral occipital infarct	Bilateral para-central scotoma upper quadrants	Prosopagnosia achromatopsia topographical loss

BD	FF	AC	LA	TA	AM	*Total*
42	38	26	94	22	41	*36*

Age	*Diagnosis*	*Field Defect*	*Perceptual Disorder*
Case 24			
63	Occlusion of basilar artery	Right homonymous hemianopia	Visual alexia

BD	FF	AC	LA	TA	AM	*Total*
42	38	26	94	22	41	*36*

Age	*Diagnosis*	*Field Defect*	*Perceptual Disorder*
Case 26			
49	Supratentorial meningioma	Concentric constriction more marked	Visual constructive defect

BD	FF	AC	LA	TA	AM	*Total*
37	33	26	11	11	50	*32*

The numbers below each case represent scores in each of six sensory efficiency tests. BD, brightness discrimination; FF, flicker fusion; AC, acuity for small objects; LA, local adaptation; TA, tachistoscopic acuity; AM, apparent movement detection.

interpretation of performance is misleading without some means of explaining the relations between the task and function level deficits. Thus, two levels of description are required, a function level and task level, and a mapping function between the two. In the hypothetical case presented, the two levels would be a measure of general brightness sensitivity determined by the cells destroyed and a measure of performance in a given test. The mapping function would be the weighting coefficient.

The above points are illustrated in the following section, which describes work carried out over a number of years on a single agnosic patient (R.C.), and concludes with a theory of his disorder based upon the notion of contour masking. In the final section, I compare R.C.'s performance with that of two other patients in the literature whose disorders can be understood in a similar manner.

4. A CASE OF APPERCEPTIVE AGNOSIA

4.1. The Patient

R.C. worked as a foreman in an iron foundry until 1975 when he suffered carbon monoxide poisoning resulting from an accident in which he was trapped for 45 minutes inside a chimney. He was unconscious for several hours and was completely blind when he regained consciouness. He gradually regained his sight over the following few weeks but was left with a severe visual impairment which was diagnosed as visual agnosia. He has been unable to work since the accident and cannot go out of the house unaccompanied. R.C.'s ability to "recognise" features of his surroundings and "get by" in a normal environment has improved dramatically over the years, especially in the first year or two following the accident. However, the view presented here is that most, perhaps all, of this long-term recovery has been a consequence of his learning to re-interpret a permanently altered phenomenal world, rather than as a consequence of restored vision.

A full ophthalmological and neuropsychological assessment of this patient has been presented elsewhere (Abadi, Kulikowski, & Meudell, 1981). He was diagnosed as having a severe agnosia with intact sensory functions apart from a small field defect and diminished low spatial frequency sensitivity. Cognitive functioning was reported normal apart from evidence early on of slight language and memory deficits which later disappeared. I examined the patient experimentally on a number of occasions between 1979 and 1983. Some of the data have been discussed elsewhere (Campion, 1984; Campion & Latto, 1985). A CAT scan (Fig. 7.2) indicated a diffuse lesion more prominent above the calcarine sulcus of the left hemisphere extending into striate and prestriate cortex. There was some involvement of the prestriate cortex of the right hemisphere. A

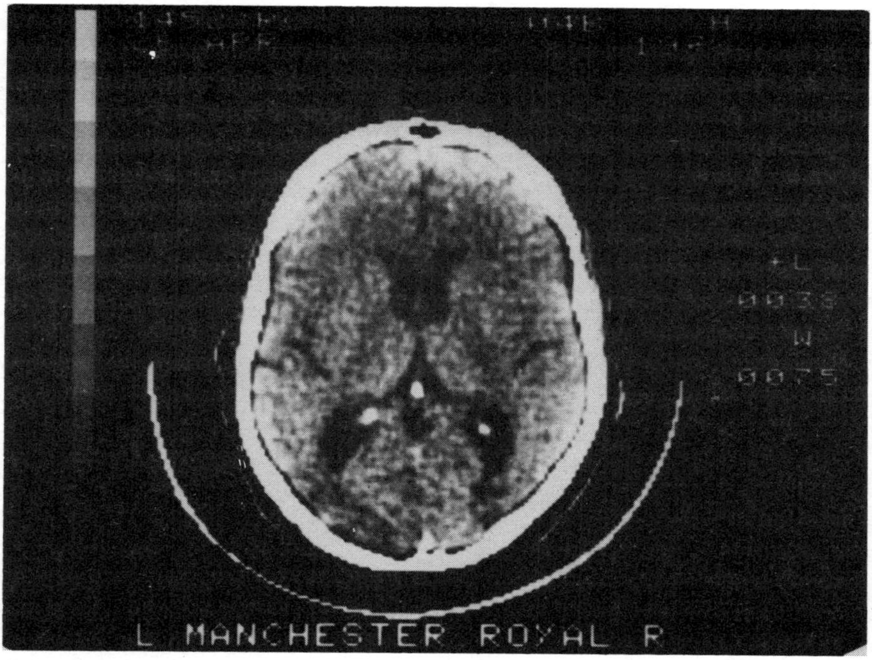

FIG. 7.2. CAT scan of R.C.'s brain recorded on 26th April 1978. The section is immediately above the calcarine sulcus. Note the low density (dark) area in the left occipital lobe involving striate and prestriate regions, and also the smaller low density patch in the prestriate region of the right hemisphere.

dynamic field plot (Fig. 7.3) revealed a right inferior defect consistent with the CAT scan. A feature of the field not noted by the earlier study was its contraction and uncertainty of response introduced by the use of an outward moving target (see Section 4.3). I originally attributed this to the altered nature of the task, together with R.C.'s generally poor vision, but I later took this to indicate that the crude dynamic plot produced by a conventional inward moving target was actually disguising the existence of a patchy field defect of a complex nature.

4.2. Behavioural Testing

4.2.1. Clinical Picture

R.C. was mentally alert and talked freely and normally. He was unable to recognise common objects placed in front of him, simple geometric shapes, the orientation of lines or grating patterns or even the number of such items (1 or 2) presented together. He was unable to name items,

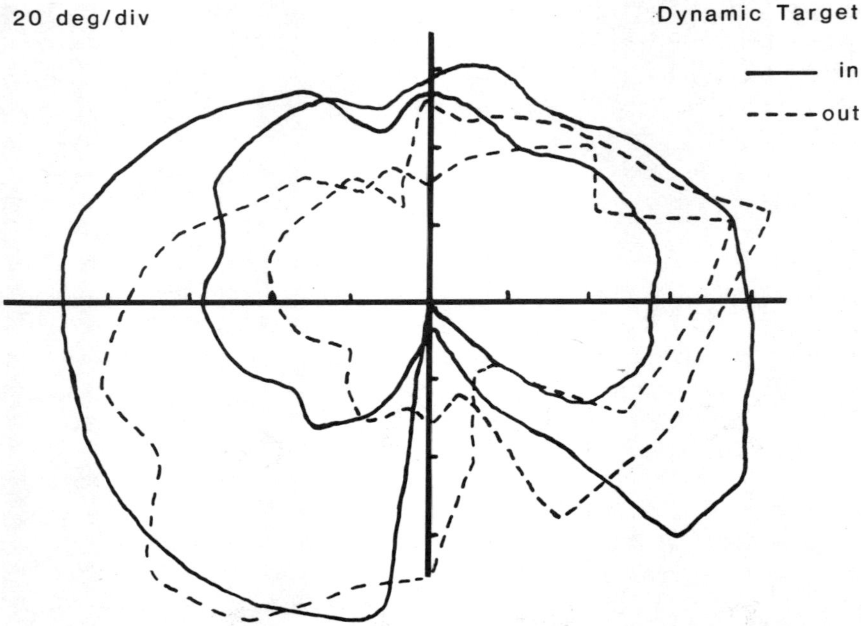

FIG. 7.3. Dynamic plot of R.C.'s visual fields using a Goldman Perimeter recorded on 7th December 1979. The target was 64mm, intensity "e". The solid lines indicate the plot for an inward moving target and the broken lines for an outward moving target. Left and right eyes are superimposed. The border of the field for the outward target was more indefinite than that for the inward target as well as being contracted. The broken line indicates the modal position from 3 or 4 determinations. The border was most indefinite along the most contracted meridian.

describe their functions or make same/different judgement between pairs presented side by side or in sequence. His agnosia would be classed as apperceptive on the grounds that he could not copy or trace items. He could not even trace along a straight line with his finger with confidence or accuracy. He could not recognise the letters shown in Fig. 7.4, nor could he trace any of these with his finger. He could, however, write some letters and numbers to command, although his performance was poor (Fig. 7.4) and it seems likely that he was using mainly proprioceptive cues. There was some indication of some residual shape discrimination in that he identified the "M" in Fig. 7.4 as "W", and said that he had been able to recognise "X"s on car number plates when they had been added as the year identifier. He could not, however, recognise the "X" shown to him in Fig. 7.4. He could readily identify letters and numbers "traced" in the palm of his hand by a finger.

In contrast to his very poor form perception, he could negotiate obstacles in the room, reach out to shake hands and manipulate objects or to

FIG. 7.4. *Top*: Letters shown to R.C. for identification and tracing. Real height 15cm. *Bottom*: Letters and numerals drawn freehand by R.C. to command. Identification is given below each figure.

reach a cup of coffee. He could readily name objects by nonvisual cues such as touch or sound. He could also comment on features of objects such as their colour or whether they were shiny or not. He could also recognise the "texture" of objects, although he found this difficult to describe. He seemed particularly sensitive to fine repetitive patterning such as the graticules on drawing instruments or the teeth on a comb. If encouraged, he could often make an accurate inference about the the nature of objects from such cues. Also, when asked to identify items, he would often move his head around as if searching for the best view, or he might move towards or away from the object as if trying to "get it in focus". This behaviour suggested that the was trying to build up a picture of the world by a kind of scanning activity.

4.2.2. Discrimination of Complex Items

To test his discrimination abilities more rigorously, R.C. was asked to name 30 line drawings of common objects from the Boston Naming Test and 27 object equivalents. Naming was untimed and he was given the correct name at the end of each trial whether he had correctly identified the item or not. Near misses such as the response "flower" for "tree" were counted as correct as it indicated that he was recognising some attributes of the item. There were four testing sessions spread over four days. Each session contained new items and some that he had failed to recognise on the previous session. Objects were identified more easily than pictures and repetition improved his performance considerably. Initially, R.C. scored 17 out of 27 for objects and 5 out of 30 for pictures. Of all the items repeated at least once he scored 16 out of 17 for objects and 8 out of 12 for pictures. Two features of R.C.'s performance must be emphasised. First, successful performance on the above tasks did not indicate normal recognition. All identifications were difficult for him and he often hesitated and was uncertain of the correctness of his responses. Secondly, he appeared to use partial cues to infer the identity of items. Objects were easier than pictures because, presumably, there were more cues available. It seems likely that there remained some limited amount of form perception because, although dependence on such an inferencing operation is abnormal, the fact that he could manage this with line drawings suggests that he was not only using non-form cues such as size, colour, and reflectance.

4.2.3. Discrimination of Simple Items

The next study probed the limits of his residual capacity by using items of simple structure and a sensitive performance measure. It also examined his discrimination of small luminance differences and desaturated hues. Pairs of stimuli were presented in random sequence and a forced choice response was required with feedback. The results (see Fig. 7.5) show that, with training, R.C. could learn to discriminate stimuli differing only in some simple spatial parameter such as orientation, also that colour and brightness discrimination were substantially impaired under these conditions. Neither of these features was discovered during clinical examination. Again, the patient's report suggested that he was not recognising the stimuli and it was only the feedback that allowed him to attach, what seemed to him a quite arbitrary verbal label, to a novel percept. For example, he reported that the vertical grating was identified because it was more "prominent" than the horizontal one. The square stimulus, R.C. said, looked like a "row of lines" and the circle like "a lot of dots". All discriminations were, of course, trivially easy for normal subjects.

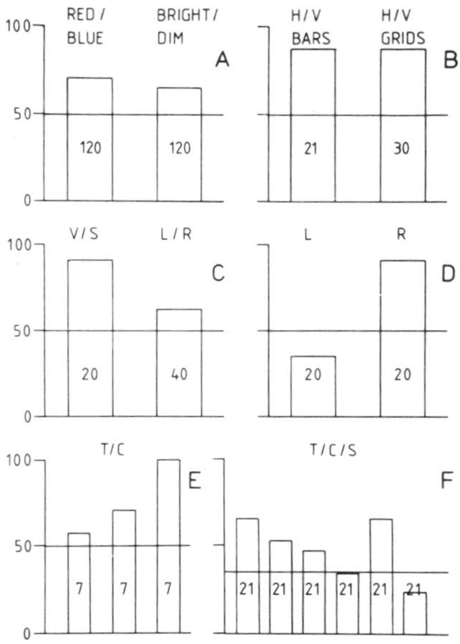

FIG. 7.5. A–E: Percentage correct forced choice judgements between pairs of stimuli. The number within each bar shows the number of trials in which stimuli were presented and the horizontal line indicates chance performance. Stimulus parameters: A: Red vs. blue plain field using Kodak filters CC30R vs. CC30B. Bright vs. dim plain field using no filter (300 cd/m^2) and Kodak neutral density filter, N.D. 0.3. Fields were 22°c.s. 22° high and 15°c.s. 22° wide. B: Horizontal vs. vertical bar (8°c.s. 22° × 2°c.s. 22°) and horizontal vs. vertical square wave gratings (3 cycles/degree, 15°c.s. 22° circular field). C: Vertical vs. slanting (45°c.s. 22°) gratings and left vs. right slanting gratings (\ vs /) parameters as above. D: Proportion of left and right slanting gratings correct. The asymmetry could have been due to a response bias but R.C. seemed much surer of the right gratings, saying that they appeared more "prominent".

4.2.4. Localisation Ability

Casual observation suggested that R.C. could localise objects adequately. However, more careful observation suggested that operations such as walking up and down steps were performed with greater deliberation and uncertainty than normal. Also, he tended to give obstacles in the room a wider berth than was necessary or usual. Surprisingly, when presented with two squares of light on a screen 50cm away from him (each 2cm across and 20cm apart, one above the other) and asked how many spots of light there were, he replied "One". When asked to touch the spot of light he leaned forward and placed his finger on the lower of the two squares accurately but with some deliberation. He was asked to keep his finger in place and see if he could see any other spots of light. This he did, but despite looking around the screen, replied that he could see no other spots of light. This appeared as some kind of visual neglect because there was no obvious sensory basis for this disturbance.

To test R.C.'s localisation ability more accurately, a special semi-circular perimeter was constructed (described in Campion, Latto, & Smith, 1983). The subject viewed binocularly a central illuminated spot. Target lights of 1°18′ diameter were switched on for 1 second at one of 20 positions in a random sequence. The subject moved a pointer pivoted in the centre of the perimeter arc, while maintaining fixation, to where he thought the light had appeared. There were 10 positions of the light (between 8° and 80° from the fixation spot) in each hemifield and 10 presentations of the light in each position. Mean response position is plotted against mean target position for each hemifield in Fig. 7.6. A z transform of the two regression coefficients reveals that they are significantly different (see caption to Fig. 7.6). Normal subjects in this task produce correlations between target and response of about 0.9 (see Campion et al., 1983). Thus, precise localisation ability is poor, and is poorer in the right visual field, the one subserved by the hemisphere most affected by the lesion according to the CAT scan.

4.2.5. Contrast Sensitivity

A study of visually evoked potentials (Campion & Latto, 1985) suggested that lesion effects had caused R.C.'s visual system to become unusually insensitive to certain spatial frequencies and orientations. Abadi et al. (1981) had reported that the patient's contrast sensitivity function (CSF) was relatively normal. However, I wished to investigate this further under conditions that would allow me to measure his CSF for different orientations of gratings and for different hemifields of presentation, to establish some relationships between the anatomical, electrophysiological, and behavioural evidence.

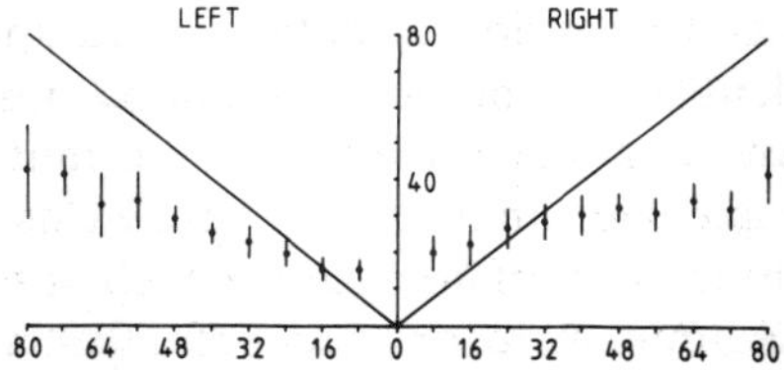

FIG. 7.6. Mean pointing responses for R.C. (vertical axis) with standard deviations (n = 8), to target positions (horizontal axis) in the left and right visual fields. Axes are labelled in degrees of visual angle. Regression equations for response (Y) on target (X) are: $Y = 0.39 + 11.4$ (left field); $Y = 0.25X + 19.3$ (right field). The two slopes are significantly different ($P < 0.001$).

Contrast thresholds were measured for horizontal and vertical gratings of six spatial frequencies (see Fig. 7.7). Stimuli were flashed for 10msec in left, right, and full fields, and the subject's task was to detect a pattern of any kind. There were five trials for each stimulus using the ascending method of limits. The average contrast value was plotted against spatial frequency for each hemifield (see Fig. 7.7). CSF was determined in this fashion for the patient and for a normal subject. Whereas the CSF showed the usual "U" shape for the normal subject, it was grossly abnormal for the patient, being virtually flat. This resulted from fairly normal thresholds for low and high spatial frequencies, but with very little variation between these extremes. In the normal subject, although there were differences in the CSF between hemifields, the full field CSF could be derived as a summation of each hemifield's response. This clearly was not the case with the patient. There were slight orientation differences in the normal subject (horizontal stimuli produced consistently higher thresholds) but these differences were consistent across spatial frequency and hemifield. In the patient, however, the CSF was quite different in shape for each orientation (although the absolute differences were small) and the extent of the differences varied between hemispheres. In the full field case, differences between orientations were virtually zero except at lower spatial frequencies. Thresholds were generally higher in the right field (subserved by the left hemisphere), and to this extent, there is some relationship between anatomical and behavioural data, but the case of the unusual CSF remains obscure. The data are important, however, in indicating, as did Bay, the importance of temporal factors in "elementary" perceptual tasks detecting deficits.

4.2.6. Orientation Discrimination

Unfortunately, the differences in Fig. 7.7 are not statistically reliable, although they do provide a tenuous link between behaviour, anatomy, and electrophysiology. However, it remained unclear how these findings related to the patient's perceptual discrimination abilities. As both electrophysiological and behavioural data showed spatial frequency sensitivity to be dependent on orientation and lateral position, I next investigated R.C.'s capacity to make forced choice orientation judgements at different spatial frequencies in the two hemifields. R.C. made forced choice orientation judgements of gratings for each of six spatial frequencies in each hemifield. Stimuli were presented for 500msec. R.C. made an orientation judgement on each trial, at the end of which he received feedback. Results are shown in Fig. 7.8. Performance was poor, but averaged across spatial frequencies, it was above chance in both hemifields, and seemed to vary with spatial frequency, and between hemifields. Statistical power was low in this study and the observed differences again

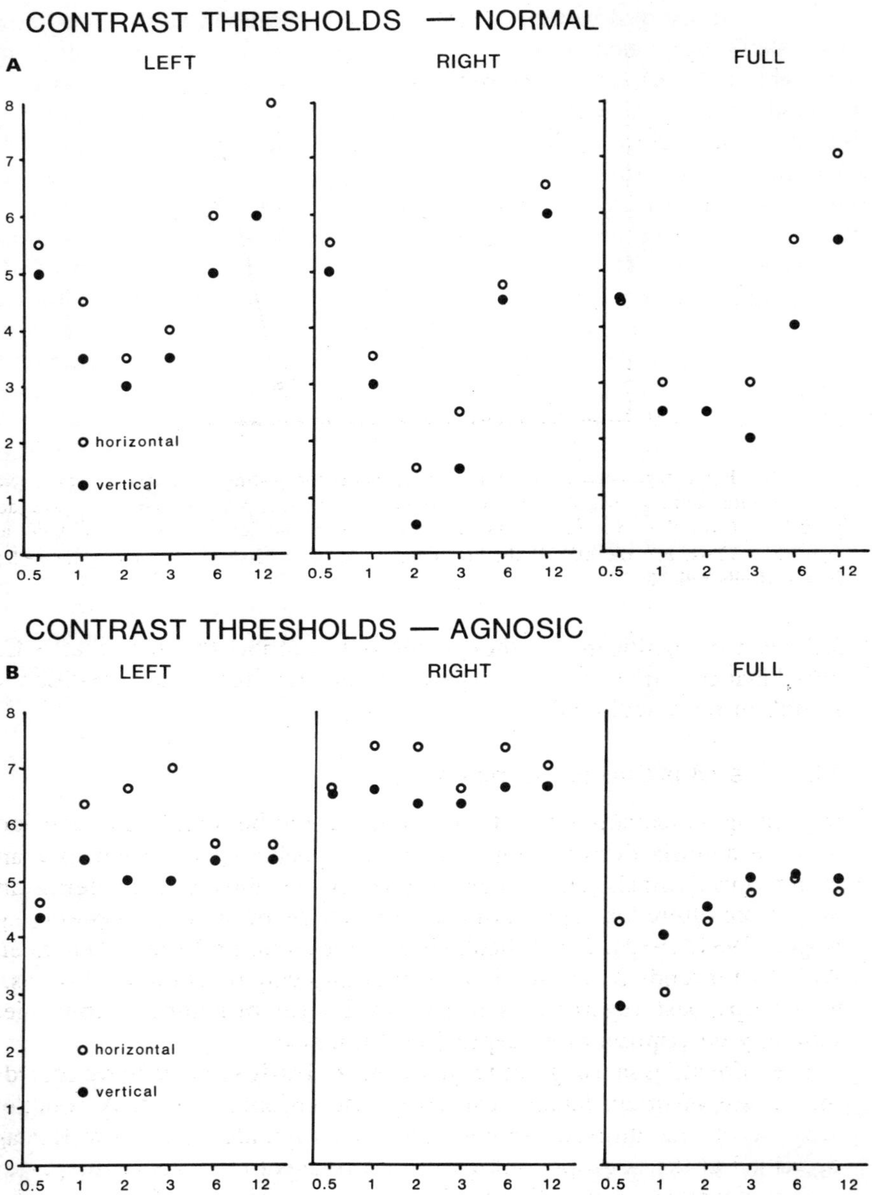

FIG. 7.7. Contrast threshold (vertical axis) to square wave gratings of 6 spatial frequencies (horizontal axis) for left, right, and full field stimulation. Orientation of gratings was horizontal (open circles) or vertical (filled circles). A, normal subject; B, agnosic patient. Thresholds are expressed in arbitrary units and spatial frequencies in cycles/degree visual angle.

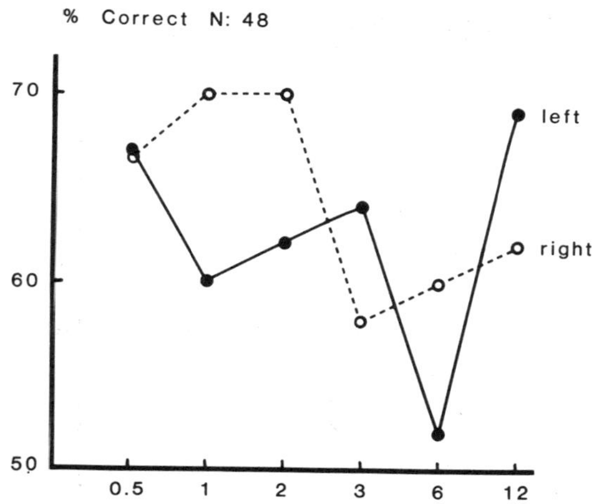

FIG. 7.8. Percentage correct orientation judgements for gratings of 6 spatial frequencies: 24 horizontal and 24 vertical stimuli were presented at each spatial frequency in a random sequence. Overall performance was above chance in the left ($z = 4.2$. $P < 0.05$) and right ($z = 22.04$, $P < 0.0005$) fields. For a single set of 48 trials, performance above 62% is statistically reliable.

fell short of significance, although the data support the view that R.C.'s performance varies with the spatial frequency and lateral position of stimuli in the visual field.

4.3. The Masking Hypothesis

In seeking an explanation of these data, it could be tempting to conclude that the agnosia derives from damage to specific spatial frequency and orientation channels. Deficits are frequently explained in these terms and indeed are offered in support of a channel model of the visual system (e.g., Regan, 1981, 1982). The difficulty here is the status of the term "channel". Although it tends to be used in a manner implying function-level status, it is perhaps best regarded as a task-level term providing a convenient summary description of perceptual performance.

The difficulties in using this term are more clearly seen when we consider the nature of brain damage caused by the lesioning agent. A complete account of the disorder should allow us to understand how damage described at the neurophysiological level relates to deficits at the perceptual performance level. From what is known of the effects of carbon monoxide intoxication at the neurological level however (e.g. Garland & Pearce, 1967), there does not seem to be any way of relating this to the concept of "channel". Although there are frequent attempts (e.g. Regan, 1981) to map the term directly onto particular classes of cortical neurone, the utility of this has not been well established. In the case presented here, we have no reason for expecting carbon monoxide to damage selected classes of cell.

From R.C.'s subjective reports and discrimination performance, it was clear that he used unusual perceptual operations to discriminate objects or grating patterns. For example, identity of objects was inferred from cues such as approximate size, shape, and colour; grating orientation was discriminated on the basis of "prominence". A consideration of these operations seemed necessary for a potential explanation. The fact that R.C. could see very fine detail, and could discriminate some stimuli differing only in shape, suggested that some sort of form perception was possible but was made difficult because of some sort of severe degradation. Why should a square, for example, look like a "row of lines" or a circle like a "lot of dots" (Section 4.2.3)? In this respect, it is interesting that R.C.'s perception of fine detail was relatively unimpaired. His acuity was normal and he could recognise features such as fine graticule markings (although we cannot be sure that inferencing was not involved here). For instance, he could readily detect fine texture features such as stippling in line drawings or pebble-dash on the side of a house. Perhaps one way of characterising his phenomenal world is to say it was such that a mass of dots continued to look like a mass of dots, whereas a coherent outline was altered to look also like a mass of dots. The patient continually asserted when questioned that his vision was "not clear", but it was "not blurred as it might appear through a frosted glass window". In consideration of this a return to the visual field plots is instructive (Fig. 7.3). Although the dynamic "inward" plot was almost identical to that of Abadi et al.'s fig. 7 (1981), the "outward" plot produced an irregular and uncertain boundary. Now, since carbon monoxide poisoning is known to cause multi-focal (peppery) infarcts of cortical tissue (Garland & Pearce, 1967) due to anoxia, it seemed possible that such infarcts within the occipital cortex had caused his visual field to become peppered with numerous minute scotomata. The size and distribution of these could perhaps cause masking or interruption of object contours at an average spatial "interruption" frequency such that acuity performance remained unimpaired, but object identification was severely disrupted. The effect would be similar to the "critical band masking" of Stromeyer and Julesz (1972), but in this case we would regard the scotomata as acting similarly to a simple mask or filter imposed on the patient's image of the world, rather than appealing to the concept of the spatial frequency channel.

To test this hypothesis, Richard Latto and I examined in detail the central portion of the patient's visual field using a sort of find grain static perimetry (Fig. 7.9A). The central portion of his field was divided into 800

1 degree squares and a spot of light was flashed in the centre of each square for 1 second while R.C. fixated a central spot monocularly. Each flash was rated for perceived brightness on a scale of 1–4. Each square was plotted with a spot whose size was inversely proportional to perceived brightness, maximum brightness leading to a square being left blank. This field plot is shown in Fig. 7.9B, from which it is clear that fluctuating light sensitivity exists over the central portion of a visual field defined as normal by conventional dynamic perimetry. This fluctuation in sensitivity could be defined by an associated spatial frequency in task-level terms. That is, it

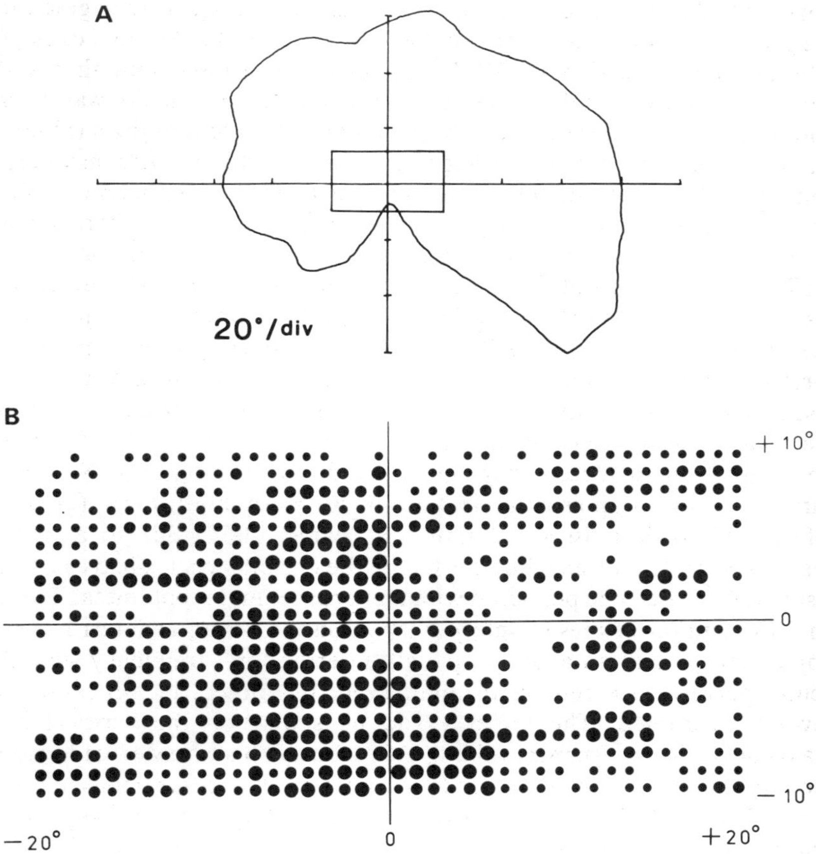

FIG. 7.9. A: The area of R.C.'s right eye visual field subjected to the fine grain static perimetry described in the text. B: The area in A with spot size indicating the rated brightness of light targets. A large spot indicates low rated brightness.

FIG. 7.10. A: Photograph of a scene, and B: the same photograph covered with a random dot mask to simulate what the world might look like to R.C. It is assumed that the patient would not actually be aware of the dots but would be left with the consequent disruption of contour necessary for form perception. Note the differential masking effect of the same mask on different objects. Thus, the child's face completely disappears, whereas the wheelbarrow remains visible. The bucket contour is disrupted to an intermediate extent.

could cause a decrement in sensitivity at specific spatial frequencies in CSF tasks. This definition allows us to specify the deficit with some precision, without committing us to explanatory notions based on "channels". The crucial question is whether spatial frequency masking expressed in these terms could completely account for the agnosic symptoms. Figure 7.10A shows a photograph of a child playing with a bucket behind whom is a wheelbarrow and Figure 7.10B, the same photograph covered with a random dot mask. I suggest that this represents the sort of image that R.C. has of the world, although he would be unaware of the dots themselves because of their cortical origin and he would be left only with their perceptual consequences. It is interesting to note the differential effect that a mask of only a single spatial frequency (in the task sense) has on the objects in the scene. The child all but disappears, the bucket becomes difficult to see, but quite a lot of the wheelbarrow remains recognisable. When this picture is shown to normal subjects who have not previously seen the unmasked version, they invariably fail to see the child and rarely see the bucket. The wheelbarrow, however, is normally described as a cart or trolley of some description. In other words, subjects tend to make inferences from partial cues in the same way agnosic patients do. The quality of the inferences is remarkably similar between the groups. There is also some anecdotal evidence that subjects can learn to adapt to the degradation and become better at "seeing" what is in the picture. This could possible be analogous to the "recovery" noted in R.C. (Abadi et al., 1981). It seems plausible that the masking effect could account for all the behavioural data but, to be taken seriously, the hypothesis would require more precise specification. An attempt at a crudely quantified test was made by attempting to simulate R.C.'s discrimination performance in a normal subject by investigating the effects of random dot masks of two different "spatial frequencies" on CSF orientation discrimination. Stimuli were tachistoscopically presented for 10msec, and followed by a random dot mask which disrupted grating detection. There were three mask conditions: "no mask", "low frequency mask", and "high frequency mask". The "spatial frequency" of the mask was varied simply by varying the average density of dots without any attempt at quantification. Both the CSF and orientation discrimination were measured. The results are given in Fig. 7.11. Different spatial frequencies of mask were found to elevate detection thresholds, depending on spatial frequency of the stimulus. The elevation is in the direction predicted by the masking hypothesis. That is, the low frequency mask elevates low frequency targets most, and the high frequency mask elevates high frequency targets most. Notice that the presence of the mask has a general flattening effect on the CSF as we saw in the case of R.C. The effect of the masks on orientation discrimination is more complex, but can perhaps best be described as a

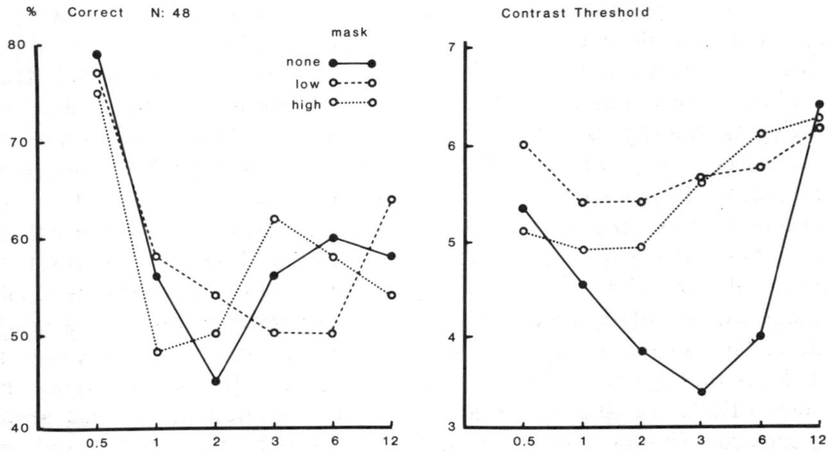

FIG. 7.11. *Left*: Percentage correct forced choice orientation judgements in a normal subject for 6 spatial frequencies (horizontal axis) under 3 masking conditions. *Right*: Contrast thresholds (vertical axis, arbitrary units) for the same subject and the same stimuli under the same masking conditions. Note the flattening of the CSF under masking conditions and the interaction between spatial frequency and mask.

shift of the performance curve towards the low frequency end with the high frequency mask, and towards the high frequency end with the low frequency mask.

Clearly, the results from these two simple experiments with a single normal subject cannot be taken as a definitive test of the masking hypothesis as an explanation of R.C.'s deficit. They do, however, serve as a crude test of the hypothesis and they produce results suggesting it is worth pursuing.

4.4. Summary of Findings and Conclusions

By traditional clinical criteria, R.C. presents as a case of apperceptive agnosia. However, experimental analyses showed that he has abnormal brightness and colour discrimination and an abnormal CSF, indicating reduced sensitivity to pattern especially in the right visual hemifield, with the degree of sensitivity depending on the orientation of the pattern. His visual field is also peppered with scotomata in a random and asymmetrical fashion.

These data, together with the electrophysiological data reported elsewhere (Campion & Latto, 1985), suggest that R.C. is least responsive to patterns in the left hemisphere where the lesion indicated by CAT scan is largest. It is suggested that the visual agnosia in this patient is caused by a simple masking of contour produced by a peppered visual field.

The key questions that arise from this research are: (1) Is the masking hypothesis true either as it stands or in some modified form? (2) Could masking explain agnosia in any other patients? (3) What implications do the findings have for an understanding of brain processes subserving visual perception? With regard to the first question, one strategy would be to continue to develop and refine testing procedures for the patient and to relate these in a more principled fashion to simulation conditions with normal subjects. However, it is somewhat salutory to consider that such a strategy would only indirectly lead to greater understanding of the visual system. This is because although we have a better view of the deficit at the task level that is often the case, and a plausible theory for linking the known effects of the lesioning agent to the deficits at this level, the construct linking the two is that of the visual field "mask", and the construct underpinning this is the "scotoma". Given our state of ignorance about what a scotoma represents in terms of striate and extrastriate damage (Campion et al., 1983), at the function level we are perhaps no further advanced. Perhaps the most significant aspect of this work, whether or not the masking hypothesis is true, is that it suggests a novel research strategy. In terms of brain structure it leads us to consider more carefully the detailed effect on the brain of different pathological conditions and to consider the full range of structures which might be affected by a given lesion, in terms both of gross and fine anatomy within a given area. In terms of function it leads us to consider more carefully the status of theoretical forms with respect to different levels of description and how these different levels might be related to structural damage.

Whereas the conventional approach seeks a commonality between patients based on gross anatomy and the high-level descriptions of function derived from clinical observation, I suggest that we should seek a commonality between patients based on a detailed knowledge of the brain lesion and a detailed knowledge of the perceptual operations involved in experimental tasks. In this way other agnosic patients who have suffered carbon monoxide poisoning should also be able to have their deficits explained by masking.

5. TWO OTHER PATIENTS

The two cases presented here are S, described by Benson and Greenberg (1969) and Efron (1969) and H.C., described by Adler (1944). They were selected because: (1) they both suffered carbon monoxide intoxication; (2) the original accounts provide sufficient detail to capture the nature of their deficits; (3) and together with R.C., they form a neat hierarchy of impairment.

5.1. Patient S

5.1.1. *Clinical Picture*

The patient, a male aged 25, suffered carbon monoxide poisoning after being exposed to gas from a leak while taking a shower.

Most of the investigation was carried out seven months after the incident. S was attentive to his surroundings and could negotiate corridors in his wheelchair. He could name colours and follow moving stimuli but he could not identify, by vision alone, familiar objects placed before him. Posture and tone were normal but he had difficulty in initiating movements. Standing, turning round, and sitting were performed awkwardly. Recent and remote memory, spontaneous speech, and comprehension of and repetition of spoken language were intact.

5.1.2. *Sensory Tests*

Visual fields were dynamically normal for white 10mm and 3mm targets. There was an inferior constriction for coloured targets.

Snellen acuity was impossible to measure, although: "He was able to indicate the orientation of a letter 'E' and detect movement of small objects at a standard distance. He could identify some familiar numbers drawn before him in small size. Optokinetic nystagmus elicited bilaterally with fine $\frac{1}{8}''$ marks on a tape. Fundoscopic examination revealed no abnormalities of the optic discs or retinae". There was a striking impersistence of gaze characterised by quasi-random wandering movement of the eyes, especially marked when inspecting an object.

S could detect small differences in size and movement of objects although these were not normal, and he could discriminate small differences in hue (7–10nm). He could also discriminate small differences in luminance (0.1 log units). He could extract a single dimension to discriminate stimuli. For example, when shown two discs of light differing in hue, luminance, and size, he could readily indicate the "brighter", "larger" or "deeper red". In spatial summation and flicker fusion there were small deviations from normal. In the case of spatial summation, threshold luminance against target size produced a curve similar to the normal, plateauing at 100$'$, but the patient's curve was elevated by 1.5 log units, indicating a reduced sensitivity to light. CFF was reduced to approximately 15Hz (about half the normal value).

5.1.3. *Perceptual Tests*

1. S could name colours but was generally unable to name objects, pictures of objects, body parts, letters, numbers, or geometrical figures. He could readily identify and name these from nonvisual cues. He inferred the nature of presented objects from colour or size cues. For example, a safety pin was "silver and shiny like a watch or nail clipper" and a rubber eraser was "a small ball". He identified a white typewritten letter on a blue background as a "beach scene". The blue background was "the ocean", the stationery was "the beach", and the print was "people seen on the beach from an airplane". If stimuli were moving, his identification was improved.

2. His problem was not confined to naming. He could not match block letters, silhouettes, or pictures to real objects. He was unable to copy letters or simple figures and could neither describe nor trace the outline of common objects.

3. He could write crude letters and numbers to request, although they were poor and contained omissions and distortions, e.g., ƽ for 5 and ∞ for 8.

4. He could count a few items such as coins or paper clips closely spaced although he could not identify them.

5. He could only select objects from a group using a cue such as colour and size he had learned to associate with the object on a previous occasion.

6. He could not recognise his doctor or family members by sight alone, or his own face in a mirror. He identified a photograph of himself but only from the colour of his military uniform. He identified a magazine cover girl as a woman because she had "no hair on her arms".

5.1.4. *Special Tests*

1. The EEG showed a persistent bilateral slowing in the parieto-occipital areas. A pneumoencephalogram showed bilateral posterior ventricular dilation.

2. Recordings of his eye movements confirmed that he failed to scan the essential parts of a scene but instead engaged in quasi-random searching movements. However, he could follow a point light source, and if this was moved systematically over a scene, the patient's recognition performance improved.

5.2. Patient H.C.

5.2.1. *Clinical Picture*

The patient, H.C., a female aged 22, suffered carbon monoxide poisoning after being trapped in a fire in a night club. She was initially blind but after two days could distinguish light from dark but no colours, and could recognise the white shapes she could see as doctors and nurses. The former she distinguished from the latter on the basis of tobacco smell and hair style. During the first two weeks she suffered from "flight of ideas", reiteration in actions and speech, but nonvisual senses, motor activity, and speech were not impaired.

5.2.2. Sensory Tests

Visual fields were defined as normal dynamically, apart from a possible slight constriction of the right lower field for colour. Fixation was difficult.

Snellen acuity was impossible to measure, but acuity measured as the maximum distance allowing the counting of three dots, was reported normal.

H.C. could recognise colours after two weeks. Before this, red and green were difficult but blue and yellow normal. There was a permanent slight impairment. For example, dark blue was always recognised as "purple". She could match colours according to shade and intensity.

5.2.3. Perceptual Tests

1. H.C. was able to write from the start but made many errors and four weeks after the incident her writing was almost normal. However, she could not copy cardboard letters put together to form words. She introduced inversions and reversals of letters but managed to correct these with difficulty. Certain letters remained always difficult to write. For example, "t" and "i" were often confused. Her touch-typing remained good although there were occasional confusions such as between "t" and "l".

2. During the first two weeks she could not recognise any letters but could recognise a few numbers such as "1", "4", and "7". She recognised, first straight lines, then curves which allowed her to infer the identity of numerals. For example, "In a 6 there is only a lower loop. If I find an upper loop then I know it is a 3".

3. Later, she could recognise all printed capitals when presented singly and most small letters. As with numbers, straight line letters were the easiest to recognise and recognition proceeded by means of extraction of partial cues, inference based on these and knowledge of the stimulus set. For example, H.C. recognised "e" "because it has a space on this side", she said, pointing to the right. When the same letter was presented upside down she said "That is a small 'a' because the space is on the other side", and she pointed to the left.

Words were identified by inferring the identity of certain letters and estimating the length of the word. Thus, when shown the word "PRESIDENT" and asked to copy it as she saw it, she wrote "PRESIDEWT" but correctly inferred that the word was in fact "PRESIDENT".

H.C. remarked that letters "look as if they are all together, as if it were just one line. I have to separate them myself". Printing with large spaces made it easier for her to separate the individual letters. She could easily identify, by touch, letters cut out of cardboard.

4. During the first month H.C. was unable to recognise simple geometric figures. For example, a circle and a triangle were both identified as the letter "A". Five weeks after the injury, she called an equilateral triangle a "big A", but when told that it was not a letter she correctly identified it as a triangle. Ultimately, she could still copy only simple shapes such as a triangle, circle, and square. She was unable to copy a hexagon. Figures with curved lines were the most difficult.

The veridicality of her perceptions was related to orientation (Adler, 1944, fig. 5.). Thus, the figure  was drawn with almost normal accuracy when she was given unlimited time. She reported that it looked like a "capital U". In other orientations she reported that the figure appeared fragmented.

H.C. was very poor at assembling red and white blocks to copy simple sample patterns, saying "The white baffles and confuses me. I always think there is something in addition", pointing to the white background beside the sample blocks.

5. Although H.C. could draw straight lines, she could not divide them correctly. When asked to divide a line in half, she traced several times along the line and marked the ends of the line over and over before making a dividing line. It seems likely that she was using proprioceptive information for this task.

6. Spontaneous drawing was grossly impaired during the first two months but improved thereafter until the fifth month. Body parts in a drawing of a girl were crudely depicted and bizarrely associated in early attempts. Final ability was good but some parts were still omitted until prompted.

7. During the first two weeks, no objects could be identified at all and the patient seemed to make random guesses. When colour perception returned, she guessed by using the colour. For example, ice cream was identified as "scrambled egg". From the third week she traced round the contour of objects with her finger and began to make inferences based on contour information alone. Thus, a coin and a compact were each identified as "a key ring".

During the second month the patient gradually became able to appreciate the third dimension. Objects were recognised by "adding up impressions", and a naive observer would fail to detect any abnormality as, in purely behavioural terms, her recognition of objects was "perfect". However, her disability could be demonstrated by tachistoscopic presentation. For example, a green toy battleship produced the following responses with the exposure times given in brackets; "a fountain pen" (1sec), "a green knife" (2sec), "a boat" (3sec).

8. During the first few weeks H.C. was unable to recognise people by sight at all, not even her husband, although she recognised other people by voice or footstep. Later on, when H.C. had fully "recovered", she was still unable to recognise by vision alone anyone whom she knew and was seeing for the first time since the incident. However, she recognised these people on subsequent meetings, but only if their presence has been significant to her activities. In brief, she could store representations of faces she had paid close attention to, but not of people who were merely incidental. This was presumably because the percept degradation she suffered from made discrimination of faces more difficult than normal and the degradation was such that representations laid down before the accident could no longer be matched to current percepts.

9. Pictures were more difficult to recognise than objects. Coloured pictures were recognised more easily than uncoloured ones. H.C. described pictures as children do, by enumerating details. During the first two months she would identify only a few items out of the whole picture. When she was shown two pictures of a boy with a sailing boat with the boy in two different postures, she identified only the boy, but denied that it was the same boy in each picture.

10. After two months H.C. could count backwards and forwards and add and subtract, but she could only multiply if the result was less than 20. During the first four months she confused multiplication, subtraction, and addition and their corresponding symbols. Final performance level left her with the ability to multiply all the single digits but still unable to carry out division. This seemed to be because, whereas in multiplication she could adopt a simple addition strategy, in division it was necessary to form a representation of the whole number. Practice did not improve her perform ance.

Although H.C. could not at first tell the time, she worked out a system used by other agnosic patients. Thus: "The 6 is below the 12 and the 9 across from the 3 on the watch. First I look for the hands and find which is the hour hand and which is the minute hand. Then I look for the numbers. I memorise that 1 means 5 minutes, 2, 10 minutes . . . and so on". H.C. still made some mistakes and confused hour and minute hands. She could indicate immediately which was the larger of two numbers but was unable to explain why this was the case. She remained with difficulties over the number of days in a week and the number of days in a year. Her appreciation of the passage of time seemed, however, normal.

5.2.4. Special Test

H.C.'s EEG was of unusually low voltage and showed no slowing with hyperventilation and no focal activity.

6. CONCLUSIONS

6.1. The Patients and the Masking Hypothesis

Each of the patients I have discussed, R.C., S, and H.C., apparently suffered carbon monoxide intoxication. R.C. seems most impaired, followed by S, and then by H.C. Unfortunately we have insuffient evidence to make judgements about degree of intoxication in each case. All three patients were initially unconscious, were completely blind on initial waking, and gradually recovered their perceptual capacities to a stable agnosic level over a period of weeks or months. There is no evidence of visual recovery beyond this sort of time span and recovery after this period is likely to have been due to relearning of permanently altered percepts. It is apparent that the perceptual world for these patients was both altered and degraded. Recognition seemed always to be by a process of inference from perceived partial cues and learned responses. We can therefore discern three possible levels at which recovery could have occurred:

1. Visual recovery (i.e., restoration of a phenomenal).
2. Perceptual learning (i.e., learning to abstract new patterns from this phenomenal world).
3. Associative learning (i.e., learning to establish the physical referents of these patterns).

It seems likely that each higher level followed an increasingly long time course in recovery. Terminology is difficult here, so it is important to make these distinctions clear. This can be done by reference to the hypothetical visual world of R.C. depicted in Fig. 7.10. The term "visual recovery" would refer to the recovery from blindness to the state depicted here. This state would set an absolute limit on perceptual learning by defining the set of cues available. The term "perceptual learning" would refer to the ability to abstract the pattern of the wheelbarrow. The term "associative learning" would refer to the learning that this pattern represented a wheelbarrow. It should be emphasised that these three terms are to be regarded as levels of description of a perceptual and not as stages in perceptual processing. The advantage of this characterisation is that it provides a low level of description for revealing the functional effects of a given lesion and a high level of description for revealing the consequences of this for perceptual performance.

There is no gross impairment in what would traditionally be called "sensory functions" in any of the patients. There is, however, a slight field defect as measured by dynamic perimetry in all patients and the inferior constriction seen in S is similar to that in R.C. Few details are given of perimetry so we cannot say with what degree of precision visual function was estimated in these procedures. The degree of observable field defect seems to be related to the severity of the agnosia, with R.C. having the greatest defect and H.C. the least. All three patients showed reduced sensitivity to luminance and colour differences, at least to some degree.

Perhaps the most significant performance deficit common to all patients was the inability to track the contours of objects with the eyes, especially if the contours were curved. It seems likely that the poor scanning behaviour was a *consequence* of the inability to perceive contour clearly rather than being its *cause*, because the patients retained the ability to follow externally driven stimuli and to scan contours by following a finger tracing the outline of figures.

In the case of R.C. it is suggested that contours could not be seen clearly because his visual field is peppered with scotomata. Could this explain the deficits in the other patients? What seems clear in these patients is that contour or form perception *per se* is not destroyed because small parts of objects can be seen clearly. The difficulty seems to lie in the simultaneous perception of a large area of contour. The patients seem to "recognise" objects by adding up all the bits they can see and making an inference, based on these, and expectations derived from the context. They find straight line contours the easiest, presumably because of the predictability of such contours. Note, in Fig. 7.10, how the straight lines of the wheelbarrow contour stand out and resist degradation whereas the limited curved contour information from the bucket, and even more so, the subtle features of the child's face, almost completely disappear. The ability of a single process—the mask—to cause the selective disruption of discrete classes of objects is an important feature of the hypothesis. The case of face recognition demonstrates how misleading clinical diagnostic terms such as "prospagnosia" may be. All the patients suffered from prospagnosia in the sense that none of them could recognise once familiar faces and relearning proved difficult or impossible. However, there is no reason to suppose this represents any sort of specific deficit. It is more likely that faces represent an important class of "objects" whose features are particularly difficult to discriminate and therefore are particularly prone to disruption. There is an important distinction to be made here between R.C. and S (the two more severe cases), and H.C. Whereas H.C. did learn to discriminate (albeit with considerable difficulty) between a limited set of faces, this was not possible in R.C. or S. The fact that the remembered faces had to be closely attended to is an indication of the difficulty of this task. Presumably the necessary perceptual and associative learning were very difficult and required a great deal of attentional effort. If the relative preservation of this capacity in H.C. is due, as suggested, to a relative reduction in contour disruption, then it can be seen how the use of a term such as "face recognition" without some understanding of the component processes involved in such a task can be misleading. A similar point can be made in relation to the inadequate scanning of object contours. Without some understanding of perceptual operations at a task level, it is not clear which of the two performances—poor scanning and poor contour perception —serves as an explanation for which. It is suggested here that both have equal status as tasks disrupted by masked object contour. The notion of masking is potentially powerful because it could explain, not only the impoverished scanning but, for example, the searching movements of the head, slow tracing movements of the finger, recognition by inference from parts, and possibly also spatial disorientation and localisation uncertainties. Together with the derived notions of perceptual and associative learning, it also allows us to understand better the nature of the recovery process. Vision to such patients could be like trying to build up a picture of the world through scanning it by means of a tube with a very narrow angle of view, but in their case they might have many different "tubes" of different sizes, randomly spaced, and perhaps introducing their own "local" distortions such as poor brightness sensitivy or poor acuity. Note that the masking hypothesis does not preclude the existence of additional deficits in, say, memory and attention. The claim is that the presence of a "mask" forces the patient towards certain perpetual strategies which may place special demands on memory and attention processes, but these processes could, of course, themselves be deficient.

I suggest that the theory, that one type of visual agnosia (at least that due to carbon monoxide intoxication) is caused by simple contour disruption through visual field masking, be regarded as a plausible means of explaining the disorder. It has the advantage that the principles involved can be made explicit and tested. It also has the potential capacity (illustrated with the three patients here) of introducing greater coherence into the complex data derived from observations.

6.2. Apperception as an Explanatory Construct

I should like to conclude this chapter by returning to the issues discussed at the beginning; to focus on the classification of visual agnosias, and to consider the utility of the term "apperceptive". The question of classification tends to present itself as "how many types are there?" For example, are there two (Lissauer, 1889), three (Warrington, 1982), five (Kertesz, this volume, Chapter 6), or six (Humphreys & Riddoch, this volume, Chapter 10)? The answer to this question must surely rest upon what a given classification is intended to achieve.

In the clinical case, presumably a given scheme should make those distinctions which are important for diagnosis, prognosis, treatment, and other clinical objectives. In the experimental neurophyschological case, however, presumably a given scheme should reflect those distinctions which are important for understanding brain function. An important principle here seems to be that not only should a classificatory term reflect "what's really there" (in the terms of Humphreys & Riddoch's, this volume, Chapter 10, it should be "empirically derived") but it should be cast at the appropriate level of description suited to its declared purpose. A symptom of failure to cast a term at the appropriate level is that we cannot recognise when we have an "instance" of it. The point is made clear (although only implicitly) in Chapter 10 by Humphreys and Riddoch with regard to the use of the term "apperceptive". The two terms used to define this term are "elementary perceptual functions" and "visual object recognition". The use of the first term leads us into the problem of trying to decide what counts as an elementary perceptual function. Is it what is going on in testing acuity and visual fields, or in Bay's "*Funktionswandel*" tests or in Ettlinger's "sensory efficiency tests"? The use of the second term leads us into the problem of trying to decide what counts as "visual object recognition". Is it what is going on when R.C. makes a forced choice discrimination between a triangle and a circle or when S identifies a slowly-drawn "O" or "X", or when H.C. (Section 5.2) reads a word by painstakingly identifying each letter, or when a patient matches a distorted view picture to a prototypical view picture in the presence of a distractor item (Humphreys & Quinlan, this volume, Chapter 3)?

The view presented in this chapter is that the difficulties are analytical rather than empirical. They arise from a failure to appreciate the need for both function-level and the task-level descriptions of performance. The function level would be regarded as "nearer to the brain" and the task level as " nearer to behaviour". Many of the difficulties in visual neuropsychology seem to derive from taking a task, deriving an abstract term which describes this, and using this abstracted (high-level term) as a (lower-level) function term. A consequence of this mismatch of levels is a tendency, when confronted with the real world of data, to either retreat into an ever-decreasing world of "idealised" constructs (e.g., Warrington's 1985 re-definition of agnosia, discussed by Humphreys & Riddoch, this volume, Chapter 3), or to suffer an uncontrolled proliferation of constructs, leading ultimately to pure empiricism (cf. Humphreys & Riddoch, chapter 10).

In the case of the term "apperceptive" it should be remembered that the empirical data supporting it comprised intact performance in relatively crude clinical sensory tests and the inability to copy shapes. The fundamental contrast here made by Lissauer (1889) was between a patient who failed to see properly and a patient who could see properly but failed to perform the associations necessary for recognition. Now, although these terms, because of their ordinary-language considerations, lack the necessary precision for our use, I suggest that Lissauer nevertheless captured an important distinction. We could therefore resurrect the term "apperceptive" in a different, more precise, guise, by relating it to the levels of recovery posited in the three patients. It may be that there is a distinct class of patients who suffer severe and permanent damage to their cortex, and hence to their phenomenal world, because of the sort of disseminated lesion suggested here. The functional damage could then be defined as apperceptive and being that damage which sets absolute limits on the degree of subsequent perceptual and associative learning. Without further exposure to the appropriate patients, it is not clear how these limits should be discerned or described, or even if this would indeed be a useful distinction to make. The objective would be to define the deficit in functional terms such that it would map onto a description of the brain damage and onto a description of deficient performance expressed at the level of the task.

The argument for descriptions at the level of the task is made because it is at this level that we can see the impact of a given lesion. Thus, I could argue that clinical accounts given of patients, such as those presented in this chapter, although informal and unprincipled, often give us a better "feel" for the nature of the deficit because they provide rich data at the level required. If we accept that the level of description is defined for us by the effects of a lesion, then it behoves us to develop terminologies at this level which aid our understanding. By adopting this position we embrace a research strategy which leads us away from the traditional empirical problems of discrimination patient classes and lesion boundaries into the analytical problems of describing brain lesions and the perceptual tasks influenced by them.

ACKNOWLEDGEMENTS

I wish to thank R.C. who acted as subject for me through many hours of tedious testing. I wish to thank Richard Abadi and Janus Kalikowski of the Department of Ophthalmic Optics, University of Manchester Institute of Science and Technology, and Peter Meudell and Andrew Mayes of the Department of Psychology, University of Manchester, who introduced me to R.C., discussed their data with me; and offered helpful advice. Richard Latto of the Department of Psychology, University of Liverpool helped greatly in the later stages of the research with R.C. Finally, I must thank Glyn Humphreys who went through each draft of the chapter very thoroughly and offered much helpful advice and direction, and Sue Godfrey who very kindly undertook to type the several versions.

REFERENCES

Abadi, R. V., Kulikowski, J. J., & Meudell, P. (1981). Visual performance in a case of visual agnosia. In M. V. van Hof and G. Mohn (Eds.), *Functional recovery from brain damage*, pp. 275–286. Amsterdam: Elsevier.

Adler, A. (1944). Disintegration and restoration of optic recognition in visual agnosia. *Archives of Neurology and Psychiatry, 51*, 243–259.

Benson, D. F. & Greenberg, J.P . (1969). Visual form agnosia. A specific deficit in visual discrimination. *Archives of Neurology, 20*, 82–89.

Bay, E. (1953). Disturbances of visual perception and their examination, *Brain, 76*, 516–550.

Campion, J. (1984). Evoked potentials and discriminative capacities in a case of visual agnosia. In R. H. Nodar and C. Barber (Eds.), *Evoked potentials*, II. The Second International Evoked Potentials Symposium, Butterworth.

Campion, J. & Latto, R. (1985). Apperceptive agnosia due to carbon monoxide poisoning. An interpretation based on critical band masking from disseminated lesions. *Behavioural Brain Research, 15*, 227–240.

Campion, J., Latto, R, & Smith, Y. M. (1983). Is blindsight an effect of scattered light, spared cortex, and near threshold vision? *The Behavioural and Brain Sciences, 6*, 423–486.

Efron, R. (1969) What is perception? In *Boston studies in the philosophy of science*, Vol. 1V, pp. 137–173. New York: Humanities Press.

Ettlinger, G. (1956). Sensory deficits in visual agnosia, *Journal of Neurology, Neurosurgery, and Psychiatry, 19*, 297–307.

Garland, H. & Pearce, J. (1967). Neurological complications of carbon monoxide poisoning, *Quarterly Journal of Medicine, 144*, 445–455.

Lissauer, H. (1889). Ein Fall von Seelenblindheit nebst einem Beitrage zur Theorie derselben. *Archiv für Psychiatrie und Nervkrankheiten, 21*, 222–270.

Marr, D. (1982). *Vision*. San Francisco: W.H. Freeman.

Mehler, J., Morton, J., & Jusczyk, P. W. (1984). On reducing language to biology. *Cognitive Neuropsychology, 1*, 83–116.

Nielsen, J. M. (1937). Unilateral cerebral dominance as related to mind blindness. *Archives of Neurology and Psychiatry, 38*, 108–135.

Regan, D. (1981). Visual psychophysical tests in multiple sclerosis as an aid to diagnosis, localisation of pathology and assessment of experimental therapy. In L. M. Proenza, J. M. Enoch, and A. Jampolsky (Eds.), *Clinical applications of visual psychophysics*. Cambridge University Press.

Regan, D. (1982). Visual information chanelling in normal and disordered vision. *Psychological Review, 89*, 407–444.

Stromeyer, C. F. & Julesz, B. (1972). Spatial frequency masking in vision: critical bands and the spread of masking. *Journal of the Optical Society, America, 62*, 1221–1232.

Warrington, E. K. (1982). Neuropsychological studies of object recognition. *Philosophical Transactions of the Royal Society, London, B298*, 15–33.

8 Object Concepts and Object Names: Some Deductions from Acquired Disorders of Word Processing

Elaine Funnell
Cognitive Neuropsychology Research Group,
Department of Psychology, Birkbeck College,
University of London, Malet Street, London WC1E 7HX, U.K.

The ability to recognise objects is basic to life. From the most lowly to the most highly developed species, survival depends upon accurately identifying objects in the surrounding world. Yet, although object recognition is a primary cognitive ability, we have, at present, only a limited understanding of the cognitive processes involved. What information makes up an object concept? How are object concepts organised? How are object names related to object concepts? These are some of the questions which need to be answered.

This chapter does not pretend to provide the answers to these questions; its aim is much more modest. It examines some of the assumptions made about object concepts; it takes a sideways look at object concepts through evidence obtained from the study of reading and related tasks; and, finally, it introduces some new evidence concerning the properties of object concepts and their relation to object names. While there is passing reference to studies of normal individuals, discussion concentrates upon evidence from the breakdown of behaviour in people who have suffered brain damage during their adult life.

1. MODULARITY AND THE DIVISION OF LABOUR

1.1 The Principle of Modularity

Over the past two decades the study of mental processes in individual brain damaged individuals has provided insights into the processing mechanisms involved in a range of different cognitive tasks: for example, in reading (e.g. Coltheart, Patterson, & Marshall, 1980; Patterson, Marshall, & Coltheart, 1985; recognising colours (Oxbury, Oxbury, & Humphrey, 1969; Beauvois, 1982; Beauvois & Saillant, 1985); recognising faces (e.g. Hay & Young, 1983); and recognising objects (e.g. Taylor & Warrington, 1971; Newcombe & Ratcliff, 1974).

One common feature stands out in the study of behaviour after brain damage: The processing involved in complex tasks appears to be shared among sets of specialised subsystems (Allport, 1985). For example, studies of the breakdown of the mental lexicon suggest that it is composed of sets of independent codes for written and spoken words, both of which are functionally separate from representations of word meanings (Morton & Patterson, 1980; Allport & Funnell, 1981; Ellis, 1982).

A system which is organised into small, functionally distinct specialist modules is efficient and economic. When properly organised, its strength lies in the fact that a change can be made easily to one part of the whole, without many compensatory changes being necessary to the rest. This is the principle of modularity as stated by Marr (1976). Of all the systems which need to adapt to change, the cognitive system involved in learning to recognise objects in the world is a most deserving candidate.

Modularity has been grasped with enthusiasm by cognitive psychologists searching for principles upon which to understand the organisation of mental knowledge. Consequently, when empirical evidence suggests that processing is organised into discrete subsystems, then the principle of modularity itself is often called upon to strengthen the arguments. Thus, modality specific semantic systems for the understanding of words, pictures, noises, etc., which are claimed from the dissociations in processing observed in brain damaged patients, appear to be supported by the principle of modularity (Shallice, 1981a).

1.2 Modularity and Models of Cognitive Processing

As Shallice (1981a) has pointed out, modularity is "implicit in flow diagrams of information transfer between processing structures". An influential example of such a model is the logogen model (Morton, 1979). When functionally independent modules within such flow diagrams are postulated on the basis of empirical evidence directed explicitly to the question of the representation of information (as for example were the priming experiments reported by Morton, 1979), then the subsystems derived may be accepted with some confidence. However, when such evidence is lacking, then the task of identifying the independent components which comprise an information processing system is not a straightforward activity. Apart from embracing the fact that a system is likely to work better if it is divided into specialised subsystems, the principle of modularity has not been used in a disciplined fashion to develop guidelines as to the psychological principles which might determine how knowledge is divided into independent components. In the absence of such guidelines, we use, in practice, a variety of different distinctions—material specificity, semantic/functional category, input vs. output domains—to motivate the separation of information into independent modules.

There is a further problem still for developing models of cognitive processing: Sometimes even interpreting the empirical data in terms of independent processes can be difficult. There are two related problems. The first concerns the development of models of cognitive function. Double dissociations are widely taken as evidence for the functional independence of (at least two) processing mechanisms. However, the nature of these mechanisms is often obscure. Dissociations may reflect the operation of functionally distinct representations of knowledge, but equally they may reflect the operation of functionally distinct access pathways to a common set of representations (Allport & Funnell, 1981). Campion (this volume, Chapter 7) draws attention to further problems for the interpretation of functional dissociations in the performance of brain damaged patients. Secondly, it is not necessarily a simple matter to decide, for any particular patient, whether it is the representations of knowledge, or the access pathways to knowledge representations, which are implicated in the performance deficits. As Riddoch and Humphreys (this volume, Chapter 4) point out: In a cascade model of processing, damage to access pathways can give rise to errors that are also typical of damage to representations of knowledge.

Modularity is not a licence to create multiple components; quite the reverse. Modularity appears to explicitly restrict the number of independent components in a system through its emphasis on efficiency when adapting to change. In particular, this seems to imply that the same information should not be represented across a range of functional units, as a change to one part of the system will require changes to other parts as well. Yet, many subsystems inferred from dissociations observed in behaviour after brain damage appear to duplicate material across separate functional units. Modality-specific semantic systems for recognising objects (Lhermitte & Beauvois, 1973), and separate sets of orthographic codes for reading and spelling (Morton, 1980; Shallice, 1981b; Ellis, 1982) are just two examples of apparently duplicated material across independent subsystems. When the principle of modularity appears to be violated in the subdivisions proposed on the basis of brain damage, then there is perhaps reason for questioning the interpretation of the evidence upon which the divisions are based.

2. CONCEPTUAL REPRESENTATIONS OF OBJECTS

2.1. Objects and Object Names

The principle of modularity predicts that a single set of conceptual representations should subserve the recognition of objects (presented in any modality) and the understanding of object names. However, Warrington and Shallice (1979) and Shallice (1985) suggest that object names and objects are understood by different systems: object names by a lexical semantic system; and objects by a visual conceptual system. The evidence in support of this comes from a patient (A.R.) who has some difficulty in naming both written picture names and pictures. A deficit in naming both pictures and words might appear to be prima facie evidence in favour of a single conceptual system for the processing of objects and object names. However, the patient responds differently to an auditory semantic prime, depending upon whether the stimulus is a word or a picture. When an auditory semantic prime word is given, naming the word is helped (in absolute terms) much more than naming the picture. The auditory prime is believed to have boosted the semantic processing of the word, but not the understanding of the picture. On the basis of this difference, the authors argue that pictures and words map onto different sets of cognitive codes.

This would be a reasonable conclusion to draw if it were certain that A.R. relied solely upon semantic processing for accessing a name for both words and pictures. However, A.R. is not equally dependent upon processing by meaning when reading aloud written picture names and naming pictures. It is clear from an analysis of his reading performance that A.R. has some ability to read aloud nonwords (5/25, 7/25) and to sound out letters—those nonwords he could successfully read aloud were those in which he could sound out all the letters. Given that the majority of his reading errors were visual errors (57%) or shared the first letter (20%), most reading responses would be likely to be phonologically fairly close to the target. Clearly, an auditory semantic prime would be very much more useful to a system that already knows something about the sound of the target (as in reading aloud picture names) than one which does not (as in picture naming). For example, the auditory clue "Egypt" would be more informative as a prompt for naming the word *pyramid*, if it were already known that the response must start with the sound /p/, than for naming a picture of a pyramid where no orthographic-phonemic clues are available for finding a name. The fact that the auditory prime only boosted word naming to the level of 50% probably reflects the fact that the patient's ability to sound out letters was impaired.

As the processes available to A.R. for reading written picture names and naming pictures are not equivalent, the fact that a semantic prime facilitates reading, but not naming, is not convincing evidence for the existence of independent conceptual systems for objects and words.

I should perhaps point out that the separation of conceptual systems for the *visual* knowledge of coloured objects and *verbal* knowledge referring to colour (Beauvois, 1982) is not in question here. In this particular division of labour, the visual conceptual system is thought to know about relationships between colours, colour matching, and the appropriate colours of objects in the world. Whereas the verbal conceptual system is thought to know about colours in terms of verbal associations, in which the colours may not be the real colours of the objects (an English example would be green bacon; meaning unsalted). Clearly, such knowledge is unlikely to be represented in a visual-conceptual system for object recognition, as green-coloured bacon does not exist—at least, not under normal circumstances. This distinction conforms to the principle of modularity, since these two conceptual systems are argued to represent different sorts of knowledge.

2.2 Object Concepts and Domains of Sensory Processing

Evidence for multiple conceptual systems for recognising *objects* comes from reports of modality-specific aphasia: optic aphasia (Lhermitte & Beauvois, 1973); bilateral tactile aphasia (Beauvois, Saillant, Meininger, & Lhermitte, 1978); and auditory aphasia (Denes & Semenza, 1975). The crucial evidence in the first two cases is that while in one modality of input (visual or tactile) the object can be named (and therefore presumably recognised; but see Section 3 for further discussion of naming as an indication of recognition), in the other modality the object cannot be named, even though the object has been recognised. Here, recognition refers to the fact that the function of the object can be adequately gestured.

On the basis of such studies, object concepts have been divided into separate systems for different modalities of input. Each subsystem being thought to entail processes for recognising the particular sensory properties of the domain in question (for example, visual or auditory or tactile information), but each also entailing knowledge of the function of the object.

The argument for separate systems is as follows. If the object has been recognised when presented in the visual modality and in the tactile modality, but is named only from the visual modality, then the system which recognises objects in the tactile modality must be different from the system which recognises objects in the visual modality. Furthermore, functional evidence, as measured by gesture, is assumed to be represented in both systems (although this is not stated explicitly).

I shall discuss recognition later (Section 3), but one point about gesture is pertinent now. Gesture has been questioned as an adequate measure of recognition by Ratcliff and Newcombe (1982) and by Riddoch and Humphreys (1985) on the basis that many gestures are insufficiently clear for items belonging to the same category to be exactly identified. Thus, for example, a mime of putting something on the foot may not be precise enough to determine whether the actor has a shoe or a sock in mind. Sometimes mimes do appear to be clear enough for the item to be specified precisely, even when the items have a number of close associates. For example, a patient studied by Schwartz, Marin, and Saffran (1979) was consistently able to give a sufficiently precise mime for a naive observer to differentiate between gestures appropriate to such functionally similar objects as a spoon (rather than a fork) or a pipe (rather than a cigarette).

Even so, there are problems in using gesture as evidence for precise recognition. First, there are many common items that cannot be differentiated by mime, for example pen and pencil, cigarette and cigar, hairbrush and comb. Any test of precise recognition judged by gesture cannot include such items. Secondly, if only items with no close functional neighbours are used (to avoid the problem of similarity in mime), the test may not be sampling at a sufficiently detailed level to pick up impairments in recognition. In word-word matching (Funnell, 1983a) and word-picture matching (Bishop & Byng, 1984) performance drops dramatically with the presence of semantic distractors. If gesture is to be used as a measure of precise recognition, then it is necessary to use only close semantic neighbours and to ensure that these can be differentiated by gesture. Furthermore, the test must be repeated to ensure that performance is consistent. To my knowledge, no tests of gesture in modality-specific aphasia have been sufficiently stringent to ensure that recognition is both precise and consistent.

Even when knowledge of the function of an object can be demonstrated, this may not be a reliable indicator of object recognition. A patient (J.B.) studied by Riddoch and Humphreys (1985) produced very precise gestures. Nevertheless, access to semantic information (functional and associative) was found to be impaired in a matching task in which distractors were both structurally and semantically similar to the target (Humphreys, Riddoch, & Quinlan, 1985). These authors suggest that the ability to gesture the use of an object does not necessarily indicate that the full semantics of the object has been activated; gesture may be determined by the structural properties of the object alone.

Sometimes objects can be named when knowledge of function is impaired: A group of patients with left hemisphere lesions could name or describe objects in pictures, but could not match the objects on the basis of their function (Warrington, 1982). However, it is possible that in this case some of the functional distinctions were difficult to make. In the only example provided, a rolled umbrella must be matched to an open umbrella, or a walking stick. Because a *rolled* umbrella can be used as a walking stick, but is inadequate for keeping off the rain, the walking stick might be chosen quite reasonably, yet erroneously, as its functional equivalent.

In total, the evidence for recognition based upon gesture is too imprecise, and too contradictory, to support in isolation the independent existence of separate modality-specific conceptual systems for the recognition of objects. It should be noted, however, that the notion (also implied by these studies) of independent modality-specific perceptual-structural representations for processing the particular properties of an object when presented to a specific sensory modality, is not in question here.

3. LEVELS OF OBJECT RECOGNITION

3.1. Object Concepts and Recognition

What do we mean when we say that someone has recognised an object? Recognition implies "knowing what something is", but this is an imprecise definition. Has all the information known about the object been retrieved, or just some? "I've seen that face before. . . Who is she? . . . How do I know her?" is a familar and often embarrassing refrain of everyday life. Yet, in a face recognition task, a photograph of this person would be classified as familiar, and therefore "recognised". It seems clear that recognition may be only partial and that, in assessing recognition, the exact information upon which it is based needs to be known.

Models of visual object recognition are helpful in this respect. Generally, visual object recognition is separated into two stages: a perceptual or structural level (Warrington, 1982; Marin, this volume, Chapter 9; Riddoch & Humphreys, this volume, Chapter 4), hereafter referred to as the *structural* level; and a symbolic-semantic, functional-associative, or categorical level (Warrington, 1982; Marin; Riddoch & Humphreys), hereafter called the *associative-functional* level. Patients are known who can recognise objects (or rather, pictures of objects) at a structural level but not at an associative-functional level (Riddoch & Humphreys and Marin, this volume). If, by analogy, the model of visual object processing is applied to the processing of objects in other sensory domains, each sensory domain would require a structural description of the physical properties of the object: For example, structural descriptions of environmental sounds for recognising auditory features of objects (Riddoch & Humphreys, 1985).

3.2. Object Recognition and Naming

3.2.1. Naming from Associative-Functional Knowledge

Most models of object recognition require that an object must be fully recognised before it can be named: That is, it must be recognised at the structural level *and* at the associative-functional level. The models referred to in Section 3.1 are of this type: They proceed from the structural level to the associative-functional level to naming, in a strictly linear manner. Naming directly on the basis of structural information only is definitely ruled out.

The structural level for the visual perception of the shape of objects has been elegantly researched by Riddoch and Humphreys (1985; this volume, Chapter 4). At this level, objects having fairly unique shapes, with few structurally similar neighbours (for example, a chair), are more likely to be recognised precisely than objects (such as a particular four-legged animal) which have many structurally similar neighbours. For this second class of object, information from the functional-associative level must assist in the precise identification of the object. Information at this level is thought to effect speed and accuracy of naming: Entry for objects that are structurally distinct is sufficiently precise to activate specific information at the associative-functional and naming level, whereas objects which are structurally indistinct, activate multiple candidates at each level, creating noise and delaying the ultimate response.

It follows from this that the entry points into the associative-functional level of information are different for the two types of objects: objects with structurally distinct shapes will enter at a point at which the individual item has been identified fairly precisely at base level (for example, a type of chair), while objects with indistinct structures will enter at category level (for example, a four-legged animal). (See Riddoch & Humphreys, Chapter 4, for a discussion of entry points into the *structural* system.)

A pertinent question here is this: If the structural description of an object with a distinct structure is precise enough to access base-level information in the conceptual system, why cannot it also access the base-level name in the naming system? If the answer is that information in the associative-functional system enhances recognition, even for structurally distinct items (making the selection of the correct name more probable), then the nature of this associative-functional knowledge is of interest.

Many assumptions are made about what an object concept entails: Sometimes these assumptions are stated explicitly in models of object recognition, and sometimes the properties are implied in the tests used to tap conceptual representations. A small set of candidate properties emerges. Function has already been mentioned: This property appears in psychological models (e.g., Seymour, 1979; Warrington, 1982; Ratcliff & Newcombe, 1982; Riddoch & Humphreys, 1985), and in tests of object recognition (Lhermitte & Beauvois, 1973; Taylor & Warrington, 1971). Associative attributes, such as location and origin (natural vs. man-made) are also included (Warringon, 1975). Knowledge of size is questioned in both pathological (e.g. Warrington, 1975) and normal investigations (e.g., Te Linde, 1982); so too is knowledge of category (e.g., animal/not animal) and knowledge of subordinate properties, (e.g., number of legs, colour, etc.).

A glance at these different properties of object concepts shows that some specify in more detail than others the precise identity of an object. I have already noted that often function cannot distinguish between different, but related items. Even where function can determine one item from another item, it is generally uninformative when distinguishing which of the many possible examples of that item one has. It cannot distinguish one pair of gloves from another, or one cat from another, unless perhaps one takes account of somewhat wider aspects of function such as "These are the gloves I wear to weddings", or "This is the cat that digs holes in our garden". However, even here, the ability to discriminate the wedding gloves, or the cat that digs, will nearly always depend ultimately on there being a discernible perceptual difference between these items and all others of the same type. Whether this is available in some structural description system, or whether it can be realised as the result of an interaction between structural description and associative-functional knowledge (as for example, one might interpret the interaction between visual and verbal memory in which a patient who has to select the correctly coloured frog thinks "Frogs are green" (conceptual information), "This colour is green" (visual information), "Therefore this is the correctly coloured frog" (Beauvois, 1982) it seems that, in most cases, recognition will ultimately depend upon access to precise perceptual-featural information. The same arguments apply to location and origin—the information is usually too general to specify the object precisely.

Size alone is even less informative about identity. First, various examples of the same type of object often vary in size and secondly, many different objects share the same sort of size. Knowledge of size, without knowledge of shape, would appear to be useless. However, knowledge of size together with knowledge of shape might be very useful for distinguishing between structurally similar items. For example, the structural description of a rat and a mouse will differ little, but knowledge of size may determine which one is present and one's subsequent action.

Functional-associative information may help to clarify the identity of an object with many structural neighbours. However, for items with structurally distinct shapes, it would appear that in moving from structural descriptions to functional-associative descriptions, information is proceeding from the precise to the more general. In many cases functional-associative information would appear to be redundant for the purposes of identifying an item which has already been precisely recognised at the structural level.

3.2.2. Naming from Structural Knowledge

Naming directly on the basis of structural descriptions of shape was first proposed by Ratcliff and Newcombe (1982) as a partial explanation for the incidence of optic aphasia. The particular idea is that a pictogen, of the same status as the logogen for a word, is able to activate a word name directly. Its role is to help to pinpoint the correct name from a range of names that an inherently imprecise conceptual description may activate. Ratcliff and Newcombe argue that if such a visual object naming route exists, then patients may be found who can name an object precisely but who cannot demonstrate precise knowledge of the conceptual properties of the object. This route would provide an object naming route analagous to the direct route in reading aloud (Schwartz, Saffran, & Marin, 1980; Funnell, 1983a).

Certain observations indeed suggest that naming directly from structural knowledge is likely to occur. First, for some shapes a structural description appears to encompass almost all the relevant conceptual knowledge. People knowing nothing of the mathematical properties of geometric shapes, such as square, rectangle, triangle, or circle, can name them nevertheless, and I would argue that such shapes are likely to be poorly endowed with functional-associative properties. Secondly, Heilman et al. (1976, 1981; cited by Ratcliff, 1985), report a patient who named 25 objects almost perfectly, but in a semantic matching task was unable to select more than half correctly. Similar patients have been reported by Kremin (1984). These patients could name objects very well (90%–94% correct) but were poor at selecting a semantically related picture (from a set of 5) to match a target picture (20%–56% correct), suggesting that while the object could be named, it could not be recognised at the associative-functional level. Unfortunately, however, while real objects were used in the naming task, pictures were used in the matching task. Because objects provide more information about identity than pictures (see Campion, this volume, Chapter 7), this evidence for direct route naming is unconvincing.

Finally, when children first use words for naming, they commonly over-extend the use of a word to name a variety of objects. In the majority of cases, the child over-extends the word to other objects which share a common perceptual (or structural) property (Clark, 1973). Clark and Clark (1977) report a range of perceptual properties which have been observed in over-extensions: for example, *shape* (moon → cake), sound (train → moving machines), and *texture* (scissors → metal objects). The fact that over-extensions are rarely based upon the functional properties of objects (Bowerman, 1975, cited in Clark & Clark, 1977) suggests that, for children learning language, the functional properties are less salient for object naming than are the perceptual properties of objects.

If there were a route for naming pictures of objects aloud on the basis of structural descriptions alone, what would be the properties of this route? Two properties suggest themselves: these are *structural similarity* and *word frequency*.

Riddoch and Humphreys argue persuasively that within the system of structural descriptions of shape, only items drawn from categories composed of structurally dissimilar items can derive a precise structural description at the base level. Thus, if object names are to be activated directly from structural descriptions, it is likely that these will be the names of structurally dissimilar items. Naming by this route should therefore show an effect of structural similarity. Secondly, the analagous direct route in reading aloud shows a strong word frequency effect (Bub, Cancelliere, & Kertesz, 1985). If this frequency effect occurs because the more frequently named the item is, the more often an association will have been made between the orthographic and phonological word forms, then the same argument might apply to object naming. Thus, naming on the basis of the structural description of objects may also be expected to show a name frequency effect.

Interestingly, Riddoch and Humphreys (this volume, Chapter 4) have studied a patient (J.B.) whose ability to recognise objects at the structural level is intact. When asked to name objects, he named most successfully pictures of objects drawn from categories composed of structurally distinct items. In addition, he named items with high frequency names most successfully. Although Riddoch and Humphreys account for these effects in terms of a linear processing model, in which naming is activated from conceptual information in a highly interactive, cascade process, the occurrence of effects of structural similarity and name frequency on object naming is exactly compatible with the properties of the hypothetical route, outlined earlier, for naming directly from structural descriptions.

4. SEMANTIC PROCESSING AND IMAGEABLE/ CONCRETE WORD CONCEPTS

4.1. Evidence from the Study of Acquired Dyslexia

Evidence that objects and object names map onto independent conceptual systems (Warrington & Shallice, 1979) has proved to be unconvincing. In consequence, as it is possible—even likely—that object names and objects share a common set of conceptual codes, then our understanding of object concepts may be increased by studying the conceptual information underlying word processing.

Studies of patients with acquired problems in processing written words have provided important insights into the nature and organisation of processes involved in word meaning. Abnormal reading has been particularly helpful in this respect. The reading system is generally considered to have two lexical processing routes from print to phonology (see Fig. 8.1). One route connects the orthographic form of the word directly with its phonological counterpart (Morton & Patterson, 1980; Schwartz et al., 1980; Funnell, 1983a; Bub et al., 1983); the other processes the word in terms of its meaning. The second route is the so-called lexical semantic route (Marshall & Newcombe, 1973; Morton & Patterson, 1980). Figure 8.1 also contains processes operating in the reverse direction, to account for the ability to write words to dictation, and to match auditory to visual words (see Allport & Funnell, 1981, for a full discussion of this model).

Evidence for the involvement of semantic processes in reading sprang initially from the study of deep dyslexic patients who make semantic errors when reading aloud: For example, *antique* → "vase". Semantic errors suggest that the written word has first activated its meaning and then, on the basis of the meaning, activated the spoken response (Marshall & Newcombe 1966, 1973; Coltheart et al., 1980). Patients are also reported who make semantic errors in writing to dictation (e.g. Assal, Buttet, & Jolivet, 1981).

Generally, deep dyslexic patients show a marked imageable/concrete-abstractness effect in reading such that abstract words are subject to greater difficulty than imageable/concrete words (Patterson & Marcel, 1977; Coltheart 1980). This dissociation led Morton and Patterson (1980) to divide the semantic system accessed by written and spoken words into two parts: an imagable concrete part and an abstract part. This separation is supported further by the appearance of a patient who is reported to show the contrasting pattern: a superior ability to read aloud abstract words (Warrington, 1981). Since the semantic system itself may be partitioned according to the nature of the information, it is unclear to what extent the lexical semantic route in reading should be considered to be a single route.

It has recently been proposed that imageability and concreteness are related to a further type of representation of a propositional nature: "ease of predication" (Jones, 1985). Ease of predication measures how easily a propositional statement about the word can be produced, for example that a dog is a mammal, that it has four legs, etc. Jones suggests that it is this information that is tapped by the lexical semantic route in reading. His evidence comes from *post hoc* analysis of the reading of two deep dyslexic

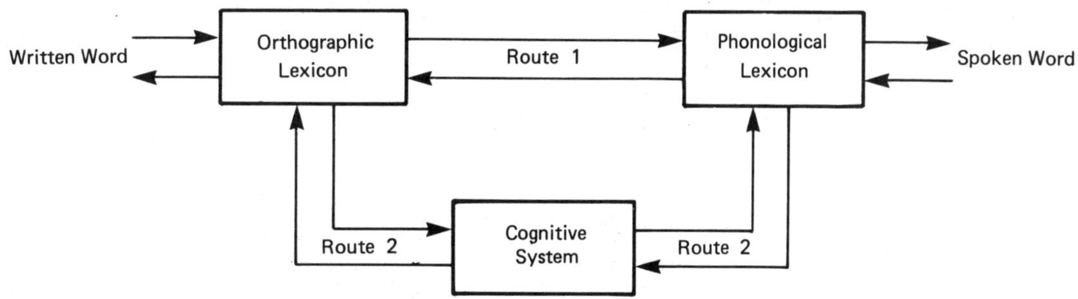

FIG. 8.1. A model of the lexical processes involved in oral reading, writing to dictation, and aural-visual matching.

patients, whose reading correlates with sensory measures of imageability and concreteness and with ease of predication. Correlations with reading performance do not allow a preference for one explanation over the other. Jones' choice of ease of predication as a better description of semantic representations is based upon the fact that it can account for two further findings: the high correlation of "categorisability" with imageability, and retrieval asymmetry for nouns and adjectives.

Ease of predication, in its emphasis upon propositional statements (an apparently verbal-semantic property), would appear to be a plausible measure of the semantic representation of *words*. In contrast, imageability and concreteness are constructs associated with sensory experience: Properties more readily associated with *objects*. To this extent, the fact that imageability and concreteness correlate at all with word processing is perhaps surprising (even if this is a consequence of correlations between these constructs with ratings on ease of predication), and suggests that words associated and objects (i.e., object names and the names of object properties), map, at some point, on to conceptual representations of a nonverbal, sensory nature.

4.2. Imageable/Concrete Word Meanings

In order to investigate further the nature of the cognitive codes underlying the processing of imageable/concrete words, an experiment was carried out in which the language performance of four patients was correlated with a variety of measures of meaning (Funnell, 1983b).

The patients were all severely impaired in speaking, reading, and writing. They were asked to carry out three tasks: reading aloud, writing to dictation, and aural-visual matching (in this task a written word was selected from a list of words to match to a single auditory word). As their ability to write *complete words* to dictation was virtually non-existent, even for highly imageable/concrete words, only performance in the reading and matching tasks will be reported here. Each task tapped the patients' ability to transcode information between orthographic and phonological forms. First, it was observed that no patient could process nonwords in any task, indicating that the ability to process information by sublexical processes was severely, perhaps totally impaired. Secondly, in reading and matching tasks, a marked word-class effect was found in which highly imageable/concrete words were processed most successfully (see Table 8.1). Two of the four patients made a considerable number of semantic errors. The remaining two patients made less than 1%.

Through a series of experiments involving spoken-to-written word matching, in which performance with semantically related and unrelated words was compared, it was established that each patient transcoded

TABLE 8.1
Percentage Correct Performance in Oral Reading and Aural-Visual (A-V) Matching

Words	*Task*	*Subjects and Scores*			
		A.L.	W.T.	C.G.	R.C.
High imageability Low frequency	Oral reading (n = 34)	65	50	47	88
	A-V matching (n = 24)	100	92	67	90
Low imageability High frequency	Oral reading (n = 40)	5	3	8	33
	A-V matching (n = 54)	35	15	11	32

imageable/concrete words between their orthographic and phonological lexical forms on the basis of semantic information, that is, by route 2 in Fig. 8.1. No other strategy was available to them. Thus, it appeared that success in processing particular classes of words in these three transcoding tasks depended upon the nature of the semantic information available. The alternative possibility, that word-class differences arose from the loss of word-class specific information in the orthographic and/or phonological systems was definitely ruled out (Funnell, 1983b; Funnell & Allport, 1987).

In order to investigate the nature of the semantic representations mediating in the processing of imageable/concrete words, an experiment was conducted in which 10 normal subjects were asked to rate *all* the words given to the patients (i.e., both highly imageable/concrete words and words low in imageability and concreteness), on various properties of word meaning. These properties included *Imageability* and *Concreteness*, widely used as descriptions of the properties of words. These variables are often argued to be very different, and claims have been made for the greater effects of one compared to the other in the reading performance of deep dyslexic patients (Richardson, 1975). However, the actual instructions given to the subjects vary very little (Paivio, Yuille, & Madican, 1968). Both stress sense experience: Imageability in terms of pictures and sounds: Concreteness in terms of objects and people. Concreteness would appear to be tapping slightly more tangible attributes of word meanings than imageability. This is confirmed by referring to Table 8.3. While ratings on Imageability and Concreteness correlate significantly with each of the sensory properties of shape, colour, sound, smell, touch, and weight (supporting the notion that there is little difference overall between the properties of Concreteness and Imageability), the ratings on shape and weight (relatively tangible properties) correlate most highly with Concreteness, while ratings on *sound* (a relatively intangible property) correlate most highly with Imageability.

As a more general measure of sense experience, and one designed to measure intrinsic sense properties rather than associated properties, another variable termed *Independence* was introduced. Here the subject was asked to rate each word according to how directly a sensory experience was evoked by a word. If the word evoked a sense experience in its own right then this represented a high degree of Independence. Alternatively, if the sense experience could be evoked only in association with a wider sense experience (that would be labelled by a different word), then that word was low in Independence. For example, a word such as *red* may produce a sensation of redness on its own, in which case it would receive a high rating on Independence, however, if it were experienced only in relation to something that is red, such as a poppy, then it would be rated low in Independence.

To derive some measure of general word meaning, independent of sensory properties, subjects were also asked to rate the words according to how easily the word could be defined (a construct referred to here as *Verbal Definition*). Defining a word seems to call for verbal propositional descriptions reminiscent of ease of predication: That is, how well factual statements can be made about the meaning of the word. Indeed, when subjects were asked later to give actual definitions of the words, they produced just the sort of factual statements which would be termed predicates by Jones (1985). Thus for the word dog, one subject said "A dog is an animal. It has four legs and a tail that wags. It lives in a kennel".

As three of the four global measures of meaning (Imageability, Concreteness, and Independence) tapped sense experience, it was decided to explore the nature of sense experience further. Eight sensory properties of objects were therefore included in further ratings, these were *colour, shape, sound, smell, taste, touch, weight, movement*. Here movement refers to the movement characteristic of the object itself: For example, the fluttering of a butterfly or the spinning of a top. Two further sensory properties were explored, this time tapping properties peculiar to the self: these were *emotion* and *self movement*. Self movement concerns any movement the subject would make in relation to the object: stirring with a spoon; running away from a tiger. Self movement is obviously related to function, since an object whose function can be mimed must have representations of self movement.

The words were rated on a scale from 0 to 7, in which *zero* meant that the word had no representation upon that dimension, *one* a small degree of representation, and *seven* a very high degree. The full word set was rated separately for each dimension in turn. This method decreased the chances of the properties of word meanings being subject to relative differences. That is, if each word had been rated on each variable in turn the subject might have weighted various properties according to relative importance. Presenting the words repeatedly, for rating on each variable, gave each measure the best chance of a detached rating.

Correlations with the patients' performance in reading aloud and aural-visual matching are given in Tables 8.2 and 8.3. These correlations show that of the four global measures of word meaning (Table 8.2), the three sensory measures (Imageability, Concreteness, and Independence) correlated significantly, and to a high degree with the patients' performance in reading aloud and aural-visual matching. It is of further interest that Independence, a measure of the direct (but unspecified) representation of sensory experience, correlated highly with patients' performance. Verbal Definition, while producing positive and significant correlations, gave a significantly lower correlation with aural-visual matching performance than the three global sensory measures.

Of the 10 sensory properties (Table 8.3), the 2 properties of the subject (subjective movement, i.e., function and emotion) produced consistently low positive correlations with the patients' performance and with the three global sensory measures of Imageability, Concreteness, and Independence. These correlations were generally significant, however, due to the large sample size. The eight sensory properties of objects (e.g., shape, colour, sound, etc.) gave generally very high positive correlations with each of the global sensory variables and with the patients' performance, all of which were significant. Apart from some correlations obtained to measures of object movement and taste, correlations between the sensory properties of

TABLE 8.2
Pearson Correlation Coefficients Obtained from Comparisons Between Four Global Measures of Meaning and Patients' Performance

Task	*Global Measures*			
	Imageability	*Concreteness*	*Independence*	*Verbal Definition*
Oral reading (110 words)	0.65	0.63	0.69	0.59
Aural-visual matching (161 words)	0.69	0.71	0.73	0.52*

Note: Group scores all given for four patients in two tasks: reading aloud and audio-visual matching. Comparisons are made across individual wards.

*Verbal definition significantly inferior to coefficients obtained to Imageability ($P < 0.02$), Concreteness and Independence ($P < 0.01$).

TABLE 8.3

Pearson Correlation Coefficients Obtained in Comparisons Between Mean Ratings on Each Sensory Dimension and Patients' Performance

	Sensory Dimensions									
	Object								*Self*	
	Shape	*Colour*	*Sound*	*Smell*	*Taste*	*Touch*	*Weight*	*Movt.*	*Emot.*	*Movt.*
1. Task										
Oral reading (110 words)	0.67	0.66	0.49	0.56	0.49	0.50	0.53	0.38*	0.26	0.17
Aural-visual matching (161 words)	0.68	0.75	0.52	0.61	0.38*	0.52	0.59	0.27*	0.24	0.27
2. *Global sensory measures* (df = 159)										
Imageability	0.78	0.86	0.70	0.72	0.52*	0.77	0.71	0.64	0.38	0.42
Concreteness	0.92	0.86	0.61	0.74	0.47**	0.76	0.87	0.69	0.18	0.36
Independence	0.91	0.87	0.67	0.74	0.48**	0.77	0.81	0.73	0.25	0.41

Note: (1) Group performance (four patients) in tests of oral reading and aura-visual matching. (2) Mean rating scores on the three global sensory dimensions. Comparisons are made across individual words.

Coefficient not significantly different from coefficients for dimensions of self: *emotion and subjective movement; **subjective movement only.

objects, patients' performance, and the global sensory measures are significantly superior to those obtained to properties of the self. In analyses based upon individual patient's performance and word categories, rather than individual words, the same pattern of results was observed (Funnell, 1983b; Funnell & Allport, 1987).

Whereas Verbal Definition correlated significantly with each of the three global sensory variables, its failure to correlate highly with the patients' performance was due to the fact that many of the words which the patients failed to transcode have relatively high ratings on Verbal Definition. Thus, the properties that enable a word to be defined, do not appear to be sufficient for the word to be transcoded by the patients in this study. If Verbal Definition is synonymous with Ease of Predication, then this result casts doubt upon the theory that the ability to encode the meaning of a word in terms of propositions is the crucial variable responsible for processing concrete/imageable words by patients who rely upon semantic information for reading aloud (Jones, 1985). The fact that Verbal Definition gave rise to significant correlations with patients' performance is probably due to the fact that it correlates highly with the three global sensory measures of Imageability, Concreteness, and Independence.

Correlations alone cannot be taken as evidence of cause and effect. However, when performance in transcoding tasks is known to depend on semantic processing, then correlations with measures of word meanings can be argued perhaps to reflect the properties of the semantic system responsible for the behaviour patterns observed. The high correlations obtained between the patients' performance and variables concerned with sense experience of the physical properties of objects, suggest that the semantic system responsible for successful transcoding between written and spoken word forms contains representations of the sensory properties of objects and events in the world.

Profiles of the full rating patterns of the sensory properties of objects (see Table 8.4) further suggest that object names are tapping a set of conceptual codes for processing the perceptible properties of objects. Although words were rated separately for each property, and semantically related words were well separated in the word lists, patterns of ratings for semantically related words are very closely similar, and appear to reflect characteristics of particular *object categories*. Interesting differences in ratings do appear which reflect the idiosyncratic properties of particular objects within a class—for example, apples are noisier (to eat) than bananas, buses are more colourful than trains, rabbits are tastier than dogs, but dogs are noisier than rabbits—on the whole the patterns appear to reflect the general characteristics of an object category. Thus, although all items in Table 8.4 (except colour names) score highly on shape—a seemingly fundamental property of "thingness"—flowers are marked by low ratings on taste, sound, and movement, but gain high ratings on colour

TABLE 8.4
Sensory Rating Profiles of Selected Semantic Co-ordinates

	Properties of objects							
Word	*Shape*	*Taste*	*Movt.*	*Sound*	*Weight*	*Colour*	*Smell*	*Touch*
Apple	6.5	6.5	1.6	3.7	5.7	6.1	5.6	5.0
Banana	6.7	6.4	1.1	1.9	5.0	6.5	6.0	5.1
Bluebell	5.1	1.7	2.7	1.1	3.5	6.7	5.2	4.1
Daffodil	6.4	2.7	3.1	1.0	4.1	6.3	5.8	4.8
Dog	5.9	2.0	5.8	5.8	5.0	4.6	5.6	5.5
Rabbit	6.1	5.0	5.8	3.0	4.5	5.1	5.2	4.0
Mouse	6.1	1.9	5.6	4.9	5.0	4.7	5.1	4.5
Boy	5.2	1.6	4.9	4.5	4.0	3.7	4.0	3.4
Girl	5.5	1.9	4.3	4.5	4.5	3.7	3.8	4.2
Man	5.6	2.0	4.7	4.2	5.3	3.7	4.3	4.1
Robin	6.3	1.2	5.3	4.8	4.5	6.3	2.9	3.4
Sparrow	6.0	1.4	5.7	4.8	4.0	4.7	2.8	3.2
Arm	5.5	1.8	5.0	1.8	4.9	3.8	2.5	4.4
Leg	5.6	2.1	4.9	1.8	5.0	3.8	2.3	4.6
Bus	6.2	0.8	5.7	5.4	5.1	5.7	4.8	3.5
Train	6.0	1.8	6.3	6.2	5.3	3.8	5.2	3.0
Bed	6.5	1.7	1.9	3.2	5.3	3.6	4.2	4.7
Chair	6.1	0.5	1.3	2.9	5.2	3.2	2.3	4.8
Table	6.6	1.5	1.5	2.3	5.8	4.3	3.3	4.5

and smell; vehicles are marked by high ratings on sound, movement, and weight; furniture by low ratings on all properties except weight and touch, and animals (in general) by all properties except taste. People appear to be a less colourful and less smelly form of animal. It is unclear what the nature of the relationship is between numerical ratings across a range of sensory properties and structural properties associated with object categories. Nevertheless, the fact that these ratings seem to capture the essence of the structural properties of particular items and particular object categories suggests that the imageable/concrete representations of meaning, onto which object names map, are composed of the sensory properties of objects in the external world.

If objects and object names map onto identical conceptual descriptions, then the properties and organisation of concepts hitherto described in relation to pictures should resemble the properties and organisation of concepts hitherto described in relation to object names. The evidence so far supports this. Processes involved in identifying pictures have been argued to divide into two functionally separable systems: one containing *structural descriptions*, the other *functional-associative* information (Section 3). The conceptual system underling object names shows the same type of distinction. The imageable/concrete properties of the semantic system—most sensitive to word-word transcoding in the patients studied here–were the sensory, or perceptible, or *structural* properties of objects: properties such as *shape, colour, sound, smell*, etc. The *functional-associative* properties of self-movement and attitude (as measured by ratings on emotion) produced consistently low correlations with performance (Tables 8.2 and 8.3).

5. SHARED CONCEPTUAL INFORMATION FOR OBJECT NAMES AND OBJECTS

Two experiments addressed directly the question of shared conceptual representations for objects and object names. These experiments introduced non-alphabetic graphic symbols to represent concepts normally expressed by single words. Three of the four patients in the study reported above (the remaining patient being unwell) were involved in Experiment 1, and one of these patients (A.L.) in Experiment 2.

5.1. Experiment 1: Associating Aural Words with Graphic Symbols

The patients were taught to associate arbitrary graphic symbols (Table 8.5) with aurally presented words and nonwords (Funnell, 1983b). The graphic symbols were unrelated pictorially and ideographically to the meaning of the words. A clear pattern of performance emerged: All three patients could only learn to associate graphic symbols with aural imageable/concrete words. They were totally unable to learn to associate graphic symbols with highly frequent aurally presented words of low imageability/concreteness (words such as *and, when,* etc), even though other tests had shown that such words were familiar to them (Funnell, 1983b; Funnell & Allport, 1987). They were also totally unable to learn to associate graphic symbols with nonwords—even when the set was reduced in size to three items only. Thus, a word-class effect was found in this experiment that mirrored the word-class effect found in the three word-word transcoding tasks reported in Section 4.2. Irrespective of the form of the material presented, or of the modality of input, these patients could transcode only that information that was able to map onto mediating imageable/concrete conceptual representations.

Graphic symbols, having no alphabetic, or phonetic characteristics, are markedly more similar to pictures than to words. Therefore it is significant that the conceptual system onto which map aural (and visual) imageable/concrete words, is also mapped onto by graphic symbols. This mapping is depicted in Fig. 8.2A.

TABLE 8.5
Graphic Symbols Paired with Words and Nonwords (Experiment 1) and Object Names and Pictures (Experiment 2)

Experiment 1

WORDS				**NONWORDS**	
High Imageable		Low Imageable			
Word	Symbol	Word	Symbol	Nonword	Symbol
pig	⊖	the	↱	doop	⤫
sport	«	how	⚭	pilt	△
hammer	∸	use	ǂ	hean	⊡
toy	⊠	make	⊻	nust	╲
shoe	♉	all	⊕	tife	⎍

Experiment 2

a) aural object name → graphic symbol → picture

Word (picture)	Symbol
cow	⍋
door	⊏
kite	
crown	•••
bus	

b) picture → graphic symbol → aural object name

Picture (word)	Symbol
tent	‖
pipe	
ball	□□□
snail	×
stool	⬣

The models in Figs. 8.2B and 8.2C represent alternative theories of the processes involved in picture naming. In Fig. 8.2B, pictures access phonological codes by an independent pathway, with no access to the imageable/concrete representations which map graphic symbols and written words (Fig. 8.1) onto phonological word forms. For the sake of simplicity, no structural or associative-functional systems for identifying pictures have been included, however, this model is consistent with the theory that words and pictures map onto independent conceptual systems (Warrington & Shallice, 1979; Shallice, 1985). In contrast, in Fig. 8.2C, pictures have direct access to the system of imageable/concrete representa-

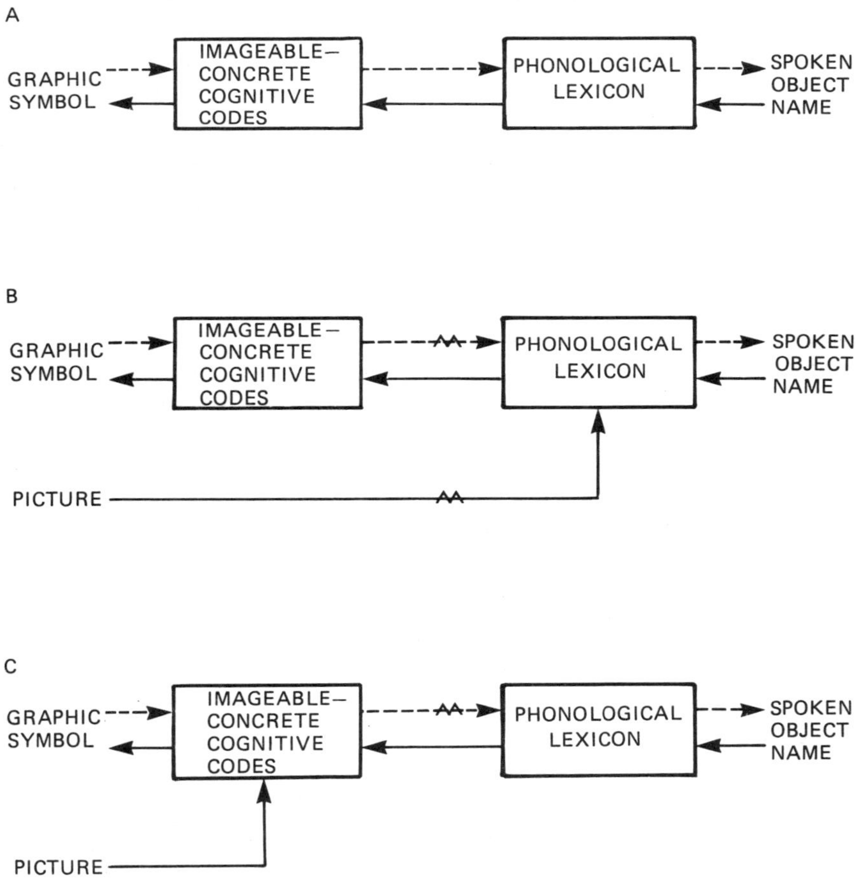

FIG. 8.2. Three processing models of mappings between spoken object names, graphic symbols, and pictures. (A) Mappings between spoken object names and graphic symbols. (B) Pictures access the phonological lexicon. (C) Pictures access the imageable/concrete cognitive codes.

tions. This is consistent with the theory that pictures, graphic symbols, written, and spoken words all map onto identical representations of meaning. These contrasting theories were pitted against each other in a further experiment involving the single patient A.L. One characteristic of A.L.—his anomia—was critical to the experimental predicitions.

A.L. is a conduction aphasic with a marked word-finding problem in spontaneous speech (less than 1% of words have clear specific reference), as well as in picture and written word naming. For example, he correctly named 22% pictures and 56% written names of 36 common objects, all with one syllable names. His problem in naming pictures was not due to a visual agnosia, as he scored very highly (130/150) on the Peabody Picture Vocabulary test. Nor was it due to a failure to identify the object. A.L. made no semantic errors in naming pictures or words in this test: His errors consisted entirely of phonemic errors (pictures, 14%; written names, 19%) and no response errors (pictures, 86%; written names, 81%).

Several observations suggest that at least part of A.L.'s word-finding difficulty lay in a severe problem in accessing phonological codes for naming (see also Allport 1983). First, he had great difficulty in verbally repeating auditory words. Secondly, giving the first phoneme of the picture of word *never* helped A.L. to produce the name, although other patients are often helped by such cues (Myers, Pease & Goodglass, 1978). Thirdly, A.L. was unable to indicate the correct number of syllables in written words and picture names to a level above chance, indicating that his word-finding problem is not arising at some stage subsequent to access to the phonological codes, for example, in processes involved in articulating the word. A.L.'s impaired ability to access the phonological codes for pictures and written words is marked as zig-zags on the models depicted in Figs. 8.2B and 8.2C. These impairments are critical to the predictions based upon the model.

The crucial experiment requires A.L. to learn to associate arbitrary graphic symbols with aurally presented object names, and then to spontaneously transfer this association to pictures of the objects, presented without forewarning. According to the hypothesis represented in Fig. 8.2B, A.L. should learn to associate graphic symbols with phonological word codes via the system of imageable/concrete representations (this was the outcome of Experiment 1). In order to associate a pictorial representation of the object (previously named) with the correct graphic symbol, A.L. would need first to access the object name in the phonological codes. However, this A.L. can do only poorly (22% in the test reported above): Thus, according to this model, A.L. should transfer associations made between aurally presented object names to pictures to a level around 25% correct. In contrast, according to the hypothesis represented in Fig. 8.2C, associations between graphic symbols and aurally presented object names should be able to transfer without error to pictures via the shared set of imageable/concrete word meanings, because in this model there is no requirement for intermediary naming.

5.2. Experiment 2: Transfer Tests—Associating Pictures with Graphic Symbols

A.L. was taught to associate graphic symbols to each of five aurally presented *names* of common objects. The graphic symbols were unrelated pictorially and ideographically to the pictured object (Table 8.5). At a second stage, he learned to write the symbol for each aural object name presented in random order. He learned to do this quickly and accurately. Then he was given a surprise transfer test in which a *picture* of the object was presented instead of its name. A.L. was asked to write down the graphic symbol appropriate to each pictured object. He responded confidently, without hesitation, and on the three successively presented test trials his responses were entirely correct (15/15).

In an alternative version of this test, A.L. was taught five new pictures of novel objects under the same conditions as Experiment 2. The associations were found to transfer without error when the picture names were spoken (in the absence of the pictures): He scored a total of 15/15 on the three successively presented trials. Although this test does not force a choice between the contrasting theories presented in Figs. 8.2B and 8.2C, as mappings from phonological word forms to pictures are apparently unimpaired (A.L.'s PVT score equals an IQ of 130), the results are included here as evidence of A.L.'s consistently perfect score across tests involving 10 different pictures and 10 different object names.

The results of these experiments support model C (Fig. 8.2), which proposes that pictured objects (and presumably also the objects themselves) map onto a system of structural-imageable/concrete representations, also accessed by graphic symbols and visually and aurally presented object names (Fig. 8.1).

The principle of modularity—here extended to preclude duplicated material—is thus upheld. Despite apparent evidence to the contrary (Warrington & Shallice, 1979), the information upon which objects and object names are identified appears, after all, to be contained within a shared system of conceptual knowledge.

REFERENCES

Allport, D. A. (1983). Language and cognition. In R. Harris (Ed.), *Approaches to language*. Oxford: Pergamon.

Allport, D. A. (1985). Distributed memory, modular subsystems and dysphasia, In S. Newman and R. Epstein (Eds.), *Current perspectives in dysphasia*. Edinburgh: Churchill Livingstone.

Allport, D. A. & Funnell, E. (1981). Components of the mental lexicon. *Philosophical Transactions of the Royal Society, London, B295*, 397–410.

Assal, G., Buttet, J., & Jolivet, R. (1981). Dissociations in aphasia: A case report. *Brain and Language, 13*, 223–241.

Beauvois, M. F. (1982). Optic aphasia: A process of interaction between vision and language. *Philosophical Transactions of the Royal Society, London, B298*, 35–47.

Beauvois, M. F. & Saillant, B. (1985). Optic aphasia for colours and colour agnosia: A distinction between visual and visuo-verbal impairments in the processing of colours. *Cognitive Neuropsychology, 2(1)*, 1–48.

Beauvois, M. F., Saillant, B., Meininger, V., & Lhermitte, F. (1978). Bilateral tactile aphasia: A tacto-verbal dysfunction. *Brain, 101*, 381–401.

Bishop, D. & Byng, S. (1984). Assessing semantic comprehension: methodological considerations, and a new clinical test. *Cognitive Neuropsychology, 1(3)*, 233–243.

Bub, D. N. Cancelliere, A., & Kertesz, A. (1985). Whole-word and analytic translation of spelling to sound in a non-semantic reader. In K. E. Patterson, J. C. Marshall, and M. Coltheart, (Eds.) *Surface dyslexia: Neuropsychological and cognitive analysis of phonological reading*, London: Lawrence Erlbaum Associates Ltd.

Clark, E. (1973). What's in a word? On the child's acquistion of semantics in his first language. In T. E. Moore (Ed.) *Cognitive development and the acquisition of language.* New York: Academic Press.

Clark. H. H. & Clark, E. V. (1977). *Psychology and language. An introduction to psycholinguistics*. New York: Harcourt Brace Jovanovich.

Coltheart, M. (1980). Deep dyslexia: a review of the syndrome. In M. Coltheart, K. Patterson, and J. C. Marshall (Eds.), *Deep dyslexia*, London: Routledge and Kegan Paul.

Coltheart, M., Patterson, K., & Marshall, J. (Eds.) (1980). *Deep dyslexia*. London: Routledge and Kegan Paul.

Denes, G. & Semenza, C. (1975). Auditory modality-specific anomia: evidence from a case of pure word-deafness. *Cortex, 11*, 401–411.

Ellis, A. W. (1982). Spelling and writing (and reading and speaking). In A.W. Ellis (Ed.), *Normality and pathology in cognitive functions.* London: Academic Press.

Funnell, E. (1983a). Phonological processes in reading: new evidence from acquired dyslexia. *British Journal of Psychology, 74*, 159–180.

Funnell, E. (1983b). *Ideographic communication and word-class differences in aphasia*. Unpublished Ph.D. Thesis. Reading University, U.K.

Funnell, E. & Allport, D. E. (1987). Non-linguistic cognition and word meanings: Neuropsychological exploration of common mechanisms. In D. A. Allport, D. G. MacKay, W. Prinz, and E. Scheerer (Eds.), *Language perception and production: Shared mechanisms in listening, speaking, reading and writing*. London: Academic Press.

Hay, C. D. & Young, A. W. (1982). The human face. In A. W. Ellis (Ed.), *Normality and pathology in cognitive functions*. London: Academic Press.

Humphreys, G. W., Riddoch, M. J., & Quinlan, P. T. (1985), Cascade processes in picture identification: Data and implications. Paper presented at the symposium on *Cognitive Neuropsychology*, Venice.

Jones, G. V. (1985). Deep dyslexia, imageability, and ease of predication. *Brain and Language, 24*, 1–19.

Kremin, H. (1984), Spared naming without comprehension. Paper presented at the *International Neuropsychological Society 7th European Conference*, Aachen, West Germany.

Lhermitte, F. & Beauvois, M. F. (1973). A visual-speech disconnexion syndrome. Report of a case with optic aphasia, agnosic alexia and colour agnosia. *Brain, 96*, 695–714.

Marr, D. (1976). Early processing of visual information. *Philosophical Transactions of the Royal Society, London, B942*, 483–519.

Marshall, J. C. & Newcombe, F. (1966). Syntactic and semantic errors in paralexia. *Neuropsychologia, 4*, 169–179.

Marshall, J. C. & Newcombe, F. (1973). Patterns of paralexia. *Journal of Psycholinguistic Research, 2*, 175–199.

Morton, J. (1979). Facilitation in word recognition. Experiments causing changes in the logogen model, In P. A. Kolers, M. Wrolstad, and H. Bouma (Eds.), *Processing of visible language*. New York: Plenum.

Morton, J. (1980). The logogen model and orthographic structure. In U. Frith (Ed.), *Cognitive processes in spelling*. London: Academic Press.

Morton, J. & Patterson, K. (1980). A new attempt at an interpretation, or, an attempt at a new interpretation. In M. Coltheart, K. Patterson, and J. C. Marshall (Eds.). *Deep dyslexia*. London: Routledge and Kegan Paul.

Myers Pease, D. & Goodglass, H. (1978). The effects of cueing on picture naming in aphasia. *Cortex, 14*, 178–189.

Newcombe, F. & Ratcliff, G. (1974). Agnosia: A disorder of object recognition. In F. Michel and B. Schott (Eds.), *Les syndromes de disconnexion calleuse chez l'homme*. Lyon: Colloque International.

Oxbury, J. M., Oxbury, S. M., & Humphrey, N. K. (1969). Varieties of colour anomia. *Brain, 92*. 847–860.

Paivio, A., Yuille, J. C., & Madican, S. A. (1968). Concreteness, imagery and meaningfulness values for 925 nouns. *Journal of Experimental Psychology, Monograph Supplement, 76*, 2–25.

Patterson, K. E. & Marcel, A. J. (1977). Aphasia, dyslexia and the phonological coding of written words. *Quarterly Journal of Experimental Psychology, 29*, 307–318.

Patterson, K. E., Marshall, J. C., & Coltheart, M. (Eds.) (1985). *Surface dyslexia: Neuropsychological and cognitive analysis of phonological reading*. London: Lawrence Erlbaum Associates Ltd.

Ratcliff, G. (1985). Agnosia and internal representations: some second thoughts. Paper presented at the symposium on *Cognitive Neuropsychology*, Venice.

Ratcliff, G. & Newcombe, F. (1982). Object recognition: Some deductions from the clinical evidence. In A. W. Ellis (Ed.), *Normality and pathology in cognitive functions*. London: Academic Press.

Richardson, J. T. E. (1975). The effect of word imageability in acquired dyslexia. *Neuropsychologia, 13*, 281–288.

Riddoch, M. J. & Humphreys, G. W. (1985). Semantic systems or system? Neuropsychologi cal evidence re-examined. Paper presented at a symposium on *Cognitive Neuropsychology*, Venice.

Schwartz, M. F. Marin, O. S. M., & Saffran, E. M. (1979). Dissociations of language function in dementia: A case study. *Brain and Language, 7*, 277–306.

Schwartz, M. F. Saffran, E. M., & Marin, O. S. M. (1980). Fractionating the reading process in dementia: evidence for word-specific print-to-sound associations. In M. Coltheart, K. Patterson, and J. C. Marshall (Eds.), *Deep dyslexia*. London: Routledge and Kegan Paul.

Seymour, P. H. K. (1979). *Human visual cognition*. London: Collier-Macmillan.

Shallice, T. (1981a). Neurological impairment of cognitive processes. *British Medical Bulletin, 37*, 187–192

Shallice, T. (1981b). Phonological agraphia and the lexical route in writing. *Brain, 104*, 413–429.

Shallice, T. (1985). Impairments of semantic processing: Multiple dissociations. In M. Coltheart, R. Job and G. Sartori (Eds.), *The cognitive neuropsychology of language*. London: Lawrence Erlbaum Associates Ltd.

Taylor, A. & Warrington, E. (1971). Visual agnosia: A single case report. *Cortex*, *7*, 152–161.

Te Linde, J. (1982). Picture-word differences in decision latency. *Journal of Experimental Psychology: Learning, Memory and Cognition, 8*, 584–598.

Warrington, E. (1975). The selective impairment of semantic memory. *Quarterly Journal of Experimental Psychology, 27*, 635–657.

Warrington, E. K. (1981). Concrete word dyslexia. *British Journal of Psychology, 72*, 175–196.

Warrington, E. (1982). Neuropsychological studies of object recognition. *Philosophical Transactions of the Royal Society, London, B298*, 15–33.

Warrington, E. K. & Shallice, T. (1979). Semantic access dyslexia. *Brain, 102*, 43–63.

9 Dementia and Visual Agnosia

Oscar S. M. Marin
Laboratory of Cognitive Neuropsychology,
Department of Neurology, Good Samaritan Hospital and Medical Center, Portland, Oregon 97210, U.S.A.

1. DEMENTIA: DEFINITIONS AND NOSOLOGY

Dementias are acquired mental disorders characterised by a progressive and largely irreversible disorganisation and deterioration of mental functions. Although the deficit is primarily cognitive, the symptomatology is by no means restricted to these functions and quite often it affects the personality and character, emotions, activity, motivation, and initiative. The progression of the disease ultimately may compromise the basic sensory and motor physiological basis of the nervous organisation. The clinical symptomatology of the dementias results from the progressive structural damage of the central nervous system that affects most severely the cortical mantle of both the neocortex and the limbic and paralimbic systems.

In recent years there is growing evidence that structural damage is accompanied, and even preceded, by important biochemical and other neurochemical functional disorders that as yet remain incompletely understood (see Francis, Palmer, Sims, Bowen, Davison, Esiri, Neary, Snowden, & Wilcock, 1985). These types of abnormalities are not only of great importance for the possible therapeutic management of dementias but also serve to explain the only approximate correlation that exists between the severity of the clinical symptomatology and the degree of morphological changes noted at the post-mortem examination or in the images obtained with the newer neuroradiological techniques of the computerised or magnetic resonance tomographies. Thus, relatively obvious symptomatology may be present in individuals whole brains show somewhat unremarkable changes in structure, while in others, severe evidence of cortical atrophy may correspond to relatively mild clinical deficits (see Schwartz, Marin, & Saffran, 1979).

The disparity between the clinical picture and structural damage should also be attributed to the fact that, particularly in the early stages of the illness, a rich reactive symptomatology may dominate the clinical picture in addition to deficits directly resulting from the cortical damage. Irritability, withdrawal, denial, displacement of blame, emotional and activity changes and, most important of all, depression, might constitute important symptomatological reactive elements in a still insightful and frustrated patient who is no longer capable of coping with the demands of his environment, family, relatives, friends, or work.

The reactive symptoms may not be restricted to emotional spheres. They may appear as cognitive deficits in the area of attention, memory, thinking, learning, and other cognitive functions and skills.

A large number of causative processes can lead to a dementia. Toxic, metabolic, infectious, or degenerative processes may affect the central nervous system primarily or exclusively, or they may affect the nervous tissue as a secondary or concomitant of other more generalised disorders of the metabolism or the hormonal systems. Common to all of them is the cerebral cortical damage that, as a rule, is bilateral and fairly diffuse, although it is recognised that some areas are more susceptible to damage. In this sense, dementia processes contrast with the unilateral and more focalised lesions that result from vascular infarcts, haemorrhages, tumours, circumscribed infections, or traumas of the central nervous system.

In general, the large majority of dementias occur in the pre-senile and senile decades of life. Although the cause may vary, the most common dementias of late life are part of the group called primary or classical dementias of degenerative type. The primary example is constituted by the dementia of Alzheimer type. The original cases were described both clinically and pathologically by Alzheimer (1907, 1911) in the pre-senile age group, and the course of the illness in these cases was particularly rapid and destructive. The loss of nerve cells in the cortical mantle, cortical atrophy, neurofibrillary tangles, senile plaques, and the reactive gliosis characterise the pathology. Soon afterwards, it was observed that the same pathological changes could be observed in numerous cases of senile individuals and most prominently so in cases of senile dementia. This latter dementia, the most common of all, tends to be less aggressive in its course and more diffuse in its clinical manifestation with a pathology qualitatively similar to Alzheimer, although usually quantitatively less severe. Because of this commonality of the pathological substratum one tends to speak today of the dementias of Alzheimer type as a group in which one can distinguish three main subgroups: the original pre-senile dementia of Alzheimer, the senile dementia of Alzheimer type (SDAT), and an intermediate variety of senile dementias with clinical features and course of the pre-senile, one that the French authors justly distinguish and call senile dementia "Alzheimerisée". One must keep in mind that this pathological-clinical differentiation is addressing the classification in its broadest terms and that from both morphological or clinical perspective there is value in discriminating several additional and more subtle subgroups which comport possible differences in course and perhaps in pathogenesis. (Mayeux, Stern & Spanton, 1985).

In general, the pre-senile dementia of Alzheimer not only is more rapidly progressive but often tends to be less symmetrical and/or may give rise to more focal areas of cortical damage. In this way, they will originate cortical syndromes with disturbances referrable to frontal, temporal or parietal lobe symptomatology, or affecting more severely, memory or aphasic or perceptual deficits. Not rarely, the structural changes tend to be quite asymmetrical with the logical consequences in the clinical manifestations.

Another pre-senile dementia, still more lobar in its lesional distribution, was described by Arnold Pick (1906), today known as Pick's pre-senile dementia. The atrophy in the typical cases affects in a remarkable way the frontal and the temporal lobes. The availability of powerful neuroradiological techniques, combined with neurobiochemical studies and with larger and more detailed neuropathological information, are rapidly changing our present nosological classifications and diagnostic and clinical criteria. This may not impact directly in the clinical neuropathological study of dementias but it will certainly change our present therapeutic and nosological views of dementia and ageing.

The dementias constitute a fairly extensive and heterogeneous clinical and pathological groups (Muñoz-Garcia, & Ludwin, 1984). For this reason the utilisation of dementia cases in neuropsychological research must be guided by careful knowledge of their various subcategories, neuropathology, and clinical characteristics. (Mayeux, Stern & Spanion, 1985). While in many cases dementias may represent excellent examples of diffuse cortical involvement in contrast to more circumscribed lesions, it is necessary to be aware of the many cases in which the lesions are rather lateralised or affect exclusively or more severely certain cortical areas (Katzman, 1981; Morris, Cole, Banker & Wright, 1984). Perhaps the best approach in the utilisation of dementias for the study of neuropsychological disorganisation is to begin by tracing a mental and cognitive profile that outlines the involvement of the main psychological parameters. The following general descriptive schema has been, in our experience, of good orientation value for research or clinical purposes—allowing to build for each case a clinical and psychopathological profile.

(a) Disorders of consciousness, general attention, and awareness.

(b) Disorders of cognitive functions, sometimes with very circumscribed deficits of specific functions; more often with a fairly diffuse and high level of compromise. Speech and language, memory, perception, praxis, learning, thinking.

(c) Disorders of the control, range, and quality of emotions.

(d) Disorders of the personality and character.

(e) Disorders of conative aspects of behaviour with alterations of the motivation, level of activity, or initiative.

(f) Disorders of the overall cognitive, personal, and social level of performance as interfered by neurotic or psychotic elements (anxiety, paranoid trends, psychological reactive depression, or compensatory features).

Given the variability of clinical and structural characteristics of dementias, even within the same diagnostic category, it is unlikely that one could easily investigate selective deficits in group studies.

2. PERCEPTUAL DISORDERS IN DEMENTIA

Disorders of perception are by no means rare clinical findings in the course of dementias. What is exceptional is to find these types of disorders in relative isolation from other neurological abnormalities or cognitive deficits. Even more unusual is to observe that the disturbance of perception is the initial clinical observable disorder, constituting the opening of the dementia process or the foreground of the clinical picture.

While the above statements are true for most of the classical dementias it is not applicable to the dementias that accompany some less frequent demyelinating and some possibly transmissible encephalopathies. Thus, it is not uncommon to observe disturbances of visual perception in cases of audanophilic leucoencephalopathies of the type that in the past was called Schilder's disease, and also in cases of subacute spongiform encephalopathies, today best known as Jakob–Creutzfeldt disease, particularly in a form originally described by Heindeinhein (1929). The clinical picture is dominated and often heralded by a progressive central disturbance of visual perception that eventually may lead to cortical blindness. In all these later cases the perceptual visual disturbance is closely related to the initial focal posterior white or grey matter cerebral involvement that often characterised these diseases. If visual perceptual disorder, agnosias, or cortical blindness are present in these infrequent subacute disorders of the central nervous system, the frequency and purity of such abnormalities is quite exceptional in the large majority of the more common disorders that are the causes of the primary dementia syndromes. Alzheimer's disease in any of its clinical presentations, Pick's disease, the dementias that accompany Huntington's chorea, or that accompany or combine with Parkinsonian syndrome, and the long list of yet not well understood primary dementia processes tend to be conditions that affect the grey matter of the cerebral hemisphere in a more diffuse manner, or tends to predominate in the more anterior frontal, temporal, and parietal cortical mantle. (For a general review of the pathological characteristics of dementias see, for example, *Greenfield's neuropathology,* Chapter 20 by Tomlinson and Corsellis, see References.) In all these cases visual perceptual disorders are uncommon as a prominent clinical feature.

3. DEMENTIAS AS A MODEL FOR NEUROPSYCHOLOGICAL RESEARCH

Although it is well recognised that even in these "classical" dementias the topographical distribution of the lesions may vary a good deal from case to case, the usual slower course of the illness, the common bilaterality of the involvement, the relative late age onset, result in clinical pictures that are quite different from those which result from more focal and acute conditions. It is useful to remember that the symptomatology, signs, symptoms, cognitive, or other deficits to be encountered as consequences of brain damage are quite variable and not exclusively dependent on the topographical localisation or the extent and size of the tissue destruction. Of equal importance is the speed and evolution in time of the alteration and the relative normalcy of the rest of the nervous substratum beyond the abnormal areas. Other more complex factors could be added such as the ontogenetic biological and functional stage of development of the central nervous system at the time of the injury, the handedness and the cerebral dominance, perhaps the sex of the injured person, and the previous special individual cognitive development achieved, the special skills acquired and, of course, the existence or not of previous central nervous system pathological conditions, potentially dormant or fully realised at the time of the present injury.

Utilising these series of factors one may attempt to characterise the clinical features of the most classical dementias and contrast them with those that result from focal cortical damage. Typically, dementias are slow evolving pathological processes with a usually insidious onset and steady progression over the course of many months and even several years. The neurobiological substratum is affected in a fairly diffuse fashion, although the ultimate result of the cortical damage may later on indicate a sometimes marked predominance in the frontal and anterior temporal neocortical mantle. In most cases, the damage is bilateral but there are cases in which there are areas so affected as to create profound asymmetries and almost focal lesions. Contemporary neuroradiological methods have allowed us to recognise such rather exceptional cases that from the clinical standpoint, manifest themselves in a manner that is indistinguishable from other focal types of lesions. The insidious onset and the temporal steady course may permit, with the exception of slow neoplasms, recognition of the eminently degenerative nature of the dementia damage.

The compromised areas suffer a process of slow and advancing loss of neurones believed to be of all types, although in some cases, the larger ones seem to be preferentially affected in the earlier stages. The neuronal loss is in most instances replaced by a variable degree of astrogliosis and the ultimate macroscopic result is a diffuse and progressive shrinkage and atrophy of the cerebral tissue. The neuropathological changes may be quite nonspecific but in some instances, such as in the group of the dementias of the Alzheimer group, the changes can be quite characteristic at neuronal level and accompanied by peculiar changes affecting the neuropile. (Neurofibrillary cell changes, neuritic or senile plaques.) The net result is finely disseminated damage that contrast with most of other focal lesions. Although the latter can be conceptualised as a total acute subtraction of an area of nervous tissue from the total biological substratum that remains largely unaffected, the dementias can be thought of as a slower and widespread alteration of the tissue by elimination of the neuronal nodes and interruption of the internal interconnectivity of the neuropile with the net resulting in a reduction density of the biological neuronal network. One can conceive focal lesions as examples of the total normal minus a modified, altered, or destroyed locus while dementias might be viewed as a haphazard and widespread "simplification" of the density of the neuronal node population and network.

I have described somewhat extensively this morphological characterisation of the dementias in order to show that many of these cases can represent conceptual models of great interest to the researcher of behaviour, particularly when contrasted with focal injuries that seem to have largely monopolised the attention of the neuropsychologist. To the above models one should add still another one of peculiar biological characteristics, namely the reversible alterations induced by encephalopathies of toxic or metabolic causes.

The characteristics of the damages in the different types of conditions that affect the central nervous system have important implications due to their clinical manifestations. Focal injuries affecting the cerebral cortex, most particularly, if they are localised at or around specific processors close to the input or output of the informational flow, can be detected as fairly steady and extensive deficits or abnormalities of performance of well-defined functions or operations. This abnormal performance is judged or even measured against the standards of normal ones, which usually are errorless and often independent from any specific pretraining of previously individually acquired proficiency. Phonological, reading, or writing errors may be induced by cultural or occasional interferences but performance of tasks of average difficulty are near perfect for a native literate speaker. Judgements regarding space parameters, perceptual discriminations, recognition of objects, or syntactic correctness may require some previous experience, but abnormal performances in these tasks following focal lesions are easy to recognise with reference to normals. Only by exception does one enter the territory of specific individually acquired skills, such as when one tries to evaluate music perception or performance. In such cases, it is extremely difficult to establish valid criterias for normal function. As a consequence we must usually content ourselves with the inventory and the measurements of what we may call the instruments of the mind and their peripheral transactions, but be extremely modest with the higher levels of the operations of the mind itself (cf. Fodor, 1983).

In contrast, the early clinical diagnosis of a dementia process rarely depends on such precise instrumental deficits. Often it is judged against a hypothetical pre-morbid level of performance or against the expected functioning for that particular individual, that time, that culture, and that circumstance. How much is "bad memory", how much is, in an ageing or stressed individual, poor learning, defective attention, increased mental fatiguability. How much is poor judgement, improverishment of associations, slowness of mental processing, reduction of mental flexibility, or dis-control of emotions to justify a diagnosis of dementia? The criteria are certainly strongly biased by the environment and culture and the dis-adjustments are to be measured more by their deviation from accepted social norm than by absolute standards. However, the real problem is how much of the function must deteriorate before it is detected or measured: How much must the brain reduce its level of functioning before one can detect the memory deficit that impedes the patient remembering, in chronological order, names of the last five Presidents of the United States or the name of the most famous teams of the national or American professional baseball leagues; how much must the lexicon be impoverished before our demented patient actually begins to exhibit clinical signs of word-finding difficulties?

It is difficult to conceive that these highly complex cognitive operations, encoded in high-level cognitive units, are to be stored or processed by the same kind of discrete processors that manipulate the elements and the basic instrumentalities of cognition. As focal lesions have been indispensable models for the discrimination and the study of these instruments (neuronal-dependent processes), the diffuse disorganisation of the biological substratum as exemplified by the dementias seems to represent formidable models for the study of higher levels of cognitive operations (network-dependent processes).

4. THE NATURE OF PERCEPTUAL DISORDERS IN DEMENTIA

4.1. Visual Agnosia

Perhaps the first person to characterise conceptually visual agnosic patients was Lissauer in 1889. Other chapters have dealt in detail with this history and here we only need to be concerned with some critical points. Lissauer proposed two classes of visual agnosic disorders: one called apperceptive and the other associative. By apperceptive agnosia he referred to the piecing together of the parts of the sensory information of the image to give the conscious perception of a whole; by association he referred to the imparting of learned meaning or ideas to the perceived image. Consequently, in his view, the inability to recognise an object could arise from failures to integrate the representation of the image or from failures to match semantic information with a normal image due to disruption in the access process or to the stored information itself.

One has to recognise that almost a century later, we can hardly improve this basic "nosological" conceptualisation which highlights the two fundamental polarities of the sensory perceptual processes. The criticisms that followed of this fundamental view were more the consequences of interpretation than of substance. Lissauer's concepts, written at the turn of the century, in a period dominated by static clinical descriptions and classifications, could only be interpreted as another nosological schema that isolated clear-cut semi-autonomous entities that merely required confirmation and precise clinico-anatomical correlations. Almost every effort to deal with the problem of visual agnosias derived from this rigid nosological perspective. Some, unable to clearly separate perceptual components from language and speech, or from other cognitive functions became sceptical, others favoured a purely sensory peripheral input disorder (Bay, 1953), while still others considered agnosias as caused *either* by disturbances in perceptual functions that have gone clinically undetected and which could be traced to primary visual sensory impairments, *or* to a generalised deterioration in intellectual functioning (Bender, 1963; Bender & Feldman, 1972). To make things even more confusing, other authors (e.g. Ettlinger, 1956) demonstrated that even a fine sensory perceptual exploration as prescribed by the "peripheralists" failed to correlate with the degree or type of the perceptual disorder or with the fact that despite the deficits, the higher levels of visual perception were well within normal ranges. (Although see Campion, this volume, Chapter 7, for further evidence on this point).

Even today, when a more dynamic understanding of this type of disorder is beginning to be accepted under the strong influences of information processing models, the interrelations between visual perceptual disorders and parallel anomalies of speech and language are intricate problems that still invite splitting nosological distinctions at clinical or more analytical neuropsychological levels (Geschwind, 1967). As we shall attempt to demonstrate such interactions between levels and codes of various types *are* to remain fuzzy. It is in their interaction that one really begins to understand the gradual and parallel flow of the information that, entering the sensory analysers, will reach and integrate with the higher levels of what Lissauer referred to as "imparting the learned meaning or ideas".

It is not the aim of this text to review the evolution of ideas in visual agnosias. The progress of the last several years are due to three main factors. First, the convincing reaffirmation that associative levels of agnosias really exist in patients in whom the inability to identify or attribute meaning to perceived objects is in dramatic contrast with their capacities to successfully describe categories by features or reproduce them in surprisingly accurate drawings (Rubens & Benson, 1971; Newcombe & Ratcliff, 1974; Hécaen & Albert, 1978). Secondly, there were studies that began to make inroads into the peculiar disturbances of perception that were encountered in agnosics that reflected stages of processing beyond feature sensory analysis and closer to identification (De Renzi, Scotti, & Spinnler, 1969; Warrington & Taylor, 1978). The studies of De Renzi et al. (1969), for instance, referred to patients with unilateral hemispherical lesions that demonstrated differential biases in tasks that depended either on perceptual analyses or on judgements based on higher associative processes. These authors presented their brain injured patients with essentially two kinds of perceptual tasks that they called predominantly perceptual and associative. A typical perceptual task required, for example, individual recognition of outlines that were contained in a model of superimposed line drawings. The associative visual task required the identification and categorisation of visual stimuli. The authors gave the following example:

> Identify as a doll a line drawing of a baby-doll and photograph of a doll. The details of the visual features of the line drawing and the photograph were obviously different but once the identification was performed it was concluded that it represented the same object. The task in this case involved less visual features themselves, but focussed mostly in a semantic process of categorization and identification.

The third factor concerns studies that have attempted to analyse and describe in greater detail the higher order perceptual disorders as they often occur in the evolution of widespread cortical involvement as observed in dementias. We now turn our attention to this last type of study.

4.2. Agnosia and Dementia

The large majority of cases of dementia of Alzheimer type or Pick's disease present an initial and chief complaint of memory loss. Dates, names, episodic memories of their recent past and, later on, important remote memories from their own life or public events are progressively involved. Meanwhile, short-term memory may remain quite intact. From this common mode of initiation, a proportion, perhaps one-third of the patient population, will add to the memory deficit an extensive and progressive word-finding difficulty that, in time, may occupy the foreground of the clinical picture leading to a severe anomia. In such cases the spontaneous vocabulary is considerably reduced and ultimately language may gradually disappear altogether leaving behind some stereotyped and automatic utterances or speech production that may even have lost its phonological and phonetic structure. Some patients may become mute. The evolution of the language disintegration may vary but in most cases, in contrast to the usual course of aphasias of receptive or other types, the clinical picture is not characterised by important abnormalities in the phonetic, phonological or syntactical aspects of language and speech. The ultimate evolution of the clinical symptomatology of patients in this group includes significant disorders of visual perception.

These perceptual abnormalities appear, as a rule, rather late and are therefore often hidden by the memory and/or the language disorder. Schwartz et al. (1979) published the results of a prolonged follow-up study of the disintegration of cognitive functions in a case of a woman affected by a dementia of Alzheimer type and of this amnestic-anomic variety. Like many other instances, the clinical picture of this 62-year-old housewife was originally dominated by a progressive inability to execute, organise, and orient herself in the performance of her daily household chores and in her own familiar environment. Later on, in addition, her language exhibited an evolving anomia without phonological errors and only occasional semantic paraphasias that led, years later, to an incomprehensible and repetitive jargon. However, she was able even at this advanced stage to sing familiar songs with normal pronunciation of the lyrics and, if willingly disposed, to count numbers up to 32. The study focused on the definition and follow-up in time of the various components of verbal communication. We paid a great deal of attention to contrast the fate of the various communicative components of her speech and language: phonology, phonetics, word reading, syntactic knowledge, vocabulary, and lexico-semantic referential relationships. To test this the patient was submitted to a number of experiments that involved matching the referential aspects of words and the ability to distinguish categories at lexical or perceptual levels. Among many tasks, the patient was asked to classify lists of types of domestic or familiar dogs, cats, or birds by providing her in some cases with the names (lexical tags) or some other times with pictures of them. It was possible to demonstrate that the patient had severe difficulty in categorising and clearly distinguishing between "dogs" and "cats". The former category had become larger and had encompassed a good number of the members of the other. The separation between "dogs" or "cats", and that of "birds" remained largely normal. What is important for our present discussion was the finding that the categorical disorganisation, that could be demonstrated in various other forms, was not restricted to lexico-semantic operations but was paralleled by equal difficulties when the stimuli were purely visual perceptual material. Thus, the same categorical deficits were present in the same characteristics when the tests were lexical (with written words) or pictorial. This suggested that the primary disorder involved the semantic memory subserving both verbal and nonverbal materials and, at the same time, demonstrating that the anomia was not merely a linguistic bystander but a meaningful component of the disorder. That anomia, a syndrome obviously due to multiple mechanisms, is frequently related to disorders of semantic cognitive level, has been confirmed by a number of other studies (Goodglass, 1980; see Riddoch & Humphreys, this volume, Chapter 4).

The study had another interesting aspect, namely the dramatic dissociation in the disorganisation of exico- and perceptual semantic levels while other linguistic or speech "instrumentalities" remained normal or nearly so until far advanced stages of the illness. Thus, not until the dementia became very advanced did the patient lose her proficiency in tasks that involved phonology, orthographic judgements, pronunciation reading criterias (see Schwartz et al., 1979), or even syntactic judgements.

The findings of this study came to highlight a previous study of three demented patients with perceptual disorders performed by Warrington (1975). Her study focused more directly and sharply on the perceptual disorder as the criteria of selection was the inability of the patients to recognise or identify common objects. At the time of the study, all three of her patients were relatively mild cases of dementia and demonstrated that their intellectual capabilities in no way could explain the deficit. On the other hand, the exploration of their elementary visual perceptual capabilities allowed Warrington to eliminate the perceptual disorders as secondary to sensory input abnormalities. The author was able to demonstrate furthermore that all three patients had severe impairments in their knowledge and categorical criterias for both the pictorial and the lexical representation of objects. The conclusion was that these cases represented selective impairments of semantic memory. A point of some importance for some later neurobiological considerations is that one of the cases of Warrington's study (case 3) was later on demonstrated to be a Pick's disease (case 4 in Cummings & Duchen, 1981), a condition that, as noted above, affects characteristically the frontal and the anterior temporal regions of the cerebral cortex with much less involvement of the rest of the neocortex.

Another study by Marin, Glenn, and Rafal (1983) provided the opportunity to explore in even greater detail the perceptual abilities of a patient with amnestic, anomic, and agnosic deficits. The patient was a 51-year-old nurse who, having developed a dementia, was studied from the second to the fifth year of her illness. The computerised tomography of her brain demonstrated a moderate degree of frontal cortical atrophy and a marked shrinkage of both anterior halves of the temporal lobes. The diagnosis of Alzheimer's pre-senile dementia or possibly Pick's disease were the most likely.

In this case we took advantage of the fact that the anomia had already progressed to the point of mutism. Except for automatic phrases that the patient repeated in all occasions in which she became excited, she remained silent but composed and attentive. This gave us the unusual opportunity to examine in great detail her cognitive abilities, focusing mostly in her perceptually based operations. Her language comprehension, oral or written, was nil and the communication was done through gestures or inducing her to continue or to imitate the examiner's behaviour.

The patient was submitted to a long list of problem solving experiments that involved language and speech, visuomotor skills, visual perceptual tasks, and visual tasks that required referental or symbolic information. A number of the tasks were taken from the Leiter Intelligence Scale, the Wechsler Adult Intelligence Scale, or the Raven's Progressive Matrices Test but another series of tests were specially created by us.

She demonstrated no spontaneous speech production other than the verbal automatisms and some very occasional echolalic production. There was no evidence of verbal comprehension or ability to understand the meaning of written words or symbols. With no signs of spontaneous writing, she was, however, able to copy letters, numbers, words, sentences, and designs of some complexity. In her copying she was strictly faithful to the model, details, size, orientation, and style of the handwriting. Thus, she copied sentences forwards or backwards, and with equal facility would copy words or sentences that made sense or were totally irrelevant and defective in the printing, orthography, or semantics. On a few occasions, however, she was able to write in correct letter order a model printed backwards or alternatively to initiate a copy of a backward printed model by the correct first letter and proceed her task from right to left.

The patient was able to match letters, numbers, strings, drawings, and photographs on the basis of strict identity of form. She was able to match designs of great complexity which she often rotated and reoriented in space. Upside down pictures of objects and individuals were thus placed in correct orientation. The same was done for coins that she separated by identity of size and design and placed in the same orientation with the same face up. Thus, in classifying coins, she separated and oriented the various values but also made two groups for the two kinds of quarters (regular and centennial celebration US25 cents).

In classifying pictures, she placed in separate groups pictures of the same subject if they had even slight variations in design or if one was in colour and the other was a black and white version. An assortment of animals was classified, after many attempts, by the predominant colour. Thus, a crocodile (greenish) ended up together with a parrot and a green insect, whereas a chimpanzee (reddish) ended up with a butterfly and a reddish spider.

The patient was able to deal correctly with colour matching and colour co-ordinating equivalencies (i.e. model blue/yellow requires copy with red/green pieces), numerosity, gradual ordering of number, size, and parts of a total. She was able to sort correctly, complex strings of letters from a given set of models, the matching often requiring reversals or changes in the orientation. In fact, our first hint about the unusual interest of this case came from the casual observation of one of us that while this speechless person was waiting to be examined, she was attentively engaged in her favourite pastime, namely solving scrambled letters puzzles. This required not only to sort the correct string of letters from the model but in this particular case the model words were printed in lower case and the strings in the letter grid were in upper case. Thus, she was able to translate lower to upper case without any trace of understanding whatsoever.

To test this unusual remaining ability further, we created grids of letters that contained strings of pronounceable or unpronounceable nonwords. We also made for her grids of "nonsense symbols": Greek letters, editorial symbols, etc. The patient was successful in the performance of all these tasks, indicating once more that the process was purely perceptually based and did not require understanding.

Sequencing of items, by size, number, or relative proportion of the elements was preserved. Matching designs or completing designs that varied along one dimension was also preserved.

The first serious failure encountered by this patient was with a card from the Raven Test. After having successfully performed with the card in which the drawing pattern changes along one single perceptual parameter there is another in which the correct answer requires the simultaneous co-ordination of two parametrical changes that are not symmetrical (two pairs of horizontal oscillating lines intersect two pairs of thick solid vertically oriented ones). In some sense, in order to select the correct alternative, it is necessary to create in one's mind a single image of the interaction of both vertical and horizontal parameters; a type of singular representation that in some ways constitutes a mental synthesis and, in this sense, not altogether different to what it might be necessary to piece together the features that constitute the representation of an object; a synthesis of perceptual elements that constitute a new unit, a symbol.

In fact, the barrier beyond which our patient was totally unable to operate was in dealing with percepts in terms of their symbolic meaning. She was incapable of matching a given pictorial set of: "man–lily–cow–cock–apple", to the corresponding pictures of "woman–daisy–horse–hen–pear", or to match a set of "hand–man's hat–shoe–baby dress–woman's hat". Similarly, she was unable to match pictures of candle and lightbulb, bucket and jar, violin and trumpet, automobile and motorcycle, ball and top. Despite her excellent performance in rather complicated perceptual tasks we never could get her to group together a printed number with the printed name of it and/or with a pictorial representation of the numerosity in terms of objects or dots (i.e. "3", "THREE", "###").

Matching familiar coins with their printed names ("Quarter", "Dime", "Nickel", "Cent") and/or with their printed value (25, 10, 0.5, 1) seemed to make no sense to her at all. This, despite the fact that on several occasions, but not always, we could engage her in ordering correctly cards with printed numbers from 1 to 10.

Several points of interest emerge from the study of this case: the basic visual perceptual instrumentalities were surprisingly well preserved. From very elementary feature perceptual discriminations to relatively complex operations of co-ordination, ordering or perceptual categorisation, or grouping she was able to perform quite correctly. There is evidence that some of the perceptual code "keyboards" were still present and were able to be displayed in order (i.e. ordering of printed numbers) or to be translated into equivalent ones (i.e. lower to upper case letters). This patient was, however, unable to deal with abstracted properties of percepts. She failed to relate pictorial representations of familiar objects that are linked by abstract parameters such as function, use, age, part of the body, sex, or categories that are not dependent directly from perceptual factors. The patient, at a more abstract level, was unable to create a mental representation of instances in which simultaneous nonreciprocal parameters need to be co-ordinated.

This case strongly suggests that the underlying disorder is in some sense semantic and not instrumental perceptual and that the abnormality is common for both the agnosic and the anomic behaviour. In this respect, one could look at the relations that exist here between perceptually based operations and their symbolic and semantic levels of integration and consider that the same gradient can be observed in the sensory aphasias along the dimensions of verbal deafness (instrumental) to deficits in language understanding, and anomia (semantic).

5. THE SPECTRUM OF VISUAL AGNOSIC SYNDROMES

It is now appropriate to attempt to consider the problem of visual agnosias in the light of recent developments and studies. Lissauer's original clinical insight was essentially correct if, instead of considering his terminology as meaning nosological fixed entities, it is considered as indicating polarities in the development of processes that go from predominantly analytical sensory instrumental processes to the co-ordination and organisation of codes and categories that are complex symbolic semantic ones (see also Kertesz and Humphreys & Riddoch, this volume).

Lesions in the early stages will originate relatively well-defined sensory deficits, and we shall continue to understand them if we are able to discriminate the elementary parameters that are utilised by the nervous system. These are not easy to decipher and not always coincidental with our natural notions of elementary features (Weiskrantz, 1974). The lesions that condition these deficits may be focal and different foci may originate deficits in different sensory parameters. The defective functions may be relatively circumscribed in character and are usually irreversible due to the fact that the biological substratum is unlikely to be duplicated elsewhere, unless there are bilateral processors doing exactly the same operations. Deficits can be compensated functionally by other overlapping processors but the exact operation is usually nonredundant. In some cases, the nonredundancy is remarkable and no other area can effectively take over the deficit left by an appropriate lesion. It is possible in such cases to observe clearly the clinical deficits. A good example of this are the central abnormalities in colour vision leading to specific disorders of colour vision, colour naming, etc. Note that it is in these instances of nonredundancy where the concepts of "deconnection" finds their best examples. The same thing cannot be observed in other cases of more compensable feature analysis of forms, shapes, angular relations, or movements (although see Zihl, von Cramon, & Mai, 1983).

All these "peripheral" disorders may result from relatively small and well-circumscribed lesions. They correspond to what we have called here neuronal-dependent processes. As expected, these areas are localised in close vicinity to each other and within the region of the primary retinotopic sensory inputs. Although there are reciprocal interconnections among themselves, they are essentially secluded from other direct motor or sensory systems.

At the other extreme are the disorders of perception we have discussed.

They are exemplified by larger, diffuse damage in predominantly associative cortical areas best represented clinically by cases of dementia. In the particular case of disorders of visual perception as discussed in this section, the most significant lesions seem to affect, most particularly, the anterior temporal cortex. Perhaps also of importance is the compromise of the frontal cortex.

Here, the focality of the lesion does not seem to be as crucial as its extent. In fact, circumscribed focal lesions in these association cortical areas may not lead to specific recognisable deficits using current neuropsychological clinical methods. For instance, it is likely that the operational codes at this level are complex units in which there are no simple features; Rather, the units operate on co-ordinated features and categorical groups. The sensory modality represented may no longer be only one and there may exist overlapping of various input types. There is often a close relation with the most powerful code available to man, namely language. Thus, parallel disorders of language and of perception should be expected and for this reason we believe that semantic disorders of visual perception as discussed in these cases are to be accompanied by a significant co-existing disorder of language of the same level of organisation, namely a lexico-semantic anomia.

The codes at this level are representations of symbols, meaningful relations, and experiences, some of which may constitute a common patrimony for all members of the species but some others may be the result of individual experiences. Rather than absence or abnormalities of specific codes or processes, one should expect disorders of the speed of processing, density of information, inaccuracy and slowness of selection or search. These are to be considered as the results of deficits in the activation of neuronal networks rather than the critical failure of a specific pathway or a neuronal processor. We have called them here network-dependent processes.

Warrington and Taylor (1978) have proposed a model for visual perceptual processing and we have extended these concepts to incorporate parallelisms with language codes (Marin et al., 1983). They are conceptual models in no conflict with what we know today of the physiological and morphological characteristics of the mammal, including the primate visual system. They accommodate well the clinical characteristics of the posterior visual agnosias as well as the cases that we have observed in our demented patients.

As it could be expected, there are a number of areas that require further specification or empirical confirmation. One such area deals with some of the intermediate stages of processing. In both Warrington and Taylor's, and in our own model, intermediate stages of perceptual processing are postulated in which the predominant functions are grouping or co-ordination of features or categorisation of them. The mechanisms determining grouping and co-ordination processes need further consideration (see Humphreys & Quinlan; Humphreys & Riddoch, this volume).

There is, for instance, very little information or clinical reports of cases of visual agnosia in whom the disorder is centred around a deficit in object perception with sparing of sensory visual feature processings and without a strong component of semantic memory involvement in which object function identity, pragmatic or contextual, and even lexical assignations are significantly spared. The agnosic patient recently reported by Davidoff and Wilson (1985) is, in this respect, of interest, particularly because of the claim made by the authors that their case had no evidence of language disorder. The single similar case that we have been able to analyse in whom sensory visual processing was reasonably good, intra-language object definitions and associations were preserved, but objects perceived could not be recognised or grouped, despite satisfactory drawings made by the patient himself. He had also an associated anomia for the same objects. The lesion in the left hemisphere was placed in the junction between occipital and temporal lobes and clearly seemed to disconnect the associations between posterior occipital and more anterior temporal cortical regions (unpublished observation). The case reported by Davidoff and Wilson (1985) is of even greater interest. For instance, this patient made matching-to-sample errors with pictures paired with either purely semantically related or purely visually related distractors. When presented later with the targets to which she had made errors and given the forced choice of either the correct name or the name of the distractor which she originally pointed to, she discriminated between targets and semantically related errors, but not between targets and visually related errors. This suggests that visual and semantic errors arose independently. The patient appeared to have difficulty accessing visual object representations, and this stage seems independent of semantic processes in object recognition. The authors correctly compare the stage of accessing visual object representations with the independent word unit stage observed in reading (Shallice & Warrington, 1980; see also Riddoch & Humphreys, this volume, Chapter 4). However, although it requires no effort to find evidence of such stages in language dissociations one cannot be but surprised by the exceptional occurrence of the parallel phenomenon in the case of pure visual object representations despite the similarly high number of possible visual object units. One needs to conclude that the problem is not yet settled.

Although the recent literature has made strong claims for specific perceptual disorders involving more or less well-circumscribed categories (i.e. perception of faces), the neurobiological basis for this perceptual grouping does not seem to be perceptual commonality of the stimuli but rather their perceptual significance for the organism. The neurobiological basis for the prosopagnosias is still a matter of debate and in our opinion it is not yet clear whether the sensory perceptual aspects of this disorder should be considered the result of a specific agnosia for faces or from an elementary early visual disorder of an element that is essentially important for the face perceptual processing. Although the argument is of course not irrefutable, the well-agreed localisation of the lesions in man in the occipital lobes, in so close relation to the other primary visual sensory processors and the constant associated disorder of colour vision, suggests that the latter interpretation may be the correct one (Sergent, this volume, Chapter 5).

It is, however, surprising that for these postulated intermediate stages there are so few clinical evidences. This seems to suggest once more that what appears to be an important element in a conceptual model may not have the same significance for the organism. There is scanty evidence that there is morphophysiological segregation of these categorical stages at the level of the brain organisation. Rather, it would seem that the organism, following its strong pragmatics, has collapsed our conceptual models and proceeds as fast as possible from the early stages of feature analysis to the integration of complex units of objects in their context and functional properties, symbol complex units which appear to be the currency of semantic memory. If that were indeed the case, many of our concepts related to abstract categories would be in fact ulterior notions, secondary deductions from and beyond the semantic stages of processing. Some of the abstract characteristics of metaphoric language and contemporary art seems to confirm this post-semantic notion.

ACKNOWLEDGEMENTS

I wish to thank the valuable assistance and collaboration of Ms. Penny Yee, cognitive psychology graduate student at the University of Oregon, Eugene, Oregon. I also thank Ms. Kathleen Hollosy for her patience in the secretarial preparation of this article.

REFERENCES

Alzheimer, A. (1907). Über eine eigenartige Erkrankung der Hirnrinde. *Zentralbl. Nervenheilk*, *30*, 177–179.

Alzheimer, A. (1911). Über eigenartige Krankheitsfälle des späteren Alters. *Zeitschrift für die gesamte Neurologie und Psychiatrie, 4,* 356–385.

Bay, E. (1953). Disturbances of visual perception and their examination. *Brain, 76,* 515–551.

Bender, M. B. (1963). Disorders of visual perception. In L. Halpern (Ed.), *Problems of dynamic neurology*, New York: Grune and Straton.

Bender, M. B. & Feldman, M. (1972). The so-called "visual agnosias". *Brain, 95,* 173–186.

Cummings, J. L. & Duchen, L. W. (1981). Kluver–Bucy Syndrome in Pick disease: Clinical pathological correlations. *Neurology, 31,* 1415–1422.

Davidoff, J. & Wilson, B. (1985). A case of visual agnosia showing a disorder of pre-semantic visual classification. *Cortex, 21,* 121–134.

De Renzi, E., Scotti, G., & Spinnler, H. (1969). Perceptual and associative disorders of visual recognition. Relationship to the side of the cerebral lesion. *Neurology, 19,* 634–642.

Ettlinger, G. (1956). Sensory deficits in visual agnosia. *Journal of Neurology, Neurosurgery and Psychiatry, 19,* 297–307.

Francis, P. T., Palmer, A. M., Sims, N. R. Bowen, D. M., Davison, A. N. Esiri, M. M., Neary, D., Snowden, J. S., & Wilcock, G. K. (1985). Neurochemical studies of early-onset Alzheimer's disease. Possible influence on treatment. *New England Journal of Medicine, 313,* 7–11.

Fodor, J. A. (1983). *The modularity of mind.* Cambridge, Mass.: MIT Press.

Geschwind, N. (1967). The varieties of naming errors. *Cortex, 3,* 97–112.

Goodglass, H. (1980). Disorders of naming following brain injury. *American Scientist, 68,* 647–655.

Hécaen, H. & Albert, M. L. (1978). *Human neuropsychology.* Chichester: John Wiley.

Heidenhain, G. (1929). Klinische und anatomische Untersuchungen über eine eigenartige Erkrankung des Zentralnervensystems im Preæsenium. *Zeitschrift für die gesamte Neurologie und Psychiatrie, 118,* 49–114.

Katzman, R. (1981). Dementia. In S. H. Appel (Ed.), *Current neurology,* Vol. 3. Chichester: John Wiley.

Lissauer, H. (1889). Ein Fall von Seelenblindheit nebst einem Beitrage zur Theorie derselben. *Archiv für Psychiatrie und Nervenkrankheiten, 21,* 222–270.

Marin, O.S.M., Glenn, C.G., & Rafal, R.D. (1983). Visual problem solving in the absence of lexical semantics: Evidences from dementia. *Brain and Cognition, 2,* 285–311.

Mayeux, R., Stern, Y., & Spanton, S. (1985). Heterogeneity in dementia of the Alzheimer type: Evidence of subgroups. *Neurology, 35,* 453–461.

Morris, J.C., Cole, M., Banker, B.Q., & Wright, D. (1984). Hereditary dysphasic dementia and the Pick–Alzheimer spectrum. *Annals of Neurology, 16,* 455–466.

Muñoz-Garcia, D. & Ludwin, S.K. (1984). Classic and generalized variants of Pick's disease: Clinicopathological, ultrastructural, and immunocytochemical comparative study. *Annals of Neurology, 16,* 467–480.

Newcombe, F. & Ratcliff, G. (1974). Agnosia: A disorder of object recognition. In F. Michael and B. Schott (Eds.), *Les syndromes de disconnexion calleuse chez l'homme.* Lyon: Colloque International.

Pick, A. (1906). Über einen weiteren Symptomenkomplex im Rahmen der Dementia senilis, bedingt durch umschriebene stärkere Hirnatrophie (gemischte Apraxie). *Monatsschrift für Psychiatrie und Neurologie, 19,* 97–108.

Rubens, A., & Benson, D.F. (1971). Associative visual agnosia. *Archives of Neurology, 24,* 305–316.

Thomlinson, B. E. & Corsellis, J. A. N. (1984). Ageing and the dementias. In J. H. Adams, J. A. N. Corsellis, and L. W. Duchen (Eds.), *Greenfield's neuropathology.* Chichester: John Wiley.

Schwartz, M.F., Marin, O.S.M., & Saffran, E.M. (1979). Dissociations of language in dementia: A case study. *Brain and Language, 7,* 277–306.

Shallice, T. & Warrington, E.K. (1980). Single and multiple component central dyslexic syndromes. In M. Coltheart, K.E. Patterson, and J.C. Marshall (Eds.), *Deep dyslexia.* London: Routledge and Kegan Paul.

Warrington, E.K. (1975). The selective impairment of semantic memory. *Quarterly Journal of Experimental Psychology, 27,* 635–657.

Warrington, E.K., & Taylor, A.M. (1978). Two categorical stages of object recognition. *Perception, 7,* 695–705.

Weiskrantz, L. (1974). The interaction between occipital and temporal cortex in vision: An overview. In F. O. Schmitt and F. G. Worden (Eds.), *The neurosciences. Third study program* Ch. 17, pp. 189–204. Cambridge, Mass.: MIT Press.

Zihl, J., von Cramon, D., & Mai, N. (1983). Selective disturbance of movement vision after bilateral brain damage. *Brain, 106,* 313–340.

10 The Fractionation of Visual Agnosia

Glyn W. Humphreys
Cognitive Neuropsychology Research Group, Department of Psychology, Birkbeck College, University of London, Malet Street, London WC1E 7HX, U.K.
M. Jane Riddoch
Department of Paramedical Sciences, North East London Polytechnic, Romford Road, Stratford, London E15 4LZ, U.K.

1. INTRODUCTION

Visual object agnosia is a marked, modality-specific deficit in visual object recognition which may occur following brain damage.[1] The classification of visual agnosia typically conforms to the classical distinction first made by Lissauer (1889), between apperceptive and associative agnosia (e.g., see Kertesz, this volume, Chapter 6; Ratcliff & Newcombe, 1982; Warrington, 1982, 1985, for some recent examples). Apperceptive agnosia is thought to be due to a disability in the construction of a stable representation of visual form, which impairs all high-order recognition processes. Associative agnosia is thought to reflect a deficit in accessing semantic (associative and functional) knowledge about an object following the derivation of an intact perceptual representation of visual form. Both types of agnosia are defined in the presence of what are thought to be intact elementary perceptual functions such as the detection of light intensity, acuity and (at least in some cases) hue.

In the present chapter, we wish to query the utility of the apperceptive-associative agnosic classification. We suggest that the classification is too simple to provide a full description of the many types of visual object recognition deficit which occur, and that it lends itself to a two-stage

[1]By recognition, here, we mean the ability to classify an object in terms of its learned functional and associative characteristics, and not the ability to access a verbal label appropriate to the object.

model which fails to specify the detailed procedures mediating object recognition. Instead, we propose a classification which reflects the complexity of the component processes involved in visual object recognition and the manner in which such processes may selectively break down. To some extent, our suggestion mirrors that of Kertesz (this volume, Chapter 6). However, Kertesz's classification of patients in terms of a multi-stage model follows classical distinctions between apperceptive and associative agnosia, whilst accounting for further classes of patients (such as optic aphasics) within this scheme. Our approach goes beyond that by discussing deficits in visual object processing within a framework of normal vision. We suggest that apperceptive and associative agnosia are syndromes which tend to obscure rather than clarify the nature of a patient's problems, and the relations between these problems and normal vision. To draw any implications from such patients for normal vision, their deficits need to be classified according to the process(es) which are disrupted

To clarify our position, we first consider the classical distinction between apperceptive and associative agnosia. We then outline an alternative, and more detailed, classification scheme.

2. APPERCEPTIVE AGNOSIA

In a clinical setting, apperceptive agnosics are classified as patients who have intact elementary perceptual functions, who have a marked deficit in visual object recognition, and who show an impaired ability to represent shape internally in tasks such as copying (where constructional deficits cannot be attributed to a constructional apraxia; see Campion, this volume, Chapter 7; Kertesz, this volume, Chapter 6).

How valid are these distinctions? Let us first consider the distinction between elementary perceptual functions and shape representation. The view that agnosic patients have intact elementary perceptual functions along with impaired representation of shape relies on three different assumptions:

1. that there are qualitative differences between elementary perceptual functions and shape representations;
2. that the relevant information is hierarchically organised and accessed serially in visual object recognition (e.g., that elementary perceptual functions must be completed prior to the engagement of other processes in object processing); and
3. that responses to the information specified at each level can be directly used for response purposes (see Fig. 10.1).

As Campion (this volume, Chapter 7) notes, assumption (3) ignores the kinds of complex decision processes which must be brought to bear in

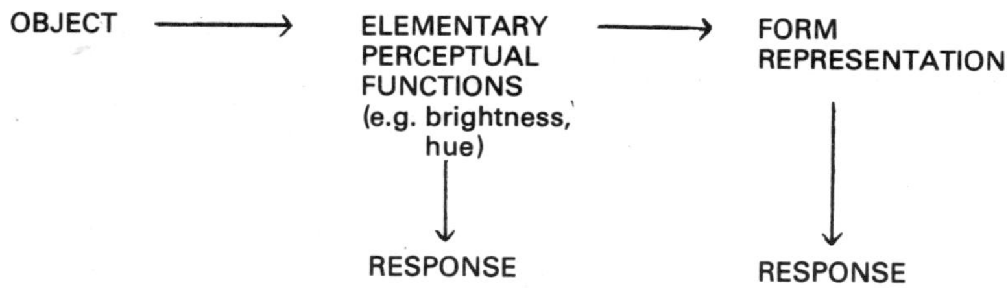

FIG. 10.1. A simple two-stage account assuming the separation of elementary and later perceptual processes.

discrimination tasks tapping each level; effectively, it is assumed that decision processes for one level of representation will not be selectively impaired. However, even in circumstances where this assumption seems reasonable, the relationship between the loss of elementary perceptual functions and shape perception is rather more difficult to establish than is perhaps commonly thought. Often, investigators rely on a secondary reference to Ettlinger's (1956) examination of elementary perceptual functions in brain damaged patients. A problem here is that, as Ettlinger notes, his tests did not include any patients who could be termed a "true case of visual object agnosia in the classical sense", and that those patients with some clinically defined perceptual deficit (such as prosopagnosia, unilateral neglect, visuo-constructive problems, or alexia) did tend to have poor brightness discrimination and acuity for small objects (see also Campion, this volume, Chapter 7; Sergent, this volume, Chapter 5). We are not saying here that deficits in shape perception are necessarily caused by impaired elementary perceptual functions (cf. Bay, 1953), but simply that the relations between the different levels of perceptual processing must be established in each patient and not assumed. That is, given a patient with what seems to be a problem in attaining an adequate internal representation of shape, it is necessary to examine fully whether or not the patient has intact elementary perceptual functions.

However, there remains a further, conceptual problem with the distinction between elementary perceptual functions and shape representation, which concerns the notion that levels of shape processing are hierarchically and serially organised. For instance, we might assume that the primitive elements in form perception are local geometric features and that the representation of whole forms are derived by building up information from this local to more global levels (as in the Pandemonium model of pattern recognition; Selfridge, 1959; see Humphreys & Quinlan, this volume, Chapter 3). In this sense, we might consider the discrimination of local form elements to be one of the elementary perceptual functions on which object recognition is based (see Fig. 10.2). Unfortunately, such a conclusion appears unwarranted, given other theoretical perspectives. Thus early

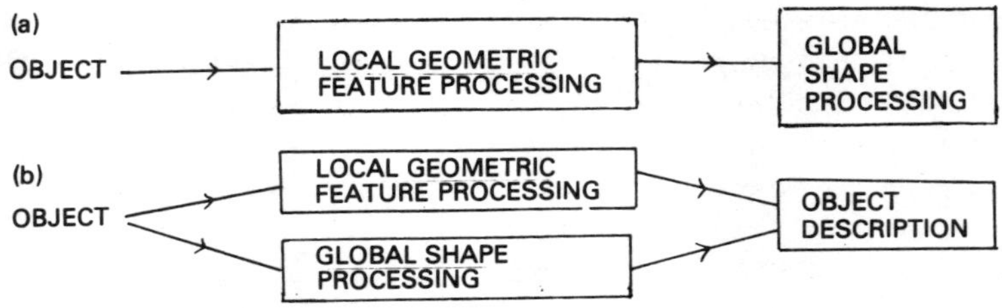

FIG. 10.2. (a) A hierarchical account of shape processing, in which global shape information is derived from the processing of local feature primitives. (b) A parallel, independent model of local and global shape processing.

processes in form perception may be conceptualised as performing an independent and parallel analysis of a limited range of spatial frequencies (e.g., Campbell & Robson, 1968), with local form information being carried by high spatial frequency components and more global form information by low spatial frequency components (see Humphreys & Quinlan, this volume, Chapter 3). A hierarchical framework for the perception of form information is not appropriate here, as both local and global features constitute the elementary perceptual primitives of such a system. The moral seems to be that, within the domain of form perception, we cannot assume a particular theoretical framework; rather the framework must be empirically derived, and, wherever possible, it should be based on converging evidence from normal as well as clinical studies.

Where then does this leave the distinction between elementary perceptual functions and form representation? One suggestion would be to draw a distinction between functions which are prerequisites for form perception (i.e., those processes which are necessary to begin cortical form perception) and those which specify or are specific to different types of form. One candidate nonform-specific function here might be brightness discrimination, whilst a form-specific function might be the loss of particular spatial frequency information (e.g., Regan, 1982). Patients who have impairments to the latter functions will be selectively deficient at tasks requiring access to specific types of form information, whilst patients with impaired nonform-specific functions will have more generalised problems over and above those encountered in the form domain.

Now, despite our caution in assuming the relations between elementary perceptual functions and patients with deficits in form perception, it seems clear that cases of selectively impaired form perception, along with intact elementary perceptual functions, have been demonstrated (at least where we draw a distinction between form-specific and nonform-specific functions mentioned earlier). Perhaps the best known example here is the case reported by Efron (1968; see also Benson & Greenberg, 1969). This patient was recovering from cortical blindness following carbon monoxide poisoning. Efron demonstrated that the patient had relatively intact discrimination of brightness and hue (at least with prolonged viewing conditions), but that he was impaired on any tasks requiring the discrimination of shape. For example, he was extremely poor at discriminating between square and oblong shapes matched for area (see Campion, this volume, Chapter 7, for a description of similar cases).

Other patients seem less grossly impaired at shape processing, though they still seem poor at achieving stable form representations. Humphreys and Quinlan (this volume, Chapter 3) have reviewed cases where patients seem to be selectively impaired at deriving representations of objects which are not viewpoint specific, so that the patients are poor at matching objects seen from different views. Such patients appear to be selectively impaired at achieving at least some forms of object constancy. Such a deficit may co-occur with relatively intact discrimination of local components of form such as line length, orientation, and size (see Humphreys & Quinlan, this volume, Chapter 3; Humphreys & Riddoch, 1984). Furthermore, different patients may be affected by particular transformations of viewpoint, with some patients affected primarily by foreshortening an object's principal axis, others by decreasing the saliency of distinctive features of objects, and others by any gross changes in depicted form relative to the canonical view for the object (Humphreys & Quinlan, this volume, Chapter 3; Humphreys & Riddoch, 1984). To label all of the above patients (including those reviewed by Campion, this volume, Chapter 7), as apperceptive agnosics fails to preserve even the major distinctions between the different patient types (e.g., between those impaired at any shape discrimination tasks and those impaired at object recognition under transformation conditions).

The above difficulty has recently been recognised by Warrington (1985), who has proposed that those patients who are impaired at shape discrimination tasks (cf. Efron, 1968; Campion, this volume, Chapter 7), should be classified as "pseudo-agnosic" and not as agnosic patients. The term apperceptive agnosic should then be confined to those patients who are unable to classify shapes across different viewing conditions. Based on this distinction, Warrington argues that apperceptive agnosics (i.e., patients impaired at classification across viewpoints) have impairments in a first categorical stage of object recognition, termed perceptual categorisation, where objects seen under different viewing conditions are assigned to a common perceptual category (Warrington, 1985; see also Warrington, 1982; Warrington & Taylor, 1978).

Unfortunately, there are problems with Warrington's (1985) attempt to re-define apperceptive agnosia. One is that the re-definition fails to accord with the classical use of the term agnosia to refer to patients with a modality-specific deficit in visual object recognition co-existing with intact elementary perceptual functions (such as brightness discrimination). In Warrington's (1985) scheme, patients with intact brightness discrimination but impaired shape discrimination would not be termed agnosic.

A second problem is that Warrington's approach tends to suggest that the processes which may be necessary for shape discrimination (e.g., grouping local form information) are qualitatively different from those involved in achieving object constancy, and that there is only one mechanism for achieving object constancy. Against this suggestion, there are grounds for arguing that object constancy may be derived by different means depending both on the stimulus and the task. Thus, different mechanisms may be invoked by objects which have a principal axis of symmetry and by those which do not have a stable axis, and different mechanisms may operate for identification tasks and for tasks requiring only the detection of invariant form information. Furthermore, at least one mechanism for achieving object constancy may involve local grouping processes which seek the best common transformation across local form elements (see Humphreys & Quinlan, this volume, Chapter 3 for further discussion of these points). We need a framework which specifies these different mechanisms.

A third problem is that we may need to distinguish between the use of stored knowledge of an object's form[2] and the use of episodic representations in perceptual classification (we use the term episodic representations here to refer to representations of form which are abstracted across viewpoint and which are created on each episode that an object is encountered; cf. Marr, 1982). This distinction is not present in Warrington's (1985) account. It is quite conceivable that a patient may have intact stored knowledge of an object's form and yet be unable to "perceptually classify" it (e.g., match it across viewpoints), and also that a patient may be unable to access stored knowledge of an object's form whilst showing good perceptual classification. An example of the former deficit would be when a patient can draw an object from memory (indicating intact knowledge of its form), whilst being unable to match it correctly across particular transformations; an example of the latter deficit would be when a patient is able to match an object across transformations and yet shows no access to stored knowledge about the object's form. A processing framework which makes a distinction between stored knowledge of object form and between episodic representations abstracted across viewpoints is given in Fig.10.3.

There is some evidence to support the above distinction. H.J.A. (Hum-

[2]Stored knowledge of an object's form may itself be separated from stored semantic knowledge about objects. Evidence for this proposition is discussed in Section 3 (see also Riddoch & Humphreys, this volume, Chapter 4).

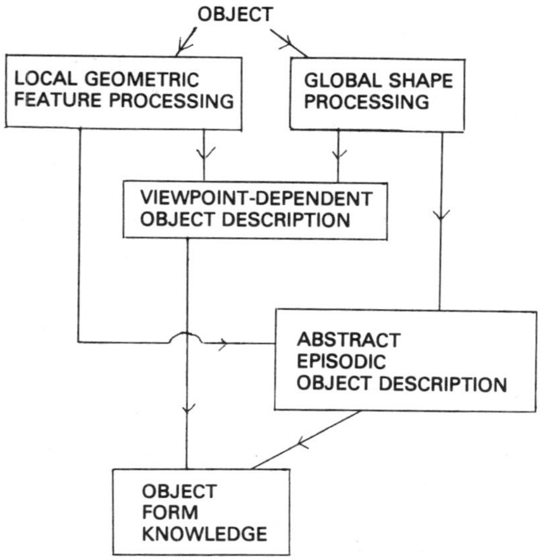

FIG. 10.3. An information processing framework specifying some of the processes involved in accessing stored knowledge of object form. It is likely that the process of forming a viewpoint-dependent object description should itself be decomposed into at least two stages: One concerned with integrating local and global shape primitives, on a 2-D co-ordinate system; and one concerned with embellishing the 2-D description with depth information (see the text).

phreys & Riddoch, 1984; Riddoch & Humphreys, in press) was good at drawing objects from memory, which may be considered a test of stored object-form knowledge. However, his performance on tasks where objects had to be matched across viewpoints was relatively impaired (when compared with non-brain damaged controls) when the objects were transformed to reduce the saliency of their most distinctive feature. Thus H.J.A. appears to be impaired at deriving at least some forms of (episodic) descriptions which are abstracted across viewpoints whilst having intact knowledge of object form. In contrast, there have been a number of reports of patients with preserved ability to match objects across viewpoints even when the patients are unable to recognise the objects (Riddoch & Humphreys, in press; Taylor & Warrington, 1971; Warrington, 1975; Warrington & Shallice, 1984). Such patients appear able to generate episodic representations which support different-view matching, and yet they remain unable to access stored knowledge of object form.

It is also possible that, normally, stored knowledge may help in the derivation of abstract episodic representations. For instance, when objects are severely transformed to make them structurally ambiguous, we may need to compare them with their stored representations in long-term memory in order to match them across two different views. An even more radical stance is to suggest that the episodic representation itself reflects the pattern of activation across a set of stored features (see Humphreys & Quinlan, this volume, Chapter 3). It follows that a patient could be impaired at "perceptual classification" for any of at least four reasons: (1) due to an inability to construct an abstract episodic description based on stimulus information; (2) due to an inability to access stored knowledge of form; (3) due to a loss of form knowledge; or (4) due to an inability to use form knowledge to "drive" object constancy.

Furthermore, it is likely that other varieties of apperceptive agnosia exist. For instance, we believe that the case of H.J.A. illustrates that recognition difficulties can reflect a specific deficit in combining information from a compound visual stimulus into an integrated perceptual whole (see also Pötzl, 1928). This impaired integrative function can co-exist with relatively intact representations of different types of shape information (so distinguishing such a patient from others with impaired processing of shape primitives; cf. Efron, 1968).

Our grounds for arguing that an integrative function may be separated from the representation of shape information *per se* are based on, amongst other things, H.J.A.'s performance on a series of tasks requiring speeded responses to visual forms which have separate local and global representations (Humphreys, Riddoch & Quinlan, 1985). In one example, H.J.A. had to identify a local letter element in a global, compound letter (see Fig. 10.4), or he had to identify the global compound letter. Using the same displays, control subjects were found to be faster to identify the global than the local letter, and their responses to the local letter were affected by the identity of the global letter (the phenomenon of "global precedence"; see Navon, 1977). H.J.A. responded roughly about as fast as the control subjects to the global letter, although his reaction times (RTs) to the local

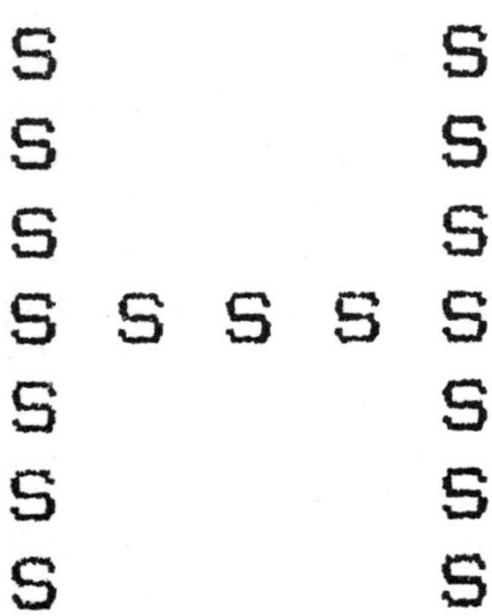

FIG. 10.4. A compound letter (after Navon, 1977).

letter were somewhat slower (632msec vs. 925msec). Furthermore, he showed no effect of the identity of the global letter on his responses to the local letter.

To account for the contrasting pattern of results with H.J.A. and the normal subjects, we need to discuss in a little more detail the kinds of processes we believe are involved in the perception of compound stimuli. Our account is close to a number of proposals recently outlined by Grossberg and Mingolla (1985a,b).

To begin with, it seems likely that in order for us to see the global letter shown in Fig.10.4, the visual system must group the local letters and mark boundaries corresponding to its edges. Such boundary marking need not give rise to a visible percept (and indeed, we do not "see" any boundary conforming to a continuous edge of such a global figure), but it would constitute a kind of labelling which states that the boundary so marked may then be used by the form identification system. That is, once the boundaries of the global form in Fig. 10.4 are marked, the form identification system can identify the form as the letter "H". We can think of this boundary-marking process as akin to the assignment of "place tokens" to a raw primal sketch, in Marr's (1982) framework. In the present case, boundary marking may be accomplished by means of locally based comparisons which register either consistency or inconsistency between local elements, with inconsistency being grounds for marking a boundary location. Clearly, there will be a large degree of inconsistency between the edges of the outmost local elements in the global figure and the blank surrounding page, leading to a rapid and efficient marking of the global boundary. The marking of the global boundary will also be supported by consistent interactions between the local letters (when they are all the same), specifying a consistent texture for the global figure. However, alternative boundary markings are also possible. For instance, boundary marking at the edges of the local elements internal to the global letter will also occur. This marking of internal boundaries will precipitate an alternative organisation of the figure to that given by marking the boundary of the global letter. Indeed, a field organised with boundaries marked at the edges of each local element would represent each local element as a separate perceptual object, and not as part of the global figure. The visual system may resolve these mutually exclusive organisations by means of co-operative and competitive interactions between the form elements. Thus the registration of consistency between the local form elements in the global figure will co-operate with a boundary marking at the edge of the global figure, while this information will compete with boundary marking between the local elements (see Fig.10.5). Normally, the system will reach a stable state with only one organisation remaining active at any one time. When the displays are constructed appropriately (e.g., with relatively small

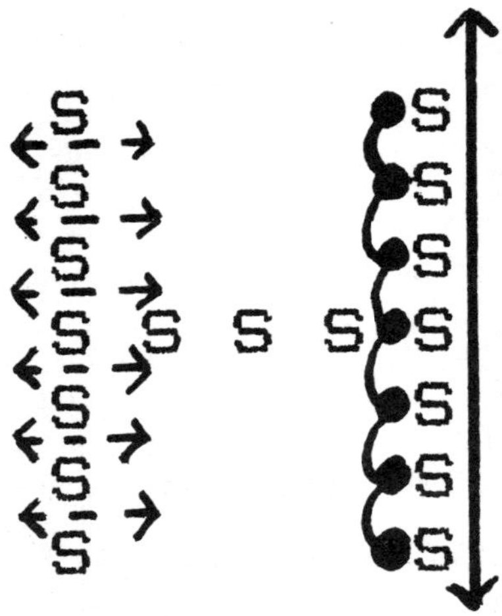

FIG. 10.5. An illustration of some of the "boundary marking" processes, which may precede the identification of a compound letter. ←→ denotes the marking of a global boundary; ←- -→ denotes the marking of the boundaries between the local letters; [symbol] denotes comparison processes which compute the similarity of the local elements.

inter-element distances and when subjects are uncertain of the location of the compound letter; cf. Grice, Canham, & Boroughs, 1983; Martin, 1979), the normal representation of a compound letter such as that shown in Figs. 10.4 and 10.5 will be of a global letter (in this case, an "H") containing a consistent texture.

We may now account for H.J.A.'s performance in either of two ways. First, his performance may be attributable to abnormal reactions within his texture-boundary-marking system. For instance, adding noise to such a system may allow boundary marking to proceed quite efficiently when there is little competition between alternative markings, whilst it might impair performance when there are a number of plausible alternative markings, when activity within the system may reach an inappropriate or unstable state. Thus global letter information may be identified relatively easily, because there is a good deal of local support (e.g., consistent texture information) for marking the global boundary and because there is little competition for alternative markings at the boundary edges (e.g., there is no "consistent" information to signal that the boundary should not be marked). In contrast, local letter information may be relatively difficult to identify because there is competition between the information specifying that boundaries can be marked between the local elements and information specifying a consistent texture. Indeed, textural consistency may be picked up between the feature constituents of the local letters and not just at the whole letter level, giving rise to a representation in which the feature constituents of the local letters are grouped and in which the individual local letters are not represented independently. According to this account, then, H.J.A. has difficulty identifying the local elements in compound stimuli either because he has difficulty segmenting the individual elements or because he segments them inappropriately. His RTs to the local letters will thus tend to be relatively long, as we observed. Indeed, his identification of the local letters may be so slow relative to his identification of the global figure that global information may have little effect on his identification responses (essentially, he may have more time to ignore the global information when identifying the local letters; see Hughes, Layton, Baird, & Lester, 1984, for a similar finding with normal subjects with very low contrast stimuli which made the local letters difficult to resolve). This account also makes the paradoxical and interesting assertion that H.J.A. typically uses local features to identify objects (see above; also Humphreys & Riddoch, 1984, 1987; Riddoch & Humphreys, in press) precisely because he has difficulty segmenting "part" information appropriately. Normally, global form information will be embellished by more local information detailing the relations between the parts of an object, etc. However, because H.J.A. has difficulty segmenting local part information, his global form representations tend to be undifferentiated and so do not support efficient object recognition; consequently, he is forced to rely on local part descriptions for identification even though his segmentation of this information is impaired. This account accords with the observation that his object identification errors typically reflect inappropriate segmentation of object parts (Riddoch & Humphreys, in press).

The alternative suggestion is that H.J.A. is impaired at extracting locally based texture information (e.g., due to some breakdown in local comparison processes). Without texture information, he may be able to direct attention to the local elements irrespective of the global letter's identity because he lacks the information specifying that the local letters are part of a more global structure. Normally, the consistent texture description may make it difficult for subjects to attend to the local elements. Nevertheless, H.J.A. may be able to respond to the global letter more quickly than the local letters because a lower spatial resolution is required (e.g., global letters may be identified using low spatial frequency information which becomes rapidly available in visual processing; e.g., Breitmeyer & Ganz, 1977). This was the view we originally favoured (Humphreys et al., 1985), and it can account for the lack of global interference on H.J.A.'s responses to local letters; however, it does not so readily explain why his local responses are abnormally slow, nor does it account for his segmentation errors in object identification.

Whichever account is adopted, the view we wish to stress is that a brain damaged patient may have a deficit in integrating and organising compound form descriptions despite having intact early processing of shape.

Feature-integration performed upon early shape primitives will yield a two-dimensional (2-D) description of a form. However, such a description will be wholely inadequate to support motor actions upon the environment, as such actions will require the accurate coding of the relative depths of the surfaces of objects (for reaching, etc.; see Marr, 1982). A further stage of processing is needed beyond feature-integration, in which depth information is assigned to the 2-D form descriptions. Evidence from the normal literature supporting the distinction between 2-D and depth-embellished representations of form, has already been discussed by Humphreys and Quinlan (this volume, Chapter 3). For our present purposes, it is also interesting to note that at least two brain damaged patients have been documented with an apparently complete loss of the ability to code information about the surfaces of objects in depth (Holmes & Horrax, 1919; G. Riddoch, 1917). In both patients, this lack of depth perception also precipitated some problems in object recognition. For instance, Holmes and Horrax's patient remarked that a glass tumbler appeared as a piece of flat glass, the shape of which varied according to how it was presented to him; he described a flight of stairs before him as "a number of straight lines on the floor"; and, when standing by a table he stated that "I would not know this is a table by looking down at it; it seems to my eyes to be at just the same level as the floor I am standing on, but when I see its legs and its edges I know it is a table". Riddoch similarly notes of his patient (Case 3, G. Riddoch, 1917) that:

> the most corpulent individual might be a moving cardboard figure, for his body is represented by an outline only. He has colour and light and shade, but still to the patient he has no protruding features; everything is perfectly flat. One of the unfortunate results of this phenomenon is that friends are recognized only by their voices. A man can be distinguished from a woman because, on account of his dress, his outline is different, and he may possibly wear a beard or a moustache.

Here then appears to be a further deficit which renders object recognition difficult. The patients appear to have good 2-D form information, but seem unable to use depth cues to create the surface based descriptions necessary for recognition on at least some occasions, like the other deficits covered in his section, it is essentially perceptual, and not associative, in nature.

3. ASSOCIATIVE AGNOSIA

A clinical distinction commonly drawn between apperceptive and associative agnosic patients is that associative agnosics may be able to produce clear copies of objects and drawings which they are unable to recognise (e.g., Kertesz, this volume, Chapter 6; Riddoch & Humphreys, in press; Warrington, 1985). Further, associative agnosics may perform relatively well on tasks requiring the matching of an object across different views (e.g., Riddoch & Humphreys, in press; Taylor & Warrington, 1971; Warrington, 1975), suggesting that such patients have intact and stable representations of form and that they are therefore differentiated from apperceptive agnosics. One theoretical interpretation of this distinction would be to maintain that recognition requires some form of semantic categorisation using stored knowledge about an object's associative and functional characteristics, and that this semantic categorisation occurs subsequently to the derivation of an intact perceptual representation of form. Associative agnosics are then thought to be impaired at semantic categorisation (cf. Warrington, 1982, 1985).

Once again, however, we believe the situation is not so straightforward. For instance, good performance on at least some tests of internal form representation does not always indicate normal perceptual performance. Thus H.J.A. (Riddoch & Humphreys, in press) is good at performing at least some forms of unusual-view matches (depending on the transformation involved; Humphreys & Riddoch, 1984), and he performs accurate copies of objects he cannot identify (Riddoch & Humphreys, in press); yet there are other grounds for maintaining that his representation of whole-object forms is far from normal (previously discussed; see also Humphreys & Riddoch, 1987; Humphreys et al., 1985; Riddoch & Humphreys, in press). To argue that a patient has sustained a relatively high-level recognition impairment will require extensive testing of lower-level perceptual functions before accepting the null hypothesis that there are no early processing impairments.

Furthermore, even if we accept that such patients do have perfectly normal perceptual processes there is a problem because different patients appear to manifest different associative deficits. These different associative deficits may reflect disruptions either to different kinds of stored knowledge about objects or to the procedures governing access to such knowledge.

One viable distinction here seems to be between stored knowledge of an object's form and stored knowledge of its functions and/or of our prior associations with it. Such a distinction is supported by at least two lines of evidence. One concerns the modality-specific repetition effects between pictures of objects which do not transfer completely to words, suggesting that the effects are not semantically-mediated (cf. Warren & Morton, 1982); a second concerns the patient (J.B.) reported by Humphreys, Riddoch, and Quinlan (in press; see also Riddoch & Humphreys, this volume, Chapter 4), who was very good at classifying pictures of objects as depicting real objects or not (an object-decision task), whilst being poor at matching associatively related objects from vision. Such a patient appears to have access to stored knowledge concerning the form of objects together with impaired access to semantic knowledge.

Given the distinction between stored knowledge about an object's form and stored semantic knowledge, it is possible that patients with relatively intact perceptual processing (e.g., up to establishing an abstract episodic representation of a whole object) may nevertheless experience object recognition difficulties for at least three reasons: (1) due to a disruption to stored pre-semantic knowledge about the object's form; (2) due to a problem in accessing the semantic system from the object form system; or (3) due to a disruption to stored semantic information about the object.

4. CLASSIFICATION AND LESION SITES

We now turn from a discussion of the relative merits of the labels apperceptive and associative agnosia in terms of how well they account for different types of visual object recognition deficit, to a discussion of how the labels have been applied to patients. We focus on the relations between patient classification and their lesion sites. Table 10.1 illustrates some cases reported within the last 20 years, together with the classification of the patient, the CAT scan, air encephalogram, and EEG findings (if any) and the visual field defect (when present).

While we recognise that there may well be no necessary relationship between the lesion site and the functional deficit (e.g., see Mehler, Morton, & Jusczyk, 1984), we might nevertheless expect that classifications should show some moderate correlation with the lesion sites. Inspection of Table 10.1 suggests that this is not the case when classifications are based on the apperceptive-associative agnosic distinction.

In some patients defined as apperceptive agnosics because they are unable to copy the objects they fail to recognise (e.g., Benson & Greenberg, 1969; Campion, this volume, Chapter 7), there is some evidence of multiple occipital infarcts, perhaps reflecting the etiology of carbon monoxide poisoning (see Campion, this volume, Chapter 7). A second group of patients, who may be classed as apperceptive agnosics because they fail to achieve adequate perceptual representations of objects seen under unusual viewing conditions (see Warrington, 1985), tend to have damage to the parietal region of the right hemisphere (Humphreys & Riddoch, 1984; Warrington, 1985; Warrington & Taylor, 1973, 1978). A third group of patients tend to have bilateral occipito-parietal-temporal lesions (e.g., Albert et al., 1975; Humphreys & Riddoch, 1984, 1987; Humphreys et al., 1985; Mack & Boller, 1977; Ratcliff & Newcombe, 1982; Wapner et al., 1978). However, unlike the first group of (apperceptive) patients, the latter patients have typically been classed as associative agnosics because of their preserved ability to copy (e.g., see Humphreys & Riddoch, 1987; Riddoch & Humphreys, in press). In a fourth group of patients, also classed as associative agnosics because of their good copying, object recognition deficits seem consequent upon unilateral damage to the posterior regions

TABLE 10.1

Classification	Reference	CAT Scan, Air Encephalogram Findings	EEG Findings	Visual Field Defects
Associative agnosia	Albert, Reches, & Silverberg (1975)	Increased uptake of radioactive material in both occipital regions posteriorly and inferiorly.	Persistent bilateral occipital showing with occasional sharp activity.	Upper quadrantic defects of the right field.
Apperceptive agnosia	Benson & Greenberg (1969)		Persistent bilateral slow wave pattern in the parieto-occipital areas.	Minimal inferior constriction bilaterally.
Apperceptive agnosia	Campion (this volume Chapter 7)	Diffuse lesion most prominant above the calcarine sulcus of the left hemisphere extending into striate and prestriate cortex of both hemispheres.		Right inferior defect.
Associative agnosia	Davidoff & Wilson (1985)	Marked dilation of the whole ventricular system, especially of the left occipital horn which extended almost to the tip of the occipital lobe. Basal cisterns were almost obliterated.		Not reported.
Associative agnosia	Humphreys & Riddoch (1984, 1987); Humphreys et al. (1985); Riddoch & Humphreys (in press)	Extensive infarct extending forward in both occipital lobes in the distribution of the posterior cerebral artery.	Normal to patterns presented to the lower visual fields.	Superior altitudinal defect of both the left and right visual fields.

TABLE 10.1 (cont.)

Classification	*Reference*	*CAT Scan, Air Encephalogram Findings*	*EEG Findings*	*Visual Field Defects*
Apperceptive agnosia (four cases)	Humphreys & Riddoch (1984); Riddoch & Humphreys (1986)	Three patients had right parietal lesions, one showed low attenuation in the posterior and inferior part of the right frontal lobe.	—	Two patients had left homonymous hemianopia; one had an inferior altitudinal defect in the left field and a lower nasal defect in the right.
Associative agnosia	Levine (1978)	Resection of the right occipital lobe.	—	Left homonymous hemianopia with macular sparing.
Apperceptive/associative agnosia	Kertesz (1979)	Deep left occipital and right frontal lesions.	More prominant theta activity and occasional sharp wave activity in the left parieto-temporal region and some irregular theta activity in the right parietal region.	Initially, a left homonymous hemianopia was questioned. Subsequent testing suggested a "spiralling" defect without hemianopia, due to excessive adaptability to stimulation.
Associative agnosia	Mack & Boller (1977)	A large left posterior lesion involving all the occipital lobe and a smaller lesion in the right inferior occipital and occipital-temporal area.	—	Right homonymous hemianopia; upper quadrant defect of the left field.

Associative agnosia	Ratcliff & Newcombe (1982)	Extensive bilateral infarction of the posterior part of the brain, mainly occipital but extending forward into the parietal and temporal lobes particularly in the right hemisphere.	—	Left homonymous hemianopia with macular sparing.
Associative agnosia	Rubens & Benson (1979)	Negative findings on CT scan, though encephalogram showed mild ventricular enlargement, greater on the left side.	Mildly abnormal.	Dense right homonymous hemianopia with macular sparing.
Associative agnosia	Taylor & Warrington (1971)	Cerebral atrophy	—	Perimetrically normal.
Associative agnosia	Wapner, Judd, & Gardner (1978)	Increased uptake bilaterally in the medial occipital region, greater on the left than the right.	Slowing in the left occipital and temporal regions.	Right homonymous hemianopia.
Associative agnosia (three cases)	Warrington (1975)	Cerebral atrophy; in one case (C.R.) there was increased uptake in the parieto-occipital region of the left hemisphere.	In one case (A.B.) there were low-voltage waves in the left posterior parietal area.	Fields full to confrontation.
Associative agnosia (four cases)	Warrington & Shallice (1984)	Widespread low attenuation maximal in both temporal lobes.	—	—

of the left hemisphere (e.g., Davidoff & Wilson, 1985; Kertesz, 1979; Rubens & Benson, 1971). There also exists a fifth group of patients with diffuse cerebral atrophy or with diffuse bilateral damage focused on the temporal lobes (e.g., following herpes simplex encephalitis) who may be classed as associative agnosics because, among other things, they may accurately classify objects presented under unusual viewing conditions and yet be unable to recognise them (e.g., Taylor & Warrington, 1971; Warrington, 1975; Warrington & Shallice, 1984). However, even with this five-category scheme it is difficult to accommodate all patients (e.g., Levine, 1978).

In emphasising the different lesion sites found in different patients, we wish to stress that neither apperceptive nor associative agnosia, as clinically defined (previously discussed), can be associated with a particular lesion site. This proposal is contrary to at least some earlier suggestions (e.g., Nielsen, 1936; Warrington, 1985), which, we believe, is due to the earlier studies examining selective types of agnosia. For instance, patients with multiple, diffuse bilateral occipital infarcts may have some problem in deriving shape descriptions (cf. Benson & Greenberg, 1969; Campion, this volume, Chapter 7); patients with right parietal damage may have some difficulty effecting particular transformations on stimulus information presented under unusual viewing conditions (Humphreys & Quinlan, this volume, Chapter 3); patients with a bilateral occipito-parietal-temporal lesion may have some problem in integrating shape descriptions (Humphreys & Riddoch, 1987; Humphreys et al., 1985); patients with unilateral left posterior damage may have some difficulty in accessing semantic information (cf. Riddoch & Humphreys, 1987; Warrington, 1985); and patients with diffuse cerebral atrophy may have impaired semantic knowledge (cf. Marin, this volume, Chapter 9). Accounts of visual object processing which maintain the involvement of only two processing stages in object recognition, apperception, and association, which can be selectively impaired by brain damage, fail to preserve the above behavioural and perhaps also anatomical distinctions.

We can add to this heterogeneous set of lesion sites found in patients previously classified as either apperceptive or associative agnosics, if we consider patients with object recognition problems because of a loss of depth perception (e.g., Holmes & Horrax, 1919; G. Riddoch, 1917). Of the two patients we are aware of who had this problem, one had bilateral lesions of both angular gyri (Holmes & Horrax, 1919); the other had only a left homonymous hemianopia, and so might be presumed to have suffered a unilateral lesion of the right occipital lobe (G. Riddoch, 1917).

We submit that little sense can be made of these anatomical data unless we specify the particular processes impaired in the different patients.

5. RE-CLASSIFYING VISUAL AGNOSIA

The theme of this chapter has been that visual object processing may be impaired in a number of rather different ways, and that we need a classification scheme which is sensitive to the different patterns of impairment which may arise. As a first step towards such a scheme, we suggest that the following distinctions be adopted. The scheme is based partly on reported behavioural differences between patients, and also partly on a theoretical framework which makes predictions about certain types of visual object processing deficits which should be observed once we have the tools to examine the deficits selectively. Of course, if these predictions fail to be fulfilled, then we may go on to question the validity of at least some of the classifications.

To begin with, let us assume that we may validly distinguish between patients who have form-specific visual processing deficits and those who have more general deficits (e.g., brightness discrimination; see Section 2). The following distinctions may then be applied to patients with form-specific deficits.

5.1. Impaired Shape Processing

This classification would be appropriate for patients whose recognition problems are attributable to deficits in processing the primitive characteristics of shape (e.g., edges at different orientations and spatial scales). Such patients would be impaired on simple shape matching tasks (e.g., physical matching; see Posner, 1978), and they would be poor at copying the objects they are unable to identify (e.g., Benson & Greenberg, 1969; Campion, this volume, Chapter 7).

5.2. Impaired Transformation Processes

This classification may be applied to patients who are able to perform simple shape matching tasks (such as physical matching), who can identify objects seen from a prototypical view, but who are impaired at identifying and matching objects seen under unusual viewing conditions (cf. Humphreys & Riddoch, 1984; Riddoch & Humphreys, 1986; Warrington & Taylor, 1973, 1978). Typically, the identification responses of such patients suggest that they are using some form of description coded within-the-plane (rather than in-depth). For instance, Fig. 10.6 shows the top view of a pepper-pot, taken so that the pot's main axis is foreshortened. Patients with impaired transformation processes may describe this as a

FIG. 10.6. A foreshortened pepper-pot (top-view) (from Humphreys & Riddoch, 1984).

button, lying within the picture plane[3] (Humphreys & Riddoch, 1984). The problem in this case seems to be that they fail to invoke the appropriate transform to code that the object is oriented in-depth. Different patients can also manifest different types of transformation problem (see Humphreys & Quinlan, this volume, Chapter 3; Riddoch & Humphreys, 1986). Such impairments would make it difficult for a patient to achieve an abstract episodic representation of an object.

5.3. Impaired Integration Processes

This classification would apply to patients who can derive adequate shape descriptions, but who are impaired at integrating the shape information at different scales (e.g., at linking local form descriptions in parallel to provide descriptions of the boundaries between different forms). Such patients should again perform relatively well at simple physical matching,

---

[3]Although patients with impaired transformation processes may code objects in unusual views as lying within-the-plane, they still seem able to assign depth to their representation. For instance, concurrently with identifying a foreshortened pepper-pot as a button, such a patient might point out that the dark rings on the surface of the "button" are holes receding in depth (see Fig. 10.6). This ability to assign depth distinguishes such patients from patients impaired at representing surface information in depth (Section 5.4). Patients with impaired transformation processes seem unable to use depth cues to "drive" the transformation required to identify an object in an unusual view, but they are not impaired at depth coding *per se*.

and they should be able to copy objects using a series of independent local form descriptions (cf. Ratcliff, 1985; Riddoch & Humphreys, in press). They will, however, be selectively impaired at tasks requiring integrated form information (cf. Humphreys et al., 1985).

5.4. Loss of Stereoscopic Vision

The two patients described respectively by Holmes and Horrax (1919) and by G. Riddoch (1917) both seemed able to derive well-integrated 2-D representations of objects, but they failed to assign depth to these representations. This impeded their ability to derive surface descriptions of objects, and so limited their ability to negotiate their environment (e.g., it would be difficult to reach appropriately for an object because the depths of its surfaces would not be coded). Such a problem will also impair object recognition where recognition is dependent on the derivation of accurate surface descriptions (as opposed to the 2-D form of an object). For instance, surface descriptions may be particularly important in the identification of individual faces, so that patients who are poor at deriving such descriptions may suffer a profound and possibly selective face recognition impairment.

5.5. Impaired Access to Form Knowledge

Up to this point, the patients we have classified have all had problems in deriving representations of form. These would be manifest on each occasion when forms are presented to them, and so they involve *episodic* form representations. Other pre-semantic deficits in visual object processing may occur because patients have difficulty in accessing or using *stored* information about visual form. For example, it may be that a patient has suffered impairments to the stored information itself. Such a deficit may be manifest in tasks such as drawing from memory (where the deficit cannot be attributed to some motor or constructional problem) and object decision (where the patient must discriminate between real and meaningless distractors; Humphreys et al., in press; Riddoch & Humphreys, 1987). In contrast, the patient may be good at matching objects across different transformations, at copying, and at tasks requiring integrated local and global form information (e.g., Humphreys et al., 1985). Importantly, such patients should show little difference between performance with familiar and with novel objects on the tasks they can accomplish.

More selective types of visual form agnosia may also be possible. For instance, it is conceivable that patients could derive normal episodic representations of a shape, that they have intact stored knowledge of object form, and yet that they are unable to access object form knowledge from the input (i.e., their problem would be specific to *accessing* form

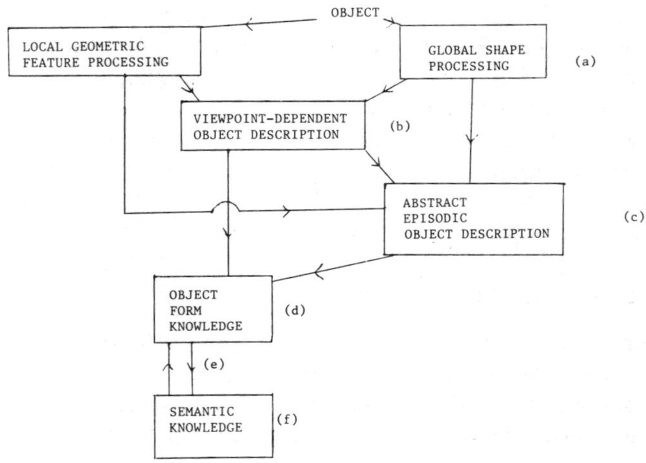

FIG. 10.7. An information processing framework specifying some of the processes involved in accessing semantic knowledge from visually presented objects. A lesion at site (a) would impair shape processing; lesions at site (b) could impair 2-D shape integration or the coding of integrated shape descriptions (due to the loss of depth perception); lesions at site (c) would impair transformation processes; lesions at site (d) would impair object form knowledge; lesions at site (e) would affect access to semantics; and lesions at site (f) would impair semantic knowledge.

knowledge). In this instance, a patient with a pure access deficit may be separated from one with a representation impairment (i.e., a patient who has lost information about the form that objects may take), by asking the patient to draw objects from memory. A patient with an access deficit should be able to draw from memory, a patient with a representation impairment should not. Patients could also be selectively impaired in certain circumstances if, despite having intact object form knowledge, they are unable to apply that knowledge to facilitate earlier processes (e.g., when objects are encountered under extreme transformation conditions; see Humphreys & Quinlan, this volume, Chapter 3).

Sartori and Job (in press) have recently documented the case of a patient who appears to have impaired stored knowledge about the form of certain objects. This patient was impaired at object decision tasks, where he tended to accept "non-objects", created by interchanging the heads and bodies of different objects, as real objects. He also tended to define some structural attributes of objects incorrectly (when asked to define objects from their names), and he would add parts incorrectly to drawings of objects. A specific account of how such a pattern of performance could be produced by damage to the object form system is offered by Riddoch and Humphreys (this volume, Chapter 4).

To the best of our knowledge no cases have yet been adequately described with a pure deficit in *accessing* the object form system. This may be because such a deficit has not been tested for hitherto, or it may be that accessing form knowledge cannot be separated from the process of generating abstract episodic representations of objects. In some sense, it may be that the application of an appropriate transform upon a given input representation is the process whereby access to object form knowledge occurs (Humphreys & Quinlan, this volume, Chapter 3).

5.6. Impaired Access to Semantics

In some cases, patients may have intact access to the object form system, and they may have intact semantic knowledge, and yet be impaired at accessing semantic knowledge visually. We have argued that this type of classification should be used to accommodate cases such as J.B. (see earlier; Humphreys et al., in press; Riddoch & Humphreys, this volume, Chapter 4). Such patients should be good at object decision tasks, good at tasks requiring access to semantic knowledge from other modalities, and poor at the latter tasks giving visual presentation. Also, the performance of such patients may be sensitive to the visual characteristics of objects, and not just their semantic characteristics, emphasising that the major source of their impairment does not reside within the semantic system (see Riddoch & Humphreys, this volume, Chapter 4).

5.7. Impaired Semantic Knowledge

It is also possible that patients may have impaired representations of semantic knowledge. Thus, Warrington (e.g., Taylor & Warrington, 1971; Warrington, 1975, 1985) has argued that impaired semantic knowledge characterises the agnosic patients she has examined with general cerebral atrophy. Whatever the merits of Warrington's case (see, for instance, Riddoch, Humphreys, Coltheart, & Funnell, in press; Shallice, in press), we would expect that a patient with agnosia consequent on a loss of semantic knowledge to show yet another differentiable pattern of performance. For example, such patients should perform well on tasks assessing pre-semantic visual object processing, including object decision tasks, whilst showing impaired recognition of the same objects. However, unlike patients with a semantic access impairment, semantic agnosic patients should primarily be sensitive to the semantic characteristics of objects. That is, the ability of such patients to match words with objects should be affected by the semantic relations between the stimuli, not by their visual similarity; also, semantic agnosic patients should generate a high proportion of naming errors which are solely semantically related to the target object.

An information processing framework which may serve to illustrate how different lesions of a componential system could generate the different types of agnosia we have suggested is depicted in Fig. 10.7.

6. CONCLUSIONS

In this chapter, we have attempted to provide guidelines for the classification of patients with object processing deficits. Our aim has not been to give a definitive classification scheme; indeed, we expect the classifications we have suggested to be further modified as our tests of object processing become more refined, and as our understanding of the complexities of the problem increase. However, in outlining even a tentative scheme we hope to have indicated the diverse ways in which brain damage can selectively impair visual object recognition. Furthermore, we believe that the kind of multi-component scheme we have proposed is open to future expansion in a way in which the classical apperceptive-associative distinction is not. For instance, if some of the distinctions we have suggested seem difficult to sustain (such as the hypothesis that certain patients may have intact knowledge of object form, an intact ability to transform data across viewpoints, and yet be unable to access form knowledge), one implication would be that certain processes are integral and not separable in visual object processing (such as transforming information across viewpoints and accessing form knowledge). Alternatively, additional distinctions may be indicated. In either case, we hope that the classification scheme indicates ways in which the categories may be altered to accommodate the deficits which occur.

ACKNOWLEDGEMENTS

The work reported in this chapter was supported by grants from the Chest, Heart and Stroke Association and from the M.R.C. to both authors, and from the E.S.R.C. to the first author. We thank Walter Sturm for encouraging us to abolish the term agnosia from our classification scheme.

REFERENCES

Albert, M. L., Reches, D., & Silverberg, R. (1975). Associative visual agnosia without alexia. *Neurology, 25,* 322–326.

Bay, E. (1953). Disturbances of visual perception and their examination. *Brain, 76,* 515–550.

Benson, D. F. & Greenberg, J. P. (1969). Visual form agnosia. *Archives of Neurology, 20,* 82–89.

Breitmeyer, B. & Ganz, L. (1977). Temporal studies with flashed gratings: Inferences about human transient and sustained channels. *Vision Research, 17,* 861–865.

Campbell, F. & Robson, J. G. (1968). Application of Fourier analysis to the visibility of gratings. *Journal of Physiology, 197,* 551–566.

Davidoff, J. & Wilson, B. (1985). A case of visual agnosia showing a disorder of pre-semantic vision classification. *Cortex, 21,* 121–134.

Efron, R. (1968). What is perception? *Boston Studies in the Philosophy of Science, 4,* 137–173.

Ettlinger, G. (1956). Sensory deficits in visual agnosia. *Journal of Neurology, Neurosurgery and Psychiatry, 19,* 297–307.

Grice, G. R., Canham, L., & Boroughs, J. M. (1983). Forest before trees? It depends where you look. *Perception & Psychophysics, 33,* 121–128.

Grossberg, S. & Mingolla, E. (1985a). Neural dynamics of form perception: Boundary completion, illusory figures and neon colour spreading. *Psychological Review, 92,* 173–211.

Grossberg, S. & Mingolla, E. (1985b) Neural dynamics of perceptual grouping: Textures, boundaries and emergent segmentations. *Perception & Psychophysics, 38,* 141–171.

Holmes, G. & Horrax, G. (1919). Disturbances of spatial orientation and visual attention with loss of stereoscopic vision. *Archives of Neurology and Psychiatry, 1,* 385–407.

Hughes, H. C., Layton, W. M., Baird, J. C., & Lester, L. S. (1984). Global precedence in visual pattern recognition. *Perception & Psychophysics, 35,* 361–371.

Humphreys, G. W. & Riddoch, M. J. (1984). Routes to object constancy: Implications from neurological impairments of object constancy. *Quarterly Journal of Experimental Psychology, 36A,* 385–415.

Humphreys, G. W. & Riddoch, M. J. (1987). *To see but not to see: A case study of visual agnosia.* London: Lawrence Erlbaum Associates Ltd.

Humphreys, G. W., Riddoch, M. J., & Quinlan, P. T. (1985). Interactive processes in perceptual organization: Evidence from visual agnosia. In M. I. Posner & O. S. M. Marin (Eds.), *Attention and performance*, Vol. XI. Hillsdale, N.J.: Lawrence Erlbaum Associates Inc.

Humphreys, G. W., Riddoch, M. J., & Quinlan, P. T. (in press) Cascade processes in picture naming. *Cognitive Neuropsychology.*

Kertesz, A. (1979). Visual agnosia: The dual deficit of perception and recognition. *Cortex, 15,* 403–419.

Levine, D. (1978). Prosopagnosia and visual object agnosia: A behavioural study. *Brain and Language, 5,* 341–365.

Lissauer, H. (1889). Ein Fall von Seelenblindheit nebst einem Beitrage zur Theorie derselben. *Archiv für Psychiatrie und Nervenkrankheiten, 21,* 222–270.

Mack, L. J. & Boller, F. (1977). Associative visual agnosia and its related deficits: The role of the minor hemisphere in assigning meaning to visual perceptions. *Neuropsychologia, 15,* 345–351.

Marr, D. (1982). *Vision.* San Fransisco: W. H. Freeman.

Martin, M. (1979). Local and global processing: The role of sparsity. *Memory and Cognition, 7,* 479–484.

Mehler, J., Morton, J., & Jusczyk, P. W. (1984). On reducing language to biology. *Cognitive Neuropsychology, 1,* 83–116.

Navon, D. (1977). Forest before trees: The precedence of global features in visual perception. *Cognitive Psychology, 9,* 353–385.

Nielsen, J. M. (1936). *Agnosia, apraxia, aphasia: Their value in cereberal localizations*. New York: Paul B. Hoeber.

Posner, M. I. (1978). *Chronometric explorations of mind.* Hillsdale, N.J.: Lawrence Erlbaum Associates Inc.

Pötzl, O. (1928). Die Aphasielehre vom Standpunkte der Klinischen Psychiatrie. In *Handbuch der Psychiatrie.* Leipzig und Wien: Franz Deuticke.

Ratcliff, G. (1985). Agnosia and internal representation. Paper presented at the *Symposium on Cognitive Neuropsychology,* Venice.

Ratcliff, G. & Newcombe, F. (1982). Object recognition: Some deductions from the clinical evidence. In A. W. Ellis (Ed.), *Normality and pathology in cognitive functions.* London: Academic Press.

Regan, D. (1982). Visual information channeling in normal and disordered vision. *Psychological Review, 89,* 407–444.
Riddoch, G. (1917). Dissociation of visual perception due to occipital injuries, with especial reference to appreciation of movements. *Brain, 40,* 15–57.
Riddoch, M. J. & Humphreys, G. W. (1986). Neurological impairments of visual object constancy: The effects of orientation and size disparities. *Cognitive Neuropsychology, 3,* 201–224.
Riddoch, M. J. & Humphreys, G. W. (1987). Visual object processing optic aphasia: A case of semantic access agnosia. *Cognitive Neuropsychology, 4,* 131–186.
Riddoch, M. J. & Humphreys, G. W. (in press). A case of integrative visual agnosia. *Brain.*
Riddoch, M. J., Humphreys, G. W., Coltheart, M., & Funnell, E. (in press) Semantic system or systems? Neuropsychological evidence re-examined. *Cognitive Neuropsychology.*
Rubens, A. & Benson, D. F. (1971). Associative visual agnosia. *Archives of Neurology and Psychiatry, 24,* 305–316.
Sartori, G. & Job, R. (in press). The oyster with four legs: A neuropsychological study on the interaction of visual and semantic information. *Cognitive Neuropsychology.*
Selfridge, O. (1959). Pandemonium: A paradigm for learning. In *Symposium on the Mechanization of Thought Processes.* London: HMSO.
Shallice, T. (in press). Specialisation within the semantic system. *Cognitive Neuropsychology.*
Taylor, A. M. & Warrington, E. K. (1971). Visual agnosia: A single case report. *Cortex, 7,* 152–161.
Wapner, W., Judd, T., & Gardner, H. (1978). Visual agnosia in an artist. *Cortex, 14,* 343–364.
Warren, C. E. J. & Morton, J. (1982). The effects of priming on picture recognition. *British Journal of Psychology, 73,* 117–130.
Warrington, E. K. (1975). The selective impairment of semantic memory. *Quarterly Journal of Experimental Psychology, 27,* 635–657.
Warrington, E. K. (1982). Neuropsychological studies of object recognition. *Philosophical Transactions of the Royal Society, London, B298,* 15–33.
Warrington, E. K. (1985). Agnosia: The impairment of object recognition. In J. A. M. Frederiks (Ed.), *Handbook of Clinical Neurology, Vol.1: Clinical Neuropsychology.* Amsterdam: Elsevier.
Warrington, E. K. & Shallice, T. (1984). Category specific semantic impairments. *Brain, 107,* 829–854.
Warrington, E. K. & Taylor, A. M. (1973). The contribution of the right parietal lobe to object recognition. *Cortex, 9,* 152–164.
Warrington, E. K. & Taylor, A. M. (1978). Two categorical stages of object recognition. *Perception, 7,* 695–705.

Author Index

Abadi, 206, 216, 220
Ackroyd, 89
Adler, 179, 182, 187, 222
Albert, 153, 162, 184, 189, 190, 269, 294–5
Albright, 152
Alford, 80
Allen, 181
Allman, 83
Allport, 55–56, 67, 73, 112, 234–235, 244, 247, 251, 253
Alzheimer, 262
Anderes, 148
Anderson, 5, 69, 71, 123
Assal, 148, 244
Atkin, 182
Attneave, 28, 31, 69

Babb, 154
Bagnara, 50
Baird 291
Balestrery, 161
Balint, 188, 191
Ballard, 5, 32
Banker, B. Q., 263
Banks, 49
Barbeito, 62
Barton, 181
Bartram, 55, 112, 119
Ballard, 6, 69
Bay, 160, 176, 178, 200–201, 203, 231, 269, 283
Beale, 63
Beaty, 161
Beauvois, 127–128, 181, 184, 185–186, 234, 235–237, 241
Beck, 5
Bender, 85, 160, 176, 190, 269
Benson, 179, 186, 189, 191, 222, 269, 284, 294–5, 297–299
Benton, 107, 160, 181, 185
Berndt, 131
Besner, 53, 109
Biederman, 48
Binford, 30
Bishop, 238
Black, 132
Blake, 47
Bobick, 25
Bodis-Wollner, 160–161, 182
Boller, 184, 190, 294, 296

Bornstein, 148, 185
Boroughs, 290
Botez, 189
Bourne, 55
Bowen, 261
Bower, 43
Bowerman 243
Boyes-Bream 116
Bradshaw 159, 162, 165
Brain, 187
Braine, 63
Breitmeyer, 61, 291
Brizzolara, 165
Brownell, 125
Bruce, 85
Bruner, 188
Bruyer, 148
Bub, 132–133, 243
Bucher, 59, 61, 67, 244
Bucy, 175
Bundensen, 52
Butler, 50
Butterworth, 136–139
Buttet, 244
Byng, 238

Caan, 85
Callagirone 137
Campbell, 284
Campion, 7, 12, 107, 160, 188, 206, 212, 221–222, 235, 242, 268, 282–283, 285, 294–5, 298
Cancelliere, 132, 243
Canham, 290
Caramazza, 131
Carey, 12, 147
Carlson, 43
Caron (A.), 43
Caron (R.), 43
Carr, 110
Cavanagh, 48, 62, 150, 152
Chain, 189
Chambers, 191
Chance, 160
Charcot, 187
Chase, 79
Chmiel, 67
Clark (E. V.), 242–243
Clark (H. H.), 242–243
Cloning, 183
Cole, M., 88, 263
Coltheart, 2, 4, 7, 53, 130, 234, 244, 303
Colombo, 150
Cooper, 50–53, 63
Corballis, 50–52, 63, 146
Coren, 37–38
Cornsweet, 47
Corsellis, 265
Cortese, 109
Corwin, 158
Cowey, 4, 83–84, 86, 88
Craik, 138
Crandall, 154
Critchley, 160, 188
Crowell, 163
Cummings, 272

Damasio (A. R.), 185
Damasio (H.), 185
Daugman, 152
Darley, 139
Davies-Jones, 87
Davidoff, 277, 295, 298
Davison, 261
Dean, 86
DeBauche, 190
Delis, 93
Denes, 237
Denny-Brown, 191
De Renzi, 88, 269
Desimone, 4, 85, 86, 152, 154
Devic, 188
De Vita, 62
Diamond, 12
Diesch, 113
Dodwell, 76–77, 82, 84
Draguns, 155
Dreher, 154
Ducarne, 189
Duchen, 272
Duncan, 67
Dunker, 76
Durso, 109

Efron, 178–179, 191, 222, 284–85, 288
Eley, 50–51
Ellis (A. W.), 135, 234–235
Ellis (R.), 55–56, 67, 112
Epstein, 54–56, 67, 73
Escourolle, 189
Esiri, 261
Ettlinger, 160–161, 178, 191, 201–204, 231, 269, 283
Evert, 110

Fairweather, 165
Farrell, 52, 78
Faulconer, 108
Favre, 148
Feldman (J. A.), 6, 44, 57, 69, 71, 160
Feldman (M.), 176, 268
Felleman, 84
Ferro, 179, 190
Fiorentini, 158
Fischer, 84
Fitzpatrick, 80
Flavell, 155
Flinchbaugh, 25
Fodor, 267
Forrest, 147
Foster, 49, 76
Franklin, 137
Francis, 261
Freedman, 147
Freiheit, 113
Freud, 176
Freund, 127, 181
Fries, 154
Frisby, 23–24
Funnell, 7, 11, 13, 128, 130, 234–235, 238, 242, 244, 246–247, 251, 253, 303
Fusillo, 184

Gainotti, 136–138
Gaffan (E. A.), 87
Gaffan (D.), 87
Ganz, 86, 291
Gardner, 297
Garland 215–216
Garner, 72, 149
Gelade, 5, 39
Gelb, 176, 179, 186–189
Gellman, 49–50
Gerade, 109
Geschwind, 163, 181, 184, 269
Gevins, 147
Gibson (E.), 76
Gibson (J.), 25, 29, 76
Giese, 23
Ginsberg, 47, 155, 158, 161
Glenn, 272
Gloning, 183
Gluck, 117
Goodglass, 107, 136, 139, 181, 256, 271
Gogel, 80
Goldblum, 179
Goldstein (A. G.), 160
Goldstein (K), 176, 179–180, 186–189
Gomori, 184, 190
Gordon, 160
Gough, 80
Graves, 179
Gray, 116
Greenberg, 179, 191, 222, 284–285, 294–295, 298–299
Greene, 63, 76
Gregory, 79
Grice, 290
Grimson, 27
Gross, (C. G.), 85–87, 152
Gross, (R. A.), 182, 190
Grossberg, 289
Grotzbach, 113
Guenther, 110

Haber, 147
Hahn, 188
Halsey, 147
Hamilton, 155
Hampson, 132
Harker, 80
Harvey, 159
Harrison, 87

Hart, 131, 133
Hartman, 80
Hatfield, 55–56
Hawryluk, 184, 190
Hay, 234
Head, 85
Hebben, 179
Hecaen, 147, 153, 162, 179, 269
Heilman, 242
Heindeinhein, 264
Hellige, 146, 158, 164
Helmholz, 54
Hildreth, 23, 26
Hinton, 5, 32, 47, 53, 63, 69–71, 82, 93, 123
Ho, 182
Hochberg, 32, 49–50
Hoff, 183
Hoffman, 25, 30
Hohle, 113
Holley-Wilcox, 80
Holmes, 88, 187, 292, 298, 301
Horn, 28
Horrax, 187, 292, 298, 301
Howard, 134–139
Huang, 25
Hubel, 5, 20, 82
Hughes, 291
Humphrey, 86, 96, 234
Humphreys, 2–6, 9, 11, 13, 32, 36, 39, 49, 58, 60, 67–69, 71, 73, 78–80, 85, 88, 89, 91–94, 107–110, 113, 119–121, 123–124, 127—130, 133, 135, 151, 154, 157–158, 160, 163, 178, 180, 182–183, 190–191, 193, 199, 230–231, 235, 238–241, 243, 275, 277, 285–288, 291—296, 298-303
Hyvarinen (J.), 150
Hyvarinen (L)., 150

Jeannerod, 188
Jeeves, 85
Job, 130, 302
Johansson, 76, 78
Johnson (C. A.), 161
Johnson (D. M.), 116
Johnson (J. E.), 158
Johnson (M. K.), 109
Jolicoeur, 51–53, 62, 80, 117–119, 124, 133
Jolivet, 244
Jones (G. V), 244, 248, 251
Jones (R. H), 163
Judd, 78, 297
Julesz, 5, 8, 61, 216
Jusczyk, 198
Jung, 176
Jusczyk, 4, 293

Kaas, 83, 154
Kaniza, 37
Kaplan, 181
Katz, 111, 116
Katzman, 263
Kapunia, 163
Kay, 163
Kellman, 43
Kelter, 113
Keltner, 161
Kertesz, 10–12, 107, 132, 178, 180, 182, 186–189, 197–198, 230, 243, 275, 281–282, 296, 298
Klatzky, 110
Kluver, 175
Kirsner, 109
Koenderink, 25
Koffka, 31, 54, 76
Kohn, 136, 139
Koriat, 53, 92
Kosslyn, 51, 117
Kremin, 128, 242
Kronauer, 152
Kulikowski, 206

Land, 5
Landau, 51–52, 62
Landis, 179, 186, 189
Lange, 176
Larsen, 52
Latto, 206, 212, 216, 222
Layton, 291
Leestma, 182
Lester, 291
Lennie, 150, 152, 154
Leventhal, 154

Levine, 184, 187, 190, 296, 298
Lewis, 163
Lhermitte, 127, 185–186, 189, 235, 237, 241
Lindsay, 44, 46
Linnankoski, 150
Lissauer, 175–176, 189, 197, 230, 232, 268, 275, 281
Livingston, 20
Lockhart, 138
Longuet-Higgins, 24–25
Lorber, 160, 164
Lovitts, 56, 67, 73
Ludwin, S. K., 263
Lupker, 110–111, 116
Luria, 189

McCauley, 110
McClelland, 5, 9, 119, 123
McCullough, 127
Mcloughin, 136
Mach, 76
Mack, 184, 190, 293, 296
Mackworth, 188
Madican, 247
Maffei, 158
Mai, 275
Mansfield, 154
Marcel, 244
Masullo, 137
Masure, 179
Marin, 7, 10–11, 13, 108, 238–239, 242, 262, 272, 277, 298
Marr, 2–5, 7–9, 17–20, 22–23, 26, 28–30, 32, 35, 47—48, 63-67, 69, 71, 87, 93, 113–114, 116–117, 122, 151, 191, 198, 234, 286, 289, 292
Marshall, 163, 191, 234, 244

Martin, 290
Mauer, 163
Mayeux, R., 263
Mayhew, 23–24
Meadows 147–148, 162, 183
Mehler, 4, 198–199, 293
Meininger, 237
Meudall, 206
Mervis, 116
Merzenich, 154
Metzler, 30, 50–52
Meyer, 80, 119
Mezzanotte, 48
Miceli, 137
Michel, 188
Milech, 109
Miller, 120
Millward, 159
Milner (A. D.), 85
Milner (B.), 161
Milner (P. M.), 157
Mingolla, 289
Minsky, 45–46
Mishkin, 85
Mistlin, 85
Monsell, 108
Moran, 4, 84, 154
Morgan, 153
Morris, J. C., 263
Morton, 4, 9, 108–109, 112, 137, 198, 234–235, 244, 292–293
Mountcastle, 152, 155
Muise, 55
Munitz, 148, 185
Muñoz-Garcia, D., 263
Munk, 175
Murphy, 116–119, 125
Myers, 256

Nagler, 152
Nagourney, 50
Nakagawa, 163
Navon, 124
Neary, 261
Nebes, 163
Neisser, 44, 46, 79, 82
Nettleton, 162
Newcombe, 127–128, 184, 234, 238, 241, 242, 244, 265, 281, 294, 297
Nielson, 189, 197, 298
Nishihara, 2, 30, 47, 63, 65, 67, 93, 113, 116–117, 122
Norcross, 182
Norman, 44, 46, 53, 57, 92

O'Boyle, 164
O'Connell, 76

Oldfield, 119
Orchard-Lisle, 134–135, 137–138
Osman, 120
O'Toole, 159
Oxbury (J. M.), 234
Oxbury (S. M.), 234

Paivio, 247
Palmer (A. M), 261
Palmer (L. A.), 83
Palmer (S. E.), 59–63, 67, 79, 89, 97
Papert, 46
Parasuraman, 161
Park, 54
Parmalee, 110
Parsons, 53, 63, 82
Pasik (P.), 191
Pasik (T.), 191
Pasnak, 80
Paterson, 5
Patterson, 9, 108, 112, 137, 159, 165, 234, 244
Pearce, 215–216
Pease, 256
Perkins, 31
Perret, 85
Pick, 263
Pillon, 189
Pinker, 44, 48
Plastow, 63
Pylyshyn, 168
Podraza, 139
Pollen, 152
Poggio, 17, 22–23, 63, 84
Poppelreuter, 176
Posner, 299
Potter (D. D.), 85
Potter (M. C.), 108
Potzl, 288
Powell, 152
Prazdny, 25
Pribram, 86
Prinzmetal, 49
Putnam, 110

Quinlan, 2–6, 9, 11, 32, 39, 49, 67, 69, 94, 108–109, 113. 123, 150, 154, 157–158, 178, 190, 231, 238, 277, 283–285, 287–288, 292–293, 298, 300, 302–303

Raab, 182
Rabin, 8
Rabinowitz, 48
Rafal, 272
Ramier, 179
Ratcliff, 88, 127, 128, 184, 234, 238, 241, 242, 269, 281, 294, 297, 301
Reches, 295
Regain, 110
Regan, 161, 215, 284
Reines, 184
Richards, 21, 30
Richardson, 247
Riddoch, (G.), 88, 292, 298, 301
Riddoch (M. J.), 6, 9, 11, 13, 36, 49, 69, 79–80, 85, 88, 89, 91–94, 107–108, 128–129, 130, 133, 160, 163, 178, 180, 182–183, 190–191, 193, 199, 230–231, 235, 238–241, 243, 271, 275, 277, 285, 287, 291–296, 298–303
Rips, 117, 125
Risberg, 147
Robertson, 93
Robson, 284
Rocha-Miranda, 85, 190
Rock, 54, 62
Rodieck, 154
Rolls, 83
Roncato, 50
Rosenquist, 83
Rosch, 79, 115–118, 124–125, 132, 133
Rosinski, 110
Ross, 186
Rubens, 162, 186, 269, 297–298
Ruddy, 80
Rumelhart, 5, 9, 123

Saffran, 108, 238, 242, 262
Saillant, 128, 184, 234, 237
Sanders, 191
Sandini, 158

Santos, 179, 190
Sartori, 130, 302
Sato, 85
Saunders, 86, 96
Scarborough, 109
Schein, 4, 84, 154
Schenk, 183
Schienfeld, 155
Schutta, 88
Schvaneveldt, 80
Schwartz (E. L.), 152
Schwartz (M. F.), 108, 238, 242, 262, 270–271
Scotti, 88, 269
Segarra, 189
Sejnowski, 5, 32, 69
Sekuler, 47
Selfridge, 46, 82, 283
Semenza, 237
Serbanescu, 189
Sergent, 9, 11–12, 36, 84, 95, 124, 146, 148, 155, 157–160, 162–165, 185, 287, 283
Seymour, 241
Shallice, 128, 130–131, 234–236, 243, 255, 257, 277, 287, 297–298, 303
Shapley, 150
Shepard, 30–31, 50–52, 63, 76, 78, 96
Shetzer, 50
Silveri, 137
Silverberg, 184, 295
Simion, 50–51
Sinclair, 159
Skroka, 148
Slobin, 117, 125
Smith (E. E.), 116–119, 125
Smith (J. E.), 120
Smith (P. A.), 85
Smith (Y. M.), 212
Snodgrass, 122, 127
Snowden, 261
Soffer, 184
Souther, 5
Spanton, S., 263
Spehlmann, 182
Sperber, 110
Spinnler, 88, 269
Spreen, 107, 181
Sroka, 185
Steiger, 50–51, 71
Stemberger, 107
Stern, Y., 263
Stevens, 3, 7–8, 11, 29, 31–36, 63, 82
Stromeyer, 216
Stumfel, 109
Sumi, 79
Sutherland, 3, 46

Tabussi, 165
Takane, 163
Taylor, 88–89, 93, 160–161, 180 234, 241, 269, 276, 285, 287, 293, 294, 297–299, 303
Te Linde, 241
Tet Braack, 183
Teuber, 160
Tipper, 67
Tomlinson, 265
Toyama, 148
Treisman, 5, 39
Tsai, 25
Turing, 19
Tusa, 83
Tyler, 80, 188

Ullman, 21, 25–26, 29, 39, 77
Umiltà, 50, 165
Underwood, 164
Ungerleider, 4, 84, 86, 154

Van Allen, 107, 185
Van Doorn, 25
Van Essen, 83–84, 86, 152, 154
Van Vliert, 183
Vanderwart, 110, 122
Vernea, 189
Von Cramon, 275
Von Grunau, 84

Walker-Smith, 159
Wallach, 76
Waltz, 32

Wapner, 36, 294, 297
Warren, 109, 112, 293
Warrington, 9, 88–89, 95, 130–131, 160–161, 180, 188, 191, 199, 230–231, 234, 236, 239, 241, 243–244, 255, 257, 269, 271, 276–277, 281, 285–287, 292–294, 297–299, 303
Waxman, 21
Weil, 110
Weiskrantz, 86, 88, 96, 191, 275
Weisstein, 47
Weller, 83, 154
White, 50
Whitfield, 164
Wiesel, 5, 82
Wilbrand, 187
Wilcock, 261
Wilkinson, 84, 87
Wills, 147
Wilson (B.), 277, 294, 298
Wilson (B. M.), 147
Wilson (C. L.), 154
Wilson (H. R.), 23
Wilson (M.), 190
Wingfield, 119
Winston, 46
Witkin, 32–33, 35
Wolkstein, 182
Wolpert, 189
Wright, D., 263
Wutzig, 113

Yantis, 120
Yin, 147–148
Yuille, 50–51, 71, 247

Zaidel, 146
Zeki, 4, 84, 154
Zihl, 275

Subject Index

alexia, 179, 181, 183, 184
algorithm, 3–6, 17–19, 23, 39
Alzheimer's disease, 262–264, 266, 270
amnesia, 187, 190
analytic/wholistic dichotomy, 149, 162–163
anomia, 107, 270–272, 274–275, 276–277
anosognosia, 187
Anton's syndrome, 187
aphasic naming, 136
apperceptive agnosia, 10, 12, 175–180, 182, 186, 188, 191–192, 197–199, 208, 230–232, 268, 275, 281–282, 285, 288, 292–294, 298
associative agnosia, 10, 12, 175–176, 179–180, 188, 192, 197–198, 268, 275, 281–282, 292–294, 298
associative knowledge (see *semantic representation*)
auditory aphasia for environmental sounds, 176
auditory aphasia, 237
auditory verbal agnosia, 176
axis based description, 30, 32, 58–59, 81–82, 91, 97

Balint's syndrome, 188
base level representation, 115–118, 124, 132–133

colour agnosia, 181, 183, 191, 277
colour anomia, 184
colour constancy, 6, 19
colour recognition (see *colour vision*)
colour vision, 4, 6, 84, 179, 184, 201, 210, 221, 225, 273, 275
conceptual knowledge (see *semantic knowledge*)
conduction aphasia, 256
connectionist theories, 5–6, 8, 32, 68–71, 96
constructional deficits (see *visuo-constructive problems*)
contextual biasing effects, 59–61
cortical blindness, 182, 264, 285

dementia, 187, 261–279
depth coding, 54–55, 287, 292, 298, 300–301

disconnection hypothesis, 181, 183, 186, 275
double dissociation, 235
dyslexia, 243–246

face perception, 147
feature detection, 45–47, 82, 283
field defects, 178–179, 181, 183, 190, 201, 204, 206–7, 216, 223–224, 231, 294–297
figure-ground discrimination, 185, 191, 291
figure-ground segmentation (see *figure-ground discrimination*)
foreshortening, 33–35, 90–93, 285
form knowledge processing deficit, 301–303
form specific processing deficit, 299
frontal lobe, 190, 263, 265, 272, 276, 296

geniculo-striate visual system, 188
gestures, 127–128, 238
grouping, 289

hemispatial neglect (see *visual neglect*)
hemispheric asymmetry, 145–146, 162, 164–168

illusions, 38
imageability, 246–257
inferior temporal lobe, 85–88, 96
integration of shape descriptions, 298
integration processing deficit, 288, 300
invarient form information, 76–79, 81–82, 84, 97, 151, 286

Jakob-Creutzfeldt disease, 264

landmark features, 49–51, 57, 81–82, 298
laterality research, 145–146, 162, 164–165, 168
levels of abstraction, 3–7, 17
local and global form information, 124, 157, 163, 283–284, 287–291, 301
localisation of function, 146, 169

mental transformations, 50–52, 77, 81–82, 298
minimal feature transforms, 90–91
mind blindness, 175
modularity, 2, 7–9, 11, 19–20, 35–39, 65, 233–235, 257
motion, 8, 19, 21, 24–26, 28, 275

non-semantic route to naming, 127, 242–243
normalisation, 45, 54–57

object decision task, 129
object form system (see *structural descriptions*)
occipital cortex, 83–84, 152, 154, 175, 184, 189–190, 198, 278, 294–295
optic aphasia, 2, 127, 181–182, 185, 192, 237, 282
optic array (see *invarient form knowledge*)
optokinetic nystagmus, 183
orthography, 108
orthographic input logogens, 112
output phonology, 119

parietal lobe, 88, 198, 294, 295–298
pattern recognition, 82
perceptual categorisation, 198, 285
perseverations, 185–186
phonological representation, 108, 112, 120, 123, 129, 131, 135–138, 140, 240, 244
Pick's pre-senile dementia, 263–264, 270–271
pictogens, 112–113
primal sketch, 61
priming studies, 109–111, 130, 132
prosopagnosia, 147–148, 179, 183–184, 190, 202, 204, 229, 277–278, 283

prototypes, 115–117, 127
prototypical views, 79, 90–92

retinal descriptions, 43–45, 55

Schilder's disease, 264
semantic access deficit, 303
semantic categorisation, 180, 198, 293
semantic deficit, 303
semantic knowledge (see *semantic representation*)
semantic lexicon, 137–138
semantic memory, 115–117, 131, 138
semantic representation, 80, 108–110, 112–113, 116, 118–119, 120–123, 128–129, 131, 134–140, 238–247, 251–253, 255, 257, 268, 271, 274, 277, 281, 286, 293–294, 298
senile dementia, 262
sensory deficits, 160, 200–206, 229, 231, 268, 271
shape discrimination failure (see *apperceptive agnosia*)
simultanagnosia, 38, 183, 189, 191
spatial frequency analysis, 47–48, 61–62, 154–159, 163—168, 212–213. 216, 220–221, 285, 291, 301
static object agnosia, 188
stereopsis, 8, 21–24, 28, 34, 87
stereo-vision deficit, 301
stereograms, random dot, 8, 23, 38
structural descriptions, 46–47, 76–79, 92, 94, 97, 108, 112–113, 119–124, 129–134, 139, 238–403, 252, 255, 257, 286, 293
structural representations (see *structural descriptions*)
subjective contours, 37–38
surface interpolation, 8, 26–28, 37
symmetry effects, 61

tachistoscopic experiments, 145–146, 162, 168
tactile aphasia, 237
tactile agnosia, 176–192
tectopulvinar visual system, 188
template theory, 44–48
temporal lobe, 166, 189–190, 263, 265, 272, 276, 297–298
texture boundary marking system, 290
texture gradients, 21, 32
texture information, 289–291
three D (3D) descriptions, 65–67
three D (3D) form information, 8, 19, 21, 25, 28
top-down effects, 79–80
transformation processing deficit, 299
two and a half D (2 1/2D) sketch, 28, 63–65

unilateral neglect (see *visual neglect*)

verbal/visuospatial dichotomy, 149
visual deprivation, 150
visual evoked responses, 183
visual form agnosia (see *apperceptive agnosia*)
visual imagery, 186–187
visual neglect, 187, 212, 283
visual/verbal conceptual (semantic) systems, 237, 241, 243, 271
visuo-constructive problems, 178, 187, 208, 262–263, 225–226, 301